ON GIVING THE SPIRITUAL EXERCISES

On Giving
the
SPIRITUAL EXERCISES

*The Early Jesuit Manuscript Directories
and the Official Directory of 1599*

Translated and edited by
Martin E. Palmer, S.J.

ST. LOUIS
THE INSTITUTE OF JESUIT SOURCES
1996

Number 14 in Series I:
Jesuit Primary Sources in English Translation

Second printing 2009

© 1996 The Institute of Jesuit Sources
3601 Lindell Boulevard
St. Louis, MO 63108
Tel.: 314-633-4622
Fax: 314-633-4623
E-mail: ijs@jesuitsources.com
Website: www.jesuitsources.com

Library of Congress Catalogue Number 95-81839
ISBN cloth 978-1-880810-17-0
      paper 978-1-880810-18-7

For my parents

Contents

Introduction

THE PRIMARY directory, or guidebook, for giving the Spiritual Exercises of St. Ignatius is of course the little book of the Exercises itself. Throughout the book St. Ignatius accompanies the matter for the retreatant's meditation or reflection with instructions to the director of the retreat. These instructions cover the selection and preparation of retreatants, the ways of adapting the Exercises to different persons and situations, the actual method for giving the successive exercises, and other information needed in guiding the retreatant.

However, these instructions are for the most part quite laconic, leaving many practical questions unanswered. In the earliest years of the Society of Jesus, when most of those giving the Exercises had been personally formed by St. Ignatius, this caused little difficulty. But with the passage of time and the rapid growth of the Society, the need became clear to make more detailed directives available in writing.

St. Ignatius himself was aware of this. The obvious recourse of expanding the book of the Exercises itself seems not to have occurred to him. He had spent over twenty years assembling and refining his text, and once it had finally been printed in an elegant Latin version (the "Vulgate") with solemn papal approval in 1548 he refused to countenance even the slightest revision.[1] Thus, the needed supplementary materials would have to be furnished in a separate guidebook, or "directory."

With this in mind, St. Ignatius himself jotted down a few notes, and had his secretary, Juan de Polanco, make a practice of bringing to him questions that arose about the Exercises and recording his answers. Another Jesuit in Rome, Juan Alonso de Vitoria, while directing a retreat under St. Ignatius' supervision, wrote an extensive account of the instructions he was given.[2] These, together with a few other early documents, make up a small body of

---

[1] In his introduction to his *Exercices Spirituels: Texte définitif (1548)* (Paris: Seuil, 1982), pp. 17-19, Jean-Claude Guy adduces an incident of 1555 recorded by Luis Gonçalves da Câmara (*Memorial*, n. 321): St. Ignatius indignantly rejected changing the tense of a verb in the Latin version to bring it closer to the Spanish original, even though the Latin (and not the Spanish!) was exposed to the charge of unorthodox teaching because of its ambiguity. The reason St. Ignatius gave was that "the Latin Exercises had been approved by the Pope."

[2] From Vitoria also we have a detailed protocol of his own election to enter the Society of Jesus, made in successive stages as prescribed by St. Ignatius. See Appendix 2.

I

material deriving directly from St. Ignatius. They form Part I of this book (Documents 1 to 6).

In the years following St. Ignatius' death in 1556, individual Jesuits in various parts of Europe wrote down and circulated occasional notes on giving the Exercises. A number of of these have survived in manuscript form. Meanwhile the project of producing a systematic directory for Jesuits was not lost sight of, although under St. Ignatius' first two successors in the generalate the press of other business prevented much progress being made. The fourth general, Everard Mercurian (1573–1580), pushed the work more vigorously, himself composing the first sketch of a systematic directory (Document 18). At Mercurian's urging, St. Ignatius' secretary and close collaborator, Juan de Polanco, also composed a substantial directory (Document 20). Polanco's is re-garded as the finest of the early directories; it exercised great influence on the final, authorized Directory of 1599.

Early in the generalate of Mercurian's successor Claudio Aquaviva (general 1581–1615), Diego Miró, another of St. Ignatius' close collaborators, following the basic outline of Polanco's work, composed a directory more in line with his own more literalist understanding of the Ignatian tradition. In manuscript form this directory achieved wide circulation among Jesuits. But it was not felt to satisfy fully the need for an official directory, which Aquaviva wished to be more broadly based.

Assembling a dossier of the various manuscript directories composed up to that point, Aquaviva sent them out to a small group of leading Jesuits for com-ment. Among these was Miró himself, whose response proved to be an even more uncompromising version of his original directory (Document 23). Another Jesuit to whom the dossier was sent, Gil González Dávila, provincial of Toledo in Spain, likewise accompanied his comments on the earlier directories with a full-scale draft of his own (Document 31).

With this wealth of materials to draw upon, Aquaviva was able in 1591 to circulate for comment a preliminary printed draft of an official directory, care-fully compiled in Rome from the earlier documents. Only in 1599, however, was this work published in its definitive form: the *Directory to the Spiritual Exercises* (Document 43). By far the fullest and most adequate of all the direc-tories, it served Jesuits in its frequent reprintings over the ensuing centuries as an authoritative guide to the practice of the Exercises. It was twice translated into English in the early twentieth century.[3]

The manuscript directories which preceded this official Directory gathered dust in archives until the nineteenth and twentieth centuries, when scholars

---

[3] W. H. Longridge, *The Spiritual Exercises of Saint Ignatius of Loyola, Translated from the Spanish with a Commentary and a Translation of the* Directorium in Exercitia (London: Robert Scott, 1919; reprinted by A. R. Mowbray, 1950); *Directory to the Spiritual Exercises of Our Holy Father Ignatius: Authorized Translation* (London: Manresa Press, 1925).

began exhuming and publishing them piecemeal. Then, in 1955, Ignacio Iparraguirre, S.J., assembled the entire body of surviving documents from before 1599 and published them, along with the official Directory itself, as volume 76 in the Monumenta Historica Societatis Iesu, entitled *Directoria Exercitiorum Spiritualium (1540–1599)*.[4]

It is substantially the materials in Iparraguirre's volume which are here translated. In addition to all the materials deriving from St. Ignatius himself, I have included all the surviving guidelines and directories up to and including the official *Directory to the Spiritual Exercises* of 1599. This constitutes the near-totality of sixteenth-century material on giving the Spiritual Exercises.

Devoid of literary pretensions and in some cases but crudely drafted notes, these guidelines and directories are straightforward and practical. They aim for the most part only at filling out St. Ignatius' own terse directives in the book of the Exercises. The ideal model envisaged is that of thirty-day Exercises being given by a Jesuit to a young man[5] who is deciding his vocation. In Exercises thus given "in full form" (Latin *exactê*), strict adherence to the Ignatian program is insisted upon, with only such modifications as limitations in the exercitant's health or mental capacity may require. Somewhat greater flexibility is foreseen, however, in the various adaptations of this standard model (Exercises of the First Week and Second Week only, Exercises "in everyday life," Exercises for Jesuits, etc.)

The reader will find here little of the modern concern with a presumedly distinctive spirituality or theology of the Spiritual Exercises. The early Jesuits, following St. Ignatius, had no thought of innovating in what subsequently came to be called spirituality, much less in theology. They aspired only to make a better organized and more concentrated use of the Church's inherited spiritual practices in order to bring a person in a relatively short time to fuller personal actualization of the Church's traditional faith—a faith that was wholly dominated by the issue of eternal salvation, both that of the retreatant and of those whom Christ might call him to "help." Indeed, what scant theoretical discussion of the Spiritual Exercises does survive from the sixteenth century is

---

[4] Iparraguirre's edition, besides being exhaustive, is heavily annotated and furnished with excellent cross-references, bibliography, and index. The research underlying this volume was exploited in Iparraguirre's history of the practice of the Spiritual Exercises in the sixteenth century: *Historia de los Ejercicios Espirituales de S. Ignacio de Loyola*, vol. 1: *Práctica de los Ejercicios de S. Ignacio de Loyola en vida de su autor* (Roma-Bilbao, 1946); vol. 2: *Desde la muerte de S. Ignacio hasta la promulgación del Directorio oficial* (Roma-Bilbao, 1954). Joseph de Guibert, S.J., briefly reviews the protracted genesis of the official Directory in his *The Jesuits: Their Spiritual Doctrine and Practice*, translated by William J. Young, S.J., and published by the Institute of Jesuit Sources (Chicago, 1964, and St. Louis, 1971 and 1994), pp. 243-247.

[5] Exercises given to women were considered a special case for which many of the practical norms given in the directories would be partly or wholly inapplicable.

devoted mainly to defending them against the charge of innovation.

Anyone, however, who is interested in getting a concrete idea of what it was like to direct or to make the Ignatian Exercises in the decisive early decades of the Society of Jesus will find in these documents, for all their unpretentiousness, a privileged source of information and insight.

★ ★ ★ ★ ★

For ease in correlating these translations with Iparraguirre's edition and its copious notes and index, I have preserved his document and paragraph numbering throughout. Reference to the Spiritual Exercises themselves is made with the modern paragraph numbers placed in square brackets.

In translating the official *Directory* of 1599 I have drawn liberally upon the version by W. H. Longridge cited above.

I wish to thank Fathers George E. Ganss, S.J., and John W. Padberg, S.J., for their encouragement and help in the preparation of this book.

PART I

DIRECTIVES STEMMING DIRECTLY FROM ST. IGNATIUS

DOCUMENT 1

Autograph Directory of St. Ignatius

This set of notes on the Exercises has been preserved in copies attested as having been taken from an original in St. Ignatius' own handwriting—hence the term "autograph." They are particularly helpful in seeing how St. Ignatius envisioned Exercises that were focused on the making of an election. (Original in Spanish.)

COPY OF A SHEET IN OUR FATHER'S HANDWRITING, TAKEN FROM THE ORIGINAL: FOR GIVING THE EXERCISES

I.

[1] The initial Annotations may be shown, and this can be more helpful than not.

[2] The place where he makes the Exercises should be where he will be least able to be seen or talk with anyone, if the Exercises are being given in full form.

[3] He should eat or drink nothing but what he has asked for.

[4] Where possible, it is better for someone other than the person giving the Exercises to hear his confession.

[5] The one giving the Exercises should always ask him about his consolation and desolation, and what he has experienced in the exercise or exercises he has made since he last spoke with him.

[6] Upon entering the three or four times of election,[1] he should remain especially secluded, not wishing to see or experience anything that is not from above.

[7] Prior to this, the director should dispose him immediately to be completely resigned to either the counsels or the commandments.

[8] So that he will be more disposed toward God's greater glory and his own greater perfection, the director should dispose him to desire the counsels over the commandments if this should be for God's greater service.

---

[1] The second method of the third time [184–187] is here also referred to as a fourth time.

[9] He should dispose him and make him realize that greater signs from God are needed for the commandments than for the counsels, inasmuch as Christ our Lord advises the counsels and places difficulty in the ownership of property that is possible in the commandments.

[10] When, upon explaining the first part [time] of the election, no basis for seeking it there can be had, he should go on to the second.

[11] In the second—by consolation and desolation—he should give a full explanation of what consolation is, going through all its aspects, viz., inner peace, spiritual joy, hope, faith, love, tears, and elevation of mind, all of which are gifts of the Holy Spirit.

[12] Desolation is the opposite, coming from the evil spirit and gifts of the same. Its components are war versus peace, sadness versus spiritual joy, hope in base things versus hope in lofty ones; similarly, base versus lofty love, dryness versus tears, wandering of mind amid base things versus elevation of mind.

II. DIRECTORY FOR THE EXERCISES OF THE SECOND WEEK, BY OUR FATHER IGNATIUS.

[13] In the case of those who in the First Week show little fervor or desire for going on to decide their state of life, it will be better not to give the exercises of the Second Week, at least for a month or two.

[14] Those who have a strong desire to go on to decide their state, after finishing their general confession, may be allowed on that day, and the day they receive Communion, to rest until the following morning without being given any exercise in the form of an exercise—although they might be given something easy, v.g., on the commandments of God.[2]

[15] The one giving the Exercises should not bring along the book of the Exercises to read to the person but should have the matter he will speak about carefully studied beforehand.

[16] If he has time, it is preferable not to bring the points written out but to explain the material and then dictate the points for the person to write in his own hand. Lacking the time for this, he can bring them to him written out and leave them. But in either case, the one giving the Exercises should explain them as they are in the book, and leave only the points succinctly put in writing.

---

[2] In a copy revised by him, Jerónimo Nadal here inserted: "for besides resting from their previous labor, they should recreate themselves, thanking God for the grace received and rejoicing and delighting in the Lord's mercy."

III. DIRECTORY FOR THE ELECTIONS

[17] First of all, it must be insisted that a person entering upon the elections do so with total resignation of his will; and, if possible, that he reach the third degree of humility, in which for his own part he is more inclined, should it be for the equal service of God, toward that which is most in accord with the counsels and example of Christ our Lord. Anyone who is not in the indifference of the second degree is not suited to enter upon the elections, and it is better to occupy him with other exercises until he reaches it.

[18] Among the three modes [times] of making an election, if God does not move him in the first he ought to dwell on the second, that of recognizing his vocation by the experience of consolations and desolations. Then, as he continues with his meditations on Christ our Lord, he should examine, when he finds himself in consolation, in which direction God is moving him; similarly in desolation. A full explanation should be given of what consolation is; i.e., spiritual joy, love, hope for things above, tears, and every interior movement which leaves the soul consoled in our Lord. The opposite of this is desolation: sadness, lack of confidence, lack of love, dryness, and so on.

[19] When no decision has been reached in the second mode, or one that is not good in the judgment of the one giving the Exercises, whose task it is to help discern the effects of the good and evil spirit, then the third manner should be resorted to—that of the discursive intellect by means of the six points.

[20] Finally, the method that follows this one can be resorted to, i.e., that of the four points—as a final resort.

[21] The person may proceed by presenting one side to God on one day and the other on the next, v.g., the counsels on one day and the commandments on the next; and noting in which direction God our Lord gives a greater indication of his divine will—like someone presenting various foods to a prince and noting which of them is to his liking.

[22] The matter proposed for deliberation is: first, whether the counsels or the commandments; secondly, if the counsels, then whether inside or outside a religious institute; thirdly, if in a religious institute, which one; fourthly, after that, when and how.[3] If it is the commandments, then in what station or style of life, etc.

[23] *Addition.* In the Second Week, where elections are dealt with, those who have already decided their state of life should not be made to deliberate on their state of life. In lieu of this deliberation, they can be offered one of two things on which they might wish to make a choice:

The first is, where it is equally for God's service and without scandal or

---

[3] For an example of an election made in these stages, see Appendix 2.

harm to the neighbor, to desire injuries, opprobrium, and abasement in all things with Christ, in order to be clothed in his livery and imitate him in this aspect of his cross. The other is to be willing to suffer patiently anything of this kind whenever it should befall him for love of Christ our Lord.[4]

---

[4] This final paragraph, in Italian, is found only in a few manuscripts, including, however, one of the oldest.

Reminders of St. Ignatius

These five remarks on the Exercises were dictated by St. Ignatius and are preserved in the handwriting of his secretary, Juan de Polanco. (Original in Spanish.)

ON EXERCISES

The following are some points which our Father Master Ignatius wants to remain by way of reminder in the book.

[1] *On Exercises:* First, a person making the Exercises should always be asked what he wants to eat, and then be given what he has requested, whether what he requests is a fowl or a mere morsel—whatever is according to his devotion. Thus, after dinner he should tell the person who clears the table or brings him dinner what he wants for supper. Similarly, after supper he should say what he will want for dinner the following day. He considers this one of the things which are most helpful.

[2] 2. As for the other penances, what is said in the Exercises should be explained to him. If he requests some instrument, such as a discipline, hairshirt, or the like, the director should ordinarily offer to give him what he asks.

[3] 3. Regarding the exercises of the First Week: the Father does not think they should be given all at one time, and has never done this. Instead, they should be given one by one, until at the end the person is making all five. Similarly with the exercises of the other Weeks.[1]

[4] 4. His view regarding the elections is this: the first point to be proposed is whether to follow the counsels or the commandments, with an explanation of the counsels: "Sell what you have, give to the poor, and follow me" [Matt 19:21]; the second, should he decide for the counsels, whether in a religious institute or not (for he could follow the counsels in hospitals, etc.); the third, if in a religious institute, which one; the fourth, having decided this, the time when he will be begin and other details.

[5] 5. Those who make only the exercises of the First Week should afterwards be given the Particular and General Examens and the First Method of Prayer.

---

[1] This seems to contradict what the Exercises say [72]. There is considerable divergence among the directories on this matter of presenting the exercises of the First Week.

Second Directory of St. Ignatius

This first attempt at a systematic directory gathers together St. Ignatius' own remarks on the Exercises. It is preserved in a copy with corrections and additions in the handwriting of St. Ignatius' secretary, Juan de Polanco, and of Jerónimo Nadal. (Original in Latin.)

JESUS
PROCEDURE FOR GIVING THE EXERCISES
IN THEIR FULL FORM

1. Order

[1] As regards the order: the Foundation should be given before anything else; second, the Examen against a particular fault; third, the General Examen [32–42]; fourth, the five-point daily Examen. Then, on the first day, the 1st exercise should be given, in the evening if possible, so that it can be begun at midnight.

[2] On the morning of the next day the 2nd exercise should be given; and on that day after dinner the 3rd and 4th exercises together. Then, if conveniently possible, on the same day after supper the Additions should be explained so that the exercitant can begin to use them in making the 1st exercise at the following midnight (which begins the third day), the 2nd at daybreak, the 3rd before dinner, and the 4th after dinner. On the third day also, if possible, the 5th exercise will be given after vespers.

[3] On the following (fourth) day, beginning at midnight, he should go through the five exercises using the Additions (these Additions should be explained more carefully when the exercitant seems not to be making much progress). That is: at midnight the 1st exercise is made, at daybreak the 2nd, after Mass the 3rd, at midafternoon the 4th, and before supper the fifth—if the exercitant is capable of this exertion.

[4] Then, at the next visit, the director should give him the examen on all the exercises and start explaining the Rules for the Discernment of Spirits for the First Week. In short, he should always be bringing the exercitant something new.

2. *Manner*

[5] As for the manner of giving exercises: the points should be given rather succinctly, not diffusely.

[6] On visiting the exercitant, an account of the points should be required. It is important to ask especially about the thing being sought in the particular exercise, v.g., contrition in the exercises on sin, etc.

[7] If the exercitant answers satisfactorily one should not stay long with him or ask him many other questions. If he is not finding what is being sought, then he should be carefully questioned about his agitations and about the Additions.

[8] The exercitant can be told to write down his ideas and movements.

3. *Number of exercises*

[9] As for the number of exercises that should be given: on the one hand it can be useful to add others to the five aforementioned exercises, such as on death, judgment, and the like, if this is needed for the person to find what he seeks, i.e., sorrow, etc. On the other hand, if he finds what he seeks through the five aforementioned exercises no others are needed.

4. *The general confession*

[10] First of all, as regards the general confession, he should not prepare for it until he has completed the aforesaid exercises.[1] As for what is said in the first point of the 2nd exercise about his examining the multitude of his sins by going through the places, times, etc., this should be a general rather a particularized examination. For a close scrutiny of fine points is not as helpful toward sorrow as is getting an overall view of one's serious sins.

[11] Secondly, while occupied in getting together this general confession, he should not be engaged in any other exercises which are not pertinent to the confession.

5. *Some notes*

[12] Note that if a person does not obey the one giving the Exercises and wants to proceed by his own judgment, one should not continue giving him the Exercises.

[13] Secondly, if some persons' mental disposition does not seem such that much fruit can be hoped for from them, it will suffice to give them the exercises of the First Week and leave them with this thirst until they give surer

---

[1] A copy used by Nadal ends this paragraph as follows: "until he has done the aforesaid exercises three or four times, especially if they produce some fruit. However, moderation must be observed, so that after the sixth day at the latest, or even after the fifth, they should prepare for the general confession even if they have experienced no sensible fruit."

warranties for expecting richer fruit.

[14] Thirdly, such persons could be given one of the Methods of Prayer, especially the first one on the ten commandments, the capital sins, etc. Then, with the practice of making the Examens mentioned earlier, they can be let go.

[15] Fourthly, how one eats and drinks contributes greatly to the elevation or lowering of the mind. Hence, so that the exercitant's sobriety and abstinence will be voluntary and adapted to his particular nature, the one giving the Exercises should tell him that after dinner he is to request what he wants prepared for his supper, and after supper what he wants for dinner the following day. The server should be told that when clearing away the tablecloth and dishes after dinner he should ask the exercitant what he wants for supper that evening, and after supper what he wants for his next dinner. He should bring exactly what was requested, whether he asks for ordinary fare or even something better, or just bread with water or wine. The one giving the Exercises, however, should take care to know what he is doing in this matter of diet so that excesses in either direction can be avoided.

[16] Fifthly, another not inconsiderable help—both because it interrupts mental exercises, which cannot be carried on too long without ill effects, and because of the benefit of humility, which is furthered by humiliation—is for each exercitant, even those used to soft living and having many servants, to sweep and if necessary sprinkle their own rooms, make up their beds, and in general engage in functions of this sort which are usually attended to by servants.

DOCUMENT 4

Directory Dictated to
Father Juan Alonso de Vitoria

The Jesuits living with St. Ignatius in Rome sometimes gave the Exercises under his supervision. He would meet with them while they were directing the Exercises to instruct them on giving the points and help them over any difficulties they met. This was his method of forming directors for the Exercises.

It was probably in 1555, on the occasion of giving the Exercises under St. Ignatius' guidance to Lorenzo Maggio, that the Spanish Jesuit Juan Alfonso de Vitoria[1] drew up this important summary of St. Ignatius' directives to him. The style and organization are Vitoria's, but there is no reason to doubt that the document faithfully renders St. Ignatius' teaching.

In the first decades of the Society this directory was held in high regard, and much of its contents passed into the official Directory of 1599. (Original in Spanish.)

NOTES ON THE EXERCISES AND HOW TO GIVE THEM,
DRAWN FROM THE ORIGINAL OF FATHER VITORIA—
DICTATED, AT LEAST IN SUBSTANCE, BY OUR FATHER
MASTER IGNATIUS OF HOLY MEMORY

[1] It does not seem advisable to encourage a person to go into seclusion for making the Exercises unless he possesses the following qualifications, or at least the more important of them. First, he should be someone who may be expected to bear considerable fruit in the Lord's household if he is called thereto. Second, even if he lacks this degree of developed capacity in skills or acquired knowledge and the like, he should at least possess the age and intelligence needed for making progress. Third, he should be in a position to make a decision regarding his own life, even for the state of perfection if God should deign to call him to it. Fourth, he should have a good and presentable appearance, etc. Fifth, he should not so strongly attached to anything that it would be hard getting him to place himself in equilibrium before God; rather,

---

[1] Appendix 2 translates Vitoria's record of his own election of a state of life, carefully executed in successive stages as prescribed by St. Ignatius in Doc. 1.22 (see Doc. 6.12.)

15

he ought to be uneasy in some respect, with a desire to know what he ought to do with himself and an uncertainty about this. Furthermore, generally speaking, the more suited a person is for the religious state and for the Society, the more suited he will be to make the closed Exercises. Persons who lack these dispositions, and who do not afford hope that they can be brought to equilibrium regarding their affairs, or who are married or religious or unqualified, should not be given the Exercises, especially when there are other persons to give them to or other legitimate occupations. However, such persons ought to be given appropriate assistance, such as the First Week; they should be urged to retire somewhere in so far as they can, except for times when they go to Mass, vespers, or to the house for receiving the Exercises. They can be given further assistance by way of exercises from the other Weeks, the Methods of Prayer and examination of conscience, and the like.

[2] A person who is a good prospect but lacks the dispositions needed for making the Exercises fruitfully should be helped along with frequent confessions, talks, and familiar conversations—but prudently, so that he will not form the suspicion that this is being done to beguile him (though this would be a holy guile and one that is praised by St. Paul: "Being crafty, I caught you by guile" [2 Cor 12:16]), for this usually arouses resentment and does no good.

[3] We have learned from experience that there is ordinarily no better way to encourage people to make the Exercises than in confession. This, however, should not be done abruptly, but at the right moment. Similarly, when in our dealings with people we can tell that they are in some way dissatisfied with the ordinary secular life they are leading (except in the case of married persons, etc.), either because their affairs are going poorly or because their parents or relatives treat them badly, or for any similar reason, then you might say to them: "I really think that for your consolation, and so that you will know how to guide yourself in all that you do, it would be very helpful for you to go into retreat for some days to make the Exercises." This idea would appeal to the person if he had been shown the wretchedness of people who labor only to please someone other than God, either for the sake of money or for any other purpose. If the person does not know what the Exercises are, you can say to him, "Here we know how to give certain exercises," etc., going on to commend the Exercises as their worth requires and giving examples of people in similar misfortunes or desolation who, after making the Exercises, were left in consolation. It is enough—indeed better—simply to give the facts without mentioning names. One should avoid saying that the person decided to enter religious life; it is better just to state that after making the Exercises he was consoled and relieved. There are many other ways of urging people to make the Exercises, and the more indirectly the better, so long as the person realizes how worthwhile the Exercises are, what great peace abides in the soul of anyone who makes them well, and what great fruit and light they provide

toward knowing how to direct one's life well and for the service of God in whatever state one is in. Examples given should be of people who did not decide to enter religious life; it is fear of the idea that they will end up entering religion, or that only religious and similar persons make the Exercises, which frequently renders people reluctant to make them.

[4] When such a person has been persuaded to make the Exercises as they should be made, it is much better if he can make them outside the house in a place that is secluded and where he would be able to hear Mass and vespers, or at least Mass.

[5] However, if he is given a room in the house, it should be in the most isolated part of the house. He should be told he is being given this room so that he will not lose any spiritual benefit for want of a place—but on the stipulation (assuming he has money to pay with) that he is being given only spiritual care and a room, along with a bed in case he has none of his own or could not bring it without difficulty. He will pay for his own food: the buyer or dispenser will keep a record of the food he gives him and what was spent on it, and after the Exercises are over will give him a full accounting.

[6] He should be told that it would be good for him to pay at the start enough or more than enough to cover his expenses, with any balance being refunded at the end—the reason for this being only that concern about providing his expenses will not get in the way of his making the Exercises well.

[7] Beginning with the day he starts the 1st exercise, the person who brings the exercitant his food should follow this procedure: when clearing the table after dinner in the forenoon he should ask the exercitant what he wants to be brought for supper, and after supper what he wants for dinner the following forenoon. He should then bring neither more nor less nor anything other than was requested; he should bring it at the exact time requested, neither earlier nor later. He should not be satisfied to let him say, "Just bring me what the brethren get." He should apologize and tell the exercitant that this would be against the procedure of the Exercises, and that he has to ask explicitly for what he wants; if all he requests is bread, or only an ounce of bread, that is what he is supposed to bring him, and nothing else. Thus, as regards quality, quantity, or time he is supposed to stick exactly to what the exercitant tells him. Furthermore, he is not to converse with him about anything other than matters connected with serving him, such as bringing his laundry, telling him that dinner is ready, or similar matters, as has been stated. In addition, he should find out when the exercitant goes to Mass, and during that time he should make his bed and clean his room and do any needed straightening up. He shall also not let anybody talk to the exercitant without the director's permission. He shall also let the director know at least once a day what and how much the exercitant has eaten, etc. Each day he shall record what he gives the exercitant so that at the end he can give him a full accounting. He shall also be most

careful to edify the exercitant with his humility, self-control, and eagerness to serve him for the sake of Jesus Christ in any needs he may have, with very evident charity and with the observance of a holy and discreet silence; he should also pray specifically for the exercitant every day, and for the director as well, so that they may both accomplish the will of God.

[8] If the director judges that it would be for the exercitant's spiritual advantage to have one of the brothers or priests visit him occasionally, he can do this. But no outsider should visit him, except where this is unavoidable.[2] If one of our men does talk with him, he should be told to converse only in a general and global way about the service of the Lord; he should say nothing that could be construed as either directly or indirectly trying to attract the person to the Society. He should not talk about the Society at all, or ask the retreatant if he has made a decision or whether he has any questions. If the retreatant attempts to ask him anything or share anything with him, he can tell him that the director will answer him and that he himself does not have permission to talk about these things. If he does have such permission, what he says should be cautious and well thought out and edifying. He should not urge him to choose one or another state, unless the exercitant already feels himself inclined to a particular state and has told him this; then he may, after careful reflection (and supposing, as I have said, that he has permission) tell the exercitant what he thinks in the presence of the Lord, if he judges that saying it at that point might confirm the exercitant in his good resolve or help him to turn away from something which is less good and to place himself back in God's hands to be guided by him. But, as I have said, he must constantly be on guard not to talk about anything which might suggest that he is trying to push him toward the Society. This would be against the rule of the Exercises and against the purity of spirit of the Society, which does not want anyone to be moved to enter the Society otherwise than by free choice and at God's will and prompting, even if he is so obviously a suitable candidate as to exclude doubt. Besides, to act otherwise would be thrusting one's own sickle into the harvest of the Lord, who at this moment wishes to dwell with the exercitant's soul at his own good pleasure. Moreover, with the exercitant having been moved at such at time by the advice or efforts of a mortal human, the door will always be open for the devil to tempt him by suggesting that had it not been for the influence of so-and-so's advice he would never have taken such a step, and that the idea came from a human being, and humans are nearly always wrong. And so the devil will always have this temptation at hand.

[9] The one giving the Exercises should be governed by the same rule. He should take care to contribute nothing of his own beyond the ministry of giving him the Exercises as they ought to be given, with a great deal of charity,

---

[2] On this point see González Dávila's comment, Doc. 31.28.

concern, and prayer. He should beseech God earnestly on the exercitant's behalf not to allow this soul to be led astray because of the sins of the one giving him the Exercises. Further, he can tell the exercitant that he should ask our Lord in prayer with all his heart for the grace, first, of not seeking either consolation or desolation in these Exercises or wanting to make them for any reason except the love of God, etc.; secondly, of being able to make the Exercises seriously, overcoming every obstacle; and thirdly, of deriving from them whatever fruit will most redound to God's glory and the good of souls, etc.

[10] ON HOW TO GIVE THE EXERCISES IN THE FIRST WEEK.

[11] 1. On the evening that the exercitant goes into retreat, all he should do is to prepare and dispose himself by prayer to make the Exercises perfectly and as a noble knight of Jesus Christ. Since it is a matter of such importance to him, he should be urged to great earnestness, for Scripture says, "Cursed be he that does the work of the Lord remissly" [Jer 48:10]; and also to be both simple as a dove, always interpreting whatever is done or said in his regard in good part, and wise as a serpent, not concealing any thoughts which the devil or the good spirit give him but instead telling them to the director so as not to be led astray. And for this, if he has not gone to confession and Communion and is accustomed to do so frequently, he may do this before beginning the Foundation, etc.

[12] He can also be told by way of remark or admonition to remember that the fruit he draws from the Exercises will be proportional to how fully he abandons himself into the Lord's hands to do with him according to his will, as Scripture says, "My son, give me your heart; and I will fill it" [Prov 23:26; Ps 81:11].

[13] 2. With an educated person the director should display greater learning, but with charity and humility.

[14] 3. This will contribute much to the exercitant's forming a high opinion of the director. For the same reason, the director should not bring the book of the Exercises along with him but come with what he has to say well prepared beforehand. He should have the exercitant write it down on the spot in a very abbreviated form, more succinctly than in the text of the Exercises.

[15] 4. As is stated in the rules, the director should not spend much time with the exercitant except where necessary. He should not speak so fully that the exercitant no longer feels a desire to know more, or gets the idea that he is incapable of working out anything more to say on his own. He should give the exercitant a starting point and a method for discovering things by himself, for this is ordinarily what is helpful.

[16] 5. It seems preferable that the director make his visit in the morning, the mind being more apt at that hour to penetrate things, etc. On the other hand, people are often in greater need in the evening, because at that time there is generally an increase of temptations and desolations, the mind being less ready for contemplation and consequently more restive and vulnerable to temptation, and hence in greater need of consolation.

[17] 6. He is accustomed to go every other day,[3] but I think this should be done only exceptionally. From my own experience, I think that it is best to make a visit once a day and no oftener unless some particular need arises. However, in the case of some very mature and settled persons, omitting one day's visit might be all right, perhaps even advantageous, etc.

[18] 7. In dealing with the exercitant he should try to maintain a holy gravity, even more so with important personages, but with tokens of great humility and charity. He should make the exercitant understand that a given thing is for his greater profit, and he should not be as the scribes and Pharisees but as one having power [see Matt 7:29].

[19] 8. In the First Week not much is needed in the case of persons who are advanced in the way of the spirit and who have long been going to confession and Communion, and who wish to find out in which state they can best serve God. Indeed, if it is possible they should complete their general confession and the whole First Week in four or five days. The opposite holds for those who are less well disposed. To bring them to lament their sins and understand how serious a matter it is to have offended God, they can be given additional exercises, such as on death, the particular judgment, the general judgment, etc.

[20] 9. In the case of such persons and of any persons who are not yet abandoned into the hands of God our Lord, etc., so that he can dispose of them and direct them toward what is best for them, and who come into the Exercises with their own plans and intentions, it is important to make every effort to rid them of this imperfection, for it is a moth which consumes the precious robe of their true vocation and utterly prevents them from discovering the truth. Anyone known to be very obstinate in this regard before entering the Exercises should not have been encouraged or allowed to make them until he had reached greater maturity by means of frequent confessions, as has been said. However, once he has begun making the Exercises we have to try to help him. A good aid for this is to keep him for some time in reflection upon the Foundation, in the Particular and General Examens, and in learning how one sins by thoughts, words, and deeds—for an additional three or four days in which to mature. If he remains quite obstinate throughout the First Week, I do not think I would proceed with him, or at least I would give him the remain-

[3] See González Dávila's comment, Doc. 31.29.

ing Exercises as expeditiously as possible. Nevertheless he should be dismissed in a way that will not cause him to give up coming for confession and for familiar and spiritual conversations. (This supposes that he is a quite promising subject and that there are no others better disposed than he upon whom to bestow your efforts.)

[21] 10. Before giving him the Foundation, the director, after himself carefully examining the twenty guidelines that are placed at the front of the Exercises for the instruction of the one giving them, should give the exercitant four of the guidelines contained there, in the following order: Annotations 1, 20 (either entire or whatever part he judges suitable), 5, and 4. Then he should give him the Foundation, explaining it in such a way that the exercitant will have a starting point for finding what he is seeking. A path should be opened for him as follows: "To help you understand the problem of making an indifferent use of the means God our Lord has given us so that we can reach the end for which he created us, and so that after grasping this you will place yourself unreservedly in his hands, since this is the foundation for finding what we are looking for, consider the following: There have been persons who took the path of religious life and did not persevere in it but refused to bend to the sweet yoke of the Lord, and have consequently gone to hell because they abandoned religious life and through their own fault died apostate. Others entered religion after having been unable to live in the world without sinning and offending God or without failing to make much progress in the Lord, etc., and they reached sanctity; if they had married they might have gone to hell. Similarly with all the other states of life, one after another: some who possessed riches have earned heaven, others who possessed riches have earned hell. Since this is so, and since the evil does not stem from the state itself, it certainly comes from our side in embarking on things unthinkingly and inclining our minds without reflecting whether this is right for the service of God, whether it is my calling, whether this is the best path for me to travel and so reach the end for which God created me. Not everyone can be a religious. The Lord says, 'He that can take, let him take it' [Matt 19:12], indicating that there are some who cannot and that those who can, if they want to be perfect, or even in a certain sense if they want to be saved, are obliged to take it, for it appears to be a precept inasmuch as he says, 'He that can take it, let him take it'—in a case where they judge that they would be unable to keep the law of God our Lord in the world or where their calling is so manifest that they are under obligation to follow it.[4] Now it is certain that since this difficulty is real, and since we do not know what is right for us, we need to abandon ourselves wholly into the hands of God our Lord. And so you must ponder well this Foundation." The Foundation can be divided up for him into three parts: (1)

---

[4] See González Dávila's criticism of this in Doc. 31.30.

the end for which God created us; (2) the means; (3) the problem of choosing among them without knowing clearly which is the right one for him, as was stated above, with the ensuing harm—so as to motivate him to place himself in an even balance.

[22] 11. If he is properly disposed, the exercitant can be given on the same day, after the Foundation, the Particular Examen which follows, along with the notes pertaining to it, since in order to sow the good seed you first have to pull up the bad weeds and thistles, etc., which is the purpose of this exercise and the one which follows for the evening. An explanation should be given to him of how many ways it is possible to sin and to merit in one's thoughts, as is stated in the Exercises. If necessary, each item can be given on its own day, for the exercitant's greater spiritual help.

[23] 12. Note that the Particular Examen should be given as soon as he has begun the Exercises, in order to uproot and exclude anything which could keep him from making them well.

[24] 13. For this purpose, one ought to explain to him before the 1st exercise four of the twenty preliminary guidelines: Annotations 3, 11, 12, and 13. He should then be told how to make a general confession by using the considerations presented there, and others if he so wishes. He should be told that in order to do this well certain exercises are given. Then, on the first day, he should be given the 1st exercise with four repetitions. After that he should be given the ten Additions for making the Exercises well. On the second day he should be given the 2nd exercise, on the third day the 3rd, with repetitions, etc. But, as was stated above, if the exercitant is a spiritual person who has already lamented his sins, etc., he can be given all the exercises in a very short time.

[25] 14. If it is seen that he is beginning to need them, the exercitant can be given the fourteen Rules for the Discernment of Spirits for the First Week, which are found near the end of the Exercises.

[26] 15. The 2nd exercise of this Week is given not for the exercitant to begin examining his conscience for confession but so that he can look in a global fashion at the many sins he has committed and at his evil past life, and experience dismay at them, come to repentance, etc.

[27] 16. When only one exercise is given on a day, it can be divided up so that he makes one or more points in each hour, with one or two repetitions of the entire exercise.

[28] 17. The one giving the Exercises ought to have read over ahead of time all the rules contained in them, and even reviewed them once or twice. In giving them he should preserve their order. This is very important. When I was giving them our Father insisted on this very strongly with me; for otherwise the director will make many mistakes and the exercitant will not make the progress he ought to make, as experience has shown.

[29] 18. As the Exercises state,[5] during his preparation for confession the exercitant should not be making any exercise; and his preparation for confession should come after he has been given all the exercises of the First Week, along with a procedure for writing down his sins and recalling them. Father Master Polanco's *Directory*[6] is very useful for this task.

[30] 19. In observing the rules or ten Additions which are given for making the Exercises well, care should be taken to have them observed very exactly, as is directed, seeing to it that there is neither excess nor too much laxity. The exercitants' characters also need to be taken into account. Melancholic persons should not be pressed too hard but given free rein with most of them; the same is true of persons who are delicate and not much used to such things. But careful thought must be given to what will be most helpful. I myself have employed leniency in these rules with some persons and it did them good; with others I used considerable strictness, but as gently as possible, and I observed that by the Lord's grace this did them good also.

---

[5] The following instructions are not in the text of the Exercises, but can be found in Doc. 3.10–11.

[6] This refers not to Polanco's directory for the Exercises (Doc. 20) but to his manual for confessors and penitents: *Breve directorium ad confessarii ac confitentis munus rite obeundeum* (Rome, 1554).

Directives and Instructions of St. Ignatius

We have gathered here directives urging the use of the Spiritual Exercises from letters commissioned by St. Ignatius during the last years of his life. They are followed by an instruction sent by him in the early 1540s to the Jesuits of Portugal and some pertinent passages from his Constitutions of the Society of Jesus. *(Original in Spanish.)*

I. From a letter of Juan de Polanco, by commission of St. Ignatius, to Father Felipe Leerno, February 3, 1554:

[1] . . . Regarding the Spiritual Exercises, our Father has asked me to send a reminder everywhere to make efforts to employ them with men and also with women (who, however, ought to come to the church to receive them). This applies to the exercises of the First Week, leaving people with one or another of the Methods of Prayer, according to their capacity.

[2] This refers to Exercises without having the persons go into seclusion but instead with their taking a few hours each day for this purpose. In this way the effectiveness of the Exercises can be communicated to a large number of people, up to the general confession and some Methods of Prayer, as has been stated.

[3] Our Father also says he wants a weekly written report on whether anything is being done with regard to the Exercises; i.e., the numbers of those who make them or have been urged to do so—just as is done with the numbers of our students.

[4] In giving the Exercises in full form there is no need to be so liberal. In fact, they should be given only to very capable subjects, such as some who are suitable for our Society or other persons of importance, because for these persons they would be particularly valuable and the time would be well spent on them.

[5] Your reverence should not be surprised at our Father's strong insistence on this matter of the Exercises. For among all the means used by our Society this one is in a special way the Society's own and one which God our Lord has made great use of for countless souls. Moreover, it was by this means that the majority of the good subjects in the Society today were drawn there from the world, so that if we wish to swell the Society's numbers with good men this would appear to be an excellent means. For married persons and other persons

24

in the world or in religious life the Exercises are likewise extremely valuable, especially the First Week. . . .

II. From a letter of Juan de Polanco, by commission of St. Ignatius, to Father Jean Pelletier, May 30, 1556:

[6] . . . Regarding the Exercises: if there is no time for giving them, it need not be done. And among the persons to whom they ought to be given those come first who might be suitable for religious life and have not yet decided on their state, as are some learned persons of talent or learning, or others who, if themselves helped, will be able to help many others—assuming the availability of time and place.

[7] The exercises of the First Week can be extended to large numbers of persons, including women and married ladies. But once they have made their general confession and have been left a memorandum and instruction on how to pray and examine their consciences, one should proceed no farther.

[8] The Second and Third Weeks are for the persons mentioned above, who are suitable to become ministers. The place for these persons could be in the college itself if they are good subjects—or in a house nearby.

[9] And since this is a means for winning a considerable number of people for God's service and very characteristic of our Society, our Father wants a brief report on whether the Exercises have been suggested or given to any one or to no one. This report can be brief, as it is for the number of students. . . .

III. From a letter of Juan de Polanco, by commission of St. Ignatius, to Father Gaspar Loarte, June 5, 1556:

[10] . . . As for giving the Exercises, in the case of women they should be given nowhere but in the public church; and unless they come every day, or every other day, the Exercises should not be given to them.

[11] As for married men and any others not suited for the religious state: they can be given the Exercises by coming to either the church or the house. Both for women and for such men the Exercises of the First Week are sufficient, with the addition of something on the manner of praying and examining their consciences.

[12] As for going on to the other Weeks, not everyone is capable of this nor is the time required well spent on everyone. Rather, this is for persons who, themselves being helped, will be able to help many others, as are in particular persons suitable to become good ministers and who have not already decided their state of life. It would be well for such persons to make the Exercises in full form, at least up to the decision. However, if they decide badly or do not cooperate, one should not proceed further even with these

persons.

[13] If a room nearby can be found for such persons, that would be preferable. An occasional good subject could also be received in our house for this purpose if there is room. If not we should manage as best we can.

[14] And if there is no opportunity for giving the Exercises, that too can be reported, viz., that the Exercises are not being given to anyone. . . .

IV. From a letter of Juan de Polanco, by commission of St. Ignatius, to Father Cesare Helmi, July 4, 1556:

[15] . . . The decision not to go beyond the exercises of the First Week can be made for one of two reasons: either because the persons making them are not capable of it and it is not worth wasting a lot of time on them, or else because the one giving the Exercises is not very experienced in giving them.

[16] Regarding the first reason: the Exercises should normally not be given to persons unsuitable for the religious life, except for those of the First Week and some Methods of Prayer.

[17] Regarding the second reason: those without personal experience of the Exercises will have a hard time giving them. However, with regard to our own men, there would be no harm in giving them the exercises of the other Weeks also, while not entering into the matter of the elections for a state of life with them. The method taught in the Exercises could, of course, be applied to some other elections, but without touching on their state of life. . . .

V. From a letter of Juan de Polanco, by commission of St. Ignatius, to Father Fulvio Androzzi, July 18, 1556:

[18] . . . Among the things which are usually of great and interior help to people your reverence knows one that is of great importance: the Exercises. I remind you then to make use of this weapon that is so familiar to our Society —although the First Week can be extended to large numbers of persons, with the addition of one or another Method of Prayer. To give the Exercises in full form one needs to find subjects who are capable and apt for helping others when they themselves have been helped; otherwise one should not go beyond the exercises of the First Week. Your reverence should keep an eye out to win over some good subjects for the Lord's service, and for them this is an excellent way. . . .

VI. Instruction of St. Ignatius to the Jesuits of Portugal (probably from the early 1540s):

To our men in Portugal, for their protection and advancement in the Lord:

[19] With the confidence in you all which I feel and with the assurance that my words will be received with the same intention and wholesome will with which I write them, I shall say a few things by way of admonition as if I were admonishing my own soul.

[20] If I were there with you I would try to write out my sermons first before giving them. I would not touch on points that were problematic or presented any difficulty, but would simply correct faults and sins in a modest and orderly way.

[21] If I gave the complete Exercises it would be to very few: to persons of learning or very eager for perfection, or of quality, or suitable for the Society.

[22] As a rule I would give the Exercises of the First Week. After the general confession I would give some Examens and normally proceed no further.

[23] I would be quite sparing in giving the elections, and only to educated persons who are very eager to make them or who could not be the source of any embarrassment to us. It sometimes happens that people leave the Exercises without having made all the profit they expected, and are tempted to say in public that we were attempting to impoverish them by urging them to poverty and religious life.

[24] I would have no dealings with young women of the common people except in church and quite publicly. On the one hand they are lightheaded and, whether true or not, such dealings often give rise to bad talk since such women are generally more inclined to be giddy and inconstant in the service of God our Lord. Later their devotions not infrequently turn either to the flesh or to weariness—to get people to give them alms for their bodily needs.

[25] If I dealt with women about spiritual things it would be with noble ladies and those against whom no evil rumor could arise. Above all I would never talk with a woman behind closed doors or in a secluded place, but in public where they can be seen, so as to forestall any criticism or suspicion.

[26] In all spiritual dealings I would strive to make a single step of safe progress rather than attempt to gain a hundred at risk of harm to myself or of conflict with the other in order to move him ahead (even though I might be very much in the right). A scandal, whether with foundation or not, does us much more harm than if we were to accomplish only half the good which God our Lord does through us, especially in times and places such as these.

[27] I would make a point of giving satisfaction to all men and women with whom I deal or speak, so that when I do this they may see in me someone who is moved by lowliness and humility and not at all insistent on my own way, especially in matters of little or no importance.

VII. From the Constitutions of the Society of Jesus:

[28] The first experiment [of the novices] consists in making the Spiritual Exercises for one month or a little more or less, that is to say, in the candidate's examining his conscience, thinking over his whole past life and making a general confession, meditating upon his sins, contemplating the events and mysteries of the life, death, resurrection, and ascension of Christ our Lord, exercising himself in praying vocally and mentally according to the capacity of the persons, as he will be instructed in our Lord, and so on (Examen, 4.10).

★

[29] After they themselves have experienced the Spiritual Exercises, they should get practice in giving them to others. Each one should know how to give an explanation of them and how to make use of this spiritual weapon, since it is obvious that our Lord has made it so effective for his service.

[30] They could begin by giving the Exercises to persons with whom less is risked, and consulting about their method of procedure with someone more experienced, noting well what he finds more useful and what less so. Their explanation of the Exercises should be such that it not only satisfies people but also moves them to desire to take advantage of the Exercises. Generally, only the exercises of the First Week ought to be given. When the Exercises are given in their entirety, it should be to exceptional persons or those who desire to decide upon their state of life (IV, 8.5 and E).

★

[31] The Spiritual Exercises should not be given in their entirety except to a few persons, namely, those of such a character that from their progress notable fruit is expected for the glory of God. But the exercises of the First Week can be made available to large numbers; and some examinations of conscience and methods of prayer (especially the first of those which are touched on in the Exercises) can also be given far more widely; for anyone who has good will seems to be capable of these exercises (VII, 4.F).

From the *Memoriale* of
Father Luis Gonçalves da Câmara

It was to the Portuguese Jesuit Luis Gonçalves da Câmara (c. 1519–1575) that St. Ignatius dictated his autobiography toward the end of his life. While serving as minister (subsuperior) under St. Ignatius at the house in Rome during the same period, Gonçalves da Câmara also kept a log of the saint's actions and sayings. Years later back in Portugal he expanded this record with further recollections. These additional comments are here given in italics.

The following excerpts from the Memoriale *relating to the Spiritual Exercises correspond to numbers 226, 254, 305–307, and 311–313 of the complete text as edited in the* Monumenta Historica Societatis Iesu, Fontes Narrativi, I. *(Original in Spanish and Portuguese.)*

[1] [February 26, 1555.] Talking of the Exercises [Father Ignatius] said that of those he knew in the Society Favre held first place in giving them, Salmerón second, then Francisco de Villanueva and Jerónimo Domènech. He also said Estrada was good at giving the First Week.

[2] One thing I will remember is how often I have noticed that in his entire manner of proceeding Father observes with exactitude the rules of the Exercises. He seems to have rooted them first in his own soul and to have drawn the rules from his own interior acts. The same can be said of Gerson[1]— living with Father seems to be nothing else than reading Gerson translated into action.

★

[3] [March 2.] The Exercises are better for someone who has not yet decided on a state of life, because then there is a greater diversity of spirits; also when someone is in temptation or distress, for the same reason. The method used in Spain for giving them in the beginning is in general good.

[4] I need to remember what Father said to me one day: that he did want anyone to go to the colleges without making the Exercises first, at least the

---

[1] At that time Jean Gerson was widely thought to be the author of the *Imitation of Christ*.

First Week with the Methods of Prayer. I must also be sure to remember to ask Father to give me his definitive views on how to give the Exercises.

★

[5] April 1. Speaking to me about the abbot's[2] Exercises, Father told me the following. First, that the rigor with which the Exercises were made today was nothing compared with how they had been given in the beginning. In those days nobody made them without going several days with nothing to eat (though no one urged this on them). Nowadays he would not dare allow more than a single day to a hardy exercitant—though he felt no scruples about the past. All the first fathers made the Exercises in full form in seclusion. The one that did the least abstinence went three days without eating or drinking a thing —except for Simão [Rodrigues], who, not wishing to interrupt his studies and being in poor health, did not leave his house or do any of these extreme austerities but was given the meditations by Father, etc.

[6] Favre made the Exercises in the suburb of Saint-Jacques in a house on the left bank, at a time when wagons could cross the Seine on the ice. Although Father used to watch to see if an exercitant's lips were sticking together in order to tell if he was not eating, when he examined Favre he discovered that he had gone six full days without eating a thing and was sleeping in his shirt on the wood they brought for his fire, which he had never lit. He was making the meditations on the snow in the courtyard. When Father discovered this he told him, "I am confident you have not sinned in this but instead have merited greatly. I will come back in less than an hour and tell you what to do." Then Father went to a nearby church to pray. His own wish was for Favre to continue without eating as long as he himself had; it would have been only a little while longer. But this desire notwithstanding, after making his prayer he did not dare to allow it. And so he went back to light him a fire and fix him something to eat.

[7] Besides his severe fast Master Francis [Xavier], because he was one of the outstanding jumpers on the Île de Paris, tightly bound his whole body and legs with a cord; thus bound and immobilized he would make the meditations.

[8] "tightly bound his whole . . ."—*Apparently during his meditations he kept getting thoughts of his jumping and the good times he had on the island, and this as a source of natural pleasure. To overcome this passion at its root he bound his limbs, mortifying them with the bonds against his agility and skill in jumping.*

[9] Pietro Codazzo, to whom Father also gave the Exercises, went three days without eating, although he was a big eater and accustomed to comforts, and a man who in Pope Clement's time had been administrator to the pope's own administrator. He came out quite well disposed and some time later decided to enter the Society.

---

[2] Girolamo Martinengo.

★

[10] [April 3.] Father thinks that persons one hopes may eventually follow the way of perfection, even if they request the Exercises, should not be given open Exercises.

[11] "Open"—*By open Exercises I mean when the exercitant is not completely withdrawn and has only a limited amount of time for the meditations, continuing to go out and attend to his affairs.*

[12] During the Exercises nothing should be given in writing.[3] Likewise one should not talk about religious life unless the commandments and counsels in general have first been presented and the person has decided for the counsels. Learning today of someone who did not follow this rule, Father said he did not know how to give them.[4]

[13] Father said that he wanted to make a directory on how the Exercises ought to be given. He said Polanco should ask him about uncertain matters at any moment, since for the Exercises he would not have to think much before answering.

Our Father later made this directory[5] and I brought a copy to this province.

---

[3] This contradicts what was said by St. Ignatius himself and many other directories; see Doc. 1.16.

[4] See Appendix 2 for Juan de Vitoria's election, which was made in the stages as prescribed here.

[5] Presumably this is our Doc. 1.

PART II

OTHER 16TH-CENTURY MANUSCRIPT DIRECTORIES

From the Writings of
Father Jerónimo Nadal

Entering the Society of Jesus in 1545, the intense Majorcan theologian Jerónimo Nadal quickly became one of St. Ignatius' closest collaborators. He was commissioned to promulgate and implement the Society's Constitutions in Spain and elsewhere. The following remarks on the Exercises are taken from his talks and regulations.

I. From his exhortations in Spain, 1554 (original in Latin[1]):

[1] However, in addition to this double concursus, one natural and one special to all believers, there is a most special concursus by which a person pursues purity of heart and perfection; and we do this, following the Church and the tradition of the Doctors, by the practice and fruit of prayer. That is, by this concursus we seek an understanding of the truths at their roots.

[2] We are assisted in this by the Exercises, upon which God has also conferred remarkable effectiveness, the principal cause of which is God's will, as in his other operations. God gives effectiveness to the words of anyone he wishes, thereby manifesting his own power. This was visible in St. Stephen's sermon: it contained hardly anything not found elsewhere in the Scriptures, yet we see it had an astounding power. The only reason we can assign for this is the will of God.

[3] We must think the same of the Exercises, which contain almost nothing that cannot be found in other books: it is from the will of God that they possess the efficacy we see.

[4] Nevertheless, one reason can be assigned by way of consequence: the Exercises give an excellent procedure for removing hindrances to perfection, following the method handed down by the holy Doctors.

For the mind is first cleansed by means of general confession, etc.—in such a way that even venial sins are carefully uprooted, and passions overcome or weakened (first part of the Exercises).

[5] He also includes the sacraments and the frequent practice of self-exami-

---

[1] The translation here follows Miguel Nicolau's transcription of this text in *Monumenta Historica Societatis Iesu, Epistolae et Monumenta P. Hieronymi Nadal,* V, pp. 90–93, rather than that given by Iparraguirre in his *Directoria.*

nation, and this with the greatest care. Nor, though apparently quite ordinary, should these examinations be despised; instead they should be highly valued. They purify the mind so that prayer will not be hindered. Note also that this examination is remarkably well organized, as is easily seen.

[6] Nor should we pass over in silence that there is in addition the power of the sacrament here, when a person resolves to go to confession and make satisfaction. . . .

[7] The method and order of the Exercises is purgation, illumination, union; and the sequence followed is the proper one, beginning humbly and without undue curiosity from the bottom, with great faith and hope.

II. From the eighth exhortation at Coimbra, 1561 (original in Spanish):

[8] Regarding the first trial [for novices], that of the Exercises: we should take them all together, or, in the case of those who are unwell in the head, little by little. The value of making them is obvious, since it takes considerable effort and skill for a person to abandon the bad habits he brought with him from the world; and for this persons are great helped by prayer, the rudiments of which they learn in the Exercises. We shall speak of this later.

[9] The Exercises are made at the beginning also to test each person's aptitude for spiritual things and for prayer, elements of such importance for our institute that it would seem that anyone completely unsuited for them should not be allowed to enter.

[10] It is also important for the superior who will guide the man to observe which Week—the First, the Second, etc.—will be most helpful for him, and to exercise him in the elements of that Week.

III. From the ordinations for the colleges (original in Spanish):

All Should Make the Exercises

[11] The *Constitutions* require that the Exercises be given to those being received into the Society, and it would seem that there can be no grounds for substituting other experiments for this, as can be done, with discretion and dispensation, in the case of the other experiments.

[12] Hence, all must go through the Exercises. Note, however, that those who have already decided to enter the Society should not be given the elections, and that we should more readily give to all the Exercises of the First Week, with a few meditations from the Second Week to introduce them to the method of meditation.

[13] However, one should not fail to give the full Exercises (without the elections, as indicated) to anyone in whom there is no evident reason why not, such as would be notable lack of capacity, clear indications that they will do no

good, mental or physical disability.

[14] The decision to give them entire or only in part, as has been stated, lies with the ordinary superior, who will consider the particulars of the case. It should be borne in mind that the Exercises are given differently as a probation than for a need on the subject's part.

[15] The Exercises given for some need will have that need as their criterion. Those given as a probation will be as follows. One should give the exercises of the First Week to those entering their initial probation, for seven or eight days during that period right at the beginning of their first probation.

[16] Together with these exercises they should make their general confession; then they will do what is further indicated in the *Constitutions*, 1, 4. Thus their first step will be the Exercises and the general confession, and their final one reconciliation and reception of the most holy Sacrament. All this can be accomplished in twelve or fifteen days, as indicated in *Constitutions*, 1, 4.

[17] The superior will decide whether to give the remaining exercises as part of the probation. However, it would seem that normally, once they have entered the house and performed some jobs, they could be given the full Exercises—assuming, as has been said, that they are capable of it.

[18] If they made the complete Exercises before the first probation, this would normally be preferable.

[19] The Exercises should not be given in the house to externs. However, we might try to have some friend with spare rooms who could put up those wishing to make the Exercises. Failing this, the Exercises might be given in an isolated room in the lower college.[2]

[20] Externs making the Exercises in the house must pay their own expenses. If possible they should not make them in the house; if they do, it should be in the lower college.

[21] When the Exercises cannot conveniently be given to an extern outside the house, then he may be given a room in the house, as far removed as possible from contact with the brethren, particularly in cases where there is a prospect of his changing his state for the Society.

[22] Normally, because of our principle of poverty, externs making the Exercises should pay their expenses. But if the college is well off, or the rector has reason to think it better to ask nothing, this can be done. Moreover, one need not ask anything if there are grounds for thinking the person will afterwards volunteer payment.

[23] The custom in Spain of making them in the house should not be changed, unless there are good accommodations elsewhere.

[24] Ought one hand over in writing the exercises that are given? Reply: It is good to dictate the points or leave them concisely written out; of course

---

[2] At Coimbra there was a second, somewhat out-of-the-way college.

they should be given a fuller explanation orally.

[25] Ought the Exercises to be given, as was formerly customary, in full rigor as regards enclosure and other matters, since it is thought that the lack of this is the reason why they are no longer so effective? Reply: It seems good to give them strictly, according to the character of the person, as is stated in Annotations 18, 19, and 20 of the Exercises.

[26] The text of the Exercises should be amended to read *etiamsi planum compertumque est.*[3]

[27] While the rules at the end of the Exercises warn against making public statements against ecclesiastical or civil authorities, although our men may admonish them of their duty in private [362], nevertheless the point of this admonition is to forestall public bitterness and detraction.

[27A] Should any such be feared, this private admonition ought to be forgone. In general one should first endeavor that the admonition be made through someone else. But if the need is urgent and there is no one who can give the admonition with the same prudence and moderation, the matter must be carried out in such a way that the admonition is by all means taken easily and produces its effect.

IV. *From the revised General Instruction of 1576 (original in Latin):*

[28] If a man experiences a loss of spirit because of dealings with externs, or has become worldly in some way and is giving little edification to the neighbor, he should endeavor to help himself by the Society's ordinary means, seriously and energetically, in gentleness of spirit.

[29] The means I refer to are the customary ones: spiritual reading, more frequent Communion, more time for prayer, and, if necessary, making all or part of the Spiritual Exercises; also doing some exterior mortifications. All this should be done following the judgment of his confessor or superior. The latter, depending upon the situation or the person's character, can alter these means or add various others; they must take care that mental dissipation or loss of devotion is not ignored.

[30] The Spiritual Exercises should be given to those who are accepted into the Society. It does not seem that there can be any justification for replacing the Exercises with other experiments or probations in the way that the other

---

[3] While Ignatius' Spanish original of rule 14 for Thinking with the Church begins, somewhat ambiguously: "Though it *be* very true that no one can be saved without being predestined . . . ," the printed Latin version (the "Vulgate") had translated: "Even if it *were* altogether ascertained and defined that . . ." Nadal directs that in the Latin copies the verb "were" be changed to "is," to avoid the impression that Ignatius doubted the standard opinion. (Because the Vulgate bore papal approval, however, Ignatius himself was unwilling to have this alteration made.)

experiments may be changed at the superior's judgment and dispensation.

[31] They should also be given to those received as temporal coadjutors, but with adaptation being made to their capacity. Thus, all should go through the Exercises—with the reservation that those who have already decided to enter the Society should not be given the elections, at least not on their state of life.

[32] One may more readily give to all the Exercises of the First Week, along with a few meditations by way of introduction to the method of meditating. However, one should not fail to give the entire Exercises (except the elections, as mentioned above) to anyone who is qualified. It does not seem that there can be any justification for failing to give all of them to persons who are qualified. This as a general rule—the ordinary superior will decide on particular cases.

[33] The Exercises are given to our men in two different ways: as both a probation and a source of spiritual help, or as a source of spiritual help only. In the first way, the exercises of the First Week are given in the first probation, or, after entrance into the second probation, the remaining exercises right away. This first way serves to test the degree of spiritual capacity in the one making the Exercises; his spiritual profit is not the only concern.

[34] The Exercises are given in the second way either because of need, when someone has become spiritually lax or weak, or also for greater spiritual fruit. This will all be at the discretion and direction of superiors.

[35] Women should not be given the Exercises without the consent of their husbands, parents, or guardians; nor nuns without the consent of their superiors. In giving them to women who are not under authority, all the greater circumspection and prudence is required. Lay women should generally be given the First Week and somewhat more, without the elections. Nuns may be given more than this, but judiciously and without the elections, at least as regards their state of life. They should be given to lay women only in the church; to nuns in the place designated by their superiors, so long as they are inside the cloister and our men outside, separated by an iron grille and curtain as is customary.

[36] Those chosen to give the Exercises should have received a talent for this, and the complete Exercises ought to be given with great exactness. When they are not given in full, the last of the guidelines at the front of the Exercises should be observed [18, 19].

[37] Any of our men who have not yet made the Exercises should do so, and in full form if in the superior's judgment their health and capacity permits. This will be without the election of a state of life; nevertheless, they could make an election on how to reach greater progress in the Society, submitting any election they make in this regard to the judgment of superiors.

[38] If possible, externs should not make the Exercises in the house. If they

are received in the house, they should pay for their own expenses. The reason why this should normally be done is deduced from the principle that we profess poverty and hence may not be prodigal in expenses to which we are not obliged. However, if the college is rich, or if the rector decides for good reasons that another course should be followed, or if there is no doubt that the person will spontaneously offer payment, none need be demanded.

[39] Where it exists, the practice of having externs make meditations within the confines of the college should not be changed, unless this can conveniently be done outside the college. However, if the Exercises are given inside the college, it should as far as possible be somewhere apart from where the brethren live.

[40] Externs who are to be given only the exercises of the First Week for making a better general confession, or who are otherwise not being given the Exercises in full form, should not be received in the house or in the college.

[41] Great care ought to be taken that men deemed likely to have a talent for giving the Exercises should themselves be given them in full form. All should know that they are extremely powerful and that immense fruit should be expected from them; that this is a palmary and extraordinarily effective ministry of the Society. Hence those with ability for this should be selected: they should first give the Exercises to our own men under superiors' supervision and instruction, and then to externs as superiors judge opportune.

Notes of St. Peter Canisius

For all their brevity, these notes preserved in the handwriting of the apostle of Germany (1521–1597) reveal much about his understanding of the Exercises. (Original in Latin).

METHOD OF GIVING THE EXERCISES

[1] Physical exercises differ from spiritual; yet they correspond nicely in many points as regards the body and the soul of the one exercising, because of their value and necessity for a person engaged in action.

[2] The purpose of the Spiritual Exercises is threefold: that a person overcome himself; not be moved by any evil affection; and direct his affections toward God.

[3] He should remember to bring a generous spirit and to offer himself wholly to his Creator.

[4] He should lay down the Foundation in three points: the purpose for which man was made; the functions of creatures; and his own behavior in the use of them.

[5] He should resolve to make both the General and Particular Examens.

[6] To say the canonical hours with greater devotion and composure.

[7] Briefly to explain the General Examen [32–42].

He should be asked how he is doing—first in the corporal aspects of the method of meditation; second, in his colloquies with God and the saints; third, in his own quest for contrition, sorrow, and tears for sins; fourth, in his resolve to offer himself wholly to his Creator; fifth, whether he experiences spiritual movements and thoughts produced by diverse spirits; and sixth, regarding the ten Additions.

From the
"Spiritual Directory of the Mixed Life"

The lengthy unpublished treatise from which the following section is taken was composed either by St. Ignatius' secretary, Juan de Polanco, or by his companion and first successor as general of the Society of Jesus, Diego Laínez. Our passage gives an adaptation of the Spiritual Exercises for a week-long retreat. The development of the points is remarkable for its breadth of vision, encompassing every level of reality. (Original in Latin.)

ON THE SPIRITUAL EXERCISES

[1] The Spiritual Exercises. They are readily and effectively given chiefly to persons who in some way are already disposed for them, v.g., persons being moved by God's inspiration to a conversion of life. Nevertheless they can also be of much help to persons perplexed or uncertain about their choice of a state of life or otherwise burdened.

[2] Nevertheless, they can be given to anyone wishing to make spiritual exercises. For God does not deny his grace to those who prepare themselves for it.

[3] *How to give them.* The preambles of the Exercises. These are the preparatory prayers and preludes to be made in every exercise or meditation. They also include the composition of place and imaginative representation of the matter of meditation. Then comes the preparatory prayer or petition for the grace of contemplating. Then come the points of the matter for meditation. Finally, the colloquies and prayer. Requirements are: solitude, freedom from worry and exterior occupations, avoidance of possible distractions and hindrances, a daily schedule, the right attitude, elevation of mind beyond the book, a guide.

[4] For brevity and convenience we have reduced these Exercises to a week. Depending on persons and situations they can be expanded to two weeks or longer.

[5] MONDAY. The points for meditation are these. Consideration of God's

omnipotence, wisdom, and goodness. Creation of heaven and the elements, of creatures, angels, men, animals, trees and plants, etc. The bliss of heaven, the fatherland, happiness, eternal life. The glory, joy, splendor and endowments of the souls and bodies of the blessed. . . . Our first parents' primitive state of innocence and justice. The twofold fall of man by original sin, concupiscence and actual sin, issuing in the woes of earth and of mankind: hunger, thirst, war, storms, cold, heat, the passions, poverty, scarcity. These points can be considered for several hours and can be enlarged upon by an experienced retreatant as well as by the guide. So also with the following points.

[6] *Consideration of oneself.* TUESDAY. Points: consideration of self and of time and place: Where are you? Who are you? Also, reflection on each phase of your life: the time, the place, the state of life, circumstances in which he then lived as a sinner in each period; the things he happened to witness, and how swiftly and unmindfully everything passed by. His state of mind then and now.

[7] *Consideration of his relations with others.* Who were the persons? What were his pursuits? In what town? In what apartment, privy, business? What situation, what state of life?

[8] *Consideration of death.* Death of friends and acquaintances, companions, relatives, neighbors, fellow-townspeople, lodgers, parents, etc.

[9] *Reading.* Job, Ecclesiasticus, Lamentations, Jeremiah and other prophets will be helpful.

[10] WEDNESDAY. Points: consideration of the transitoriness and vanishing of the ancients. First, people: the Hebrews, Greeks, Romans; kings, philosophers. Secondly, structures: palaces, theaters, castles, towers, citadels, and cities —Rome, Carthage, Troy, Constantinople, Jerusalem, Babylon.

[11] *Consideration of earthly realities.* The third consideration is of realities now. First, earthly ones: citadels, castles, villages, where there are so many families, men, women, children, servants, living not in solitude but for themselves, vainly wasting their lives on worldly pursuits and rarely thinking of God.

[12] Secondly, spiritual realities: monasteries, houses, chapels, churches, hospices, hermitages—in different places: towns, mountains, forests, hills, wildernesses, where numerous religious render service to God.

[13] Elevation of eyes and mind beyond the book and the buildings in the vicinity out to the horizon: the countryside, harvests, forests, rivers, provinces —the whole geography of the world. From there lift your mind and eyes to the heavens. A global view of the world in all its variety and woes.

[14] THURSDAY. The points for consideration are these. Think over and weigh each of my own vices and sins throughout my life—the places, times,

persons, and other circumstances, as above on Tuesday.

[15] Secondly, examples of God's vengeance. God's judgments and justice. Sins before conversion: sins of heart, tongue, deed, omission. Sins since conversion. Penance, contrition, confession, satisfaction and restitution. Fasting, prayer, watching, disciplines, good and helpful actions. Amendment. Faith, hope, charity.

[16] The third consideration is of death: its hour uncertain, suspected, unprovided. Preceding illness, wrenching of nature, awareness of sin, disorder of whole body, expectation of demons, shortness of life, loss of joys, separation from loved ones, accusation of the soul, fear, burial, mourning, being forgotten.

[17] FRIDAY. Points: The first consideration is of hell. Deep and formless chaos. A place of shadows, fire, smoke. Darkness, cries, shrieks, wails, blasphemies, noise, stench, eternal torments: cold, heat. Terrifying sights. Sufferings. Punishment of each sin, loss of the vision of God.

[18] The second consideration is of the judgment. Terrifying signs: lightning, thunderclaps, shaking of stars and elements. The angel's trumpet, resurrection, fear, appearance before heavenly court and demons. Examination, separation, deserts of one's deeds, manifestation of one's conscience. Sentence.

[19] SATURDAY. The points are these. Repetition and reprise of the fall of man from Thursday. The first consideration is of mankind's redemption and the life of Christ. First, recall Christ's humanity: annunciation, conception, birth, baptism, public life and preaching, betrayal, last supper, washing of feet, entering the Garden, arrest, accusation, scourging, crowning, crucifixion, death, burial. But in all these consider the words and deeds of Christ, together with his virtues: his humility, poverty, patience, obedience, sparingness, charity, chastity, prayer.

[20] Secondly, contemplate Christ's divinity: prophecies, signs and miracles at his birth, transfiguration, miracles, resurrection, ascension, sending of Holy Spirit, appearances.

[21] Thirdly, lives of saints: the humility and greatness of spirit of the apostles, martyrs, confessors, virgins, monastic fathers, hermits. Their wanderings, sufferings, shipwrecks, hunger, thirst, temptations, falls; their virtues: poverty, patience, longsuffering. Miracles, martyrdoms, endurance of wrongs, tortures, contempt, teeth of beasts. Places: churches, catacombs, caves, tombs, etc. Reflect on all these.

[22] SUNDAY. We have reserved this day for the end out of regard for the joyful meditation of the mysteries especially suited to it.

[23] *Eternal life.* Consider eternal life. Contemplate and praise the holy Trinity. Also God's power, wisdom, goodness. Other topics of consideration

and contemplation: glory, reward, joy, endowments. . . .

[24] *Reward.* Reward of the blessed: consolation, divine sonship, kingdom, possession. Glorification of the blessed: wisdom, friendship, honor, power, assurance, joy, eternity, vision, splendor, song, aureole.

[25] As stated above, these exercises can be shortened or lengthened according to persons, occupations, time, and convenience. During the Exercises doubts and perplexities can be resolved, v.g., regarding the choice of a state of life, pursuits, conversion, carrying out good works, giving alms; change or abandonment of occupations; making vows, entering religion, ordering one's associations and one's household. Here also is the place for discernment of spirits, for knowing by what spirits the exercitant is troubled or tried.

Counsels of Father Duarte Pereyra

Father Duarte Pereyra (1527–1587) was a novice-master in Spain for most of his active life in the Society of Jesus. He himself made the Exercises under Francisco Villanueva, considered by St. Ignatius the best at giving them after Pierre Favre and Alfonso Salmerón (see Doc 6.1). The following directives are excerpted from a treatise (about 1562) which also includes his own meditations and other comments on the Exercises. (Original in Spanish).

PREFACE

[1] Knowing how to give the Exercises well is a matter of great service to God our Lord because of its great benefit to souls, as experience has abundantly shown. Hence, it is very important that the Society have men who know how to exercise this ministry—so characteristic of the Society—with the competence it requires.

[2] For much harm has been done by persons giving the Exercises who did not know how to do it. Doing it well is difficult, at least for those just starting out. For it is clear that they will not immediately grasp the articulation between the First and Second Weeks, their harmony and correspondence, which seems more divine than human.

[3] For it is not easy to grasp how the Foundation of the Exercises contains the foundation of the election, and how from that point on the exercitant is beginning to be prepared for the election, which has as its foundation the indifference which is such an essential element there. Accordingly, because of this and other difficulties in this matter, a superior decided that a father who had been exercising this ministry for many years[1] should note down some guidelines and clarifications for those starting out in this ministry. And this is why he has done so, setting down here some remarks on how he gave the Exercises. Anyone wishing to take advantage of them will here find the matter; he himself will provide the form according to the gifts which the Lord bestows on him.

[4] He will find a number of propositions against which some have objected (unjustifiably, because the teaching is plain and clear) here grounded in the teaching St. Thomas—thus sparing him a certain amount of study and labor.

---

[1] Pereyra himself.

[5] In my treatment of the Second Week I have put down verbatim a discussion I had with a learned and distinguished doctor of theology who, though recognizing that our Lord was calling him to religious life, fiercely resisted this vocation. It was a gracious discussion and it turned out well for the man, who eventually received from the Lord a very special grace so that he responded to his vocation by entering the religious order to which he had been called, living and dying there with great edification and now, as we may believe, enjoying his God in heaven. And to heaven may the Lord deign to bring us all, so that all together we may behold him clearly, love him, and enjoy him, praising him for ever and ever. Amen.

[CHAPTER 1]
[6] SOME COUNSELS FOR THE ONE WHO WILL GIVE THE EXERCISES, HELPFUL FOR THOSE STARTING OUT TO GIVE THEM, REGARDING THE FIRST TWO WEEKS

In the name of the Lord

[7] The first thing to note is that the one giving the Exercises should give great attention to the quality of the person to whom he is giving them, taking into account his age, education, intelligence, temperament, etc. For the Exercises must be given in a form adapted to the characteristics of different persons, as our Father of happy memory remarks in the Annotations [18].

[8] Let us assume I am giving the Exercises to a highly educated person, a doctor of theology, whom I desire that God our Lord should call to the state of perfection, since it seems to me that he would give great service to our Lord in that state. Let us also assume that he asks to be given the complete Exercises.

[9] Now the first thing that this father would do was to explain to the person what the term Exercises means: it means any method of examining one's conscience, any method of meditating, praying, contemplating, praying vocally as well as inwardly, and finally any other spiritual operation. For just as we call taking a walk, hiking, running, or jumping physical exercises, so here we call these spiritual activities spiritual exercises. Holy King David used this term when he said: "And I meditated in the night with my own heart; and I was exercised and swept my spirit" [Ps 77:7]—where he was apparently speaking of the examination of conscience.

With these preliminaries he would then launch into the Exercises

[10] And then he would launch into the Exercises and dispose the person for them, telling how the Exercises were a highly effective means for bringing a person to knowledge of his God and Creator and to knowledge of himself, and how they were all the more effective in proportion as the person receiving them disposed himself to take advantage of them. . . .

Humility

[11] And a very important virtue for a person's disposing himself (through the Lord's grace) to have the divine Majesty communicate himself will be the virtue of humility. According to St. Thomas, this is a virtue which makes a person inclined and eager to subject himself to God for God's own sake and to man for God's sake.

[12] This virtue arises from knowledge of God and knowledge of oneself. For by realizing one's own nothingness and God's infinite being, one's own lowliness and God's sublimity, one's own poverty and God's wealth, one's own weakness and God's omnipotence, one's own ignorance and God's infinite wisdom, a person comes to say: "Abyss calls unto abyss" [Ps 42:8]. The abyss of human wretchedness calls out to the abyss of God's infinite perfections, and this prompts us to subject ourselves to God. . . .

[13] And then he must made to understand how the benefit he gets from the Exercises depends in great part on his communicating himself to the one giving them, rendering him an account of his manner of proceeding in prayer, of the questions and difficulties that occur to him, of whatever hinders his progress, and of whatever our Lord communicates to him.

[14] The director should make clear in this matter that he does not wish to know any sinful thoughts or desires, but only what is needed to direct him for his advancement, to help him with remedies against temptations from the devil, both the clear and manifest as well as those concealed under the appearance of good when the devil transforms himself into an angel of light. Just as a physician cannot cure a patient unless the latter discloses to him the causes of his sickness, so a spiritual physician cannot help him unless he communicates himself to him.

Practical versus theoretical knowledge.

[15] Here it is very important to get him to understand the difference between knowing a thing speculatively and knowing it practically. A physician can *say* what milk is—its essence and accidents, with all its qualities and properties—but not *savor* or taste it like a nursing infant; the latter cannot *say* what milk is but does *savor* it. Similarly, this divine wisdom is very different from theoretical knowledge; it is a savoring wisdom which gives one a taste of the things of God, a practical and loving knowledge which ignites and enkindles the will. . . .

[CHAPTER 2]
THE GOAL OF THE FIRST WEEK.

[16] Once the exercitant has been disposed by means of these consider-ations, he should be told what is the first thing we should try to achieve, what is the goal. For this, we could explain to him how the Exercises contain four Weeks which deal with different matters, as will be seen when we have put them into practice, and how three of these correspond to what the doctors call the purgative, illuminative, and unitive lives; and how just as each of these lives has its own purpose which it strives to achieve, so also each of these three Weeks, which we will now begin with the Lord's help to discuss, has its own purpose.

[17] Now the aim sought in the First Week with the Lord's grace is for a person to know himself, and by knowing himself to know that he has gone astray, trod the path of his own perdition, walked apart from his God and his entire good. This knowledge will beget a strong desire to remedy this situation, which will be by achieving genuine penitence.

[18] And for this he should be told how the root and cause of human perdition stems from the want of this knowledge, so that a person is alienated from himself; and how the opposite of this will produce, with the Lord's help, his good and his remedy.

Prayer and meditation

[19] Now what we must do is take steps to enter interiorly into self-knowledge, since we have said that it is from the root of self-knowledge, with the Lord's grace, that must spring our good and our remedy, as we see in the Prodigal Son. An essential and effective means for this is prayer, joined with meditation. . . .

[20] I have explained that the purpose of this First Week is for a person to enter interiorly into self-knowledge, for from the root of self-knowledge, with the Lord's grace, must spring our good, and how this goal corresponds to the goal of the purgative life, which corresponds to this First Week. This goal consists in a great loathing for sin because it is an offense against God, and an effective purpose of amendment; in a loathing for oneself; in a love for con-tempt of self; and in a strong desire for genuine penitence, giving rise, with God's grace, to the practice of penance. And for this purpose we have taken meditation and prayer as a means, and we have seen how important this is as a remedy for a person's evils and how it has been a means for self-knowledge.

Another means

[21] Now with the Lord's helps I will discuss another means for a person to enter into himself and know himself. Here Aristotle says there are two modes of demonstration: *propter quid,* and *quia*—two ways of knowing a thing: by its *causes* or by its *effects.* He says that we know a thing when we know its causes ("True knowledge is knowing a thing through its causes") and he posits four of these: efficient, final, exemplary, and material. Now since in the Foundation of the Exercises both modes of knowing man are given—by causes as well as by effects—we will begin to discuss this.

[22] The Foundation begins: "Man is created to praise his God, to reverence and serve him, and by so doing attain to his end."

The Foundation

[23] The first point, self-knowledge through one's causes (*propter quid*) is comprised in the statement that man is created. To create is to make something from nothing; and from this we will derive the four causes of the human person: efficient, final, exemplary and material. . . . Then it is said that God created him to praise and serve him . . . and that this is done not only with the heart but also with the tongue and with works, ascribing to God and to his grace the gifts we have received, performing all our works for his glory and honor. The reverence and homage owed to this Lord is called *latria,* an homage owed to God alone. This is rendered to God, as St. Augustine says,[2] by faith, hope, and charity. For these give rise to the virtues and gifts, and thus to obedience and observance of his commandments and of all that human beings are bound to.

[24] This constitutes the first part of the Foundation. The second is recognition that everything God has created in this world—all creatures—were for the sake of man and to help him and to be means for achieving this end for which he was created. . . .

[25] Now let us turn to practice, and to how we ought to employ these means for the our goal of self-knowledge. Let us place before our eyes this end for which God created man, and let us look at ourselves in it as in a mirror which shows us what is clean and what is dirty, what is orderly and what is disordered. . . .

---

[2] *Encheiridion* 1.3.

Comparing the means with the end

[26] So now, looking at ourselves in the mirror of this end, let us begin comparing the means with the end, to see and recognize the correspondence or lack of it between the means we have used and this end, comparing with the end our use of all creatures. How have I made use of them so that they would be means for my achieving this end?—food, clothing, property, honor, office, dignities; my senses, faculties, health; imagination, irascible and concupiscible appetites, memory, understanding, will; thoughts and desires, words and actions; how have I used faith, hope, and charity; the sacraments, the blood of Christ and all his exemplary actions done for our imitation; and in fine all God's gifts?

[27] Then I should ponder the lack of correspondence between all these means given us by the Lord and the end for which he gave them to us. In this way we will recognize the disorder of our lives and begin to know ourselves and begin to enter into ourselves: "And returning to himself he said," etc. [Luke 15:17]. This will give rise to a desire for the remedy, which is genuine penitence.

[28] And this is the second way for knowing oneself by the effects, as we know a tree by its fruits. . . .

Indifference

[29] The third point of this presupposition and foundation of the Exercises is that it is essential for a person to make himself indifferent to all created things (so far as this is allowed to the liberty of our free will and not forbidden), so that for our part we do not desire health rather than sickness, riches rather than poverty, honor rather than dishonor, long life rather than short, and so in all other matters, choosing only that will help us toward the end for which we were created.

[30] Regarding this we should pay close attention to what our Father of happy memory says in Annotations 5, 15, and 16, because this is a crucial point on which much needs to be done. This indifference is an abandonment whereby a person places himself in the hands of his God and Lord, saying: "My Lord and my Creator: here you behold, O Lord, all my liberty, all my powers, my senses and my body and all that I have. I place it all in your hands. Dispose of it and of me as is most for your glory and honor and the salvation of my soul."

[31] Doing this genuinely with all our heart helps greatly toward God's communicating himself to us, because we are opening the door of the heart for the Lord to work great things in it. . . .

[32] And so explaining the Foundation in this way and having the exercitant meditate it for an entire day, pointing out to him the three points mentioned above: the first on self-knowledge through causes, the second on self-

knowledge through effects, and the third on indifference—this concludes the Foundation.

Examen

[33] Next one should explain to him the General and Particular Examens before the meditations. Explaining them to him just as they are written, one should show him how essential both of them are. . . .

First meditation

[34] Now we can begin presenting the 1st meditation, that of the three powers. It is so called because the acts of all three powers are used in it: memory, understanding, and will. It comprises the preparatory prayer common to all the exercises, two preludes, three points, and a colloquy. On the occasion of this exercise all these elements should be explained once and for all for the remaining meditations. . . .

[35] Now we must explain how the purpose of the meditations we will now be presenting is to achieve the two things we discussed in the Foundation. The first of these is self-knowledge, coming to an awareness of the disorder in our lives by comparing the means with the end, as we indicated previously. There we said that the end of this First Week was that of the purgative life, which consists in self-knowledge by knowing oneself a sinner, an offender of God's Majesty; knowing oneself a traitor inasmuch as mortal sin is properly a treason committed against his Majesty, since by it, as far as a person can, he makes into his god the creature for which he deserts his own God, and would wish that God were not God; for all this is comprised in a mortal sin, as the doctors tell us.

[36] From this he ought to derive a loathing for himself, recognizing himself as his own enemy, as is evident from his actions, which are the actions of a true enemy: to deprive his soul of spiritual life by expelling God from his heart, to receive Satan into it, to deprive himself of the grace of his God, of the virtues and gifts, and in fine of his whole good—these are the actions of an enemy.

[37] This should give rise to a loathing for sin because it is an offense committed against his God.

[38] This should give rise to strong and effectual desires for genuine penitence and a wish to avenge upon himself the offenses against his God, and in fine from this a love for self-contempt, a desire that all creatures should treat him badly, for this is what is owed to a sinner for having offended and insulted his God so far as he was able. Cajetan says: "The sinner behaves as an enemy toward God," for by what he does he aims to rob God of being, life and all his perfections: all this is included in mortal sin.

[39] The second matter treated in the Foundation was the indifference and

abandonment that a person should have as regards things which can have a good or bad purpose and which a person can use well or ill. For this is the second thing which a person making the Exercises of the First Week must endeavor to achieve with the Lord's grace; and the one giving the Exercises must endeavor with the Lord's grace to draw the exercitant in every way possible to this indifference, inasmuch as a good election, and the proper disposition for it, depends upon this. And if he perceives the exercitant to be attached to anything which hinders this indifference, he must sincerely strive, both in his conversations and through the exercises, to give him one push after another until the Lord through his goodness draws him to it. He should note that this is one of the most essential points of the Exercises.

[40] For upon this depends the matter of the election which is so seriously dealt with in the Second Week. It is to this election that everything preceding seems to be geared, as to a point so crucial for the salvation of his soul as it is to receive his state of life from the hand of God and not motivated by any disordered passion or attachment.

[41] Note that during the First Week he should not be told what this indifference is ordered to, but only when nothing further can be done in the Second Week. For if he knew, he would perhaps lack the courage to pursue it, not clearly understanding it. Thus it is to these two matters that the exercises of the First Week are ordered, and the director should carefully ask an account of them.

CHAPTER 3
[42] AN ACCOUNT SHOULD BE ASKED EACH DAY ABOUT THE FOLLOWING MATTERS, OR SOME OF THEM

1. How he is doing with his prayer.
2. How with his recollection and attention.
3. Questions that occur to him and that he has.
4. Things standing in the way of his advance.
5. What our Lord is communicating to him.
6. Temptations, since this is a time when they are experienced more than before.
7. How he is doing as regards knowledge of his past life.
8. How he is doing as regards loathing for the cause of such evil to him, viz., sin and himself as the cause of sin.
9. How he is doing as regards a desire to perform satisfaction to his God for the insults committed against his Majesty.
10. How he is doing as regards indifference and self-abandonment in placing himself in God's hands so that the Lord may dispose of him and of his affairs as is most for God's glory and honor and the good of his soul.

11. What most hinders him in the matter of indifference, trying to get this out of him in detail so as to help him get rid of it: whether it is honor, wealth, a position, a personal attachment. This is very important for knowing how to help him in this matter.

How it would be good for the one going to give the Exercises to prepare himself so that the Lord may act through him and make of him a suitable instrument

[43] This is an essential point. For this it would be good for him to try hard to have a right intention in this ministry, desiring or seeking therein nothing except what is for the greater honor and glory of the Lord and the greater good of the person's soul. It is the task of charity to bring it about that one seeks not himself or any interest of his own but only the glory of his God, "for charity seeks not what is its own but what is of Christ Jesus" [see 1 Cor 13:5]. Moreover, perfect charity goes even further, bringing a person not only not to seek his self-interest but to seek the glory and honor of God; and not only that, but to seek what will be *more* for the glory and honor of his God. Of the soul which regards this Lord with this straight eye, the Song of Songs says: "You have wounded my heart, my sister, my spouse, with one of your eyes" [4:9].

[44] The second point is that he should place no reliance upon himself or upon his own strength and efforts, and great reliance upon the Lord and upon the special help which God has promised the members of the Society for carrying out their ministries. The grace of religion is a special help and concursus of God for carrying out the ministries of the order, and particularly this ministry, just as we have seen and every day continue to see how much our Lord has worked in souls through this means, in which our Lord will not let us down unless we place some obstacle from our side. In this regard, note that the devil will certainly battle against God in this work and throw up obstacles like a Goliath, for he knows the benefits which a soul can derive from the Exercises. And so with the Lord's grace one ought to go forth as a David and say: "You come against me with spear and sword, but I come against you in the name of the Lord of hosts" [1 Sam 17:45]. You, Satan, enemy of God, come against me relying on your strength, but I come against you relying on the strength of my God, in whom I have placed all my hope and trust, and whose glory and honor I seek, so that "I can do all things in him who strengthens me" [Phil 4:13].

[45] Thirdly, he should endeavor to make the exercise himself first and meditate it before giving it to the exercitant, so as to be able to give it more forcefully and effectively. For this it would be helpful, when possible, to make a little use beforehand of the discipline, as was done by one director through whom the Lord in his goodness wrought great things in the Exercises, such as

the conversion of great sinners. Thus the benefit to the exercitant depends very much upon the one giving the Exercises. For it is clear that a person who is more advanced and more fervent in the love of God, who has greater zeal for God's honor and for the progress of souls, will accordingly achieve more results: "Zeal for your house has consumed me," etc. [Ps 69:10].

The Additions, a great help for making the Exercises better and achieving what one desires

[46] It would seem that the Additions should be given after the exercitant has made at least the 1st exercise of the three powers and the exercise on sins, having practiced each of these meditations for its full day, doing them four times a day, twice in the morning and twice in the afternoon—in the first hour after rising in the morning, then before dinner, etc. This is because the exercitant will by then have a desire for means to make the exercises better and more systematically; and also because at this point the meditations and exercises he has already made will have aroused in him devotion and a wish to do some penance and to achieve genuine contrition for his sins. Hence now rather than earlier seems a good moment.

[47] And he should be instructed on how necessary for this purpose are corporal austerities such as fasts, disciplines and hairshirts, night-watches, rough bed, etc. For the Lord gives to each one the grace of the Lord, and it would seem that a person disposes himself for this better if he strives and labors to achieve it not only with his spirit but also with his body.

Other matters on which to instruct the exercitant

[48] Regarding meditation, he should be told to endeavor to avoid in this exercise too much intellectual speculation and to try to handle this matter with the affections of the will rather than reasonings and speculations of the mind. For this, one should be aware that the intellect both helps and can hinder the working of the will, which is love for divine things. For, while it is necessary for the intellect to precede the will, guiding it and giving it knowledge of what it is to love, nevertheless when the speculation is excessive it hinders the affections of the will, for it does not allow it room or time to work. The reason for this is that the energy of the soul is finite and limited, so that the more it invests in one direction the less remains for the other. . . .

He should also be instructed that there are two chief impediments to prayer

[49] These are the assaults of extraneous thoughts and the lack of consolation and devotion. For both one must provide him with correctives so that he will know how to act in both situations. First, as regards the assaults of vexatious thoughts which distract us and rob us of attention in prayer.

[50] This brings punishment upon a person, for at the time allotted for

dealing with his God he turns his back at the most favorable moment and walks off. And certainly when this happens through one's own fault, negligence, and carelessness, it is right that he be punished, for punishment is best used where there is guilt.

[51] However, when this is not through our guilt but because of damaged nature, as frequently occurs, there is no reason for receiving much punishment, since nature has become so disordered through sin that the lower powers do not perfectly obey the higher part of the soul, i.e., reason and will, and hence the imagination wanders from home without leave and no one notices it. This is such a natural and ordinary thing that no matter how perfect persons may be they cannot be wholly free of this weakness. . . .

[CHAPTER 4]
THE SECOND WEEK OF THE EXERCISES:
"I AM THE WAY, THE TRUTH, AND THE LIFE"

[52] So far in the First Week we have dealt with seeking sorrow for our sins, knowledge of self, indifference, etc.; and by the Lord's goodness we have reached the point where you have gone to confession and received the Blessed Sacrament. Now, having left behind the old man and the old life, we need to clothe ourselves with the new man and deal with the new life which we are to live in the brief span of life remaining to us. This we will now discuss with the Lord's help.

[53] For this, a great help will be the indifference which our Lord in his goodness has bestowed on you, together with a longing that our Lord will inspire and move you to what will be for the greater honor and glory of his divine Majesty and the salvation of your soul.

[54] And for this we will now be going into the life of Christ our Lord, who says in St. John's Gospel, "I am the way, the truth, and the life." . . .

Now let us see how we shall travel by this way which is Christ our Lord

[55] We do this in three manners: by knowing him, by loving him, and by imitating him in the exemplary actions which the Son of God performed so that we might imitate him in them. As regards the first, viz., the knowledge we ought to have of Christ our Lord as God and as man: already, through God's goodness, we have through the light of faith sufficient knowledge to save our souls, provided it is a living faith which causes one to act out of love.

[56] And as for the second: the truths taught us by faith about who Christ is in himself and who he is and has been for us, when well considered and pondered through the Lord's grace, beget love, which should lead to imitation of his virtues; and this must be the goal of this Week; for this is the goal of the illuminative life to which this Week corresponds: aspiring to love for Christ

our Lord and striving to grow continually in this love, for it is this which leads to the third element, imitation.

[57] Thus, this "way" is the natural-born Son of God, the second person of the most holy Trinity, true God and man, redeemer and savior of the world. And who will not yearn to travel by a way so lovely and delightful, with such a goal at the end? The feet by which we are to travel on this way, as we have said, are the understanding and will, good thoughts and desires. St. Augustine: *Pondus meum amor meus; eo feror quocumque feror* ("My love is my weight; wherever I am borne, it is my love that bears me there")[3]

[58] This is the matter of the Second Week: coming to knowledge of Christ our Lord. Not only to know him but to love him, and as far as we are able with the Lord's grace to imitate his virtues. This is what St. Paul says: "Clothe yourselves with our Lord Jesus Christ" [Rom 13:14]. We do this by imitating his poverty, his humility, his patience, his obedience—in fine, by following his virtues. To clothe oneself with Christ is to represent the person of Christ as far as is possible to a human being with the Lord's grace.

[59] For now since he became man, "taking the form of a slave," [Phil 2:7] he has walked in steps that we can imitate; he took these steps then so that we would imitate him in them and be able to fulfill our desire to be like God: "You shall be like gods" [Gen 3:5]. And holy King David said: "They have seen your goings, O God, the goings of my God, of my king who is in his sanctuary" [Ps 68:25]. These are the steps the Son of God took from heaven into the Virgin's womb, from the Virgin's womb to the stable, from the stable to the circumcision, from there to the Temple, from there to Egypt, to the desert, and, ultimately, to the cross. To the imitation of these steps the prince of the apostles, St. Peter, urges us, saying: "Christ suffered for us, leaving us an example, that you might follow in his footsteps" [1 Pet 2:21].

[60] Now let us enter upon the meditations of the life of Christ our Lord, which we will take as means for obtaining with the Lord's help the end of which we have spoken, setting it before ourselves as a target at which we will aim all our arrows.

Much attention needs to be given to how to give the exercises of the Second Week, for it is difficult

[61] The order this father used was the following. The first day he gave the exercise on the Incarnation and the Nativity.

[62] The second day those on the Shepherds and on the King,[4] since it is here that the King first begins to call people.

[63] The third day the exercise on the Circumcision, and the Three

---

[3] *Confessions* xiii.9.

[4] Note Pereyra's disregard of the order of the key meditations of the Second Week.

different Kinds of Persons, because this exercise demands detaching ourselves, and if this is painful for us, so was the circumcision for Christ.

[64] The fourth day the exercise on the Kings, and the Three Degrees of Humility for us to offer to the Lord in place of the three gifts.

[65] The fifth day the exercise on [the Presentation in] the Temple, together with the first [time of] election in the form of points for him to meditate on.

[66] The sixth day the exercise on the Flight into Egypt and that on his remaining behind in the Temple.

[67] The seventh day the exercises on the Baptism and on the Desert.

[68] The eighth day proceeding through the life of Christ our Lord up to the Calling of Apostles, giving the exercise on the Two Standards at this point, or later on, reserving the final [time of] election for when the person is seen to be properly disposed to conclude an election. The order in which these exercises are given depends greatly upon the exercitant's disposition, on how he is doing with the first way of making an election.

[69] Before going into detail on the days, two things should be mentioned here which will be of value for all the exercises of the Second Week.

[70] The first is to instruct him about the statement toward the end of the point that "I should apply this to myself, drawing fruit from it." He should endeavor with the Lord's grace to draw one or all of three things: love, fear, and confusion. Thus, from knowledge of the goodness of God shining forth therein and of the benefit done to me, I will derive love; from my ingratitude toward this Lord I will draw confusion; and likewise fear, lest I now fail to take advantage of this great goodness, for it all might end up being more for my condemnation. In the love is included desire to imitate Christ our Lord, since, as we have said, love gives rise to the desire to imitate.

Regarding the colloquy to be made at the end of the exercise

[71] Here one should proceed thus: at the end of the exercise one should add to the particular benefit I am thinking about in the meditation all the other benefits of creation, conservation, government, redemption, vocation, as well as all the others—recognizing how I am insufficient to give thanks to the Lord not only for the particular benefit but even more for such a great number of them. I will call upon all creatures to help me praise and thank God, since I am incapable of doing this for so many benefits, saying, "All you works of the Lord, bless the Lord," etc. [Dan 3:57].

[72] And I will say with holy King David, "What shall I render to the Lord for all that he has rendered to me?" [Ps 116.12], and with an affection of gratitude I will make an offering to the Lord of myself and of all that is mine, saying: "Lord my God, here you see all my liberty, memory, understanding, and will, my soul and my body, all that I have. Do with it and with me

whatever you wish, for this is what I wish. I also offer to you, my God, eternal Father, the merits of your most holy Son, our redeemer Jesus Christ, his Incarnation, his life and death," etc. I will conclude with the third element, which is the petition. Here I will ask for the virtues I most need, and for what I wish at this moment, which is for him to show me his will; and I will end asking love for him with the deepest affections I can muster, saying: "O my God, O my Lord, O my entire good, when shall I love you with all my heart, all my feelings, etc.?"

[73] This is treated by our Father in the exercises on the King and in the exercise on the Love of God, for it is good to proceed entirely in accord with them.

[74] *And going into detail on the days of the Second Week*

[75] The way of giving the exercise will be, as our Father says, that one briefly gives the story of the exercise and its points. And what the person giving the exercise needs most to point out for him should always be points geared to the end being pursued, which is knowledge of Christ our Lord, love and imitation of him, correspondence to his calling. . . .

Here he should be instructed that after completing the fourth and final hour of prayer in the afternoon he should sum up of what he has drawn from the four hours of prayer made during that day

[76] This was treated above in the First Week when discussing how to ask an account. Here an account can be asked of the following:

[77] What our Lord has communicated to him with respect to light and knowledge of himself, of his God, of the benefits and mercies conferred upon him, and the devotion imparted to him.

[78] How he is doing in the matter of desires to imitate this Lord, desires to battle under his standard.

[79] How he is doing as to indifference, in regard to placing himself in the Lord's hands so that he may dispose of him and of all that is his in the way most for God's honor and glory and the good of his soul.

[80] An endeavor should be made to learn what he is most attached to, what is his principal hindrance, so as to try to help him break free of this attachment, until the Lord brings him to genuine indifference and self-abandonment.

[81] How he is doing as regards his desire to come to the right conclusion in a matter of such importance as receiving a state of life from the hand of God.

Regarding the second day of the Second Week

[82] Here he used to set up the exercise on the King in this way. He would say how the children born to an earthly king are not born kings and are not born with discretion or the use of reason, so that to become kings they must spend many years before they will be able to have the prudence needed to govern. But this is not the case with the child Jesus, for he was born a king, as the kings acknowledged when they said, "Where is he who was born king of the Jews?" [Matt 2:2].

[83] Secondly, he does not have to wait any time or years for the use of reason or for prudence and discretion, since this child was blessed from the moment of his conception, for at that very instant he beheld the divine essence; and so he is most wise, most prudent, most powerful; he is the king who governs heaven and earth and is obeyed by creatures, for he is true God and man.

[84] And this child, a king from the crib, is beginning to wage war upon the world, the devil, and the flesh; he is already summoning people—shepherds, kings.

[85] Here one can present the exercise on the King; and how the Church here is called militant and in heaven triumphant, for here it has struggle, there victory, triumph, and crown. Here there are two violently opposed armies, Lucifer's and Christ our Lord's: terrifying is the hatred of Lucifer and his devils for Christ our Lord, and so for those who belong to him; hence the struggle of both to get people to fight under their standards, etc.

The exercise on the Shepherds

[86] Regarding this exercise, one should reflect on who the persons were whom God chose to be the first to receive from the angels the good news of the gospel. They were shepherds—poor, ignorant fellows doing their job of watching their flock by night. He did not choose for this the wealthy people in Jerusalem, or the learned, or the noble, or those who had their consolation and comfort on earth.

[87] How they responded to the divine vocation, the divine call: "The shepherds said to each other, 'Let us go over to Bethlehem,' etc. And they came in haste, etc." [see Luke 2:14]. What obstacles will others find in responding to this call? How they will be held back by honor, wealth, comfort, human wisdom, etc.

[88] Then, how those in the household of the Lord who are to be promoted to higher vocations are the ones who do what lies in themselves, giving a good account of their duties and of the lesser calling in which God had first employed them. Thus we see how he called Moses, who was whistling to his sheep like a good and conscientious shepherd, leading them to the thickest and

remotest parts of the desert; God called him to be the ruler of his people. God called David to the kingdom when he was busy with his father's livestock. Saul was called when he was looking for his father's asses, etc. Upon such persons God confers great favors.

[89] At nightfall, when asking an account in this way of the day that has gone by, one should try to learn how he is doing as regards desire and strength for responding to the inspirations of God and the calling of the Lord.

[90] And if he perceives in him resistance and repugnance toward the state of perfection, in a case where it is clear that God is calling him, he should try to help him in this, with the Lord's grace. For this, the following will be helpful.

[91] The great harm that will inevitably follow to someone who refuses to conform his will to God's, for God's will is the first and infallible rule, since, being the primal will, it has no other will by which to be governed and all other wills must be governed by it. Hence, it must be the criterion and rule of every will—and this whether a person likes it or not.

[92] For if he refuses to follow the order of God's mercy he will feel that of God's justice; for by refusing to follow this divine will, the first rule, he will necessarily follow his own will, the cause of all evil, the root and source of all perdition. . . .

Third day

[93] Here one can present to him the exercise of the Three different Kinds of Men. Each has acquired ten thousand ducats, and not with the purpose and pure intention which they ought to have of the service of God and good of their souls; and now they want to have God's approval and to be saved, getting rid of the disordered affection they feel toward the property, which constitutes a hindrance to their salvation.

[94] One should strongly emphasize the great danger incurred by the first two, so that with the Lord's grace the person may place himself in the third degree; and I ought to strive with the Lord's grace to bring him to desire that our Lord should call him to what is more perfect, to what is more for God's honor and glory and the greater good of his soul. Our Father instructs him to ask for this in the exercise of the King, and here in this exercise.

[95] Thirdly, the prayer for what is desired, viz., the grace to choose what will be most pleasing to God and most salutary for myself. Hence, urge him not to be satisfied with a service of God that is good, or one that is better, but only with one that is perfect, according to St. Paul's words: "I beseech you by the mercy of God to present your bodies a living sacrifice, pleasing to God, etc., that you may prove what is the good, acceptable, and perfect will of God" [Rom 12:1–2].

[96] Here one will discover if the exercitant is attached to anything—

whether money or some honor or position, etc.—and see how he is doing as regards indifference, for this will be the touchstone. Here begins to emerge the purpose of the indifference which our Father placed in the Foundation of the First Week. Here the sagacity of the Exercises—which appears more divine than human—begins to become clear, viz., bringing a person to indifference, to abandoning himself into the hands of his God with a desire to choose and adopt what will be for God's greater glory and honor and for the greater good of his soul, for it is this that the soul yearns for because of its great capacity for good, in the awareness that only this can fill its capacity.

[97] And thus, when our Lord has granted this indifference he normally calls the soul to what is most perfect; and to this the soul is normally moved by reason, even though it is true that the conclusion, "This is better and more perfect; therefore it is better for me," does not follow unless there intervenes a calling from the Lord; for whatever state God calls a person to is best for him even if it is not the most perfect in itself; this will relieve a person who was beginning to feel under pressure. . . .

The exercise on the Circumcision

[98] . . . This exercise seems highly appropriate for this day, and can be presented as follows. Here our King and our Creator and Lord, our great commander, shows us the arms his soldiers must fight with to conquer their enemies—the devil, the world, and the flesh. These arms are humility, patience, obedience, etc.

[99] Hence the example he gives us of obedience and humility: he so humbled himself that for our example and cure he even obeyed this onerous precept of the law, taking the mark of a sinner, not caring that because of the mark he took he would be considered a sinner. . . .

The fourth day of this Week

[100] He can be given the exercise on the Kings together with the Three Degrees of Humility. Regarding the first: how they responded to God's call— "We saw his star and have come to adore him" [Matt 2:2]; seeing the star and recognizing through the prompting of the Holy Spirit that it was a sign of God, they set out immediately, breaking through all difficulties that might arise, which would be neither few nor inconsiderable. . . .

The Three Degrees of Humility

[101] They should be given in the form of a meditation and exercise.

[102] The composition will be to see this humble child in a low and humble place, in great poverty, in order thereby to move our hearts to love this virtue of humility and poverty of spirit.

[103] Petition: to beseech the Queen of Angels to obtain from the Lord

grace so that I may offer to his divine Majesty these three degrees of humility.

[104] The three degrees of humility will serve as three points for me to meditate, as I contemplate the examples of this given to us by these holy men.

[105] Here, how Christ our Lord as man subjected and humbled himself not only before the eternal Father but also before human beings, and not only before the Virgin and Joseph but also before sinners, humbling himself to be baptized by his servant St. John.

[106] Further, he humbled himself to the point of wishing to be considered a sinner, as in his circumcision and baptism, assuming the mark of a sinner; and finally he humbled himself to the point of being considered a fool, as happened in his passion. By means of this example I will strive to humble myself as much as possible, in imitation of my God and Lord and entire good.

[107] Beseech the Queen of Angels to obtain for me grace from the Lord for this, remembering the humility by which she so pleased the Lord; in her canticle of the Magnificat she spoke of two things: the Lord's mercy and the means for obtaining it—humility.

The fifth day of this Week.

[108] On this day one can give the exercise on when the Lord was presented in the Temple. . . .

The first election be given on this day in the form of a meditation as follows

[109] The usual preparatory prayer.

[110] The composition will be of that the exercise presented today: the Presentation of the Son of God in the Temple.

[111] Thirdly, to ask the Lord to give me the grace to incline my heart, however great its repugnance, to what I shall ascertain to be his will, to the point where makes of me a sacrifice pleasing to his divine Majesty.

[112] Fourthly, to go through the election as through points, pondering each point in it. . . .

[113] Very appropriate here would be the exercise on the Two Standards of the two supreme commanders, as regards both the summoning of the soldiers and the exercise's teaching on poverty of spirit, which goes well with the calling of poor men, for it is good that those who preach poverty be themselves poor; and those who preach poverty of spirit ought to be poor in spirit.

[114] One should explain that this state is higher than that of the rich. Thus says the glorious apostle St. James: "Let the brother of low condition glory in his exaltation, and the rich in his being low" [James 1:9]. For the state of the poor is closer to that of Christ our Lord and his mother than is the state of the rich; James also says: "Hearken, my dearest brethren: has not God chosen the poor in this world, rich in faith, and heirs of the kingdom which God has promised to those who love him?" [James 2:5]. These are the chosen ones of

God, the heirs of his kingdom, the truly rich with true spiritual, heavenly, and eternal riches.

[115] And when this exercise has been reached, and this Week is coming to its end, it is also to hoped that our Lord will have come to the end with the person who desires what God desires of him, and desires to follow his vocation; and thus, to conclude his election, one need only give him the final election, so that thereby through the Lord's grace he may come to a complete conclusion and decide for this state with an efficacious determination to carry it into act.

[116] Everything stated above I said verbatim during the Second Week to a distinguished and learned person, a doctor of theology, who in his concluding election decided to be a religious, having received a very special grace from the Lord so that he made a vow to join the Society; and in this way he lived and died in the Society in a most exemplary and edifying fashion; and now we may believe that he is in glory rejoicing in his God. And may God deign to bring us all to glory so that we may all together see him clearly, love him, enjoy him, and praise him for an eternity. Amen. This took place in Jesús del Monte in the year of the Lord 1562.

Method of Giving the Exercises Dictated by Father Alfonso Ruiz

Father Alfonso Ruiz (1530–1599) worked as superior and novice-master in Spain, Italy (where one of his novices was St. Stanislaus Kostka), and South America. For a time he was part of a committee charged with drafting an official directory to the Exercises for the Society of Jesus.

The following guidelines of Father Ruiz were recorded by Fabio de Fabi (ca. 1545–1615), his successor as novice master in Rome, possibly around 1568. (Original in Latin).

METHOD FOR GIVING THE EXERCISES
WHICH I GOT FROM FATHER RUIZ

[1] First, he should read the instructions of Father Ignatius so as to be able to follow their precepts more carefully while still moderating and adapting certain of them in accord with the exercitant's character and situation.

[2] Secondly, he should explain to the person wishing to make the Exercises what their purpose is, viz., that he should strive to order his life and dispose his mind to understand and carry out God's will more perfectly. He should tell the disciple to become interiorly recollected, enter into reflection, and have a hunger for colloquy and converse with God. If this is done God is accustomed to communicate many things.

[3] He should lay aside all his other affairs and concerns and should work solely on his own salvation and solid grounding in spirit and the right state of life. If all throughout the year confessors aim and strive to get nothing else than this from their penitents, how much more will one who gives the Exercises do the same.

[4] Thirdly, one who gives the Exercises should be altogether unreliant on his own intelligence; he should rely wholly on God. He should commend the whole business to God, pray, and ask the prayers of others for his disciple. He should talk little with him, except where he judges it would be helpful for dispelling melancholy, furthering his bodily health, or bringing temptations to light. He should warn the exercitant that he ought to take no notice of the director's person—all he will find is an inept and unworthy instrument of

God's grace, blemished with many faults. Instead he should recognize God as
the source of every good thing.

[5] He should take everything told him as coming from an angel sent by
God. Not with human wisdom and prudence but with a simple eye, he should
receive it as intended for him by God, however simple the thing may be.

[6] The director should converse with him familiarly, deal with him trust-
fully, and win over his goodwill so that he will be entirely open with him. He
should tell him to write down briefly the points and course of his meditation,
not worrying about these during the prayer itself but gathering and preserving
them in the examination after the prayer.

[7] Those who are negligent or tepid should be stirred up by means of
penance, for example, by surreptitiously leaving a discipline or hairshirt in their
room. (This requires special tact, particularly when dealing with persons from
north of the Alps.) The more fervent, on the other hand, should be particularly
questioned about matters of sleep and food, and held in check.

[8] Fourthly, the first thing is to give the Foundation to be meditated for a
period of time without prescribing any length or method of preparation. Then
the exercitant should be visited: if he got nothing out of it he should be told to
do it again. In the evening he should be given the Additions and the five-point
General Examen, and then for the following day the 1st meditation or exercise
of the three powers, and so learn the use of the three powers in meditation.

[9] He should spend an hour on each meditation, even if he goes through
four different ones in a single day and repeats them each day up until his
confession. Meanwhile he should be getting ready for his confession, and
complete it by the end of the First Week.

[10] The Rules for the Discernment of Spirits should be given to the more
capable.

[11] Fifthly, the meditation on the King is the first in the Second Week,
which in the Incarnation and Nativity can be practiced for two hours, although
the remaining mysteries of Christ's life should take only one hour each. The
application of the five senses is best made while meditating the mystery itself
rather than in a separate exercise.

[12] Sixthly, meditation on the Passion demands the greatest care: its fruit
is great.

[13] The exercise on Spiritual Love should be given only at the end, since
it pertains to the unitive life.

[14] Seventhly, a man who has entered or been admitted to the Society, or
who has taken vows, should be given nothing on the election. The election
should be given to others—but taking extreme care not to give the exercitant
the impression that one is attempting to persuade him to anything. This care
should be preserved all throughout the Exercises of a person who undertakes
them with the intention of deliberating about his state of life.

Summary of an Anonymous Instruction

The anonymous instruction of which this document is a summary was quite probably by Jerónimo Nadal (1507–1580). Although the original instruction is no longer extant, it was used by Father Gil González Dávila in composing his own directory (see Doc. 31). (Original in Latin).

EXCERPTED FROM THE INSTRUCTION
OF AN UNKNOWN AUTHOR

[1] *Notes on the Exercises, drawn from an instruction*

[2] I. Meaning of the term Exercises. II. Usefulness; fruit. III. Method for giving and receiving them.

[I.]

[3] The director, with a cheerful face, should make the Sign of the Cross. Then he should explain to the person who with a generous spirit is about to make the Exercises what is meant by the term Exercises, etc.

[4] II. THEN HE SHOULD EXPLAIN THEIR FRUITS.

[5] To our own men in the Society we can say that it was through the Exercises that the Society had its beginning, and that they were given by God to Ignatius when he was doing penance and praying. In the same way Ignatius himself, in his zeal for the salvation of souls, later gathered others to whom he gave them, prompted, as we may religiously believe, by this impulse from God to give the same Exercises to others. During his subsequent studies at Paris he gathered other companions by means of the Exercises; and at the Society's beginning anyone wishing to be admitted to the Society was tested by this means. Hence, in the *Constitutions* regarding those being examined it is one of the experiments [*Constitutions*, Examen, 4.10].

[6] To those not of the Society we can speak of the nature and extent of the fruits received by numerous persons—both learned and unlearned, religious and secular, young and old, men and women, virtuous and dissolute, etc. Although with differing degrees of progress, all reached great clarity of mind

and light in the spiritual path as well as an excellent will and fervor in the Spirit of God.

[7] Indeed, it seems that the Holy Spirit is clearly at work in those who make them, giving knowledge of sins, sorrow for them, a will to change one's life, contempt for the world, desire for mortification, etc. Those who have been more engaged in giving the Exercises with the requisite care have experienced these things.

[8] Indeed, there seems to be a unique grace and gift which the Lord has bestowed on the Society for giving these Exercises; it appears that God cooperates in a special way with our men in giving them.

[9] Once the terms have been explained and the fruits set forth, in case the person receiving them might have any remaining doubts, some of the causes of these fruits can be mentioned.

[10] First, of the three ways by which a person can be helped in the spiritual life—reading, hearing the word of God, and meditation and prayer—it is the last mentioned which is the highest and most effective. We know by experience that even when we talk often about something or hear it we do not savor it as much as when we meditate on it, etc. Use the example of someone who sees food, someone who touches it, and someone who tastes it: the third will have a stronger . . ., etc.

[11] Second cause: the director of the Exercises is a living voice, one which will be all the more effective to the degree that the person is more disposed and secluded from distractions.

[12] Third cause: along with hearing the points, the exercitant also has a short written text of them to read, without a multiplicity of other things. Thus, reading, hearing, and meditation all work together.

[13] Fourth cause: because, as we are told by the saints, particularly St. Vincent [Ferrer] in his book on the spiritual way, no one should think he will make progress in the way of the spirit unless he has a master and teacher therein.[1] For just as in other arts and sciences . . ., etc., how much more in this way which is beset by so many dangers, difficulties, deceits of the devil, etc. Hence the one giving the Exercises is a guide who points out the safer and easier way, and with greater fruit. Likewise, the Lord is most pleased with the humility shown in a more learned person's being taught by an unlearned one—as has been the experience of some scholars of the orders of St. Dominic and St. Jerome, who received remarkable benefits. And we should believe that the greater the exercitant's humility—in thinking that he knows nothing and in having great reverence for the director, etc., through whom God will frequently teach him many things, etc.—the richer without doubt will be the

---

[1] *Treatise on the Spiritual Life*, translated by T. A. Dixon, O.P. (Westminster, MD: Newman Bookshop, 1944), ch. 4 (pp. 13–14).

fruits he receives.

[14] A fifth cause is that the exercitant lays aside all his other affairs, associations, recreations, and comforts; and devotes himself totally to God. Upon such persons God is accustomed to bestow his gifts, graces, secrets, etc. Hence the more he withdraws from these human comforts and affairs the more generous he will find God toward him.

[15] It is helpful, however, to have a secluded place, time, scheduled hours, in which to deal with God.

[16] III. METHOD.

[17] There are multiple methods of giving the Exercises, for various types of people.

1. They are given in full form to those who withdraw for a month from all affairs, etc., to a place away from their own house where they have someone serve or bring them their meals and can hear Mass without disturbance and make five and a half hours of meditation, etc.

[18] This method is used with very promising young men—along with the elections, since they have not yet chosen their state in life.

[19] 2. They can be given in less full form in a room in our own house, where they make four and a half hours along with the Examen. This method is more common with our own men who are already in the Society or desire admission; it is done in one of our colleges or houses, in a secluded room with other facilities, etc.

[20] 3. Others, who lack these facilities, or the leisure to go into complete retreat, or this amount of time, are given three, two, or one hour of exercises according to the person's convenience. This will be beneficial for anyone, but more for those who devote the greatest time and fervor to it.

[21] Those who have already chosen a state which is immutable, such as married persons and religious, should not be given the elections; however, efforts should be made to have them reform and strive for perfection as far as they are able.

[22] Women will be given the exercises in church. It will suffice for them to come two or three times to receive them, if this can be done without causing talk. If it might cause talk it will suffice for them to come once, but make two hours of exercises.

[23] *The disposition required in an exercitant is the following*

[24] 1. They should approach them with great desire and fervor, as befits a matter of such great importance. It is sometimes helpful not to give the Exercises right away but to test their desire by putting off giving them the Exercises.

[25] 2. Particularly in those who wish to choose a state of life, there should be a genuine and great resignation of themselves to the will of God: "Lord, what would you have me do?" [Acts 9:6].

[26] 3. Great attentiveness in trying to understand the exercises which are given them, and care in writing down the points immediately, and much more in performing them, omitting nothing of what is presented to them.

[27] 4. They should have a very open heart, concealing nothing from the director, neither their desolation nor their consolation. They should desire to be entirely guided by the one giving the Exercises.

[28] 5. Note that at the beginning, especially if they are not used to meditating, they often experience numerous distractions, difficulty in applying their mind, and temptations. And so they need to keep going with patience and trust in the Lord, in hope that if they persevere they will obtain greater facility and help from the Lord.

[29] 6. While making the Exercises the exercitant should have no other books and should not wish to pursue any other meditations but work on these alone as if no others were in existence or known by him; he should concentrate his whole mind on these, etc. The usual books for exercitants are lives of the saints and Gerson's *Imitation of Christ*.

[30] 7. He should expend greater care and effort on acts of the affections than on those of the understanding. His endeavor and concern should not be so much to dilate and expand on the points where a lot of thoughts or a variety of ideas come or are supplied to him, as is the case with some more active minds. Rather his concern ought to be to apply them to the will: he should desire and strive to have his affections moved. This moving of the affections of great, indeed paramount, importance.

[31] 8. A person who is not used to giving the Exercises should first peruse the Annotations at the front of the Spiritual Exercises, etc.

Counsels of Father Jerónimo Domènech for Making the Exercises Well

According to St. Ignatius one of the ablest directors of the Exercises was Jerónimo Domènech (1516–1592). He served for a time as St. Ignatius' secretary, and it was he who gave the Exercises to Jerónimo Nadal. For many years he governed the Society in Sicily.

These brief remarks were noted down by Fabio de Fabi when Domènech gave the Exercises to him and his fellow scholastics at the Roman College in 1569. (Original in Latin.)

POINTS TO BE OBSERVED
FOR MAKING THE SPIRITUAL EXERCISES FRUITFULLY

[1] To call upon the most Holy Trinity that we may make the Exercises fruitfully and with progress of our soul.

[2] To take the attitude that you had never read, known, or heard any of the things that will be presented to you, desiring to learn them afresh for the salvation of your soul.

[3] To regard the person giving you the Exercises as an angel come down from heaven, impelled by compassion to communicate to you what pertains to the salvation of your soul.

[4] To understand what a spiritual exercise is: nothing other than a certain way and method of examining one's conscience, reforming the powers of the soul, and choosing a definite state of life, leading to knowledge of God and self.

And it is called spiritual exercise by analogy with physical exercise.

For just as through physical exercise ill humors are consumed, raw and undigested food is digested, the blood is purified and renewed; so through spiritual exercises the powers of the soul, both higher and lower, external and internal, are renewed, and a person ultimately reaches that true purity of soul which is the goal of our life.

[5] Further, in the Exercises one must employ the two faculties of understanding and will, but the latter more than the former.

[6] You should always judge your neighbor favorably, putting a good construction upon everything in case he should he say or do something untoward.

[7] Since you now have full leisure to do what is right, shake off all sluggishness and negligence and spend the time granted you well, with all eagerness and diligence.

[8] It will be extremely helpful to offer to your Creator all your effort and entire spirit, so that he may dispose of all that is yours according to his divine will and not your own, and as he knows to be for his greater glory and your good.

Notes on Meditation
by Father Jerónimo Domènech

The following notes, taken by a Jesuit student who made the Exercises under Domènech at the Roman College in 1569, are particularly rich in spiritual instruction. (Original in Latin).

SOME NOTES TO BE OBSERVED
IN THE MEDITATIONS GIVEN BELOW

[1] He should take care to grasp well and remember the points he is to meditate on, so that they will come to mind quickly and readily during the hour of meditation itself.

[2] He should understand the end and fruit to be garnered in each meditation so that he may acquire it, keeping his eye on this target throughout the entire meditation.

[3] He should know that although each exercise or meditation has its own special and immediate purpose, v.g., humility, contrition, trust, fear, etc., it is nevertheless the special property of every meditation to direct us toward love of God as its ultimate end and primary fruit, in order that we may thus reach that blessed union in which our will is entirely subordinated and united with God's so that we become one spirit and one will with him; for to this, as to our ultimate goal, all our meditations, prayers, and operations are directed.

[4] Before going to meditate he should ask himself whether he is conscious of possessing the spirit of freedom proper to God's adopted sons, and of possessing spiritual joy, as well as abandonment of self to God. Should he find himself lacking in one of these three conditions he ought to try as diligently and as earnestly as he can to acquire it so as to proceed to his meditation accompanied by these attitudes. For acquiring them it will be very helpful for him to say beforehand, with suitable attention, reverence, and devotion, the verses: "Turn your face from my sins," etc., down to "I shall teach the wicked," etc. [Ps 51:11ff].

[5] He should strive hard to enter into himself and to shut the door on all other thoughts. And so, before beginning the meditation, he should for a short

time advert briefly to what he is about to do, viz., be present in prayer before
the throne of almighty God and in the sight of all the holy angels and blessed
spirits, with the eyes of all focused on him alone and watching to see how he
bears himself in an action of such moment and in a matter of such importance
for his own salvation. He should frequently come back to this reflection during
the course of his meditation so that he will continue praying with the proper
reverence, attention, and devotion.

[6] When distracted by a variety of thoughts, or oppressed by various
spiritual desolations and griefs, he should be careful not to fall into impatience
or faintheartedness. Rather, he should turn humbly upon himself and acknowledge his own wretchedness and worthlessness, making use of various colloquies
either with his own soul or with God; then he should go back to the points of
the meditation.

[7] He should particularly beware of employing in his meditation any
violent effort of head, heart, or faculties for the purpose of securing attention,
tears, or consolation out of the meditation. This will do no good. In fact he
will tire himself out, become deterred from prayer, and have greater difficulty
in returning to meditation once the intellect and the other faculties of the soul
perceive they are being so severely strained. Instead, he should patiently wait
for the Lord to come and shower him with the rays of his splendor. He should
behave like someone who, in the faint light of dawn, deeply yearns to see the
content of a picture he holds in his hands, eagerly awaiting the sun's rays and
turning the picture again and again toward where the approaching light will
enable him to see it better. Meditating in this fashion, he keeps turning over
the points interiorly in different ways, ardently longing for spiritual light to
come. He should keep beseeching strongly until aroused to attention and
devotion. Meanwhile, until the light comes he should wait for it with great
desire—yet patiently, recognizing that he is unworthy to be visited by so great
a Lord and illuminated by the Holy Spirit.

[8] One should not try to imagine the presence of the divine Majesty up in
heaven or to lift up the intellect to his presence dwelling there. For only with
greatest difficulty could a person establish and fix an imaginative picture of this
sort without the cooperation and straining of his mind (a thing altogether to be
avoided). Instead, he should focus on the throne of God and the presence of
his entire heavenly court within himself. For it is written: "The kingdom
of God is within you" [Luke 17:21], and "Do I not fill all heaven and earth?"
[Jer 23:24]—so that God is more intimately present to us than we are to ourselves, for "in him we live and move and have our being" [Acts 17:28].

[9] It is very helpful to review and briefly prepare the points from the
previous day so that one can readily gather from them matter for meditation
and allow one's meditating to be guided by the Holy Spirit himself, setting no
boundaries to him but rather continuing with those points where through the

Spirit's motion one receives greater profit, such as consolation, movement, or illumination of mind. One should not pass on to another point as long as this action of the Spirit lasts, but should gather the fruit to which one is invited by the Holy Spirit.

Different people, in fact, gather different fruits from the same meditation and the same point, depending on what the Spirit is pleased to grant to each. From one and the same point a beginner will get one thing, a person moving forward another, and someone who is perfect still another.

[10] And it is not sufficient to have material prepared for the days' meditation. It is necessary also to know some clear and definite method and order of meditating, so as the more easily, attentively, and fruitfully to get at the marrow hidden deep within the points. One should employ this method and order of meditating unless (as has been said) the kindness of the Lord and the anointing of the Holy Spirit supersedes it with another.

There is no one method of meditation common to all, nor can any one definite method be prescribed as suitable for a given type of meditation; for holy persons meditate in different ways. Different persons should use different methods, just as they have different goals. From this there arise various degrees of contemplation. What can be said on this topic in a general way and for common use is found in the three types of meditating presented by our Father Ignatius of blessed memory in his book of the Exercises.

Common to all three, however, is that the three powers of the soul are to be applied to the points—and sometimes even the senses when the matter is accessible to them. Thus, for example, with his memory a person should recall the points themselves and carefully weigh their meaning. Then he should use his understanding to consider, reason about, ruminate, and expand on them. Finally, he should be moved in his will by eliciting from the reasoning of the intellect various acts appropriate to the end of the particular meditation, v.g., fear, wonder, humility, confusion, love, etc., so as to arrive at that union mentioned above. And since meditation's fruit lies especially in acts of the will, these should accordingly be much more frequent than acts of the understanding, which bear little fruit unless subordinated to acts of the will.

Notes for a Directory
by Father Diego Miró

Miró's full-scale directory, commissioned by Father General Mercurian, is given below (Doc. 23). The following are some earlier notes which he wrote for a directory. The italic references after the entries refer to the corresponding paragraphs in Miró's full directory. (Original in Latin.)

OUTLINE OF A DIRECTORY FOR GIVING THE EXERCISES, BY FATHER DIEGO MIRÓ

[1] For giving the Spiritual Exercises the following passages from the *Constitutions* will be helpful: IV, 8.5 and E; VII, 4.8 and F; IV, 10.10; I, 4.D; Examen, 4.10; III, 1.20 and R; Examen, 4.41; and elsewhere as indicated in the index printed in the new *Constitutions*.

[2] The one giving the Exercises should have experienced them himself, have studied the whole book, and have at his fingertips the matter he is giving. *[Doc. 23.6]*

[3] There should be a single person giving the Exercises; where because of need there are two, they should not disagree with each other. *[Doc 23.11]*

[4] The one giving the Exercises should give the points from memory, or else give them in writing (see Annotation 20 [Vulgate]). *[Doc. 23.12]*

[5] The more willingly one makes the Exercises the more fruitful they will be; also the reverse *[Doc. 23.16]*

[6] Before giving the Foundation, Annotations 1, 5, 17, and 20 should be given. *[Doc. 23.25]*

[7] The exercises should be given in the order in which they occur (see Annotation 20); otherwise they will do the exercitant no good, as Father Ignatius used to say. *[Doc. 23.15]*

[8] First, the Foundation should be given, as a goal set up to which sins are an obstacle and toward which are directed the exercises of the First Week, the consideration of sins, the Particular Examination of conscience and especially of those sins that weigh one down more heavily, and the General Examen [32–42] for coming to an awareness of all one's sins. *[Doc. 23.27]*

Secondly, the 1st, 2nd, and 3rd exercises should be given. *[Doc. 23.36]*

[9] The tenth Addition on penance is left to the exercitant's freedom.

[10] It is helpful for the exercitant to sweep his own room, make up his bed, etc. *[Doc. 23.125]*

[11] He should visit the exercitant once or twice after meals, since it is not a time of meditation and he may need some consolation; this is the time to ask an account of the points of the exercise.

[12] If he will not obey, the Exercises should not be continued.

[13] It is better if someone other than the one giving the Exercises hears his confession *[Doc. 23.48]*. In private confessions the use of the Exercises should be discreetly recommended. This has led to many vocations to religious life. For who is suitable to make the Exercises, see Annotations 18–20.

[14] Father Ignatius used to say that during the Second Week, when a person enters the three times of election, he should go into greater than usual seclusion, so that he will neither see nor hear anything that is not heavenly and from God. *[Doc. 23.84]*

[15] A person who is about to make an elections should be given a careful explanation of consolation and desolation, as set down in the Rules for the Discernment of Spirits. *[Doc. 23.85]*

[16] The one making an election should lay the counsels before God one day and the commandments the next, intent only upon seeing which God prefers, like someone offering dishes to a prince. *[Doc. 23.89]*

[17] Upon completion of the exercises, these and similar instructions can be given: the continual presence of God; ejaculatory prayers; a right intention in all things: consideration of God's benefits; consideration of our end and of sins; lamenting our own and others' sins; rumination of Scripture texts. *[Doc. 23.135–40]*

[18] If he remains in the world he should pray in the morning on the life and passion of Christ using the method of the Exercises; make an examination of conscience morning and evening; say the rosary; receive the sacraments using a definite spiritual method; cultivate devotion to the saints, his guardian angel, and his patron saint; read spiritual books; and help his neighbor according to his capacity. *[Doc. 23.142–145]*

DOCUMENT 16

Report of Father Antonio Valentino

Antonio Valentino (1540–1611) worked as novice master in Italy for twenty-six years. He was requested to write a report on how he formed his novices; it begins with an account of how he gave them the Spiritual Exercises. (Original in Italian.)

CHAPTER 1: THE SPIRITUAL EXERCISES

[1] During the first probation, then, I try to get to know the novices' spirit and intention, giving them the papal bulls and the usual *Examen*,[1] examining them as required by the Institute and the Rules. If I discover no impediment, I go on to the other tests of the second probation, trying to get to know them better and give them a spiritual foundation by the use of the customary means of the Society: the Spiritual Exercises, the general confession, exhortations on the Institute and the Rules, abnegation of their own judgment and will, and the other virtues, especially obedience, humility, and simplicity.

[2] As for the Exercises, I take care to avoid giving them during the coldest or hottest seasons, also taking into account the capacity, age, and strength of each. I keep the same order given by Father Ignatius of holy memory, although not in all cases with the full rigor of five hours of prayer a day and getting up at night.

[3] However, I adapt myself to their capacity—orally and with some written Additions—to open up their understanding and arouse the affections, so that they will then put into practice what they have meditated and not imagine that meditation consists in beautiful ideas.

[4] For this purpose I explain to them the aim of each Week of the Exercises, following what Father Peter Favre says in his *Memoriale*,[2] viz., that, just as each of the four Weeks has a different subject-matter, so each Week has a different purpose. In the First Week what is sought is hatred for sin and consequently the denial of one's self-will, mother of this horrible monster.

---

[1] The account of the Jesuit vocation prefixed to the *Constitutions*, for presentation to those applying to enter the Society during their "first probation," an introductory period before admission to the novitiate proper, or "second probation."

[2] In this and the following six paragraphs Valentino gives the substance of Favre's remarks on the different Weeks in his *Memoriale*, n. 303. See Monumenta Historica Societatis Iesu, *Fabri Monumenta* (Madrid, 1914), pp. 639–40.

78

Hence it is suitable, in accord with the subject-matter of sins, to ask in the colloquies at the end of the meditation for the three graces. First, a true knowledge of and contrition for the sins of one's whole past life. Second, a true knowledge of the way in which I should order my life in the future. Third, a firm purpose of true amendment, and a true ordering of my life for the future.

[5] In the Second Week the aim of the contemplations is the imitation of Christ's life which is being contemplated. Hence, in the principal colloquies with the Blessed Virgin, Christ, and the eternal Father, another three graces are requested. First, denial of self. Second, contempt for the world. Third, perfect love for the service of Christ our Lord—for there are many who imagine they have good thoughts about the service of Christ and love his person, but who do not find so pleasing the duties and occupations in which this service consists.

[6] And so these persons often, not without consolation, have many thoughts about the things of Christ, his life, his virtues and perfection, but never give any thought to the many works by which this Lord desires to be served and imitated by his ministers, so that where he was they too might be— they who one day will be where he is now in heaven, who first was in the stable and on the cross and now is in glory.

[7] The purpose of the Third Week is affectively having compassion with Christ and effectively suffering something for love of him, corresponding to the matter of his holy passion. Hence, in the colloquies three graces are asked. First, compassion with Christ in his physical sufferings. Second, compassion with Christ in his poverty, nakedness, and abandonment by all those dear to him, even to the point of being forsaken by the Father. Third, compassion in his insults and ignominies, with a desire to follow him not only to the table, as many do, but also to the cross, as only a few do who are true lovers, who stand firm with him in trials. For there are many persons who do not have or know how to have this sentiment in their spirit and in their body, fleeing the cross like demons and loving honors and whatever the world loves and not what Christ our Lord—and he crucified—loved and embraced.

[8] In the Fourth Week, according to the subject-matter, the purpose and aim is perfection in prayer and action, having God through long practice always gently before one's eyes, being mindful of him when we think, speak, or act. For in this way God comes to be everything in everything, and in this way one does all his actions in God's presence, as Father Ignatius wishes, and in a way we behold God in all things, as we find in the beautiful Contemplation on Spiritual Love.

[9] To this end we strive to know Christ glorious and glorified, and we ask three graces that comprise many goods. First, as regards the reward, love of God and of Christ. Second, a full and perfect joy in Christ alone. Third, the true peace which cannot be had except in him alone and from him alone. In

this way, by the beautiful sequence of the Exercises, the novices start from the
holy fear of God which is the beginning of wisdom, and passing through desire
for the Christian virtues, end up with love for God and a desire to know him
perfectly and to be united with him as they should, seeking him alone in
all things.

[10] Then I teach them our Father Ignatius' method of meditating and
acting in each exercise, joining meditation with prayer, with this difference
between them, that meditation is a kind of disposing cause for prayer, and
prayer a kind of effect of meditation.

[11] And so I divide each exercise into four parts: first, the preparatory
prayer; second, the preludes; third, the points; fourth, the colloquies. In the
preparatory prayer a person briefly presents to God his intention and asks his
help, seeking glory and grace: glory for God and grace for himself.

[12] St. Bonaventure's beautiful advice is helpful for this: "Let the devout
soul, inflamed with desire to contemplate God, kneel in spirit before the
throne of the most blessed Trinity; let it knock humbly; let it request wisely
the strengthening power of God the Father to keep it from being crushed by
labor, the guiding wisdom of God the Son to keep it from the guiles of error
that would sway it from the truth; the comforting love and mercy of God the
Holy Spirit to keep it from being overcome by weariness and somehow falling
off from the meditation it has begun and from the praise and glory of God it
has intended"[3] This preparation can serve again at the beginning of each
activity.

[13] In the preludes, since they are a sort of preamble to the meditation, a
person begins gently by recalling the history, and then passes on to the physical
picturing of the mystery in the imagination, and from there to the understanding of the points by deep and steady reflection. This way of proceeding is
natural for human beings and quite suitable for beginners, who proceed more
by the senses and imagination than by the intellect.

[14] It is true that those more advanced and practiced, by elevation of the
mind to God, move directly to the point of truth and the nerve of the affection. Thus St. Bonaventure says on this matter: "There is a kind of meditation
which rises from what is lower to what is higher. However there is another
kind that descends from what is higher to what is lower. This is far nobler and
more lovely, and it is more easily obtained by fire of love, which can be
achieved in two ways, one common and the other mystical and secret. The
first is by way of investigation and elevation; it begins with lower things,
ascending to the summit by prolonged exercise. For example, the way of
loving God by use of previous meditation is this. First the faithful disciple by

---

[3] St. Bonaventure, *Soliloquy on the Four Spiritual Exercises*, in *The Works of Bonaventure*,
tr. José de Vinck, vol. III (Paterson N.J.: St. Anthony Guild Press, 1966), p. 36. The Latin
original is in Quaracchi, vol. 8, 28.

his exterior sense or eye beholds exterior creatures; then, by rising somewhat, he deposits in his imagination what he has perceived with his outer eye. Then, rising higher, by thinking and comparing, he finds a single creative cause of all things. This is how the philosophers arrived at a knowledge of God; through seeing the vast magnitude, beautiful order, and great usefulness of creatures, they came unerringly to a knowledge of a single, mighty Creator—and this by the power of the soul which is called reason, higher than the exterior sense and the imagination. Finally, from this consideration of creatures a certain habit is deposited by the foregoing in the intellect, where the original foundation in creatures is left behind, and, not so much by the contemplation of creatures as by a radiance shed into the mind by God, it is more nobly elevated to the contemplation of divine things; and this is called the intellective power or intellect, which consists solely in pure meditation.

"Finally, all meditation which is not seconded by an affection of love is vain. Such was the meditation of the philosophers: though they knew God they did not glorify him as God but became vain in their thoughts [see Rom 1:21].

"The other way of rising to God is far nobler than all these and easier to have. It is called unitive wisdom, consisting in a loving desire by upward-surging fiery affections, that is, by frequent jaculatory prayers."[4]

[15] St. Augustine says: "The Egyptian fathers are said to have prayers that are frequent but very short and speedily launched, lest the attention which is so important for a person who prays, watchfully aroused, should by excessive prolongation be dissipated and dulled."[5]

[16] It is true that in these preludes we should not dwell too much on physical images, as do children or animals, but like rational human beings pass from visible things to invisible, except of course for the humanity of Christ, which is a door of the divinity, in which as in a mirror the angels long to look and in which we ought to look at ourselves, imagining him who was beautiful beyond the sons of men [see Ps 45:3] under different images at different times: as a lovely infant, as a youth, as a mature man, as nailed to the cross, as laid in the tomb, as glorious and rising like the dawn; in different guises at different times: as a pilgrim "making as if to go farther" [Luke 24:28], as one praying, "spending the night in prayer to God" [Luke 6:12], as a humble servant who "went down with them and was subject to them" [Luke 2:51], etc.

[17] As for consideration of the points, it is not good to wander aimlessly though a variety of ideas but to consider definite and organized topics—not many but few and well penetrated, so that we strive to feel and almost see them, and in good time stay the foot of the intellect and move forward with

---

[4] Pseudo-Bonaventure.

[5] Letter 130.10.

the foot of the affections, striving to get some fruit for ourselves from the topics considered.

[18] Patience and perseverance are needed to drive away bothersome images and temptations; a good practice is to ignore and despise them, focusing on one's own business.

[19] Among other things, it is very good to consider God in prayer as a Father for whom we have reverential fear and filial love and trust, asking him for whatever is needed or helpful for us.

[20] The meditation should end with prayer, and the devotion attained should be preserved by silence and humility; spiritual profit should be shown by avoidance of sins, eagerness in doing good, and longing for perfection.

[21] For this purpose, every exercise ends with a colloquy and with the Our Father, when the heart is warm, the affections aroused, and the attention directed in the second person immediately to God present there. This movement is most perfect and effective, as St. Bonaventure says: "A right intention is moved in three ways: sometimes *for* God, sometimes *toward* God, and sometimes *into* God. It is moved *for* God in action performed chiefly for his sake, even though we may not be thinking of him at the moment. It is moved *toward* God in reading, meditating, and conversing about God, because then our mind is occupied with God himself, though we do not direct our attention to him in the second person. It is moved *into* God by prayer when the mind thinks of him and addresses him in the second person, embracing him and clinging to him with devout affection."[6]

[22] Hence we can say that the colloquy is the tongue of the heart, which brings forth with feeling the five utterances of which St. Paul speaks: prayer, petition, obsecration, thanksgiving, and praise of God [1 Tim 2:1]. But the Our Father at the end of the colloquy is like a divine tongue of Christ himself, devised with infinite wisdom, filled with sentiments of a child of God. It has three parts: exordium, body, and conclusion.

[23] The exordium aims at six attitudes in the person praying. Attention, trust, and humility and filial fear are expressed in "Father." Charity and shared love are expressed in "Our." Elevation of the mind to God is expressed in "Who art in heaven." The sixth attitude is reverence for this great Lord in the presence of the whole court of heaven.

[24] Attention is of four kinds: first, to the letter; second, to the meaning of the letter and significance of the word (hence Father Ignatius' beautiful Methods of Prayer); third, to the end, i.e., to the reason why we are praying, such as the honor of God, forgiveness of sins, grace, or eternal glory; fourth, to the person we are praying to, i.e., God, whose presence in this way we learn to have always before our eyes, either in his humanity or in his divinity. For we

---

[6] Pseudo-Bonaventure.

can have him present either in the height of heaven, or before our eyes, or within us; or under the image of father, lord, physician, or spouse, etc.

[25] The second part of the Our Father, its body, contains seven petitions of wonderful order, brevity, and force. And the conclusion is the "Amen," which serves as a confirmation of what has gone before, as though unifying the mind completely in a single word. These hints will suffice.

[26] As for the general way of considering the mysteries of Christ in order to imitate his virtues, particularly his humility, obedience, and charity, it is as follows. First a person beholds with the eye of faith and reason the event contained in the history, with the circumstances of persons and places, and makes himself as present to the mystery—or the mystery as present to himself— as if he saw everything with his own eyes and heard what was being said.

[27] Second, he focuses on the person of Christ, true God and true man, as he suffers or performs a given action. He makes some reflection for himself, considering how his divine nature allows the human nature to suffer, even forgoing for himself the help which he gives to others.

[28] Third, one should consider the way Christ suffers or acts: his virtues of humility, meekness, patience, severity toward himself and kindliness toward others, obedience to God; and one should strive to imitate Christ.

[29] One should consider the reasons why he suffers or acts: the honor of God; our own instruction, motivation, and salvation. Also Christ's own motivation: measureless love and longing for our supreme happiness. One should consider what return we ought to make to him, ending with a prayer corresponding to the movements engendered by the meditation and the like.

[30] In particular, in the Foundation of the Exercises on the end of the creation of man, the novice should endeavor to lay a solid foundation in knowledge, love, and desire of the glory of God for which he was created. He should remember that according to all the holy Fathers the purpose and immediate aim of every spiritual exercise should be always before our eyes, like a target, viz., purity of heart as the ultimate disposition for having perfection, which consists in charity, which the Apostle calls the end of the law and the bond of perfection. It makes us one spirit with God through union of wills, willing and not willing the same as God and our superiors, resulting in our own blessedness and God's glory in us, which is our final end.

[31] So long as we are uncertain what God's and our superiors' will is, we must remain in perfect indifference of will, waiting to be moved and praying that he will give us light to know his will, saying twice over with the Prophet, "My heart is ready, O God, my heart is ready" [Ps 108:2].

[32] Having caught sight of the star, we will follow it with the three magi until we find Christ in the stable, that is, until we become children again with childlike simplicity, humility, and perfect self-denial, in the least place, below everyone else in the service of God. Here is where the magi found Christ, not

in royal palaces. This indifference is highly praised by Adam in his homily on the Three Kings,[7] where he says that it is an excellent means for grasping the will of God in prayer and holy exercises, as Father Ignatius of blessed memory teaches those who want to make an election of a state of life and discover their own vocation.

[33] Adam writes: "Behold, magi came from the east to Jerusalem, etc. They were not bound to their place or country, to flesh or blood. We are bound by all these. We want to serve God, but in this place, in this town, among our relatives, among our friends, etc. This is to follow not the guidance of the shining star but the affections of corrupt flesh. This is not 'My heart is ready, O God, my heart is ready.' It was not enough for the Prophet to say, 'My heart is ready'; he added a second 'ready.' Why—except to indicate that he was ready for every eventuality, happy or sad, pleasant or painful? This must be the attitude of a person who wants to find where the star is calling him to go. The star is a light from heaven poured into the mind and enabling us to know the newborn savior, Christ the Lord, showing us the way that leads to him, with its many vicissitudes.

"If you want to know where this star is calling you, do this. Strip your heart bare: try to cleanse it of every affection binding you carnally to flesh, blood, place, country, or any other thing. When you have done this, when you have reached the point where you feel yourself ready for anything that happens, ready to follow wherever God calls (this is an indispensable first step), then seize opportune moments to make your spirit present to God, free of all impediment. First behold the wisdom of his Majesty, then what his supreme Majesty underwent for your sake, and finally how you will pour out your heart before God. And when you say nothing you will be saying much, and the whole content of your speech will be this: 'Here I am,' i.e., 'What would you have me do?,' etc. When you have done this, if not immediately then at least in the end with passion, you will feel yourself so strongly drawn, impelled, and urged in a given direction that you will only be able to say, 'This is where I am called, this is where I must go.' This is certainly what the magi did, and this is the third point which the evangelist wants us to see in his description of the event: 'Behold, magi from the East came to Jerusalem, saying, "Where is he who is born king of the Jews?" ' "

[34] This is the best foundation for the spiritual life, and the background of Father Ignatius' beautiful rule[8] that when someone wants something from a superior, in order to know whether he is proceeding in accord with God's will he should, before making his request, place himself in perfect indifference of

---

[7] This is probably Adam of Dryburgh, a twelfth-century preacher. The homily cited has not been found.

[8] See *Constitutions of the Society of Jesus*, III 1.26.

will, and then betake himself to prayer. Then, if he concludes he ought to present it to the superior he should do so, leaving all concern about it to him in the conviction that whatever he disposes, having understood the matter, is what God disposes. Anyone who kept this rule would never be troubled about anything but would abide in continual peace and tranquillity of mind.

[35] In order not to go on too long, I will not enter into the individual exercises, but merely remark that one should not fail to teach the novices how to examine themselves, make their confession, and pray according to the methods of the Exercises, explaining to them the Rules for Discerning the Movements of various Spirits, leading them through the First Week by consideration of the four last things in such a way that they will not hate sin out of fear of punishment like slaves, nor love virtue out of hope of reward like hirelings, but do so motivated by pure love and the glory of the divine Goodness like good sons.

[36] And although fear is proper to beginners, causing them to hate and flee sin, nevertheless to move forward in the spirit of love is proper to our Society. But since there is such variety of minds and bodily constitutions, and since the charity of beginners differs from that of those going forward or the more advanced, it follows that different exercises are more suitable for different persons. The First Week is more appropriate for the newly converted—those who, in the purgative way, still feel the prick of conscience and cry out with the Prophet: "Pierce my flesh with your fear, for I am afraid of your judgments" [Ps 119:120].

[37] Hence, at the beginning these persons locate their perfection almost wholly in penance and mortification of the flesh. But progressing to purity and joy of conscience through the Examen and general confession with true contrition, satisfaction, and amendment of their sins, they discover, once purified, a greater light. At this point the Second Week, in the illuminative way, better suits them; they discover another more perfect kind of mortification—a mortification of the person as such, i.e., of their own sense, judgment, and will, through genuine and entire indifference and abandonment of themselves into the hands of obedience, entrusting themselves totally to God's providence and will, in imitation of Christ, whom they behold humbled and subject not only to the Father's law but also to the commands of his mother and of Joseph, etc.

[38] Here they begin to discover the perfection of our Society's institute, grounded totally on the firm rock of obedience, both to the Supreme Pontiff and to all other subordinate superiors, and directed to one's own and one's neighbors' salvation and perfection, with all our well-ordered and powerful means. Here they see that "obedience is better than sacrifice" [1 Sam 15:22] and that eating by obedience is better than fasting by one's own will.

[39] Finally, as they grow more perfect in this virtue of obedience, they also grow more perfect in charity, the goal of religious life. This charity, as

found in beginners, those making progress, and the perfect, causes the first to hate sin; the second to long for virtue, particularly obedience so as to do the will of God in all things and in the best way; and the third to love God purely for his own sake, seeking his glory in all things by the ordered way of obedience, and loving the neighbor for love of God, working for his salvation in all the ways which obedience will ordain.

[40] The first have as a first principle hatred of sin; on its basis they perform all their good actions to expel sin with all its roots, making use of the ordered means of the Society to this effect, such as the General, Particular, and daily Examinations of conscience, confession, etc. The second have an ardent desire for virtue as the principle of their actions. The third have love for God as the first principle of their every thought, word, and deed.

[41] Beginners bend all their efforts to stripping off the old man, those making progress to putting on the new man so they can appear in public and deal with people in an edifying way for the help of souls, while the perfect, already clothed in the wedding garment, long ardently for union with God as their final end and strive to bring all souls to this end; themselves aflame, they inflame others with love of God, cooperating with God in bringing souls back to him—a work that is most divine and proper to our Society—as our first fathers did.

[42] Hence I lay much stress on the Exercises and devote the greatest attention and effort to them. I give them to a number of men at once and at the best seasons, since, not having a great deal of mental stamina, I cannot be engaged in this toil all the time.

[43] I also have the exercitants occasionally confer together in my presence: they share their way of proceeding in the Exercises and anything that can be said for the instruction and edification of the others (omitting private matters which each one tells me in his individual conference). This gives rise to spiritual knowledge and practice in living well, and they get to see the manifold operation of the Holy Spirit, who in meditation on a single topic brings persons to the same end by different routes, as by different lines to the same center, with all of them hitting on truth and virtue. In this way they become experienced in spiritual matters by learning from one another.

Instructions Attributed to
Father Paul Hoffaeus

Paul Hoffaeus (ca. 1525–1608), named as they author of these instructions, entered the Society shortly before St. Ignatius' death and was for twelve years provincial of Upper Germany and for ten years assistant for German affairs to the superior general. Unfortunately there are grounds for doubting that Hoffaeus is in fact the author of this directory. (Original in Latin.)

INSTRUCTIONS FOR THE DIRECTOR OF THE EXERCISES, BY REVEREND FATHER PAUL HOFFAEUS, PRIEST OF THE SOCIETY OF JESUS AND PROVINCIAL SUPERIOR IN GERMANY

[1] Since not all those desiring to make the Exercises can have the same way of life, constitution, health, mental capacity, or leisure, the director must carefully adapt a special procedure for each individual, as regards not only content but also method and time-schedule.

[2] *Different classes of persons and how they should make the Exercises*

[3] The first class comprises uneducated persons who are largely incapable of meditation. Instead of the exercises, it will be enough to give them the Particular Examen, the General Examen with its five points, and a method for receiving Communion, attending Mass, and praying, along with sufficient catechetical instruction on the main and more essential elements of the Christian religion, especially moral teaching. In lieu of an exercise, they will also spend a half hour a day on the first Method of Prayer.

[4] The second class are persons somewhat but only slightly more capable than the preceding. These can be given all of the above (if they are not yet familiar with them) together with the exercises of the First Week adapted to their capacity, for them to spend two hours a day on.

[5] The third are those who, though intelligent and educated, are impeded by public or other affairs and concerns. These can be given, along with the Foundation of the Exercises, all the exercises of the First Week and as many

mysteries of Christ's life as they wish, along with the twofold examination of conscience, the methods of prayer and for frequent confession and Communion, and the Contemplation for Obtaining Spiritual Love. They will, however, have only an hour of meditation each day (unless they wish and are able to do more) and two separate quarter-hour examinations of conscience.

[6] The fourth class are those who have sufficient capacity but do not wish to choose a state of life. Apart from the material on the election, these can do all the other exercises and everything else in the book of the Exercises for as long a period and as many hours a day as they wish.

[7] The fifth are those who do desire to choose a state of life. These, in addition to the exercises of the First Week and the instructions on the election, should be given as many of the remaining exercises as their situation or occupations, and also their strength and willingness, will bear; they should spend as many hours on the exercises as they wish.

[8] The sixth class are those who want to make the complete Exercises in full form for five hours a day. These should follow the procedure outlined in the book of the Exercises.

[9] The seventh are those who, while having the capacity, want no more from the Exercises than the complete cleansing of their consciences through a general confession. After settling on the number of hours with them, one should give them the examinations of conscience, the Methods of Prayer and the Contemplation for Obtaining Spiritual Love, along with the exercises of the First Week with their usual requirements.

[10] The eighth class are our own scholastics, whether novices or not. These can be given the same as the fourth class, following, however, the judgment or provisions of superiors.

[11] The ninth are our coadjutors, whether novices or not. These should be given more or less the same as the second group.

[12] However, if the coadjutors are capable of meditation they should be given the same as the scholastics, particularly if they desire this. Normally, however, they should be assigned an hour and a half of physical activity in silence each day before and after dinner, especially if they cannot read.

[13] All those in the first seven classes should be discreetly urged to resolve that for the rest of their life they will go to confession every week and to Communion every other week, or even weekly if so moved.

[14] The final two groups, however, should be enjoined, at least toward the end of the Exercises, to make a general confession and go at least once to Communion.

[15] They should likewise be told to make the Contemplation on Spiritual Love and the Three Methods of Prayer and, by way of epilogue at the end of the Exercises, to devote at least a full day, depending on their condition, to the better ordering of their life; to planning their daily religious activities, vocal and

mental prayer, spiritual ejaculations, and other devotions; and to devising certain reminders to help them remember at stated times to perform some exercise of divine worship or on mysteries of the life and benefits of Christ.

[16] For experience shows that a good many persons are frequently willing and to do a number of excellent things for the their own spiritual advancement, but, having no method or system and no reminders to stimulate them to duties of piety and devotion, end up doing none of these things, or else doing them so confusedly that it gradually begets distaste and neglect.

[17] However, care must be taken that they do not overburden themselves with too many different devotions. Instead, under their director's guidance, they should start off with a few modest things, adding others later if it seems good in the Lord.

[18] It would also be a good idea, where needed, to renew one's program of devotions several times a year at the major feasts.

[19] It is useful for extern seculars to read a book on the four last things[1] during the time preceding the general confession, one on contempt for the world[2] during the time of the election, and after the election (or after the general confession if they make no election) the *Imitation of Christ*.

[20] Finally, it was not without good reason that Father Ignatius prescribed the use of devout colloquies at the end of each exercise. For slower minds, this opens the way to mental prayer, where we often bog down. Hence I would deem that use of these colloquies should be strongly inculcated and taught to our scholastics and brothers.

[21] *The distribution of time for making the Exercises*

[22] While the Spiritual Exercises are divided into four Weeks—the first on sins, judgment, and the pains of hell; the second on the life of Jesus Christ our Lord up to his solemn entrance into Jerusalem on Palm Sunday; the third on his Passion; and the fourth on his Resurrection and Ascension—this does not mean that the Weeks must necessarily run for seven or eight days. People are slower or quicker at finding what they seek, v.g., in the First Week contrition, sorrow, and tears for their sins, and terror at the severity of judgment and punishment. Hence the Weeks sometimes need to be lengthened or shortened. However, the full and complete Exercises are generally finished in thirty days, more or less.

---

[1] The best known of these was Denis the Carthusian's *De quattuor hominis novissimis liber*.

[2] The *De contemptu mundi* of Pope Innocent III (Lotario de' Conti di Segni) was widely used among the early Jesuits. English versions: *On the Misery of the Human Condition*, tr. Margaret Mary Dietz (Indianapolis/New York: Bobbs–Merrill, 1969); *De Miseria Condicionis Humanae*, ed. Robert E. Lewis (Athens, Georgia: University of Georgia Press, 1978).

[23] With our own brethren, however, who are seeking renewal of spirit through the Exercises in the midst of their studies or other occupations, I think that ten or twelve days will generally suffice.

[24] However, I do not think that an extern should be allowed to make an election unless he commits himself to spend at least twelve or fifteen days in the Exercises.

[25] There are various ways of dividing up the hours, depending on the person's strength, intelligence, and occupations. Some can do only a half hour at a time, others a full hour. Some can only do one hour a day; others more, up to five.

[26] For our own brethren who have occupations I would advise prescribing no more than four hours; for externs in Germany no more than three unless they themselves request it or there are particularly strong reasons.

[27] *Additional general remarks: For the superior as regards exercitants*

[28] Before he accepts externs for the Exercises, he should find out from them whether they will be satisfied with our food and drink. To avoid burdening the college, he should inform the person where advisable that, not for our profit but on account of our poverty, he should make appropriate payment for his food and drink.

[29] Those about to leave may (with a certain selectivity) be invited to our table, spending a seemly recreation with the fathers and being sent off in the Lord.

[30] When three or more of our brethren make the Exercises in common, they may take their meals at first or second table. During this period the reading in common and other activities in the dining room should be judiciously adapted for them.

[31] *For the one serving extern exercitants*

He should find out who the exercitants enjoy talking with, but never call anyone to talk with them without the director's approval. He should make sure that prayers are frequently being offered to God for them, either by himself or by another. He should let them know the times when they are supposed to start or end any activity. He should inform the director when he thinks they are treating themselves too austerely or need a walk in the garden. He will take care to provide his own services and whatever else is needed at stated times and on a definite, reliable schedule. He will make sure that, if several persons are likely to be making an election at the same time, they will not confer with each other; for this reason, they should go to different Masses where they will not meet. However, they may hear [say?] their own Masses at the same time.

[32] *For the one serving our own brethren making the Exercises*

He will make sure that the exercitants do not converse with any of our men or with each other, even at the time of recreation. Anything they ask him in writing he should show to the director. He should provide for the brethren everything prescribed above for the one serving extern exercitants, by way of time schedules, services, and preventing excessive austerity.

[33] When several brethren are making the Exercises together under the same director, he should give a common signal for the beginning and end of the meditation, for Mass, and for the conferences. He should also give a signal at 9:30 in the morning and at 1:30 and 4:30 in the afternoon for the common repetition and the giving of new material. He will make sure that their recreation is not disturbed by others. He will send them out into the garden for relaxation every day or every other day, giving them a time to return as the director will indicate.

[34] *For the director of the Exercises*

He should carefully observe Annotation 15 of our Reverend Father Ignatius of blessed memory, viz., *[the text of the Annotation follows]*.

[35] Those who converse with exercitants should know what kind of Exercises they are making at the time so that they can adapt their conversations accordingly. Without having consulted the director, no one should offer exercitants books to read, nor should they obtrude anything having to do with the Society upon them—indeed they should not readily answer questions when asked, particularly about the Society, but recommend that they ask the director alone about these things.

[36] To intelligent persons with experience in meditation, he should narrate the history faithfully, explaining its main lines only briefly and in passing so that the exercitant can reason and reflect about it in meditation on his own. In this way, if he himself discovers anything which sheds light or gives a deeper insight into the mystery, either through his own thinking or through God's enlightening his mind, he will derive greater relish and richer benefit than if someone else had profusely narrated and explained the matter to him. Not abundance of knowledge but an interior sense and taste is what satisfies the soul's desire.

[37] However, those who are slower and unaccustomed to meditate ordinarily waste their time and hours in the Exercises unless they are given a fuller explanation of the material, with something different for each repetition. This will help enkindle their spirits and at the same time accustom them to make similar considerations on their own. Thus, while intelligent persons usually enjoy their own discoveries rather than those of others, slower and more inexperienced persons find it more helpful and gratifying to be guided by

the director and to have their minds illuminated and hearts inflamed with his light, rather than to cast about in their own darkness, with no order or system, in long, fruitless meandering.

[There follows the text of Annotations 7–11, 16, and 17.]

[38] *The exercitant should be informed of the purpose, method, and practice of the Exercises*

[Annotations 1, 3, and 5 are quoted here.]

Since a definite prescribed length of time is to be spent on each exercise, it is important that the exercitant find peace of mind in knowing that he has spent more rather than less time on it. The devil frequently tries to get people to shorten the time set for prayer or meditation.

[The gist of Annotation 13 is given here.]

[39] When the exercitant is in deep consolation and fervor, he should avoid making any sudden, unconsidered promise or vow. Careful attention must be given to all the positive and negative factors that might affect the execution of what he is about to promise.

[40] The exercitant's progress in the spiritual life will be the greater the more thoroughly he withdraws from all friends, acquaintances, and concerns for human affairs, v.g., if he leaves his previous lodgings and moves to a more secluded house or cell. This withdrawal and seclusion has three main advantages:

[41] First, by withdrawing from friends and others close to him and from affairs not perfectly ordained to the service of God, he merits no little grace in God's eyes.

[42] Second, with his mind thus less distracted than before in various directions, and focused on the consideration of one thing, viz., the service of God his creator and the welfare of his own soul, he will have much freer and less encumbered use of his natural powers in seeking what he so much desires.

[43] Third, the more the soul secludes and isolates itself, the more it is rendered apt to seek and attain its creator and Lord; and the closer it comes to him, the better disposed it is to receive the gifts of the divine Goodness.

[44] *Daily schedule for those making the Exercises for three hours a day*

[45] They arise at 4:00 in the morning. Upon awaking, they should resolve to avoid some particular fault, and think about the matter of the day's meditation; meanwhile they should take care of their needs.

[46] From 4:30 to 5:50 they should meditate on the assigned matter.

[47] Sometime between 5:45 and 7:45 they should hear Mass.

[48] At the time indicated to them, they should make another hour's meditation before dinner.

[49] For a quarter of an hour before dinner they should examine their

conscience.

[50] Any free time between the morning meditation and dinner should be devoted to prayer, spiritual reading, preparing for confession, or making notes on what struck them during meditation.

[51] After dinner they should have least an hour's recreation.

[52] From 2:30 to 3:30 they should meditate.

[53] After supper they should have recreation until 8:00 p.m.

[54] At 8:30 p.m. they should examine their conscience for a quarter of an hour, after recitation of the Litanies.

[55] Those making four hours a day should be assigned two hours after dinner by adding to the above three meditations another from 4:30 to 5:30 p.m.

[56] This schedule can be modified: v.g., doing an hour from 4:30 to 5:30 a.m., from 9:00 to 10:00 or 9:30; likewise from 3:00 to 4:00 or 3:30, and from 6:00 to 7:00 or 6:30.

[57] *Daily schedule for our own men making the Exercises*

[58] Strict and uninterrupted silence.

If they want to ask or tell the one taking care of them anything, they should do so in writing.

[59] They should take their meals in their own rooms. They should take recreation at the usual hours, but away from the usual places of recreation, each one alone and in silence, either sitting or walking outside their rooms, or even in their rooms if advisable.

[60] The rest of their schedule will be the same as for extern exercitants, whether they are to meditate for three, four, or five hours.

[61] If three or four men are making the Exercises under a single director who because of other duties does not have time to give them each a separate retreat, they should still make no more than three or four hours of exercises, with an additional hour for conferences, if advisable, viz., from 4:30 to 5:30 p.m. Furthermore, he should, if advisable, review for all of them together the matter he expounded to them individually, so as to fix it in their memory, since he cannot easily give it to each one in writing—although at least one copy should be posted in some common place.

[62] The rest the their schedule should be the same as for those mentioned above.

[63] However, with fathers who are more advanced, capable, and experienced, the matter for meditation can be left in writing to for them read for themselves, without need of a director or guide.

[64] *Daily schedule with half-hour exercises for persons of the first class*

[65] From 4:30 to 5:00 a.m. they should use the first Method of Prayer as they had been instructed the previous evening.

[66] After 5:00, after reviewing the previous prayer with the director, they should be given an explanation of the mysteries and ceremonies of the Mass. Then, if possible, they should hear three Masses, not one right after another, applying the earlier explanation of the mysteries.

[67] In between the Masses they should straighten and sweep their rooms. Any remaining time should be devoted to prayer and spiritual reading, or to writing.

[68] After the Masses, they should, if needed, be given sufficient matter for two more periods using the first Method of Prayer, and immediately afterwards spend a second half hour on the matter just given.

[69] After that, they can read, write, work, or walk until the time for the Examen.

[70] They will take their dinner at the time of first table.

They will have recreation until 1:00 p.m.

Until 2:00 they will read, pray, write, or do some work.

[71] They will use their Method of Prayer again from 2:00 to 2:30.

[72] Then, if the director sees fit, they could go to a nearby church for vespers, but without talking to anybody while outside.

[73] Before 4:00 p.m. they will be given an explanation on the mysteries of the rosary, using this for prayer from 4:00 to 4:30.

Until 6:00 they can read, write, or work. Then they will spend a quarter of an hour in prayer before supper.

They will take supper at the time of first table, and then take recreation until 8:00.

[74] Then some matter for the first Method of Prayer will be explained to them for the following morning's meditation.

After recitation of the Litanies, and a quarter of an hour's examination of conscience at 8:30, they will go to bed.

[75] Upon one completion of the first Method of Prayer, it can be repeated. Once sufficient explanation has been given on using the Method of Prayer, hearing Mass, and reciting the rosary, further elements of the catechism should be given. However, all of this has to be measured by the director's discretion and the exercitant's capacity—and let the same be said here for all other persons as well. Similarly, the Additions should be given as the director judges suitable.

[76] *Schedule for the First Week with two hours of meditation, for persons of the second class*

From 4:30 to 5:30 a.m., leaving out the Foundation, they will meditate the remaining exercises of the First Week in order.

They will hear two Masses, but not one right after the other.

During the time between Masses they will do the same as the first class.

[77] When they have finished the Masses and reviewed the previous meditation, the director should give them the same program of instruction as the first group if they are still insufficiently familiar with these matters, beginning with the mysteries of the Mass and the rosary. The rest of the time until the Examen should be spent reading, praying, preparing their general confession, working, or walking.

[78] Their examination of conscience and dinner will be at the same time as the first class.

Recreation will go until 12:30.

From then until 1:30 they will do the same as from their morning instruction to the Examen.

[79] At 2:00, after reviewing their previous meditation with the director, they should be given a different or the same meditation.

Then, with the director's approval, they can go to a nearby church for vespers.

[80] From 3:00 to 4:00 they will meditate.

At 4:30 they will be given an instruction of the above-mentioned topics.

[81] From 5:00 to 5:30 they will say the rosary, reflecting on the mysteries. Then they will do some work until the final quarter of an hour before supper, which they will spend in prayer.

[82] They will have supper at the time of first table, then recreation until 8:00. Then, after reviewing their meditation with the director, they will be given a new exercise.

[83] After the recitation of the Litanies and the examination of conscience, they will go to bed.

The other Additions can be adapted for them as the director sees fit.

[84] *Schedule for Exercises with a single hour of meditation*

This is suitable for persons with public duties. Upon arising, they will do the same as the others.

[85] They will devote some specified convenient hour during the morning to meditation, and two quarter hours a day to the examination of conscience.

[86] At any other free periods during the day they will hear one or two Masses, attend vespers, pray, prepare their confession, read, and write down their devotions. The director will also instruct them on prayer, on frequent and

worthy confession and Communion, and on procedures for improving their
lives.

[87] They should also endeavor, so far as their occupations allow, to remain
in a definite place at home and observe whatever practices or Additions they
director thinks they can keep. Since they will be spending most of the time of
the Exercises in their own households, any other schedule can hardly be
prescribed for them.

[88] *Schedule for Exercises with four or five hours*

Throughout the Exercises, apart from dividing the topics up into more
hours, the distribution of the material into individual days and hours should be
no different from the schedule given immediately below for Exercises with
three hours. However, a full day should be spent on the Foundation of the
Exercises.

[89] However, since our brethren do not usually get much benefit from the
exercises on sin and hell, they can shorten the time spent on them by omitting
the repetitions, should they wish to go on to other matters and not dwell
on these.

[90] *Schedule for Exercises with three hours a day*

First day

[91] On the evening before, they should be given admonitions on the
method and purpose of the Exercises, along with the Foundation of the
Exercises for the first hour of the morning assigned by the director for meditation the next day.

[92] During the second meditation period of the forenoon, they should
again meditate on the Foundation, but should first review their morning
meditation at some suitable time with the director before they are given any
new matter. They should give this account of the previous exercise to the
director regularly. For this second hour he will give a fresh explanation of the
Foundation, along with the method for making the Particular Examen. It
should be noted that anytime the exercitant is told to spend a second hour
doing the same meditation, he ought to be given a fresh and different explanation of it by the director.

[93] During the third hour of meditation (the final one, which the director
will assign for 5:00 p.m.), they should meditate the Foundation once more,
after giving an account of the second meditation at a suitable time and receiving a fresh explanation of the Foundation for this hour, along with a procedure
for the General Examen.

Second day

[94] For the first hour, after an account of the last meditation of the previous day, they should be given the 1st exercise, on sins, together with the Additions.

For the second hour, they should be given the exercise on personal sins, along with the document about the advantages of a general confession and Communion [44].

For the third hour, they should be given the 3rd exercise, which is simply a repetition of the two preceding ones; likewise the general examination of conscience for use in preparing one's confession.

Third day

[95] For the first hour, the exercise on death (unless the director judges he should repeat the exercise of the 3rd meditation one or more times) or on discerning movements in the soul.

For the second hour, the exercise on particular judgment, unless it seems better follow the book of the Exercises and proceed to the meditation on hell —or to repeat the meditation on death instead.

For the third hour, the general judgment, unless one prefers to make a joint repetition of the meditations on death and particular judgment.

Fourth day

[96] For the first hour, on hell, or at least a repetition of the meditation on the general judgment.

For the second hour, purgatory or a repetition on hell.

For the third hour, a repetition on purgatory, or else a serious beginning of the preparation for the general confession.

This entire day should be devoted to seriously preparing the general confession, and the labor of meditating should be relaxed somewhat.

[89] When, as indicated above, on the earlier days need may have arisen for the Rules appropriate to the First Week for the Discernment of Movements in the soul, these ought to be explained; however, they can also be explained along with the exercise for the first hour of the third day without waiting until they are needed.

On the following morning the general confession should be made; externs will be free to chose any confessor they prefer.

Fifth day

[98] The morning is for the confession, as already said.

For the second afternoon hour, the contemplation on the Kingdom of Christ and the eternal King.

For the third hour, this contemplation should be repeated—unless the

general confession has taken up so much time that this contemplation can only
be made once in the afternoon.

Sixth day

[99] On the previous evening, the meditation on the Lord's Incarnation
should be given for the first hour of the following day, together with the
general scheme of the exercises on the life of Christ. At the same time the
new, somewhat modified notes or Additions will be given.

For the second hour, no meditation should be assigned and the time left
free to be spent on holy Communion. Only something on drawing fruit from
the meditation of the mysteries of Christ should be given.

For the third hour, the method for applying the five senses to the history
of the previous meditation or mystery should be given.

Seventh day

[100] For the first hour, on Christ's Nativity.

For the second, an application of the senses to the history of Christ's
Nativity, unless the exercitant prefers a straight repetition of the mystery
without the simple application of the senses.

Eighth day

[101] For the first hour, an application of the senses or a straight repetition
on the Three Kings, unless the exercitant prefers to go on to another mystery.

For the second, either the Flight into Egypt, the return, the Presentation of
the Lord in the Temple, or what Jesus Christ did until his thirtieth year.

For the third, the meditation on the boy Jesus at the age of twelve should
be given, but only where there is a prospect of the exercitant's choosing his
state of life; otherwise he can do a different exercise—or even this one.

At any time the director thinks right, he should give the guidelines for
knowing good and evil spirits that correspond to the Second Week, unless he
prefers to give them along with the second application of the senses or repetition on the eighth day.

Ninth day

[102] For the first hour, the exercise on the Two Standards, with their
preamble for considering different states of life, to help gradually prepare the
exercitant's mind for the election.

For the second and third hours, a repetition of the exercise on the Two
Standards.

Tenth day

[103] For the first hour, the Three different Classes of Persons.

For the second, passing over somewhat the material about the election, on the Lord's departure to the Jordan and his Baptism.

For the third, an application of the senses or a straight repetition on the history of the Baptism, ending with the three colloquies from the exercise on the Two Standards.

Eleventh day

[104] For the first hour, the Temptation in the Desert.

For the second, the Calling of the Apostles.

For the third, the Eight Beatitudes.

The colloquies for these three exercises will be the three from the Standards, which should be used at the end of the other mysteries of the life of Christ, provided the exercitant wishes or needs to spend more days meditating further mysteries before making the election. All the mysteries given around the time of the election should be religiously accommodated to the coming election—but discreetly, lest too much insistence render the matter offensive and suspect.

Twelfth day

[105] For the first hour, the Three Modes of Humility.

For the second and third, a repetition on the Modes of Humility, together with the instruction or preamble for making a good election and the introduction on the matters for election. To these can be added, if it would help the exercitant, the two lists[3] of various states and responsibilities in the world, with their different perfections.

Thirteenth day

[106] For the first, second, and third hours, the method for making a good election should be given, along with the five salutary counsels at its fifth point, for a more correct reasoning process.[4] At the same time a written document on the third time of election should be given.

This entire day, and even more, should the exercitant wish, ought to be spent on all these considerations, until the election is concluded.

[107] The director should occasionally visit the exercitant so that, should any temptation arise that requires it, he can better direct and help him by means of exercises devised specifically to deal with the temptation. This should be done throughout the Exercises, whenever temptations arise that demand it. However, if someone not intending to choose a state of life would rather pass

---

[3] Which lists are referred to here is unknown.

[4] This is confusing. Probably the "method for making a good election" is the *first* procedure of the third way [178–183], while the "five salutary counsels" are the four rules and note that make up the *second* procedure of the third way [184–188].

over the early exercises on the life of Christ given above starting on the seventh day, so that instead he can meditate on the Lord's Passion and the other mysteries of Christ, this should be allowed him, preserving the same order, however, and continuing the Exercises as long as the exercitant is willing.

Short Instruction on Giving the Exercises, Probably by Father Everard Mercurian

Everard Mercurian (1514–1580) served from 1573 to 1580 as fourth superior general of the Society of Jesus. It was largely due to his efforts that the official directory was able to be published nearly twenty years after his death. The following text, almost certainly Father Mercurian's work, represents a major step toward a systematic directory. Unique to this directory are suggestions on giving the Exercises to schoolboys, nos. 62–73. (Original in Latin.)

BRIEF INSTRUCTION ON GIVING THE SPIRITUAL EXERCISES, TAKEN LARGELY FROM THE BOOK OF THE EXERCISES ITSELF, TOUCHING ONLY ON A FEW POINTS FOR DIRECTORS

[1] We shall first discuss the excellence or dignity, the utility, and the necessity, of these Spiritual Exercises. Secondly, their nature and parts. Thirdly, to whom they may be given, and which exercises to which persons. Fourthly, the method of giving the Exercises themselves. Fifthly, where needed we shall briefly run through the individual exercises commenting on various points.

Their excellence, or dignity, utility, and necessity

[2] 1. They are by our order's original founder, whose life and precepts we ought to follow and imitate.

[3] 2. Christ himself gave these Exercises to our Father Ignatius, and more or less in the very order and manner in which they are written. And the reason for their power and effectiveness is that they are from Christ, etc.[1]

[4] 3. In this they resemble the sacred Scriptures to a great extent. Merely read, the sacred Scriptures barely move anyone; but when meditated and pondered they are replete with mysteries. Similarly with the Exercises: when merely read, they obviously contain good precepts but move no one very

---

[1] Father Gil González Dávila (see Doc. 31.30) found this paragraph and the first sentence of the next lacking in modesty.

much; when made, however, they are extraordinarily powerful and effective for the conversion of souls and spiritual fruit, as experience shows.

[5] This why the Exercises should not be handed out for people to read. Anyone who asks for them should be urged to make them first, for reading them will do him little good and will partly prevent their helping him if he later desires to make them.

[6] The Exercises were printed solely for the use of our own men who have to give them and not for the copies to be handed out to others, as the letter prefixed to the Exercises[2] warns. They might possibly be given for reading to an individual who is perfect and much experienced in prayer, especially if he is a friend and has the nature of the Exercises explained to him.

[7] 4. It was through these Exercises that Father Ignatius brought the first ten fathers of our Society to Christ and to the Society, and through them countless others.

[8] 5. Today, wherever the use of these Exercises flourishes, great results are visible among the people and among our own men. By means of these Exercises hundreds, not to say thousands, of persons have entered other religious orders and large numbers have entered our own. Of those who remained in the world, many hundreds also have ordered or improved their lives.

[9] 6. The Exercises have been approved by the pope after previous examination, as is stated in the bull of approbation[3] at the beginning; they are thus highly safe and trustworthy.

[10] 7. The same papal bull renders abundant testimony to the Exercises, declaring them full of piety and holiness. An even greater indication of their value and excellence is that the pope himself urges all Christians to make them, etc. (The text could be given verbatim, if wished.)

[11] 8. It is thus essential for our own men not only to have experienced the Exercises themselves—that is of primary importance—but also to know how to give them, since they are a special and unique instrument of the Society.

What the Spiritual Exercises are

[12] "By the name of spiritual exercises is understood any method of examining one's own conscience; also of meditating, contemplating, praying mentally and vocally, and finally any other spiritual operations," etc. down to "are called spiritual exercises"—as is stated in Annotation 1. (Look this up and copy it verbatim.)

In a word, then, spiritual exercises comprise all our mental activities having to do with God: whether knowing God and the things of God with our intel-

---

[2] A preface, presumably by Polanco, to the first printed version of the Exercises, the Latin Vulgate of 1548.

[3] Paul III's *Pastoralis officii*, also prefixed to the Vulgate edition.

lect; loving him with our will and experiencing other divine affections; repressing and subjugating our senses, appetites, and body for his sake; or doing anything else at all for the sake of God. Thus, a spiritual exercise is a spiritual activity of our mind for the sake of God. Moreover, to deserve the name of exercise it must not be merely momentary but steady and persistent.

Division or distribution of the Exercises into parts: What parts do they have?

[13] 1. The Spiritual Exercises are divided into three parts: the purgative part or way, the illuminative, and the perfective. This division is mentioned in some texts of the Exercises [10] and is the one traditional with the doctors and with perfect spiritual men, including St. Dionysius in the *Celestial Hierarchy* and the *Ecclesiastical Hierarchy,* where he divides all hierarchical acts into those of cleansing, enlightening, and perfecting.[4]

[14] 2. In case someone may not understand these divisions, the following explanation may help. There are in our souls spiritual evils: errors in our intellect and sins—along with wicked habits, affections, and imperfections—in our will. The removal of these evils is called the purging of our soul or mind. Errors in the intellect are removed through catechetical instruction, as when a heretic or unbeliever is freed from his errors. This aspect of purgation is not handled in the Exercises, which are written only for a Catholic who has already come to faith. The other part of purgation is that which removes sins and wicked habits and affections of the mind, and this is given and contained in the First Week of the Exercises, which is entirely aimed at rooting out these sins by presenting first of all the Examen and general confession, and the knowledge of sins along with their gravity and penalty.

[15] 3. Then, after the removal of errors in the intellect and of sins, it remains, first, for the intellect to be illuminated, so that it can know God and the things of God (i.e., divine realities) and also itself along with the vanity and baseness of human realities. For the will does not move toward what it does not know. This is the second part, which is called illuminative. Its beginnings are given in the Second Week of the Exercises, where one begins to meditate Christ's life, incarnation, nativity, etc., up to his passion. In addition, a person is led to know his own baseness as well as that of all things of this life and world, and is stirred up to follow Christ his leader under his banner, and is shown not only which state of life and way is good but also which is perfect, in order to choose it should the Lord call. With the choice of this state and life, the Second Week concludes.

[16] 4. The next thing, once the intellect has been thus enlightened and the election made, is for the will to be perfected so that it may grow in virtues even to perfect charity, which is the ultimate stage of perfection. A person

---

[4] See Pseudo-Dionysius, *Celestial Hierarchy* 3.

becomes perfect in this way when he grows more in humility and becomes more humble; when he grows in patience, obedience, fortitude, and in all the virtues; and when finally in faith, hope, and charity he gives himself to this perfection.

The Fourth and final Week, aimed entirely at kindling love for God, thus begins with meditation on the Resurrection, all the way to the conclusion of Christ's life and mysteries. Then the exercise on the Love of God is given, as well as the higher Rules for the Discernment of Spirits and the Methods of Prayer. This phase of progress also includes, I believe, the preceding Third Week, which is wholly concerned with the passion and love of the Lord; there all the virtues are increased and a living model of all the virtues and of all perfection is given in Christ our redeemer on the cross.

[17] 5. Finally, once the person has reached perfection he goes out to make others perfect, i.e., to help his neighbor. Hence, at the end of the Exercises some rules are given for thinking with the orthodox Church in mind and word, particularly in these times of ours, so that we can directly oppose the heresies of our day.

[18] 6. In conclusion, however, we should note that these three parts are not so distinct that they do not to some extent blend into each other. Even during the purgation from sins in the First Week there is a kind of illumination, viz., through knowledge of sin, of oneself, and of God's justice. To some extent there is even a perfecting—through the increase or acquisition especially of those virtues opposed to the person's vices, as well as of contrition over sins for the sake of God and for love of him. Similarly, in the course of being enlightened with knowledge of Christ and God, which begins in the Second Week, attention is also given to the purging of sins: we are always looking out of the corner of our eye, so to speak, in order to remove any sins that may remain; this is why the examination of conscience is never given up. Here also there is a striving toward perfection by the augmenting of virtues and love of God. And finally, when at the conclusion perfection is being concentrated on —i.e., love of God and of the other virtues—one also reaches the highest degree of illumination in the knowledge of God and divine things; and there are always some residual sins, affections, or imperfections that need to be purged and rooted out. Nevertheless it is still true that in the first part the main and primary concern is purgation, i.e., the uprooting of sins; and this belongs by its very nature primarily to the First Week. After that the emphasis is on illumination, and in the third place on perfection.

[19] *Which exercises to give to which persons. First, uneducated persons: the following exercises in the following order*

[20] 1. They should be given the Particular Examen; perhaps also the Foundation.

[21] 2. The General Examen [32–42] for making a general confession.

[22] 3. The method for making a daily examination of conscience.

[23] 4. The method of praying for a half hour in the morning by consideration of the commandments of God and the deadly sins.

[24] 5. The first Method of Prayer as given at the end of the Exercises. It is especially suitable for uneducated and illiterate persons. They can also be given meditation on Christ's passion, selecting some of the principal mysteries: his bloody sweat, scourging, crowning, carrying the cross, crucifixion, being taken down in the arms of the Virgin; or a meditation on the fifteen mysteries of the rosary. About this time they might also be given, or told orally, some of the Annotations which apply to them.

[25] 6. They should confess once a week and go to Communion at least every other week and be given a method for going to confession and Communion well.

[26] 7. They should be given an explanation of the individual commandments of God and the Church, the deadly sins, the five senses, the works of mercy, and the three powers of the soul. These explanations should be given one at a time as they meditate on them individually.

[27] 8. Finally, once dismissed, they should keep up the following pattern of life if they remain in the world: (1) They should pray for a half hour in the morning on the subjects mentioned. (2) They should make the General Examen either before or after dinner, as well as after supper. (3) They should go to weekly confession and Communion. In addition they can be given some vocal prayers, or rosary.

[28] *With weak or sickly persons from whom not much results are hoped for, the following order will be used*

[29] 1. Some of the easier exercises of the First Week, up through the confession.

[30] 2. Then some examinations of conscience.

[31] 3. A method for confession and frequent Communion.

[32] 4. With these persons one should not go on to the election, especially where there are other people to receive the Exercises from whom greater results are hoped for. However, if the weak or sickly person is learned or has some experience in mental prayer we can give him all the exercises of the First Week along with some meditations on the life of Christ.

[33] *If the person is intelligent or educated but hindered by public affairs or other obstacles, as with a magistrate or father of a family*

[34] 1. We will try to get from him at least an hour and a half each day. We will give him some of the Annotations pertaining to the exercitant for him to look at and think about.

[35] 2. He should be given the Foundation, for an hour on two or three days. He should try to put it into practice, performing all his actions for this final end and doing only what conduces to it. He should renew this intention at the beginning of at least his principal activities.

[36] 3. The Particular Examen for a half hour.

[37] 4. The General Examen [32–42], with a method for going to confession and receiving the Blessed Sacrament. He should make a general confession.

[38] 5. In the morning, afterwards, for three days he will be given an hour's meditation on the three sins, using the three powers of the soul—the first day on the first sin, the second day on the second, and the third day on the third, as is found in the 1st exercise of the First Week.

[39] 6. For a further three days, at the same hour, he should make a second exercise on the penalty due to sin, i.e., hell, with another exercise on the gravity and penalty of sins.

[40] 7. After that, similarly with death and judgment.

[41] 8. During the time of these meditations one should also dictate to him the ten Additions of the First Week for making the Exercises better, for they contain excellent recommendations for meditating correctly.

[42] 9. The same procedure should be used with the mysteries of our Lord Jesus Christ; although perhaps later, when he is more practiced, he might meditate a mystery for one day, repeating the meditation the next day with the exercise of the five senses.

[43] *If the person is intelligent or educated, free from occupations, and desirous of obtaining the greatest possible results from the Exercises*

[44] 1. He should be given all the exercises in the order in which they occur.

[45] 2. He should write out the main points to keep from forgetting them.

[46] 3. We will indicate below how to give the individual exercises to these and other persons.

If the person is a religious from another order than ours

[47] 1. If the religious is not given to mental prayer he should be treated like any of the persons in the world of whom we have spoken.

[48] 2. If he is given to mental prayer, we can go quickly through the First Week on the purgation of sins and concentrate more intensely on how to meditate the whole life of Christ.

[49] 3. They should also be given all the remaining exercises in sequence, along with the Additions and the Rules for the Discernment of Spirits, and finally the exercise on the Love of God, as well as a further exercise on eternal happiness, even though this is not in the book of the Exercises.

[50] 4. He should also be shown the second Method of Prayer so that, after having become thoroughly experienced in the life and mysteries of Christ he can if he wishes practice this Method of Prayer using the Lord's Prayer, the Hail Mary, a psalm or canticle or Gospel, or any other text which can be meditated in this fashion.

[51] 5. He should not be given the election of a state of life lest he be unsettled. But he should be shown everything said about the election so that he can read and learn how it should be made by persons who do not yet have a fixed and unchangeable state of life.

[52] He could be given an election between two virtues; or between the second and third degrees of humility as presented in a meditation of the Second Week; or whether he would rather be dissolved and be with Christ or remain longer and serve him; or something of that nature.

[53] 6. After completion of the Exercises he could be given the book of the Exercises to read for himself and go forward by making his own exercises.

[54] 7. Finally, when he has made some progress in studying the book of the Exercises he could be taught how to give them to others.

[55] *If the person is a religious of our Society of Jesus*

[56] These will be either novices or older religious. The latter will be either temporal coadjutors and less gifted persons or else persons with more gifts and learning. They will either have made at least the First Week once or not yet have made the Exercises, even after having spent some time in the Society and made considerable progress in prayer and devotion. We shall treat each case separately.

[57] Novices just entering the Society who have sufficient intelligence, education, and strength should if possible be given the complete Exercises in order. If not, they should be given at least the First Week and the beginning of the Second, where they should be given practice in the method for meditating the life of Christ, especially with some of the chief mysteries of Christ's life.

[58] With intelligent temporal coadjutors one could perhaps give the First Week and then the First Method of Prayer, giving them an explanation of the commandments and sins one by one, three each day. Then the exercise on the Standards, the Nativity and Shepherds, the Resurrection, and the Assumption and Coronation of the Blessed Virgin—or else the mysteries of the rosary, which are about the same.

With less educated coadjutors, follow the procedure indicated above for uneducated persons.

[59] If our men have made the complete Exercises once, they should read the book of the Exercises for themselves, ponder and make them on their own, and pick out what is helpful for them. They should also learn to give the Exercises.

[60] For those of our men who have made only the First Week, especially if they are devout, the procedure outlined for religious who are spiritually advanced and given to prayer would seem suitable. Thus, they should finish the First Week quickly, on the second or third day making a general confession since their last. Then, after finishing the First Week, they should make great progress in meditating the life of Christ, and be given thorough practice, etc., as we said of the religious above.

[61] If one of our men has not made the Exercises but nevertheless has progressed spiritually, such as someone who has been a considerable time in the Society, particularly if his health is not good, he should read the Exercises on his own and ponder them, so that he can go forward and meditate on them. He should, however, have the help of someone who is experienced in the Exercises to direct him.

[62] *If they are boys*

[63] Boys (roughly seven to twelve), such as many of our pupils who go to monthly confession, can be given some exercises at least once or twice a week, depending on their capacity. These would of course not be in the form of meditations since they would not know how to meditate. But they could be given a saying for them to call to mind frequently or to spend five minutes or so on in the morning, for that is as long as boys can keep their imagination from wandering.

[64] It would seem they could be given especially some or all of the following topics, which boys usually like and find most moving and helpful.

They can be given some vocal prayers to recite every day in the morning and the evening, v.g., the Our Father, Hail Mary, Hail Holy Queen, the Creed; also prayers to the Blessed Virgin or the rosary.

[65] The daily General Examen in the evening.

[66] The Foundation on our final end.

[67] Death, judgment, hell, paradise (although they are usually more moved and attracted by thoughts of death and paradise than of hell).

[68] The Nativity, Shepherds, and Kings.

[69] Christ's Passion.

[70] The Blessed Virgin's Assumption and Coronation.

[71] The gifts of God.

[72] Likewise the lives of the saints, which they can be assigned to read for themselves. They can be given models, especially those who were holy from earliest childhood. Similarly devotion to the virgins and angels, such as their

own angel, etc.

[73] Finally, the can be given some particularly good sayings of the holy Fathers on certain virtues, v.g., virginity, penance, etc. They can learn these and have them in writing and memorize them. They can be given pictures to keep before their eyes in their rooms, or buy their own. Boys enjoy pictures a lot and are moved by them.

[74] *If they are women*

[75] The same method mentioned for use with boys can be employed with women, especially those who come to confession to our men; or else the method for uneducated persons.

[76] With women of high mental and spiritual quality one can use the procedure described for men who are intelligent or educated but occupied with business: they should be given an hour and a half or two hours.

[77] A nun at liberty to spend the whole day in meditation, and of high mental and spiritual quality, might be given the Exercises completely and seriously, though I doubt this would be frequent.

[78] Care should be taken not to give them anything in writing in such a way that anyone could claim that our men are passing letters rather than giving the Exercises.

[79] *Giving the individual exercises*

[80] *Before the meditation.* Read the exercises in the book of the Exercises itself and think them over carefully. In fact, at the beginning of each Week one ought to read that entire Week in the book of the Exercises.

[81] The director should meditate the exercise he is about to give, and ask the Lord Jesus for grace of picking out as well as possible from what he has meditated the most helpful things to say to the exercitant.

[82] He should ask the exercitant how he proceeded in the previous exercise, what he felt, etc. He should help him and give advice, assistance, etc., where needed. He should give a brief oral explanation of the upcoming meditation or exercise he is to make.

[83] Afterwards it should be given succinctly in writing. Since not every director is capable of making a short and convenient summary of the exercises and of setting down the main points clearly and in a form useful for meditation, it will be a good idea to use the ones in Italian that are current in the Society; I believe these summaries are by Father Polanco, or even by Father Ignatius himself.[5]

[84] The exercitant receives the next text in writing. He reads and thinks about it, and copies it out.

---

[5] Several of these summaries are given in our Document 20 bis.

[85] When he goes to bed at night he reads the morning exercise. Lying in bed, he reviews for the space of a Hail Mary the time of his arising and the topic of his meditation. On awaking he immediately recalls it and prepares himself for prayer. During and after meditation he should first prepare himself in this way.

[86] He makes the exercise; i.e., he meditates for a full hour, either kneeling or in any other way that helps him meditate with greater attention and devotion.

[87] Afterwards, for about a quarter of an hour, he examines how it went. If it went badly he notes the causes in order to avoid them; if well, he thanks God and continues the same way.

[88] He also notes what he experienced: his affections, trains of thought, consolations, etc., so that he can briefly report them to the director and afterwards write them up in a very brief form to keep them in mind.

[89] He gives a brief report to the director on how it went, what he did and experienced. The latter guides him, and in this way they move through the succeeding exercises.

[90] For correctly giving the Exercises to others the most essential thing is for one to have previously made and thoroughly meditated them himself, and then re-meditate them just before giving them.

It is important also to have read the book of the Exercises itself and to have carefully and thoroughly studied it beforehand, and then to do this again when giving the Exercises; and finally, to be experienced, i.e., have given the Exercises a certain number of times.

[91] *Some general guidelines for the director*

[92] He visits the exercitant twice, or at least once, a day.

[93] Upon learning how the exercise went he should never sharply reprehend or disapprove what the exercitant has done or what took place in meditation. This is very harmful and discourages the exercitant. Instead he should gently teach and instruct him how to proceed in the future. Neither should he praise him too much, so that he will not get proud. He should moderately indicate his approval and encourage the exercitant.

[94] The place for making the Exercises should be secluded and private. It is preferable for the exercitant to talk with no one at all except the director. He should stay shut in his room, at least if he wants to make the Exercises seriously and profit much by them, so that he can deal alone with God.

[95] The Exercises should last approximately thirty days, or twenty, or eighteen—or eight if only the First Week is being made. On occasion it could be forty days.[6]

---

[6] As in the Exercises given by St. Ignatius to Dr. Pedro Ortiz at Monte Cassino.

[96] For each day during the full Exercises five hours of meditation are prescribed: at midnight, at daybreak, around the time of Mass, at midafternoon, and before supper. In addition, after each exercise he should spend a quarter of an hour thinking back and examining how it went, as is stated in the book of the Exercises.

[97] He should also make the Particular Examen after dinner and supper.

[98] Others, who are less robust or who have less time available, can be given four hours, omitting the midnight exercise; or else three hours: one at daybreak or the hour of Mass and two in the afternoon; or certainly two hours, one in the morning and one in the afternoon. At the very least they should be given one hour, especially upon arising at daybreak, along with another half hour for the General or Particular Examen as we indicated above for persons occupied with important business.

[99] The posture can be kneeling, prostrate, standing, sitting decently, walking about, or any other position compatible with decency and reverence which allows the greatest devotion and attention, as indicated in the book of the Exercises. In general, however, the best posture is kneeling. If he cannot kneel for the whole time he should at least kneel for a short time at the beginning, and afterwards stand or sit. Praying prostrate, provided devotion urges him and it does no harm, or if he is otherwise used to the practice, may be done for a short period, but not often since it tends to perturb the memory and intelligence. Walking about is more appropriate while examining afterward how the exercise went. But the spirit should always be prostrate and humble with due reverence, etc. The eyes should be closed or else fixed motionlessly upon some unvarying spot.

[100] Repetitions of the exercises should be made as follows. After two exercises he should make a repetition of both in the following third hour, especially on the points where he experienced some consolation or desolation. Sometimes he is given a single exercise and told to repeat it, and then a second one in the same way. Sometimes even two repetitions are made if in some exercise he continues to experience great consolation or some other Godward affection. This has been the practice especially in the First Week.

[101] Exercises might sometimes be changed around if the exercitant's needs or utility requires. Some can also be omitted.

[102] The First and other Weeks can be lengthened or shortened, as indicated in the fourth Annotation, since some people find contrition sooner, others later. Some people also acquire devotion and skill in meditating more quickly or slowly than others.

[103] The Additions should be given at the appropriate time and place.

[104] The Rules for the Discernment of Spirits should be used and also given at the appropriate time. They are especially needed in the First and Second Weeks, particularly at the moment of choosing a state of life.

[105] Some penances should be enjoined, as stated in the Addition for the First Week (quote this and examine it). When the meditation is not going properly but is dry and barren, it is a good idea to change the type of penance immediately for two or three days, as is stated in the same place. It is also good to examine and eliminate the causes. Another help is to give some instruction on how to meditate, pointing out some elements to think about, such as the causes, effects, or relevance of the mystery, or certain virtues which can be descried there, and other things which are easy to find. Finally, it is helpful to urge the exercitant to persevere even when dry and barren, for God will eventually come if he humbly perseveres and does not give up his prayer and spiritual exercises.

[106] When the Exercises are finished he should be left with the following program of life for the future, which he ought to be putting into practice even during the time of the Exercises.

The program of life with which a person is left after the Exercises could be for the most part the following

[107] He should always preserve the presence of God in one of the following ways. He can keep Christ's most sacred humanity before his eyes as if seeing Christ before him always on the cross, or else by picturing the mystery he had meditated that morning. He can carry the likeness or image of the crucified Christ in his heart, gazing on it there; or else the Blessed Virgin with Christ in her arms. Or he can see him in heaven at the Father's right hand where he sits and beholds us; or in heaven governing all things from there; or in every place, including where we are, creating, preserving, and ruling all things. Or we can have him present within ourselves and in the essence of our soul, where he gives it essence and life and being, etc. Or any other manner of beholding that seems best.

[108] While doing this he should make frequent use of jaculatory prayers, at least before—or during and after as well—all his more important activities. For example, he can give thanks, ask grace and help in acting, refer what he does to God, praise God, pray for himself and his neighbor, etc. If a religious, he can daily renew his vows when he goes to Communion or hears Mass.

[109] He should apply to all his actions the practice of the final end, doing everything for God and his glory and no other motive. He should resolve in the morning to do this and again several times during the day, and should be carrying this out continuously, or almost continuously—beholding God with intellectual vision, or contemplating him with intellectual consideration, or recalling him often with his memory—or, even more perfectly, resolving always to do the best thing he can in every place and time for the greater glory of God, according to St. Paul's words: "Whether you eat or drink or do anything else, do everything for the glory of God" [1 Cor 10:31]. And he

should act in this way always, or at least strive toward it as best he can.

[110] Note: we must do everything for God, both principally for his own sake, i.e., out of pure love of charity, as well as for the benefits we have received, i.e., out of gratitude—and out of these two motives rather than out of fear of hell or hope of eternal glory, although we should sometimes aid ourselves with these motives also.

[111] Since they now know how to meditate they should keep up this practice well by meditating on the life and mysteries of Christ for one, two, or more hours each day. In addition they should make the twofold Examen before dinner and after supper. In fact, they should make a briefer examination occasionally after either recreation or other activities.

[112] They should have particular devotion to some saints, virgins, and angels, including their own guardian angel; to the angels of the Society and the college, to their name-saints, and above all to the Blessed Virgin.

[113] They should take particular care to grow in the virtues, especially those which are the underpinnings of the spiritual life and most pleasing to God, v.g., humility, obedience, patience, poverty, bodily purity and chastity, and mental reverence and love for superiors; but especially love of God and Christ and the Blessed Virgin. It would be good to concentrate more carefully on one particular virtue they especially desire, and then to move on in succession to others.

[114] He should also occasionally read devotional books which will help him, especially Gerson's *Imitation of Christ* and Luis de Granada's book on prayer[7] and other works: also the New and Old Testaments if he has some learning—not out of mere desire to know but in order to profit thereby and meditate.

[115] He should attend to his bodily comportment, using the Rules of Modesty.

[116] When he has reached a somewhat higher level of perfection he can afterwards (depending on how God moves him in accord with his talents and state of life) move out toward helping his neighbor in some spiritual or corporal work of mercy in hospitals, prisons, etc.; or by preaching, teaching catechism, giving the Spiritual Exercises themselves, etc., hearing confessions, etc.

[117] Which and what kind of meditation and prayer should be used we explained in a general way in our last exhortation at Padua, and can be found there. I left it with Father Charles in the form of a list on a sheet of paper.

[118] Lack of time has prevented me from writing down some remarks on the particular exercises of the First, Second, and Fourth Weeks.

---

[7] Luis de Granada, O.P., *Libro de oración y meditación* (1566). A 1582 English translation entitled *Of Prayer and Meditation* is reproduced as vol. 64 in the English Recusant Literature collection (Menston, Yorkshire: Scolar Press, 1971).

Counsels of Father Everard Mercurian to Fabio de Fabi

Father Mercurian's secretary, Antonio Possevino, wrote on the manuscript of these notes: "Very short counsels but full of content, given to Father Fabio de Fabi when he was novice master." (Original in Latin.)

[1] The Society's Spiritual Exercises are profitably received and given in the following manner—and to the same end all our order's other activities and ministries ought to be directed: preaching, administration of the sacraments, teaching.

[2] First. The Foundation places before our eyes man's end: to know God and, knowing him, to reverence, love, and serve him. This is common to every human being—good and wicked, believers and unbelievers, etc. Relevant to this are the topics of our creation, preservation, redemption, etc., so that each person, knowing his end, might devote his life, his actions, and all creatures to obtaining it. This applies to persons of every kind, capacity, and condition; and each one must be instructed, in accordance with his state, so that he will use the lawful and proper means for this end.

[3] The first thing, then, which must be done is to remove obstacles by penitence, so that having paid our debts and been freed from fetters, we may the more freely achieve our end. Hence the exercitant is immediately given the Examen for coming to an awareness of his sins of thought, word, and deed. Directly afterwards he is given the meditation on sins, so that through knowledge and detestation of them they may be wiped out through genuine penitence. Then we are directed by the example of the life of Christ the Lord, and taught a way of regulating our own life. In the same place, those lacking a definite state of life and desiring to choose one are given ways of election by means of the points for that purpose. Those already in a definite state, assuming it is a good and useful one, are given ways of confirming and perfecting themselves in that state. Finally, Methods of Prayer are given, so that they will have some procedure and instruction for practicing prayer.

[4] Likewise those who hear confessions, preach, and teach school should make earnest efforts to guide souls to their end by this path. In every circumstance they should have this goal of the Society clearly in mind, aiding others

to their salvation and eternal blessedness, as has been stated regarding the Spiritual Exercises—so that in this way greater knowledge of our Lord may be had in every circumstance and action of ours, and the name of God be more greatly glorified. The Exercises may seem in a way to be dry and tasteless. But very frequently—indeed always if they are made properly—the produce extremely abundant fruit. Sometimes just the consideration of the Foundation suffices to bring a whole soul to amendment and reform as it recollects itself and dwells persistently upon its end.

[5] We should keep the manner of giving the Exercises simply and in the same order as prescribed by Father Ignatius in his instructions. This manner was kept by Father Ignatius, Fathers Laínez, Favre, Paschase, etc.

[6] The repetitions of the exercises may seem superfluous, but in fact are extremely valuable. First, they exercise one in patience and obedience. Secondly, they help reach the fruit sought in meditation. It often happens that retreatants, intrigued by the novelty of the topics, browse aimlessly among them. The repetitions are aimed at curtailing such digressions and getting the retreatant to go back over the same materials more frequently, examine them more thoroughly, and so retain them better.

[7] Over the four Weeks of the Exercises, instruction is given on the entire range of matters which can be meditated. Hence it is valuable for our own men and all other religious to go through them all.

[8] Exercitants should be fully instructed in how to apply their powers in meditation: their understanding, memory, and will. Otherwise they will not know what to do. For the rest however, the history itself should be given as succinctly as possible.

[9] Our Spiritual Exercises comprise everything on the topic of the election which can be found in all the doctors and saints regarding this point. Indeed, much of what the Exercises provide, especially on the three times of election, is new and unprecedented.[1] The third time, based on reflection with in a time of mental tranquility, is remarkable and full of genuine wisdom.

[10] The Spiritual Exercises are remarkably effective in leading up to this. For since their primary purpose is to bring a person to his end—blessedness— they first point out this end; then cleanse the soul from sins by penitence; and finally instruct the soul how to reach its end by love, to which we are stirred up by consideration of God's works and of Christ's incarnation, his dwelling among us, and his work of redemption.

[11] The meditation on the King, however, is not given to externs unless they are going to make a choice of a definite state of life.

---

[1] Gil González Dávila (Doc. 31.20) found these claims open to the charge of exaggeration.

Directory of
Father Juan Alfonso de Polanco

As St. Ignatius' secretary and intimate collaborator, Juan Alfonso de Polanco was in a privileged position to learn the saint's mind on giving the Exercises; in fact, he was instructed by St. Ignatius to submit to him any questions about the Exercises with a view to eventually composing a directory. The following directory, completed many years after St. Ignatius' death, is generally considered the finest of those which preceded the official Directory. *For Father Gil González Dávila's high opinion of it, see Doc. 21.2. (Original in Latin.)*

[1] FATHER POLANCO'S DIRECTORY FOR GIVING THE SPIRITUAL EXERCISES

PROLOGUE TO THE MEMBERS OF THE SOCIETY

[2] Among the most effective means used by the Society from the very beginning for the end of its institute (viz., the glory of God and the progress of souls) the Exercises certainly hold pride of place. Of course, the administration of the sacraments of penance and the Eucharist, the preaching of the word of God, the catechizing of children and unlettered persons, the formation of youth in learning and piety, and other works of charity, have all with the cooperation of God's grace been widely developed. Nevertheless, the Exercises are a kind of synthesis which includes all these other means. The Exercises penetrate the inmost recesses of the soul and its powers, powerfully disposing them to receive God's grace. Correspondingly, they have garnered into the Lord's barns a more abundant, solid, and enduring harvest. Through them too persons have been called and sent out into the Lord's vineyard who can there make use of all the other means for gathering fruit.

A witness to this is our Father Ignatius of happy memory: through these Exercises he was taught and enlightened by God and made great progress at the beginning of his conversion. Other witnesses are our first fathers, who through the Exercises received the spirit of the Lord and the grace of their vocation. Further witnesses are almost all of us who followed in the first fathers' footsteps; through the Exercises we were brought by God's providence to despise this world, love the things of eternity, and embrace the same institute as they.

Witnesses also are laymen and laywomen of every condition, as well as clergy. Helped by our men through the use of the Exercises to a knowledge of God and of themselves, they have achieved remarkable, even notorious, alteration and reform of their lives. Witnesses are the numerous men and women religious of different orders who could not be brought back to the observance of their institute by public preaching, private exhortation, fear of punishment, or awe of authority, but who through the influence of the Exercises were brought of their own free will, even eagerly, to lead a life that was spiritual and consonant with their religious vocation and profession.

In view of the value of these Exercises as testified to by so many persons inside and outside the Society, as well as by the Apostolic See in the Society's charters and in specific approbation conferred on the Exercises, and seeing that the Exercises have been granted by God's grace to our Society as its own special spiritual weapon for the outstanding progress of souls, it does not seem right that we who are held by our institute to labor for this progress should loose sight of them or handle them negligently. Rather, we ought to make great efforts to train ourselves how to use them well and make them effective for our neighbor's good and the glory of God.

In accordance, then, with the decree of the General Congregation,[1] the injunction of our Father General Everard, and the intention of our Father Ignatius (who began this directory but never completed it), I have undertaken the toil of compiling this work for the benefit of our men who give the Exercises. May the pious reader take this toil in good part, and if himself granted any lights in this regard by the Lord, let him in his charity make it available to others.

[3] CHAPTER 1: REASONS WHY PEOPLE EXPERIENCE SUCH
REMARKABLE PROGRESS IN THE SPIRITUAL EXERCISES

[4] Not without reason, there are persons who wonder what accounts for the fact that the Exercises are able in so short a time to bring about such extraordinary progress in the spiritual life and such remarkable transformations of life and behavior, and in a sense of the entire person. On closer inspection, however, it is not difficult to grasp the cause of this lavish outpouring of the grace of God—from whom comes every best and every perfect gift. Anyone who thinks of God loftily and reverently, as is meet, ought to hold this of him above all: that the sun is not so ready to shed its light, or any other secondary cause to produce its natural effect, as God himself, the sun of all wisdom and justice, entirely free but also by his very nature (which is goodness) utterly

---

[1] General Congregation I, decree 107.

generous, is ready to enlighten and perfect our minds with the rays of his grace. In fact, we ought to hold that within the limits of his creatures' capacity he is on his part more eager to bestow greater gifts than lesser ones, as beseems his divine majesty and magnificence. The reason why people nevertheless receive little or no grace is because they block out the rays of God's goodness by the cloud of their sins; or else because, turning to things that are base and earthly, they fail to turn their minds and hearts to welcome the inflow of God's gifts; or because, at the least, they dispose themselves for his gifts listlessly and offhandedly and so fail to win any grace, or any great grace, from a Giver whose sovereign generosity is nevertheless coupled with sovereign justice.

[5] Now if, with God's grace, we are to dispose ourselves well to receive great gifts from him, three things especially seem required of us. First, that out of a heart which is truly generous and worthy of our adoption by our eternal Father, and out of a right intention of pleasing him, we strive after things that are truly great. Second, that we strive to obtain these things by the means that are appropriate and have been ordained by divine providence. Third, that we duly cooperate with divine providence by contributing energetic efforts of our own and doing all that lies in our own power, as is fitting, in order to obtain them.

[6] Now when the Spiritual Exercises are made as they should be, these three requirements are remarkably well met. First of all, the things aimed at and sought in the Exercises are such as truly befit sons of God; viz., that the soul be cleansed of its sins and vices, as well as of their aftereffects, and be disposed and strengthened to remain pure in the future; that the soul receive light to know the goodness, wisdom, mercy and justice of Christ our supreme mediator and our redemption, and of the eternal Father; that it be equipped for making a choice of the state and way of life that will lead to the final goal of our happiness and God's glory, and also for discerning which spirits help or hinder along the way; and finally that it be brought to perfection in what pertains to kindling within us the fire of divine love and performing our actions rightly in any state of life whatever out of a sincere impulse of love for God. Can anyone aim at things better or nobler than these?

[7] We also find the second requirement fully met in the Exercises, viz., that the best and most effective means toward this goal be made use of. Such is the meditation made in the Exercises, meditation on matters of great import, arranged in a highly organized sequence. Such also is the type of prayer taught in the Exercises, a prayer suitable for training both beginners and those who are advancing. Such also is the use of the sacraments of penance and the Eucharist, along with a method for receiving them well (especially by means of a general confession). Such also is the chastisement of the body through abstinence and other austerities, which (together with the regulation of one's eating) are explained in the Exercises. Such also is the submission of the exercitant to the

advice and guidance of a prudent director. Further such means, finally, are the rules given for examining one's conscience well, discerning various spirits, making correct choices according to God's will, making a religious disposal of one's property, diagnosing scruples, and thinking correctly with the Catholic Church. It is by these instruments or means that God's providence has willed that people cooperate with him to attain the best results, as is testified by Sacred Scripture and the lives of the saints.

[8] The third requirement too—that we make strenuous efforts of our own to cooperate with God's grace—is outstandingly well met in the Exercises, especially when they are made in full form. First of all, obstacles which could arise from persons or affairs are eliminated when the exercitant chooses a suitable place where he can enjoy solitude and be concerned only with himself and God. Further, a person gives considerable evidence of a great determination to advance spiritually when he sets aside every other concern and concentrates all his thoughts and actions exclusively on this. Yet this determination is also accompanied by hope of making this great progress, by total abandonment of himself into God's hands, by humble acceptance of direction, and by hard, serious work and personal efforts for his own advancement. Normally, the more a person does these things the more God's goodness bestows grace. Moreover, the soul's entire force, with all its various powers, is concentrated and brought to bear solely on its spiritual progress; thus concentrated, its power, both in intellect and in affection, becomes stronger. Good thoughts and desires once conceived are not allowed to drop but are followed through to some definite good conclusion. The exercitant carefully reflects and examines himself on his performance of the Exercises, so that he can continue doing what has been successful and rectify what has not. In conclusion, his activities to dispose himself for great progress are both highly intensive and well calculated to achieve their goal. Whoever does these things is making an all-out effort and doing everything in human power to obtain rich graces from God. It stands to reason that the limitless goodness of God, after first bringing a person to use these aids for disposing himself to receive the influx of grace, would shower him with graces both rich and abundant, in accord with his own bountifulness. This then is the source of the extraordinary and marvelous "change of the right hand of the Most High" evident in those who make the Exercises. In just a month they reach greater enlightenment on their state of life, deeper knowledge of themselves and God, purer and more burning love for God and eternal realities, and greater and more solid advance in every interior gift, than they had previously gained over many years of working less intensely and disposing themselves less thoroughly. And once God's action has wrought such a change in their hearts, what wonder if the change shows in their entire outward life as well?

[9] Chapter 2: Four Ways of Giving the Exercises
to Four Different Categories of Persons

[10] However, the Spiritual Exercises should be given only to selected persons, and discernment should be used in deciding how to give them to each individual. Annotations 18–20 in the book of the Exercises cast much light on this. To be more specific, however, four categories of exercitants should be distinguished. The first comprises those for whom you judge it sufficient that they make a limited degree of progress, either because they are less endowed with intelligence and judgment, or because a certain amount of instruction in the spiritual path seems to be all they need, or because it appears that little fruit can be expected from them, or because they do not have the leisure, or because it is not advisable to spend a lot of time on them. Such persons should be given (1) the Particular Examen against their more pressing faults, (2) the General as well as the Daily Examen, (3) instruction in using the first Method of Prayer for a half hour daily, with instruction on the commandments (if they are unfamiliar with them) and the deadly sins, and (4) an exhortation to go to confession weekly if conveniently possible and to Communion every two weeks, unless weekly Communion seems preferable. They could also be given any of the Additions that might be appropriate for them.

[11] The second category comprises those who have sufficient intelligence to understand the Exercises but who are disposed only to spend eight or ten days in cleansing their conscience and receiving some instruction on how to improve their lives within their present state. If they are free, and are willing and able to spend these days entirely on the Exercises in one of our houses or elsewhere, they can be given the Foundation, the Examens, and all the exercises of the First Week up through the general confession and Communion. At the same time they should be given the Additions just as in the complete Exercises. If needed, the Rules for the Discernment of Spirits pertaining to the First Week can be explained to them.

[12] Secondly, they can be given the first Method of Prayer as found in the Fourth Week. The third Method could also be helpful for them.

[13] Thirdly, they should be urged to confession and Communion, as mentioned above.

[14] Fourthly, where it is seen to be necessary or strongly indicated, they can be given some of the Rules for Distributing Alms, Discerning Scruples, Thinking with the Catholic Church, or Regulating their Diet, so far as is deemed useful and time allows. Then they can be let go. In cases where they are unable to devote the time exclusively to the Exercises, they should be given the Exercises of the First Week in the manner described below for the third category, together with whichever of the above mentioned rules can be helpful for them, along with the exhortation to frequent confession and Communion.

Thereupon they may be let go.

[15] The third category comprises those who, on the one hand, have suffi-cient intelligence and can be expected to derive not inconsiderable profit from the Exercises, but who, because impeded by public affairs or other legitimate reasons, are not free to give the full amount of time demanded by the Exer-cises. They are persons for whom it is impossible or undesirable to leave their homes and withdraw to a place of seclusion away from contact with others and the hurly-burly of affairs. Such persons should remain in their usual place of residence. They should be visited there by the director, or else (for the sake of secrecy) themselves come to our house to some pre-arranged place. These persons should first be given the Foundation, which they ought to ponder for a day or two, dedicating some suitable time to this.

Second, they should be given the Particular Examen, to be applied to their more pressing faults. They should be given the little Additions that go along with it, and for at least one further day spend a half hour on it after dinner and supper (in addition to the resolution in the morning).

Third, they should be shown how to make a general examination of their conscience for a general confession. They should also be given the daily Exa-men to practice for a day or two, along with a method for receiving holy Communion well.

Fourth, they should be given the 1st exercise of the First Week. They should meditate it for three days, spending at least an hour a day on it. They should also begin to have some of the ten Additions explained to them.

Fifth, they should be given the 2nd exercise, on the review of their sins, which they ought to ponder for the same number of days and hours. More of the Additions should be explained.

Sixth, they should be given the exercise on the penalty for sin, which they should also make for three hours over three days. Any remaining Additions should be explained to them. Such persons are not given the 3rd and 4th exercises; these being repetitions of the first two exercises, their place is taken by the three days of meditation spent on each. If it seems called for, the exerci-tants can also be given further exercises along the same line, for example, on death and judgment. This should be done where it is really necessary; in cases where the three meditations produce sufficient contrition for their sins, the extra meditations are not needed. If greater contrition is desired, further meditations along the same line can be added. Where applicable to the exerci-tant, the Rules for the Discernment of Spirits pertaining to the First Week can be explained.

Seventh, they should then make a general confession and (if they are not priests) receive Communion. Priests may celebrate Mass even earlier if so moved. After that, where it is judged good for the exercitants to continue the Exercises past the First Week, they can be given meditations on the life of

Christ from the Second, Third and Fourth Weeks, to be made similarly for two or three days each. The Additions for these can also be given. Persons of this third category can be given anything from the complete Exercises warranted by their character and the time available.

[16] In cases where the exercitant wishes to deal with the question of relinquishing or accepting some office or of choosing a state of life, he should also during the Second Week be given the Exercises that pertain to the election. But unless such a person proves outstandingly well disposed and attains true self-abandonment in seeking God's will, it would be better (especially in the matter of choosing a state of life) not to press on to a decision but to put it off to another time when he will be freer from any influence of self-love. Where such persons do seem ready to make an election, they should follow the directives given below.

[17] If persons in this third category wish to spend more than one hour a day on the Exercises, i.e., an hour in the morning, another in the afternoon, and a third at night, then they can complete this type of Exercises sooner and can more closely approximate the Exercises made in the full form, to the extent this will be deemed appropriate in each case.

[18] Should a person, after making the First Week in this way and having tasted the Spirit of God, then be disposed to make the rest of the Exercises in full form and can do this without difficulty, it would be good to do so, especially where the choice of a state of life is to be made.

[19] The fourth category comprises those who are sufficiently free from all other occupations to dedicate themselves exclusively to making the complete Exercises and who also appear both capable of bearing more abundant fruit for the glory of God and sincerely desirous of making progress. These persons, especially if they wish to make a decision about their life according to God's will, should be given the Exercises in the full form detailed below.

[20] CHAPTER 3: THINGS TO BE DONE BEFORE STARTING
BY A PERSON WHO WISHES TO MAKE THE COMPLETE EXERCISES

[21] In the case of persons who wish to make the Exercises in the full form, certain matters need to be attended to before they start in order for them to dispose themselves better to receive God's grace. They should first of all be instructed in the purpose of the Exercises. They can be given the Annotations which head the twenty in the book of the Exercises, or whichever part of them seems applicable. This is to assure, first, that each one undertake this business of his own advancement with a spirit of generosity, of desire for great progress in spiritual things, and of great confidence in God's goodness.

[22] Second, that he resolve to cooperate energetically with God's grace to the extent of his powers, and determine to bend all his strength and effort to

receiving it, with the Lord's help.

[23] Third, that he strive for this purpose to place his entire will and all his affections in God's hands, generously entrusting himself to the Lord and genuinely seeking his good pleasure and perfect will.

[24] Fourth, that if conveniently possible he should dispose himself for the influx of God's grace by giving alms to the poor and to pious works, as well as by getting others to pray for him.

[25] Fifth, that he extract himself from all other affairs and concerns by either suspending, concluding, or handing them over to others, so that he will be able to withdraw his mind from them completely and devote himself exclusively to the business of his own salvation and progress, attentive to nothing but God and himself.

[26] The better to do this, a suitable place should be selected where he will not be seen or interrupted by family and friends or by any other persons he habitually deals with. It should also be a place where he has facilities for hearing Mass and vespers if he wishes, for walking, and for freely carrying out all the activities of the Exercises. It should be a place convenient for the director to visit, and where the exercitant can have anything he desires by way of food or drink brought to him without his needing to worry about it. If necessary, he can be given the reasons listed in Annotation 20 on the advantages of choosing a secluded place of this sort, whether in one of our houses or elsewhere.

[27] Note that in cases where there is the option of assigning various of our men to give a person the Exercises, account should be taken of the exercitant's intelligence, learning, prudence, and even feelings, so that as far as possible he can be assigned a director who will enjoy his respect and liking, and who, all things considered, will be the best suited to direct him.

[28] CHAPTER 4: GENERAL RESPONSIBILITIES OF ANYONE ASSIGNED TO GIVE THE FULL EXERCISES

[29] There are some prescriptions that are general and applicable to the Exercises throughout, and others more specific to the individual Weeks.

1. In general, the director should take care that both he and the exercitant prepare themselves to cooperate fully with God's grace, striving earnestly to do all they can, the director to bring down God's grace and the exercitant to receive it. For this, it will help if the director desires with ardent charity to see the exercitant's salvation and spiritual progress for the sake of God's glory and out of a wish to see God's will accomplished in the exercitant as perfectly as possible. It will also help if the director, recognizing that while of his own power he is unable to produce this supernatural operation of grace in the exercitant he is nevertheless able to obtain this power from the infinite goodness of

God and cooperate with it, will earnestly pray for the exercitant throughout
the Exercises, remembering him in his Masses, particularly at moments of special need. He should beg the prayers of others as well.

[30] 2. At suitable moments the director should remind the exercitant to lift
the eyes of longing and trust to the source of every good thing, and make use
of every means to obtain his grace, in such a way that he places his hope not
in the means themselves but in the goodness and generosity of the Lord. While
realizing that God's providence requires the exercitant's earnest cooperation by
making use of the means, the exercitant should nevertheless fix the anchor of
his confidence not in these means but in him who is the Giver of every good
gift. These means (which ought to be recalled to the exercitant at suitable
moments) are those listed back in chapter 2, which dispose a person for the
reception of abundant grace from God through his own vigorous efforts.

[31] 3. Unless he already knows the exercitant, the director should try to
get information about his intelligence, character, and temperament, either from
others or through tactful questioning of the exercitant. In this way he will
better be able to adapt himself to the exercitant. To grave and learned persons
he should speak succinctly and learnedly; to persons of little spiritual experience, with greater fullness. To both kinds he should set forth the Exercises in
a clear and orderly fashion. It is important, however, that while allowing for
differences in the intelligence, learning, or experience of his exercitants, the
director should, on the one hand, avoid explaining the points too fully—both
so that the exercitant may have greater relish in what he himself discovers (see
Annotation 2) and so that more room may be left for lights and movements
from above; on the other hand, he should avoid being overly brief and
schematic, but should give enough to ensure that the exercitant understands the
points correctly and is able to see his way into the meditation.

[32] 4. If the exercitant can write, it will be an aid to his memory to dictate
the points of the Exercises to him in the form presented at the end of this
instruction.[2] This should follow after giving a somewhat fuller oral explanation,
as indicated above. In principle, dictating the points and having the exercitant
perform the humble task of writing them out in his own hand is preferable to
giving him the points in writing. Sometimes, however, it is preferable to give
them to the exercitant already written out, v.g., because time presses, or
because the exercitant's handwriting is poor, or because the director does not
have the points memorized. In any case, the director should always explain the
points from memory, so as not to lose the respect owed to him as a master.
If he gives the impression of being inexperienced in this ministry he will forfeit
credit with the exercitant. In rare cases where he does not leave written points
because the exercitant is perhaps illiterate, he should go over the points he has

---

[2] See Doc. 20 bis for a selection of these.

given a second time, and if necessary have the exercitant repeat them after him.

[33] 5. In accordance with Annotation 3, the director should remind the exercitant to practice greater reverence in the colloquies and other prayers than while meditating. Although one normally deals with God in both, still it is in the prayers that we more properly speak with him, whether vocally or in our heart, to a greater extent than while merely thinking. Besides, there are times when the meditation is not about God.

[34] 6. The exercitant should be aware that, as was said in chapter 1, one of the most powerful means for meriting God's grace is the humility he shows in submitting to the director's instruction and placing his trust in him. Conversely, overconfidence in self, concealment of his thoughts from the director, or refusal to follow his advice can be the cause of making poor progress or of going astray. For any person it is spiritual good sense to seek out a judge in his own affairs other than himself, as was said in chapter 1. But this spiritual guidance by another is especially necessary when a person inexperienced in the spiritual life embarks on the path of the Spirit. The doctors even counsel not setting foot on this path rather than doing so without a master. Hence, the exercitant should disclose to the director how he is making the exercises and should give him an account of them. In this way, if he has failed to understand anything fully, he can be instructed. His insights and illuminations can be subjected to scrutiny. His desolations and consolations can be discerned. And he can be helped with advice on any penances he does or temptations that beset him.

[35] 7. The director likewise should be careful to visit the exercitant at the proper times, to ask an account of the exercises made since his last visit along with his manner of meditating and using the Additions, and to monitor the illuminations of the exercitant's understanding and the movements of his affections. Thus, if the exercitant is going forward nicely, the director can give his confirmation. If not, he can inquire how carefully he is making the exercises and Additions. If the exercitant's understanding is so weak or spiritually inexperienced that he cannot find matter for meditation, the director can get him started by giving him a few ideas to work on. On the other hand, if the exercitant overstresses the intellect and fails to exercise his affections, the director can instruct him to advance with equal strides in both, and if he veers too much to one side can set him straight. If the exercitant has any doubts or questions, the director can answer them. Especially with the intelligent and learned he can anticipate questions by explaining the reason for some of the things he says, especially when proposing things that may seem novel to the exercitant. If the exercitant is lukewarm in making the exercises and Additions, the director can spur him on. If he is trying too hard the director can restrain him. If he is in desolation the director can console him. If he is flooded with consolations the director can sift them. If he is agitated by temptations or

diverse spirits, the director should make the inquiries needed for the discernment of spirits, applying the rules for the First Week with some persons and
those for the Second with others, according to Annotations 9 and 10.

[36] 8. The director should lay special emphasis on the Addition about
making a reflection and examination after each exercise, and should take care
that the exercitant puts this into practice.

[37] 9. If the director notices that the exercitant is finding a full hour on
each exercise too long, either because of his inexperience in meditating or
because of temptations, he should urge him to overcome himself and persevere
even beyond an hour, especially when experiencing desolation (see Annotations 12 and 13).

[38] 10. As for food and drink, the exercitant should be given only what he
asks for, unless the director sees that he is going to extremes in either direction.
In that case the director should suggest what discretion and charity demand.

[39] 11. The exercitant should not be told in a given Week, day, or even
exercise, anything that will come up in a later Week, day, or exercise, so that
he will not be concerned about the future and consequently derive less fruit
from the present.

[40] 12. In periods of intense devotion the exercitant should be warned
against making any vows (especially if he has shown himself to be impetuous or
unsteady). Vows, however good and holy, need to be made with deliberation
so that they may be a more pleasing oblation to God and be kept with greater
steadfastness.

[41] 13. Though the Exercises are divided into four Weeks, the Weeks are
not to be computed by a fixed number of days. Each Week should be ended
when the exercitant has achieved the aim sought in that Week. Thus, the First
Week should be brought to a close when he has reached sufficient knowledge
of his sins and contrition for them and appears ready for his general confession.
The Second Week should be ended when he has made substantial progress in
meditating the life of Christ, or, if he has entered upon elections, when he has
apparently ascertained God's will in them. The Third Week should be ended
when it is clear that he has sufficiently practiced meditating on the Lord's
Passion and has gained a good understanding of the method he is to use in
meditating on it in the future. The Fourth Week is completed when he is
judged to have made sufficient progress in the exercises on the Resurrection
and on Enkindling the Love of God, as well as the Methods of Prayer. Hence,
gauging by the goal of each Week (and taking other circumstances into
consideration as well), the number of exercises given in each Week can be
more or fewer, as can also the number of days spent on each.

[42] 14. Although the points of the exercises can be explained orally in
greater fullness, and reasons given for various things that are proposed to the
exercitant, nevertheless only those things should be left with him in writing (as

has been said) which will aid his memory in actually performing the exercises. Such texts are given at the end of this instruction. Other materials from the book of the Exercises should not be given; they are rather for the director's guidance. The points can be left either in the vernacular or in Latin. Explanations should be given and texts left with the exercitant according to the latter's needs and the director's convenience.

[43] 15. Although given in the Third Week, the Rules for the Regulation of Eating can be used whenever the director sees that the exercitant needs or can be helped by them. The same holds for the Rules for Discerning Scruples at the end of the Exercises. The Rules for Distributing Alms seem appropriate for the end of the Second Week, those for Thinking with the Catholic Church for the end of the Exercises. In general, it can be said that these four sets of rules should not be given to everyone but only to those who need them and to whom it seems worthwhile to give them.

[44] CHAPTER 5: REMARKS ON THE FIRST WEEK

[45] 1. At the very outset, the exercitant should be given the consideration of man's final end. This is called the Foundation, because the entire moral structure is erected upon it. The points should be briefly explained and the exercitant told to turn the consideration upon himself, i.e., upon the stance he has taken with regard to the end and the means up till now and the stance he wishes to take for the future.

[46] 2. In the second meeting the exercitant should be given the Particular Examen. He should be told that in every person there is generally one or another predominant sin or defect which is the source of many others. And even should there more than one such fault, still it is best to engage in single combat with just one or another at a time, taking up arms against it with special attention. Once it has been vanquished or substantially weakened, we can direct this special effort against another. In any case, the director should suggest that the exercitant make this Examen against his most pressing fault and then go on to the others in succession. In the meantime, of course, he should strengthen his resolve against all his other sins and faults in general.

[47] 3. Whether to dictate the four Additions of the Examen [27–31] or merely to explain them orally can be left to the director's discretion. With more mature men, dictation should be accompanied by some explanation of the reasons for the Examen's value. One reason is that it is easier to overcome an evil habit when one frequently turns his mind to the actions or omission he wants to be freed from, renews his resolution, and stiffens his will against the defect. Another reason is that by making this steady effort a person does what lies in his own power and merits from God the grace to be freed of the fault. For as a general rule God's grace is granted in proportion to our own effort.

[48] 4. With educated persons it will be enough simply to mention what is said in the Exercises about thoughts, words, and deeds. The less educated will need a fuller explanation. However, these matters should not be left in writing unless the person requests it or shows a special need for it. In both cases the person should be told that there are additional ways of sinning by word, and that while those mentioned in the Exercises are the common ones, others can be found in authors who treat expressly of this subject.

[49] 5. The daily five-point Examen should be dictated as it stands. The practice of this Examen will be facilitated by what is said in the book about sins of thought, word, and deed.

[50] 6. The advantages of a general confession of one's whole life should be orally explained when, after the exercises given below, the moment has come to raise the topic of the general confession.

[51] 7. Regarding the exercises of the First Week, note the following. First, they should be given one at a time (except for the 3rd and 4th, which can be given together). This is so that each can be clearly retained in the mind and carried out by itself.

Secondly, the directions given after the 5th exercise, about making the exercises at stated hours (midnight, daybreak, etc.), should be put into effect not when the exercises are first being explained, but after the complete set has been given.

Thirdly, as regards the second colloquy of the 3rd and 4th exercises, where Christ is addressed as mediator to obtain from the Father the graces mentioned there, an explanation ought to be given to less well educated persons. They should be told that while it is true that in his divine nature, by which he is equal to the Father, it is Christ's role to bestow grace and not to ask for it, nevertheless in his human nature, by which he is less than the Father, he can ask graces from the Father, from himself in his own divine nature, and from the Holy Spirit. This is evident in the prayer *Anima Christi* ("Soul of Christ") given in the exercise: it is addressed to Christ according to the human nature he has assumed. (Note, however, that there is no necessity for giving the exercitant the *Anima Christi* if some other prayer clearly suits him better.)

[52] 8. The following procedure can be used for giving the Additions. Addition 1 can be given along with the 1st exercise, and 3 and 4 after it. Additions 2, 5, and 6 can be given with the 2nd exercise; 7, 8, and 9 with the 3rd; 10 with the 5th. If some other way of dividing them up seems preferable, however, there is nothing wrong with that, provided all the rest are given along with the 5th exercise, so that from the following midnight the complete five exercises with their Additions can begin to be made.

[53] 9. The time spent in giving the exercises should as a general rule be as short as conveniently possible (supposing that they are given one by one, with each being put into practice before the next is given). If the exercitant is

staying in our house, or near enough to be frequently visited by the director without difficulty, the following schedule can be used. The 1st exercise can be given in the evening, to be made in the first prayer period. The 2nd exercise can be given in the morning, to be made before dinner. The 3rd can be given after dinner, to be made at midafternoon. The 5th can be given after mid-afternoon so it can be made before supper. Then the exercitant should be told that on the following day he should make the 1st exercise at midnight, the 2nd at daybreak, the 3rd before dinner, the 4th at midafternoon, and the 5th before supper. For the remaining days of the Week it will suffice to visit the exercitant once a day and question him about how he is doing; and also because it is good to give something new at each visit: either some relevant material from the notes that follow the Additions [87–90], or something from the Rules for the Discernment of Spirits that would apply to the First Week, or from the Rules on Scruples, or other matters deemed suitable to the particular person. However, nothing except the exercises and Additions should be left in writing. If the exercitant is staying some distance away, two visits at the beginning will suffice. At an evening visit the exercitant should be given the 1st exercise, to be made at daybreak. In the morning he should be given the 2nd exercise to be made before dinner, and the 3rd to be made after dinner, along with the 4th, which is a repetition of the 3rd. The following day, either before or after dinner, he should be given the 5th exercise and told to begin making the full five exercises on the following day, beginning at midnight.

[54] 10. While visiting the exercitant after the latter has made the exercises for a full day, the director should note whether he ought to repeat the same exercises on the following day. Normally this will be the case. If the exercitant is finding in the exercises he is making the grace he seeks—contrition for his sins—and if he shows himself willing to go over the same exercises, the director should give no new material. Instead, he should explain what is indicated in the first note after Addition 10 about the threefold fruit of exterior penance. If the exercitant himself requests a hairshirt or a discipline, it should be given to him. If, even when the value of penance is explained to him, he makes no such request, and is obviously not doing anything by way of external chastisement of the body in matters of food, bed, etc., then he should be asked if he wants to do any. There are persons who are willing but too shy to ask. One of the first fathers used to leave a discipline in the exercitant's room as if he had accidentally dropped it, by way of inviting the exercitant to use it of his own accord. How far to go in this matter is left to the director's discretion. Taking into consideration the circumstances of the exercitant, he will decide whether to encourage him to bodily self-chastisement or perhaps to restrain him if he is going to excess.

[55] 11. It may be that when visiting the exercitant on succeeding days the director will detect that he is starting to find repetition of the same set of

exercises tedious but still needs further work on obtaining contrition for his sins. The director can then give him meditations on death, judgment, and similar matters along the same line in lieu of some of the original five, as may seem advisable in the Lord.

[56] 12. Whether by remaining with the first five exercises or making additional ones, when the exercitant seems to have obtained the goal of this Week, i.e., knowledge of his sins and contrition for them, and to have worked hard at this and to have cooperated with God's grace by means of the exercises and Additions, he can be told to get ready for his general confession. He should continue the regular exercises, or a part of them, and devote the rest of his time to recalling his sins—in writing if he so wishes. It is generally considered preferable that he make this confession to someone other than the director. But if his own devotion, or the lack of priests, or some other important consideration warrants it, he can confess to the director.

[57] 13. The exercitant should be told that even if he brought books with him, during this First Week he should not read them but should instead concentrate his thoughts and affections on cleansing his conscience through the exercises for arousing contrition; and (if his location and his seclusion lend themselves to this and there is no fear of his getting into conversations with other people) that he should rather spend his time hearing or saying Mass and attending other divine offices, should he be so inclined, as is suggested in Annotation 20.

[58] 14. Even though the fourteen rules for the First Week on discerning motions of the soul be not dictated or even orally explained in their entirety, nevertheless the director should employ an explanation of some of them, viz., those which he sees the exercitant in need of for his encouragement, instruction, or consolation as may be indicated by various movements of the soul that are observed in him, or as the exercitant himself requests, or as is needed for his spiritual advancement.

[59] 15. In this and the following Weeks, the schedule of exercises (midnight, daybreak, etc.) can be varied, and the hour-long period lengthened or on occasion somewhat shortened, according to the individual's physical and spiritual condition. Nevertheless, during the First Week one should not readily cut down the number of five exercises or shorten the hour-long periods.

[60] In proposing the 2nd exercise, the meditation on personal sins, the director should warn the exercitant against going into too much detail on the first point, where he goes through the various periods, occupations, locations, etc. The place for this is later, when he will prepare himself more carefully for his general confession. In this exercise it suffices to recall and place before his eyes those of his sins that are more serious and more conducive to confusion and sorrow.

[61] CHAPTER 6: THINGS TO KEEP IN MIND REGARDING
THE EXERCISES OF THE SECOND WEEK

[62] 1. Upon completion of the general confession, when it is time for the exercitant to move on, he should be allowed to catch his breath by giving him the meditation on the Kingdom of Christ to be made twice, once in the morning and once in the evening. On that day nothing else should be given. Then, toward evening, he should be given the exercise on the Incarnation to be made the next day at daybreak. On the next day itself, in the morning, he should be given the exercise on the Nativity, to be made before dinner and toward midafternoon.

Alternatively, the exercise on the Incarnation could be given and made after he has made the exercise on the Kingdom once. Then the meditation on the Kingdom could be made a second time before the Nativity is given. Then the 3rd and 5th exercises can be given together, with the 3rd being made about midafternoon and the 5th before supper. On that day the 4th exercise (a repetition of the third) should be omitted, and the exercitant told that on the following day (which, although now the third day since his general confession, is called the "first" because it is the first day when the full five exercises on the life of Christ are made) he should do the Incarnation at midnight, the Nativity at daybreak, the 3rd exercise before dinner, the 4th at midafternoon, and the 5th before supper. In any case the times for proposing the exercises should be distributed in such a way that, with either the 3rd and 5th exercises being given together or the 5th by itself (along with one or other of the Additions which are changed in the Second Week), the exercitant can begin the "first day," making the meditation on the Incarnation at midnight and the others in the succeeding periods as indicated above.

[63] 2. In cases where the exercitant seems fatigued or not finding as much relish as he might wish in the exercises, even though in good condition physically, the schedule of meditations might well be relaxed for him. In this case he would not need to rise at midnight but would make the 1st exercise at daybreak, the 2nd before dinner, and the 3rd and 5th in the remaining two hours. The 4th, which in all the Weeks is a repetition of the 3rd, would then be dropped.

[64] 3. He should be told that after his meditations in this and the following Weeks he may do some reading. This reading should be calculated more to nourish his piety than to exercise his intellect—for example, something from the Gospel, or from Bernard, or from Jean Gerson's *Imitation of Christ*. But if the books treat the mysteries of Christ he should read nothing about topics which he will be meditating later, but limit himself to the mysteries already meditated; for it would not hurt to read treatments of the latter in the Gospels or other religious books.

[65] 4. The 5th exercise, the application of the senses, can either be understood as referring to the imaginative senses, and this would hold for a person with less experience in meditation, such as those to whom the Exercises are most commonly given; or they can be understood as pertaining to the senses of the higher intellect or mind, and this is appropriate for those who are more advanced and have experience of the contemplative life. If the senses are understood in the first way, there is no difficulty with using the imagination to visualize the persons and their circumstances or to listen to the words they speak or may suitably be imagined to speak. There is also little problem with the sense of touch when we imagine ourselves kissing Christ's footprints or garments. In imagining ourselves to kiss anything further, however, let the imagining be accompanied by reverence. For instance, considering Christ as our true and sovereign pontiff, we might kiss his feet, since we kiss the feet of his vicars, Peter and his successors, because they hold Christ's place. Or, considering Christ as our supreme and true father, king, and lord, one might kiss his hand, since here on earth children and subjects kiss the hands of their fathers, kings, and lords. As for the senses of smell and taste, beyond the imagination one should ascend to the mind, considering the sweet odor of God's gifts inasmuch as they are at a distance, and the taste of his gifts inasmuch as they are present in the holy soul and refresh it with their sweetness. Moreover, in this kind of meditations the imagining of smells and tastes that are accessible to the bodily senses leads a person onward to the exercise of these inner senses of the mind.

[66] 5. In interpreting these senses as mental and pertaining to the higher part of the mind, we can follow the teaching of St. Bonaventure in chapter 4 of his *Journey of the Mind to God*, and explain them as referring to the soul in which the image of God, through his grace, has been restored by means of faith, hope and charity. When through faith the soul believes in Christ, then through him, the uncreated Word who is the splendor of the Father and the brightness of eternal light, the soul recovers and exercises its spiritual power of sight, by which it can behold the radiance of Light itself. In this way, Christ is the soul's truth. When through faith the soul believes in Christ as the Word made flesh who teaches us what pertains to our salvation and perfection, then through him the soul recovers its sense of hearing for the reception of his words. In this fashion, Christ is the soul's way. And when by hope the soul sighs to receive Christ as the Word breathed into it, dwelling in us by his gifts and inviting us to more excellent charisms and ultimately to complete enjoyment of him, then through its yearning and hope the soul recovers its spiritual sense of smell, which it exercises by running in the odors of Christ's ointment. In this way Christ is the soul's life. When by charity the soul is conjoined to Christ as the Word made flesh, receiving a kind of delight from him even in this wayfaring state and tasting how sweet the Lord is, then it recovers and

exercises its spiritual sense of taste. And when it embraces him and passes over into him by the pure love which transforms the soul into Christ and will not allow it be torn away from him or have any other object of thought or love but himself unless it be for his sake and in him, then the soul recovers and exercises its spiritual sense of touch.

The director's prudence will dictate the measure in which these matters should be brought up or gone into.[3]

[67] 6. When giving the 1st exercise, on the Incarnation, one should explain the preludes to the exercitant, instructing him to make the preparatory prayer and three preludes in the same fashion throughout the other exercises of this and the subsequent Weeks, with the appropriate changes of matter. When giving the 2nd exercise, on the Nativity, one should also, after explaining the three points and colloquy, instruct the exercitant to continue using the same method—i.e., the consideration of the persons, words and actions, along with the colloquy—even though the matter will vary. Similarly in giving the 3rd, 4th, and 5th exercises: the exercitant should be told to retain the same method throughout the mysteries which follow, changing the matter. Thus for the remaining mysteries it will suffice to give the exercitant the matter for meditation and instruct him to use the method of the first day.

[68] 7. The Additions which change for this Week—viz., 2, 3, 6, 7, and 10 —can be divided up and all explained in the course of giving the exercises of the first day; or else any remaining ones can be explained on the second day if this is advisable. Like the exercises themselves, they can be dictated.

[69] 8. After the first day of this Week it will suffice to visit the exercitant once a day about midafternoon, so long as only the mysteries of Christ are being done. During the elections it will be good to visit him twice a day if the director has time. Two mysteries can be given at a time, to be meditated for the whole of the following day, although the exercitant should of course meditate the second mystery only after having done the first. However, if the exercitant is staying in our own house he can be given the 1st exercise at about midafternoon, to be made during the night, and then given the 2nd exercise in the morning. This will be easier if he is only making four hours of meditation. But there is no objection to giving two exercises at a time when the director is not free to come twice on the same day.

[70] 9. The exercise of the third day, on how Jesus was subject to his parents, can include consideration of his entire private life, i.e., up to his thirtieth year—with the exception, however, of the immediately following mystery on the story of his dealings at the age of twelve with the wise men in the Temple and then with his mother; this mystery receives a special consideration of its

---

[3] The teaching on the spiritual senses was criticized by Gil González Dávila as too subtle for the ordinary retreatant (see Doc. 31.14), and was dropped in the official directory of 1599 even though it had been included in the first draft.

own. And when one wishes to give the mysteries of Christ, after the first day he should turn to the back of the Exercises where the mysteries are given divided up into points. There is no need to make a summary of these: directors ought to have the book of the Exercises in their hands, and it is to be hoped that they will be fully familiar with its contents and use. For those more experienced in meditating it will suffice to give the points as found there, instructing the exercitant (as we stated above) to use the same method as on the first day. Those with less experience will need more detailed help in adapting the preludes to the matter and in distinguishing the three points: visualizing the persons with their circumstances, hearing what they say, and considering their actions—together with the colloquy. In the same way the method for the 3rd and 5th exercises should be explained until the exercitant is able to carry out the meditation unaided upon being simply given the mystery.

[71] 10. It should cause no surprise that the days listed for this Week run to twelve (besides the day, or rather two days, which precede the "first day"). A good part of this Week will be taken up by the exercises for the election. Hence, after the meditations of the third day and those of the fourth day (for which no special mystery is assigned, but instead the Two Standards and the Three Classes of Men), only a single meditation is given per day. However, if no election of a state of life or of some other serious matter is being made, two meditations a day can be given and the Week thus shortened—besides the provision, mentioned in the first note after the list of meditations for the twelve days [162], for adapting to the exercitant's ability or need by adding further meditations, v.g., on the Visitation, the Shepherds, the Circumcision, etc., or by omitting some of the mysteries listed there. Moreover, there is the possibility of combining topics for consideration on a single day—for instance the Shepherds with the Nativity, etc.—if the exercitant does not find enough matter in a single topic to fill his hour profitably.

[72] 11. A person with less facility in meditating the mysteries of Christ and apparently in need more assistance can be told that after reflecting on the third point, viz., what the persons are doing, he should turn his attention to *how* they are doing it and *why*. According to the teaching and experience of religious and holy persons, this will help open the way to fruitful meditation. If the exercitant is doing well, there is no need to give him this hint, and he should be left to himself and to God.

Class 8 → [73] CHAPTER 7: GENERAL REMARKS ABOUT THE ELECTION, BEFORE DESCENDING TO PARTICULARS → ¶ 92

[74] 1. The indication in the Exercises that discussion of the election should begin from the contemplation of the third day to that of the fifth day inclusive-

ly[4] is to be understood not so much of the days themselves as of the meditations assigned to them. For if you look at the days of the Second Week, you will see that before you get to the "first" day, i.e., the day on which all five exercises are first made together, you have to spend two or three days proposing the exercises on the Kingdom of Christ, the Incarnation, and the Nativity, with the repetitions and application of the senses. So what is meant is that the time to begin treating the election is either the day one gives the exercise on the boy Jesus' remaining in the Temple at the age of twelve or else the day one gives the exercise on his coming from Nazareth to be baptized (this would be the fifth day, since even though this meditation follows immediately upon the preceding one, the sequence is interrupted by the fourth day devoted to the Two Standards and the Three Classes of Men). The reason for beginning to deal with the election at this point is indicated in the introduction to the consideration of different states of life [135]. In being subject to his parents Christ gave an example of the ordinary state of life; and in leaving his parents to go to the Temple he exhibited the second state, that of pursuing the perfection of the evangelical counsels. Hence this is a good point at which to raise the issue of considering the state in which we ought to serve God. (Not that he went from Nazareth to the Temple without his parents' knowledge—in fact, he went up in their company; but when they were leaving the place where they stayed in Jerusalem to return to Nazareth, he parted from them and went to the Temple, being a boy twelve years old.)

[75] 2. This introduction [135] should be explained orally (not dictated) when it is clear that the exercitant is desirous of dealing with his state of life. If this is not clear, then either here or after the exercise on the Standards in the fourth day (an exercise valuable even for those with no intention of entering an election) the director can still bring the matter up in cases where the exercitant seems apt for a more perfect state and is not already in an unchangeable one, or also if in the director's judgment he ought to make a serious deliberation not on his state of life but on some other important matter regarding his own or the common welfare. If the exercitant is disposed to do this, the director should proceed with him as he would with someone who from the start had declared his intention of doing so. If the exercitant is unwilling or it would be better not to treat either his state of life or any other important election, and it still seems good to continue with him, he should go on directly to the meditation on the Baptism.

[76] 3. Throughout the period of the election, the meditations on the life of Christ are not suspended, as we indicated above, but interspersed with the exercises on the election. However, no particular mystery of Christ should be

---

[4] This indication is not present in the Autograph or the Vulgate, but was in the Vienna edition of the Exercises used by Polanco.

given on the fourth day. If four exercises are made on that day, they should be the Standards at daybreak, before dinner and at midafternoon, with the Three Classes of Men before supper. If five are made, the meditation on the Standards should be made at midnight and at daybreak, with two repetitions, one before dinner and one at midafternoon, as indicated in the note after the meditation on the Standards [148].

The observation after the meditation on the Three Classes of Men, viz., that in case of a feeling of repugnance for actual poverty one should pray to God for an inclination to it, should be explained (not dictated) to the exercitant. The reason for this is the same one that leads us (as the Philosopher says) to straighten a stick by bending it in the opposite direction.[5]

The exercitant should also be told that, since Christ said it was difficult for those who possess money to enter into life, a person needs stronger signs of God's will to stay in the ordinary state (the way of the commandments) than to choose the way of the counsels, the way which Christ, who is eternal Wisdom, advises (without commanding) us to follow. For it is unquestionably the safer and more perfect state. Hence, the exercitant ought for his part to be more inclined to the way of the counsels than to that of the commandments, if it should be what God prefers. However, since not everyone is able to accept this saying, and the Lord does not call everyone to the state of the counsels, we must carefully investigate what the Lord's will is, in the manner that is indicated below.

[77] 4. On the fifth day, after the assigned contemplation on Christ's departure from Nazareth and Baptism (whether made at midnight or at daybreak), the exercitant should be given the Three Modes of Humility so that he can spend the entire day pondering them. He should devote two or three full hours to thinking about them and making the attached colloquies. Outside these periods as well, instead of reading anything, he should ponder the same topic. The note at the end of the meditation for the fifth day [160], directing that the examens after dinner and supper should be made on faults in the meditations, should be understood to apply to both the meditations on Christ's mysteries and the other exercises pertaining to the election.

[78] 5. Toward evening of the fifth day, after the director has asked an account of what the exercitant did during the day, he should try to see if his attitude is such that he is ready to undertake the election. This readiness would consist in an abandonment of his will into God's hands as regards following either the path of the commandments or that of the counsels, being in a kind of even balance—or rather, in being for his own part more inclined to the counsels should he see it to be God's will. But if it is obvious that he is more inclined to the commandments and shrinks from the way of the counsels, then

---

[5] *Nichomachean Ethics* ii.9.

he is not properly disposed and there is no hope of his making a good election. His attitude of aversion from the more perfect way and his inclination toward the less perfect will sway his intellect to think up reasons in conformity with it. Such persons should not be taken into the three times of election. However, they may be given the exercise of the sixth day to make on the day following, and have explained to them (orally, not in dictation) the introductions to making a choice of a way of life [169] and to matters about which a choice should be made [170ff]. They should be told to repeat the meditations on the Three Classes of Men and the Three Modes of Humility, and to try to dispose themselves to beg God for abandonment to him, asking (as said above) that if it is equally or more pleasing to God, he might incline them to desire to choose the counsels over the commandments.

[79] 6. After dinner on the sixth day, the director should visit him and try to ascertain if he has achieved, or is on his way toward achieving, abandonment to God, or is instead receding from it. If he sees that the exercitant has regressed or failed to make any progress he should not go on to the three times of election but should give up the election and give him some other exercises which he deems suitable for the time being. Or, if he judges it not worthwhile to continue the Exercises with him, he should tactfully seek some opportunity, either then or shortly after, of letting him go. If the exercitant is making progress toward abandonment but has still not reached it, he can be given some other exercise of the Second or Third Week and urged to do all he can to obtain from the Lord perfect abandonment. As soon as he has reached it and is ready to undertake the three times of election, special care should be taken that he be isolated from all influences which could keep him from an authentic election. So far as possible, he should not see or hear anything which does not come from above, descending from the Father of lights.

[80] Chapter 8: Details of the Election

[81] 1. If the director determines that the exercitant should proceed to an election, he should give him the exercise of the seventh day and also (in case he will not be returning the next morning) that of the eighth day. Thus the exercitant should make the two meditations in succession, followed by one or two repetitions. Meanwhile, he should be having the first and second times of election explained to him, but not the material which follows regarding the third. The director should explain the first time in passing, and go on to the second, i.e., seeking God's will in the matter under deliberation by the experience of consolations and desolations.

The director should explain clearly what consolation is, going into particulars: that it is interior spiritual joy, peace of mind, hope fixed in God and aimed at lofty things, faith in God and directed to higher things, the experience of holy love (love for eternal realities), tears begotten therefrom, elevation of the mind to God—all these being gifts of the Holy Spirit. He should also explain what desolation is: sadness, disturbance of mind, hope in earthly things and persons, faith in them, love of low and unworthy things, experience of being dry and weighed downward toward earthly things—all these being opposed to the things mentioned above since they stem from the evil spirit. This whole matter should be explained orally, not dictated.

[82] 2. If an election is to be made regarding the exercitant's state in life, the first step (since what is the better thing considered abstractly is not the better thing for every individual) is to raise the question whether he ought to embrace the way of the counsels, of which Christ said, "If you wish to be perfect, go sell what you have and give to the poor, and come follow me"; or the ordinary way of the precepts, of which Christ said, "If you wish to enter life, keep the commandments." The exercitant should be instructed thus: during his meditations and colloquies, without any reasonings on his own part, he should place himself in God's presence, and there set before his mind's eye the way of the counsels. Then he should watch to see if he feels in his soul any movements of consolation or desolation regarding this way. He should do the same while setting before himself the way of the precepts. No specific exercise is required for this; in the course of his usual meditations and prayers, as we have just stated, he should bring this matter up before God, utterly renouncing his own will and yearning to experience interiorly what the will of God is. Outside the times of the usual exercises he should continue mulling this matter over and watching in the same way for the above mentioned movements, not attending to his own personal reflections but disposing himself as best he can to receive the inspirations of the Holy Spirit.

When the director comes, he should ask an account of these movements. If he detects signs of the good or evil spirit, he should use the Rules for Discerning Spirits, but especially those of the Second Week. He should explain to the exercitant as much as he judges necessary for the latter's guidance or—if need be—encouragement. If the exercitant seems to be moving well along this path, the director should give him another meditation and instruct him to repeat the same procedure regarding the election under consideration, to test whether the same movements persist or are replaced by contrary ones. Should the director subsequently return and discover that the same movements persist and apparently stem from the good spirit, then he has grounds for confirming the election. If contrary motions have supervened, the director should strive by means of the aforementioned rules to discern what the will of God is in the matter at issue, viz., whether to follow the way of the counsels or that of the precepts. If by this means a satisfactory election seems to have been reached on the first question, then the second should be brought up, viz., whether the exercitant should follow Christ's counsels in religious life or outside it. For by means of poverty and chastity, without obedience, a person might keep a part of the counsels by serving in hospitals or performing other holy works. Should he choose religious life, then he should choose between the contemplative and the mixed life, and the specific religious order.

[83] 3. If the election is not achieved by means of this second time, the exercitant having experienced no noteworthy interior movements, or else movements in both directions, then the modes of the third time must be used. Here the exercitant calmly places before himself his final end and asks himself what means he most ought to choose according to God's will in order to reach that end. As with the second time, he should first ask whether he ought to choose the way of the counsels or the way of the precepts; secondly, whether inside or outside religious life; and thirdly, if in religious life, whether in a contemplative or mixed order, and in which particular order. Both the first and second modes of this third time should be explained, so that for each of the questions, once he has come to a conclusion using the first mode, he should spend a further hour going over it again using the second mode. An identical result from both is a sufficient sign of a good election. When, in this third time, a person is engaged in the process of reflection needed to make an election, it will be more than enough for him to make a single meditation from among those of the Second Week, with one repetition; the rest of the time he will be thinking about his election. He should also be told to write down the motives impelling him in either direction, so that he can go over them with the director and be better guided by him.

[84] 4. When, upon being given an account of the exercitant's reflection, the director finds that the latter has been proceeding correctly and solidly, he should give his approval. If in either the second or third time he sees that the reflection is proceeding or the will receiving impulses from some false principle or from the admixture of some affection or spirit which is not good, he should warn and instruct him against drawing a bad or false conclusion from bad or false principles, and so making a bad election. However, the director should take care that his own inclinations do not lead him to push the person making the election in one direction rather than another. He should realize that his duty is to dispose the creature so that he can be taught by his Creator—whether by inspiration and movement of his affections or by the mental reflection spoken of above. The director should leave to God the whole business of calling the one making the election to this or to that state of life—in which God alone is able to give him perseverance and perfection.

[85] 5. Note the following: On the one hand, the second time of election is superior to the third, so long as it is clear that God is the source of the movements, enlightenments, or consolations being infused into the soul of the person making the election; for in this way God makes his will known more immediately by these effects of grace than by the reasoning process of the third

time. Nevertheless, if it is not evident that the spirit moving the exercitant in this way is from God, and there is some doubt in either the exercitant or the director or both about whether the enlightenments and spiritual consolations are from the good spirit or from the evil spirit masquerading as an angel of light—at least to some extent—then, even after an election has been concluded in the second time, it can be tested by the two modes of the third time. For these modes both bring the natural powers into play and at the same time dispose a person for a supernatural movement and enlightenment from God. Hence, one who has made the election in this way can answer quite well to God for his decision, inasmuch as he has done what lay in his power to learn God's will after proving unable to learn it with certainty in the second time. Of course, if God's will became evident in the second time then it would be superfluous to seek it in the third: a greater light than human reason would then have guided and enlightened his mind and moved his affections. But if the same election were to emerge from both the second and third times, the two lights, supernatural and natural, would have furnished quite sufficient assurance.

[86] 6. In asking the exercitant for an account of his election, whether in the second or the third time, the director should be alert to see if his disposition is correct, i.e., whether or not he is more inclined to the more perfect way or is at least in a kind of balance where he is ready to choose whichever way better leads to his final end and is more pleasing to God. However, if he detects that the exercitant is inclined to the less perfect course, even though he may have shown a proper disposition before entering upon the election, then the election process should be stopped until his attitude has been rectified. Otherwise there would be little grounds for expecting such an election to be a good one, however many reasons and movements may have prompted it. For if his affection tends toward what is less perfect, there is good cause for fearing that it is inclined by a spirit which is not good; yet if it is so inclined, there is obviously a danger of its drawing reason to its side rather than being drawn to the side of reason. It is different if his affection leans toward the more perfect, for such a spirit is not from flesh and blood, and it is unlikely that such an inclination comes from the evil spirit; and if it is from God, it will not be a hindrance to knowing God's will. In cases where a person inclined to what is more perfect makes an election that is apparently against reason, the election should be tested by the first and second modes of the third time (and not merely by the Rules for the Discernment of Spirits), for the greater satisfaction of exercitant and director.

[87] 7. Whatever election is made in the second or third times, the exercitant should be warned, especially if he seems ardent and of a rash or volatile character, against making any vows while he is in the Exercises. However, if he has made his election with mature deliberation and great clarity (especially if his age and character give no grounds for suspicion of fickleness), and wishes to

confirm his election with a vow to protect it against the attacks of the devil, the flesh, and the world, then the director cannot and should not forbid him— just as he should in no way encourage him to do so.

[88] 8. In the case where one choice is made during the second time, and then, there being some doubt whether the movement was from God, the two modes of the third time are proposed and result in the contrary choice, the two choices should be carefully tested by means of the Rules for Discerning Spirits, by right reason, and by sound doctrine. The motives impelling either way should be weighed. If it is quite clear that reason is in favor of the choice made in the third time, it is safer to go with the latter, because of the director's uncertainty whether the movements in the second time were from God or not. On the other hand, if the reasons in favor of the election in the third time are weak, and the movements of the second time emerge more clearly as deriving from the good spirit and are not in conflict with right reason, then preference should be given to the election made in the second time. Even though originally God's will was not clear in this election, it is possible for it to become clear after more careful examination and scrutiny, with the additional testimony of reason.

[89] 9. The director should remember that an election cannot be made in this third time, even where there was a lack of clarity about God's will in the second, if the exercitant's soul is still being agitated by various movements, for both modes of the third time require calm and peace so that the soul can bring its own powers into play. Such a exercitant can be detained in other exercises of the Second or Third Week until his peace of mind returns; without it he should not proceed to an election of any serious matter, because it would very likely not prove to have been made correctly.

[90] 10. The points for both modes of election in the third time should be dictated; and when, as indicated in the final point, the exercitant betakes himself to prayer after completing the election, he should note whether he experiences from the Lord internal confirmation of the election he has made. Any movements or enlightenments from above which he experiences in prayer should be examined by the Rules for Discernment of Spirits. If signs of the good spirit are detected and there is confirmation of the election made by reasoning, this should be deemed sufficient grounds for believing that God's will has been discovered. If there occur at this point movements, feelings, or illuminations of the mind which weaken the election made by reasoning, and these appear upon examination to be from an evil or doubtful spirit, then the election should not be changed; for this kind of temptation might be the work of the devil. But if there is clear evidence of a movement or enlightenment by the good spirit from on high running contrary to the election made, this is a sign that the reasoning was done badly, and that the election needs to be remade. But if in this prayer at the end of the election there is no noteworthy

movement one way or another either in the affections or in the intellect, and the exercitant's will continues to persevere in the choice made on the basis of reasoning, he should not change his election but should conclude that God intended that his will be discovered through rational reflection. Moreover, if his choice is confirmed by the second mode of the third time after having been already reached through the first mode, he should be all the more convinced that he has found God's will.

[91] 11. The first point of the second mode of election [184] states that it is good for the exercitant to have a thorough awareness that any inclination he feels toward the object of his choice stems from love of God alone. Note that the text says that this "is good" (convenit)—for this kind of choice is made perfectly when the motive is love of God alone. But if love for God, while being the chief motive, is nevertheless not the sole one but is accompanied by other motives in favor of the same choice which do not conflict with the love of God and are good in themselves—v.g., one's own spiritual consolation, considerations of health, or the like—this is no reason for condemning the election. However, the other motives besides God himself should not be the chief ones, and ought themselves to be subordinated to love of God.

[92] 12. In cases where the exercitant has no decision to make about taking up or abandoning a state of life or an office, but the director still judges that he ought to deal with correcting or reforming his way of life and his affairs (either because the director feels under obligation to the exercitant to render him this holy service or because he believes the exercitant's spiritual progress would be important for helping other people), the following procedure should be used. Not omitting the other exercises of the Second or Third Weeks, the exercitant should be asked to reflect on what is said after the third time of election regarding one's household, expenditures, etc. [189]. Besides the exercises preparatory to the election (Two Standards, Three Classes of Men, Three Degrees of Humility, Introduction to Making a Choice of a Way of Life), which it would be helpful, even if not absolutely necessary, to make first, he should use the two modes of making an election in the third time (rather than the second time), and these should be dictated to him. After going through one point he should move on to the next in the same hour or a later one, depending on the degree of importance or difficulty of the decision. This material on amending one's life in whatever state should not be dictated to him; an oral explanation suffices.

[93] CHAPTER 9: REMARKS ON THE THIRD WEEK

[94] 1. What is said in the first point about looking at the persons at the supper, and in the second about listening to their conversation, appears not to jibe fully with the history in the first prelude, which mentions not the supper

alone but also the washing of feet, the confecting of the Blessed Sacrament, and the discourse after the supper. Reply: all the topics mentioned in the prelude may be proposed for meditation in a single exercise, and what is said about beholding the persons at the supper, listening to their words, and observing their actions, should be applied also to the other words and actions which occurred there and not just to the events of the supper itself. Of course, the supper, the footwashing, and the confecting of the Blessed Sacrament are normally plenty for a single exercise, and that is why other matters are not mentioned in the points. On the other hand, there is nothing wrong with the history's being broader in scope (in a general way) than the meditation itself, which is restricted to the smaller number of points which can conveniently be pondered in a single exercise.

[95] 2. As the third prelude indicates, the grace especially sought in the exercises of the Lord's passion are compassionating sorrow, indignation against ourselves, and confusion at our Lord's suffering for us. These affections are of great value not only for beginners but for all, even those with experience in contemplation, especially when we wish to honor Christ's humiliation, afflictions and sorrows by recalling them with gratitude and embracing similar pains —at least by sympathy with him. Nevertheless, other holy affections should not be excluded, especially those which occur to our minds when we turn upon ourselves what we meditate. Such affections are love, hope, longing to imitate him in patience, humility, obedience, charity, etc.

[96] 3. Note that during repetitions, both in this as well as in the preceding and following Weeks, we should not only dwell on those points where we had greater relish in the preceding meditations, but also devote more time and more careful consideration to points which we had earlier passed over more quickly while dwelling on others.

[97] 4. Of the four notes given after the 2nd exercise [204–207], only the third should be dictated. It suffices to explain the others orally. As for the meditations of the following days, unless some special reason demands otherwise, only each day's points should be dictated, as they are indicated in the back of the book where the mysteries of Christ's life are given. With persons of greater experience, however, it will suffice to indicate the mysteries to be meditated as there set forth, with instructions to continue using the same method which was given in the 1st exercise. With persons of less experience, there should be further explanation of the method of looking at the persons, hearing their words, and pondering their actions; where these are many, the instructor should point out which ones to concentrate on. The instructor should have all the other notes in the book of the Exercises well studied, and he should be completely familiar with the book itself or a compendium of it. (The remarks made in this directory are meant to elucidate the book itself and its method, not substitute for it.)

[98] 5. The Rules for Regulating one's Diet given at the end of the Third Week should not be dictated but explained orally. These rules should not be given all at once but piecemeal. Nor should this be given to every person in the same way, but with discernment. Some persons with bigger appetites and stronger constitutions have more need to restrain their appetite and their use of food; others not so much. Especially as regards the fourth rule, the director should be careful about to whom and in what fashion he explains it, and how they use it, so as to avoid excess. The time for giving these rules is not just in the Third Week. Some of them may well be given in the earlier Weeks if the exercitant indicates that he needs them or the director notices that he does. If, however, they have not been explained earlier, they ought to be explained during this Week, since fewer instructions (apart from the exercises themselves) are given in this Week than in the others, and so the director will have more time for explaining them, since it is good for him to bring something fresh on his visits to the exercitant.

[99] CHAPTER 10: REMARKS ON THE FOURTH WEEK

[100] 1. The notes after the 1st exercise of the Fourth Week should not be dictated (except perhaps for the changes in the Additions, so they can be more easily remembered); it suffices to explain them orally. The remark in the third note about including more or fewer points in the meditation applies to exercises not only of this Week but of the others as well. Moreover, however many points they are divided into, if the exercitant finds what he seeks in just one or two of them there is no reason for him to rush through the others. But at the close of the hour (or longer if he is meditating for a more extended period) he should move on to one or more of the colloquies. In the repetitions he will be able to meditate the scanted points more fully, and if he wishes direct his colloquy to a different person than before; for example, if to the Father in the 1st exercise, then in the other to the Son or Holy Spirit, or to the Blessed Virgin, or to two or even three together, as his devotion demands.

[101] 2. In the Contemplation for Arousing Love it is stated (1) that love depends on actions more than words, and (2) that it consists in a mutual sharing of resources, things and works. "Depends" here means "shows itself," since the proper effects of love are actions more than words. As for love's consisting in a sharing of resources and so forth, this does not mean that such sharing is love's essence, but rather its effect. For love itself properly consists in the affection of the lover considered as an act or passion in him. But since to love is to will the other's good, its effect and goal is the good we wish for the beloved, whether in the sharing of our resources or of other goods with him. Hence the words of St. Gregory that have become proverbial: "The proof of love is the performance of deeds," and "Where love is present it does great

deeds, and where it does no deeds it is not present."[6] The love meant here is the love of friendship, not the love of desire by which we are said to love things we want for our own sakes, v.g., pleasure, wealth, and the like.

[102] 3. This exercise for Arousing Love can be given after the exercitant is a day or two into the mysteries of the Resurrection (understood to include the mysteries of Pentecost and the Ascension as well). He can spend an hour on one of these mysteries and then a second on the meditation for Arousing Love. Because the four points are extremely pregnant, if a single point suffices for an hour he can take up one or more of the others in a subsequent hour. The colloquy should be added at the end of the meditation even if all the points have not been worked through. However, should it be deemed preferable to separate the mysteries of the Resurrection from the exercise for Arousing Love, then the mysteries up to the Ascension and Pentecost can be completed in the first two or three days, and then this exercise made throughout the hours of the entire third or fourth day—ensuring that some days of the Fourth Week are left over for practicing the Methods of Prayer.

[103] CHAPTER 11: REMARKS ON THE METHODS OF PRAYER

[104] As it stands, the first Method seems suited especially for simple persons—those concerned less with deep meditation on the commandments, the capital sins, the powers of the soul and the senses, than they are with practical living: how they have behaved hitherto and wish to behave rightly in the future regarding these matters, in order to ask pardon for their transgressions and grace to do what they ought. This prayer is halfway between vocal and mental, sharing in the characteristics of both but leaning rather toward the mental.

It is stated that each commandment or sin should be dwelt upon for about the space of three Our Fathers as normally recited. But if a person finds relish on a given point or thinks it would be of value to spend more time there, nothing prevents his doing so. And if he cannot get through all the commandments or sins in the hour (or whatever amount of time is set for this prayer) he can stop wherever he was toward the end of the prescribed period and conclude with a colloquy to God. In the next period he can pick up where he left off.

[105] But when this first Method of Prayer is given to a person whose senses are more practiced and who is apter for deeper meditation on such topics, the following procedure can be given to him for the commandments. After the third Addition and the preparatory prayer which is given there [239–240], he should first reflect on how holy and good the commandment is

---

[6] Gregory the Great, *Hom. in Ev.* ii.30.

in itself; secondly, on how profitable a thing it is to keep it; and thirdly, on how he has kept it hitherto. Then follows a colloquy, grieving over his poor observance and entreating forgiveness, resolving to keep the commandment in the future, and asking grace for this. If the hour is not yet over, he can go on to the next commandment, following the same procedure. When the scheduled time is up he should stop, and continue with the remaining points in the next period. If on a given point he sees he has not sinned, he can move on more quickly, especially through the third step; and in the colloquy he should thank God, resolve to continue avoiding that sin in the future, and ask grace for this.

In moving on to the capital sins, he should make the appropriate changes but follow the same procedure. Thus, in the first point he will meditate on how evil is the sin of pride and how rightly forbidden; in the second on how harmful it is not to avoid this sin; and in the third, on how well he has avoided it hitherto. He will follow this with a prayer. Then he should move on to the succeeding sins, dwelling more on any point where he judges he has greater need.

For the powers of the soul and the senses, after the preparatory prayer the first point will be to reflect on how precious and valuable to us is the power of the intellect; the second, to reflect on the end for which it was given us and on how Christ or our Lady made use of it; the third, to reflect on how we ourselves have used our intellect, grieving over our misuse of it and purposing to amend and to imitate the exemplar we have taken as our model. Then follows a colloquy, asking forgiveness for our sins and the grace to use this gift of God well in the future. The same should be done with the other powers and the senses. This procedure might be extended to include the power of speech and even of motion (gait and gesture) insofar as these involve modesty and edification.

[106] As to the second Method of Prayer, two remarks may be made. First, when a single word does not yield an idea that can be meditated, a phrase may be taken instead, for example, "Who art in heaven" or "Hallowed be thy name" and the other petitions of the Our Father. (The expressions "Father" and "Our Father" each offer plenty of material for a person to ponder prayerfully and dwell upon with mind and heart.) Not only the prayers indicated but also many psalms offer suitable material for this method of praying. The second remark is this: when the director sees that the exercitant is making this prayer successfully, he should not wait until he has gone through all the prayers but instruct him to continue with this Method at a future date. This applies to the first Method as well, but because of the greater variety of procedures there, individual exercises may be devoted to the commandments, the capital sins, the powers of the soul, and the senses, to the extent that time permits. And then, in case the director does not propose each of the prayers separately for a separate exercise, he should at least dictate them so that the formula which the

exercitant is to use may be adequately remembered.

[107] Only two remarks need be made about the third Method of Prayer. First, this is also a method intermediate between vocal and mental prayer, with the intervals between breaths giving the person time to penetrate more deeply with his mind into the truth contained in the words of the prayer, and to be moved in his affections toward the realities he has understood. A second remark is that the intervals of breathing are not to be understood so strictly as to exclude dwelling on a word somewhat longer than the space of a breath (especially for rapid breathers). But one ought to dwell on the words approximately as long as is normally needed to take a breath. If a person wishes to tarry for a deeper penetration with mind and heart, he will thereby be approximating the second Method of Prayer. After one or two trials of this Method of Prayer, once the director has seen how the exercitant is doing and has given any needed further instructions, this kind of prayer need not be prolonged. The director can then urge the exercitant to use in the future whichever Method of Prayer he has experienced to be most helpful.

[108] Although these three Methods of Prayer are given here, one should not imagine that others are excluded—not simply those taught by the Holy Spirit but also those suggested by spiritually experienced men on the basis of their own practice and of sound doctrine, or those which each individual has discovered in his own experience to be of value for his progress. But meanwhile these three are suitable—one more than another according to personal differences or even according to different situations of the same person at different times.

[109] CHAPTER 12: OBSERVATIONS ON THE DISCERNMENT
OF SCRUPLES AND FOLLOWING THE RULES
FOR THINKING CORRECTLY WITH THE CATHOLIC CHURCH

[110] 1. Unless the exercitant is troubled by scruples there is no reason for giving him the notes on the Discernment of Scruples. If he is troubled by scruples in the first sense indicated [346], i.e., if he defines some action as sinful which actually is not, he should not only be set right with regard to the particular error but also warned against being so quick to make this kind of judgment in the future. The reason for this (apart from the useless torment of conscience over his past actions) is that in acting against such a conscience, even though the action were objectively not sinful, he would be committing sin. For this reason, he should be told to abide within the limits of his doubt (if the matter is doubtful) and strive for the time being to refrain from performing the action. But if he is informed by learned men that the action is in no way sinful, then he must altogether set aside his judgment of conscience and convince himself that there is no sin involved, relying on the authority of other

trustworthy persons rather than on his own thinking. This procedure should be seriously urged in both the first and the second kinds of scruples.

[111] 2. Where the exercitant is seen to have an overly delicate or an overly coarse conscience, the fourth note [349] should be explained to him—or that part of it which is applicable. He should also be urged to try to move from his extreme position toward a mean, trying to achieve this by inclining toward the opposite extreme, as indicated in the fifth note [350]. This itself, of course, should be done moderately and always with a view to achieving a mean. It suffices to give these matters (as well as the matter of the sixth note) orally rather than in writing.

[112] 3. As regards the rules for thinking with the Catholic Church, it should be noted that these rightly commend those things which are attacked and called into disrepute in books, sermons, and conversations by the heretics of our times or by those with heretical leanings. Hence these rules should be especially recommended as an antidote for those who live in places, and deal with persons, suspect of heresy. The usefulness of these rules lies not only in helping people to avoid falling into error by thinking differently or so expressing themselves publicly or privately in speech and writing, but also in helping to detect in the statements and writings of others deviations from the Catholic Church's mode of thinking and speaking, and to put other people on their guard against them. For this reason, these rules should not just be transmitted orally but should be given to the exercitant in written form, especially in such places as have been mentioned.

[113] The statement in the tenth rule that "it may be profitable to discuss their bad conduct with those who can apply a remedy" [362] should be taken to apply where evils of some gravity certainly exist, where there is no likelihood that others have undertaken or are willing to undertake this duty of charity, and where there is hope that some good will ensue from bringing the matter to the attention of those who can remedy it.

From Polanco's Summaries of Points for the Exercitant

Instead of being given the book of the Exercises, the exercitant had the points and instructions for upcoming exercises dictated or handed to him one by one during the director's visits. Polanco's summaries were widely used for this purpose. For the most part they are simply the text of the Exercises slightly abridged. We give here his outline of the Foundation, showing the division into four points. We also give his texts for the meditations on death, judgment, and the penalties of sin. These three meditations are not found in the book of the Exercises but are mentioned in the Vulgate edition of 1548 after the 5th exercise of the First Week [71]; in fact their use seems to have been an ordinary thing.

SUMMARY OF THOSE EXERCISES WHICH SHOULD BE LEFT IN WRITING ALTHOUGH MORE FULLY EXPLAINED BY WORD OF MOUTH

[1] THE FOUNDATION

First. Man was created for this end, that he might praise and reverence his God, and by serving him be saved.

Second. The other things were created on earth for man's sake, to help him to the aforesaid end.

Third. From this it follows that creatures are to be used or abstained from insofar as they help or hinder him toward his end.

Fourth. Hence, as far as we are able, we ought to be indifferent toward all created things, and not seek health more than sickness, riches more than poverty, honor more than contempt, a long life more than a short one; instead, of all these things we ought to desire those more which lead us more to our end.

[10] SIXTH EXERCISE: MEDITATION ON DEATH

After the preparatory prayer and prelude as given in the 1st exercise, the second prelude will be to ask the grace of meditating profitably upon death.

First point. Consider that all men, no matter what their condition, must inevitably meet death; and also that the hour of death is utterly uncertain—when a person arises from bed he does not know if he will reach the evening, and when he goes to bed he does not know if he will arise the following morning.

Second point. In death we must leave behind all the things which are loved in this world, as well as all the things people pursue with great care, toil, and danger—and even our body itself. When the soul departs from the body, nothing follows it except our good or evil works—for our salvation or damnation.

Third point. Reflect that at the hour of death one's senses are most often dulled and one's mind so hindered by pain or the vehemence of the illness that even practiced persons are barely able to keep their minds concentrated on what is needful for their salvation. The evil spirits, on the other hand, then attack in great force. There is, moreover, fear of the judge before whose tribunal the dying person will be haled to give an accounting of his life.

Finish with a colloquy to Christ, asking that he deign to forgive my sins and thus prepare me to be able to await death without fear. Our Father; Hail Mary.

[11] SEVENTH EXERCISE: MEDITATION ON JUDGMENT

After the preparatory prayer and prelude as in the preceding exercise, the second prelude will be to ask the grace of reflecting well upon both the general judgment and my own particular judgment.

First point. Consider that before the tribunal of Christ our every thought, feeling, word, work, and omission will be laid bare and exposed. Reflect upon what a detailed accounting we shall have to give for every item—and this weighed against all the gifts we have received from God: natural gifts of soul and body as well as supernatural gifts of grace, virtues, and all the helps bestowed by God, including even external goods.

Second point. Consider that we shall have to await that supremely important verdict by which we shall either obtain eternal happiness or undergo perpetual misery, depending upon our good or evil disposition at our departure from this life.

Third point. Our judge then will be inflexible in righteousness, and no one can either escape or resist him, since he is almighty; nor hide anything from him, since not only outward acts but even the inmost recesses of the heart are exposed to the gaze of his wisdom. And so this judge will not let an idle word pass by without scrutiny, nor a single evil deed without punishment. He will be both judge and plaintiff, since it is against him that sins are committed.

Fourth point. This trial will be of the most rigorous justice. There will be a host of prosecutors but no friend or advocate for the person who has died in mortal sin. What then must I do, I who stand convicted of so many crimes against God's majesty? I must use the time of this life, where the judgment of mercy holds sway, to turn and beg for mercy.

I will end with a colloquy to Christ our mediator, or to the Blessed Virgin, asking them to obtain mercy for me. Our Father; Hail Mary.

[12] EIGHTH EXERCISE: MEDITATION ON ETERNAL PUNISHMENT

The preparatory prayer and first prelude as above.

The second prelude will be to ask the grace of making a good meditation on the penalty of sin.

First point. Consider what is lost by any mortal sin, viz., in this life God's grace and all the infused virtues, as well as all one's merits and spiritual consolation; but in the next life the eternal happiness for which man was created and redeemed. This latter suffering, the worst of all, is what is called the punishment or suffering of loss.

Second point. Consider what is incurred, viz., liability to the eternal punishment in hell called the pain of the senses. Its bitterness should be weighed: horrible sights, hideous cries, unendurable stench, unending hunger and thirst, unquenchable flames. All this is outward; inwardly there is the worm of conscience, everlasting shame.

Third point. Reflect upon the total sum of suffering in every limb, every sense, every power of the soul. One who finds it so hard to endure pain in a single limb—how will he be able to bear such universal torments?

Fourth point. Consider that this pain is continuous: without intermission, without alleviation, without end. If anyone would be unwilling to endure a severe fever or acute pain in the side uninterruptedly for just a few years even if it would make him lord of the world, how will he endure the everlasting pains of hell?

Final point. Consider the senselessness of those who, for the sake of some slight pleasure or advantage which inclines them toward sin, expose themselves to the risk of so enormous a disaster—a disaster which is the just consequence of every mortal sin and is inescapable for anyone dying in sin.

I will address my colloquy to Christ, humbly begging his forgiveness and thanking him that he has not thus far punished me. I will ask the grace to avoid sin in the future, along with the punishment which ensues upon it.

Answers of Father Lawrence Nicolai

A Norwegian and a convert from Lutheranism, Father Lawrence Nicolai (1538–1622) taught theology and other subjects for many years in northern and eastern Europe. Around 1587 he replied to a set of questions about his method of giving the Exercises. Their spontaneous and personal character sets them apart from of the other directories. (Original in Latin.)

BRIEF REPLY OF REVEREND FATHER LAWRENCE THE NORWEGIAN, PRIEST OF THE SOCIETY OF JESUS, TO SOME QUESTIONS ON GIVING THE SPIRITUAL EXERCISES

[1] *Question 1: How many hours a day do you give, and what schedule do you follow?*

Usually four hours. The first is in the morning from 5:00 to 6:00. The second is from 9:30 to 10:30, so that they will have a half hour of recollection before dinner at 11:00. The third hour was from 2:00 to 3:00. The fourth was from 4:30 to 5:30. With those who seemed up to it (and I was careful not to appear to pressure them) I added an hour at night during the First Week. With others I not only dispensed with this hour but, when their health or excessive exertion required it, cut back some of the daytime hours to make the Exercises more enjoyable and profitable.

[2] *Question 2: How many and which exercises in each Week?*

Neither question can be answered definitely, since exercitants vary so much. Some finish the individual Weeks more slowly, others more quickly. Some make the repetitions readily, others find them quite tedious. Again, some need further stimulation, while others obtain the fruit of the exercises from just a few considerations. Finally, some are more capable, others less.

[3] So I never used to regulate the Exercises by the time. Instead, I regulated the time by the Exercises and the Exercises by the needs of the exer-

citant. I gave slower persons all the time they needed to obtain the fruit, which I always took to mean obtaining the end indicated in the second preamble of the current exercise. I tried to persuade people who seemed impatient with the repetitions to make them anyway by pointing out their value and necessity. With others I used to mix in some new material, especially geared toward the affections, to make it look like a fresh meditation for them. But when I saw this was not working, I used to give two exercises at a time for repetition, especially in the exercises on the life of Christ.

[4] With those who needed more stimulation or who found the Exercises boring (although this happened mainly with persons who had already made the Exercises once before or with those who had deserted the spiritual life for the flesh), I sometimes used to sharpen the exercises with some sort of explanation, supplying reasons or relating a relevant story. Other times I would put in a few apt passages culled from Scriptures and present these as fresh exercises to meditate, or I would construct entirely new exercises in the same style as the others.

[5] With more delicate-seeming persons I would immediately cut back these and other usual exercises. I used to give to more capable persons higher, more penetrating, and more perfect things which I kept back from others.

[6] As for the exercises which should be given in each Week, that depends on the purpose of the Week. I will describe my own practice in a general way.

[7] In the First Week, that of penitence, what is looked for is sorrow for sins and an effective resolve to live a new life. So I used to use whatever exercises I thought would achieve this, always taking the individual's personality into account. This Week is brought to a conclusion by the general confession; making this confession well is very important for reordering one's whole life.

[8] I learned by experience that for many people the long-drawn-out preparation for the general confession often dispels the depth of affection they have obtained during the First Week. Hence, I used to have them on their own make an hour's meditation from one of the earlier exercises of the Week; for others I would myself make up a new exercise for the purpose and give it to them. After the confession I used to give them Christ's parable about the demon that was expelled and wandered in waterless places.

[9] The main goal of the Second Week is light to follow Christ correctly as well as to know and be drawn toward a particular state of life in imitation of Christ's life. Here, then, I would use as many exercises as I thought would suffice. My own goal during this Week was to give each person, to the extent of his capacities, a rational presentation of perfect virtue and of the royal highway to it, and to help him have a love for it; and then to bring him to complete indifference. As for the choice of a particular state, I would leave the person to God.

[10] However, I saw that there was a way for the director, by giving information about different religious orders and by indirect suggestion, to cooperate with God's grace so that they might seek the religious state. But no one can teach how to do this, and it is often dangerous to try it because it will often alienate the persons instead; and if they do choose religious life it might be through human agency rather than the grace of a calling.

[11] However, if I did have this gift from God, I would deem myself obliged to observe the following. First, I would always have to keep the intention of never pushing anyone except where God is drawing him. Then, throughout the Exercises I would be on the watch for signs of a vocation. If these are present I would try in the exercises and conversations to get a clearer idea of whether he had the gift of a vocation. This can be discussed more openly, of course, with regard to the *end* of a vocation; for generally people begin to feel attracted first to the end of a certain state, and afterwards to the means. When I achieved this I would cautiously move ahead.

[12] The aim of the Third Week is the death of our vicious affections and attraction to Christ the man and to imitation of him in every virtue. Here, then, as Reverend Father Ignatius prescribed, I propose the whole of Christ's passion in the form of a summary. I also used to insert exercises to instruct them on purity of intention and genuine Christian virtues.

[13] The aim of the Fourth Week is the affection of divine love and a certain union with God. A person is brought to this by consideration of Christ in glory and of God's own perfection and great gifts to us. So in this Week I made use of exercises which would unite the heart to God and render it freer and more prompt in both mental and exterior operations. But enough on this question.

[14] *Question 3: Which exercises do you give to people wishing to choose a state of life whom you would wish to see members of our Society?*

I try to give them the exercises of the First Week perfectly. In the Second Week I carefully give them the exercises on the election. I do put in some exercises—just a few—on the life of Christ. However, if they make their choice without reasoning process I do not give the exercise on the method of making an election[1] unless I have reserves about their election, but only the second method [of the third time] by way of testing the election already made. After the election, I give only a summary of the Passion from the Third Week and some things on the virtues of special importance to us, especially obedience. From the Fourth Week I give only the second and third Methods of Prayer.

---

[1] That is, if they make the election in the first or second time he does not give the first method of the third time.

[15] My idea in giving them the Exercises in this way was so that if they decline spiritually they can later be restored. If they come with their decision already made, or already accepted for the Society, I gave them little more than the First Week and the Lord's passion.

[16] *Question 4: Which exercises do you give to persons who have already chosen their state of life and want to change it for the better?*

It depends on whether I thought them suited for that state or more suited for another. If I thought they had made a good choice, I did not use the exercises pertaining to the election but simply applied a part or the entirety of the Exercises to their state, as Reverend Father Ignatius advises in the Exercises.

[17] If I thought they were suited for a different state, or had certainly chosen a religious order which did not suit them or for which I thought they were unfit, I would give them the exercises of the Second Week with more care and try to restore them to indifference, emphasizing with them the importance of choosing carefully, or at least of testing whether their original choice was good.

[18] *Question 5: Which exercises do you give to members of our own or other orders who want to go forward in spirit?*

I gave these persons the First Week as far as needed. I adapted all the exercises of the Second Week to making an election of becoming perfect in their own state of life, altering a bit some of the exercises. I gave the remaining Weeks in full, depending upon the person. Here, however, it would be good to take note of their main faults and direct some meditations against these.

[19] *Question 6: Do you give all the Exercises to the unlearned just as to the learned, or only some of them, and which ones especially in which Week?*

Learned persons I classify as capable, and I give them the full Exercises unless there is some reason why not. To the unlearned I give the Exercises so far as I deem them capable. If I see they are unsuited for choosing a state of life I omit this matter and adapt the remainder. People I saw would obtain no particular benefit I was reluctant to admit to the Exercises; I tried to help them outside the Exercises by means of a general confession.

[20] *Question 7: Do you examine the exercitant after each exercise of each Week, and on what points in particular?*

I always ask how they fared and whether they were satisfied. To more mature persons I explain the point of the exercise so that they themselves will be able to tell whether they have attained its real fruit. I also urge them to tell me freely about the fruit they experience so that I will have a better idea how to adapt the Exercises to them, or so that I might share with them any thoughts I might have from God on how to preserve the fruit they have received. That is about as far as I go with these persons, lest I seem obtrusive.

[21] Other persons I question freely, but making sure they understand why I do this so they will not be annoyed. I ask them about other things as well, not just about the aim of the exercise. I ask them about distractions, boredom, the Examen and other things laid down in the Additions, but only so far as I think is needed; however, I do ask about these things if they are making little or no progress. I advise all to pick out from each exercise some devout resolution for the improvement of their life, in the light of the faults and tendencies they have had since childhood.

[22] *Question 8: Do you have them write down the results of their Exercises? Of each individual exercise?*

I urge them to note down their holy resolutions, lights, and devout affections, together with the reasons and motives. They should try to express in few words the main point of the whole fruit so that later they can use it to renew their spirit.

[23] *Question 9: Which and how many spiritual books do you give the exercitants in each Week?*

In the First Week I give books which call to penitence, such as the book of exemplary stories by Marcus Marulus[2] (though this book is good for all the Weeks), Denis the Carthusian on the Last Things,[3] Innocent III and Denis the Carthusian on Contempt for the World,[4] the Directory[5] and the like. But I only give a few at a time.

In the Second Week I give some of the above books, such as on Contempt for the World and the Directory, for the sake of their remedies for sins. To

---

[2] Marcus Marulus (Marulić; 1450–1524), *How to Live Well, by the Example of the Saints.* This work by a Croation lay spiritual writer was much used by the early Jesuits; it was almost the only book Francis Xavier carried with him in addition to his breviary.

[3] Denis the Carthusian (Denys van Leewen, Denys Ryckel; 1402–1471), *De quattuor hominis novissimis.*

[4] Innocent III (Lotario de' Conti di Segni), *De contemptu mundi;* also called *De miseria condicionis humanae* (English translations by Robert E. Lewis [Athens, Georgia: University of Georgia Press, 1978] and Margaret Mary Dietz [Indianapolis/New York: Bobbs–Merrill, 1969]); Denis the Carthusian, *De arcta via salutis ac mundi.*

[5] Juan de Polanco, S.J., *Breve directorium ad confessarii ac confitentis munus rite obeundum* (Rome, 1554). This is a manual for penitents and confessors.

these I add the New Testament, Thomas à Kempis on the *Imitation of Christ,* Bonaventure's life of Christ[6] and the like.

For the Third Week I give Tauler on the Passion,[7] and similar books. If needed, I sometimes give one of Luigi Lipomani's volumes on the lives of the saints.[8]

[24] The director, on the other hand, should carefully read the book of the Exercises, especially the part on the discernment of spirits. Useful also is a little book—by a certain Gerard of Zutphen,[9] I believe—on reformation of life and spiritual ascents. Also the shorter works of St. Bonaventure,[10] and those which treat the virtues, so that one can have a clear idea of the nature of each virtue.

[25] *Question 10: What has your experience shown you to be the more usual impediments, distractions, or disturbances of exercitants? What remedies do you use?*

I have found it to be a major impediment when they come to the Exercises with a definite intention not to alter some decision they have already made, and this without deliberation and for the most part because of an inordinate affection or because they want to avoid a particular state. So before I accept them for the Exercises I examine whether they have made any serious decision about their state of life, and how they made it. I then ask them if they are clear that this is a vocation from God, and on what grounds.

[26] If they are not altogether certain, I ask whether, if God should call them elsewhere, they are ready to follow his grace wherever he may end up calling them. Then I point out to them the necessity of this resolve, and encourage them to form it, showing how smooth and easy it is to follow God

---

[6] For this widely read work attributed to St. Bonaventure, see St. Bonaventure: *Life of our Lord and Savior Jesus Christ,* translated from the original Latin (New York: P.J. Kenedy and Sons, [1881]); also *Meditations on the Life of Christ: An Illustrated Manuscript of the Fourteenth Century,* translated by Isa Ragusa (Princeton, New Jersey: Princeton University Press, 1961).

[7] *Meditations on the Life and Passion of our Lord Jesus Christ Attributed to John Tauler, Dominican Friar,* translated by A. P. J. Cruikshank, 4th ed. with preface by Bertrand Wilberforce, O.P. (Westminster: Art and Book Company, 1904).

[8] *De vitis Sanctorum* (1551).

[9] Gerard Zerbolt of Zutphen, *De spiritualibus ascensionibus.* A new translation of this work has appeared in *Devotio Moderna: The Basic Writings,* trans. and intr. by John Van Engen, pref. by Heiko A. Oberman, Classics of Western Spirituality (New York: Paulist Press, 1988), pp. 243–315.

[10] See *The Works of Bonaventure, Cardinal, Seraphic Doctor, and Saint,* translated by José de Vinck, 4 vols. (Paterson, N.J.: St. Anthony Guild Press, 1960–66); and *The Soul's Journey to God; The Tree of Life; The Life of St. Francis,* translation and introduction by Ewert Cousins, preface by Ignatius Brady, O.F.M., Classics of Western Spirituality (New York: Paulist Press, 1978).

wherever he calls. If I do not succeed in getting this from them I would hardly accept them for the Exercises—except perhaps to the First Week in hope of an improvement in their attitude.

[27] Another impediment is if they have set a time limit, especially if they have decided to leave before three weeks are up. I think they have to make up their minds to spend at least that much time if they are to make the Exercises really well. So before I accept such persons I tell them to arrange their affairs so that the pressure of time will not prevent good results.

[28] A third impediment is when all they want from the Exercises is to have a lot of insights, or to help other people. Therefore I tell them that the fruit of the Exercises consists in bringing our affections into conformity with what we know, and that in the Exercises the main point is their personal transformation, it being sufficient to be concerned in a general way about helping others.

[29] A fourth impediment is when they think themselves very wise and reserve to themselves the right to pass judgment on everything. People like this I would hardly accept for the Exercises; they are generally incorrigible. Or else, during the Exercises when asking them what fruit they have had, or on some other occasion, I say things which implicitly put them down, bringing ideas of my own. Other times I openly point out to them their ignorance and pride, but I usually try to do this in a teasing way.

[30] A fifth impediment is when they will not stay within the bounds of the assigned meditation. Then I point out to them that the Exercises have a plan, and that the fruit of each exercise is like a course of bricks progressively building up the spiritual edifice.

[31] A sixth is when I find people who look on the Exercises as something excessively harsh and rigorous. Accordingly, I do not give these persons the Additions. Instead, I point out the main ones little by little—not prescribing them but showing how helpful they will be if the person wants to observe them. Likewise, I do not deprive these people of light, nor do I say anything about penances unless I see they are ready. I try to be as cheerful as possible with them, visit them more frequently, and in general handle them like cracked eggs until they become firmer.

[32] With great men also I never or rarely give the Additions. I avoid all small details and always try to treat them liberally and with a certain deference. With great as well as learned men I avoid the appearance of teaching them, except for things it is clear they need to learn. Other matters I suggest indirectly, saying that such and such a thought had occurred to me during the Exercises, or that I had thought of something which they might well reflect upon at this point.

[33] Against all distractions, I urge them from the beginning to form the habit of thinking that they are doing everything in the presence of God and

that he is watching to see how seriously we are engaged in the business of our own salvation.

[34] *Question 11: Which exercises do you give to married persons? To religious? To physicians? To lawyers?*

Common to all of these are the exercises of the First Week. Where it is judged good to give the remaining Weeks, these are the same as for other persons, with the exception of the Second Week. I have already mentioned what I do with religious in place of the election. With other persons also I concentrate on the end of their vocation, on how it contributes to God's glory and how they cooperate with God in their responsibilities. Then I set this end before them and in place of the election I try to get them to orient themselves and everything they have toward this end as perfectly as they can. This is also the point of what Father Ignatius has in the Exercises about the disposition of one's household and goods. I also try to get an idea of these persons' faults and remedy these where occasion offers by applying exercises to them.

[35] *Question 12: How many hours a day do you visit an exercitant?*

A director of the Exercises has to be unsparing of his time. My practice has been to visit each person four times a day. If you give the material for several hours [of prayer] at once, people are likely to become restless and open to distractions. In addition, every time I come, even if they are only going to be making a repetition, I try to bring something new. I never say what they will be doing in a subsequent hour, because people like things fresh, and knowing what lies down the road causes distractions. I also make an effort not to seem to be treating them on the fly. No matter how busy I am I deal with them in a leisurely way, and I do whatever I can for their consolation. If I do happen to be pressed for time, I promise to talk with them later at greater length, and make sure that I do.

[36] *Question 13: Do you send anybody to the exercitants at recreation time to have spiritual conversations with them?*

Sometimes I send someone, but usually I go myself. If I do send someone, I try to send a person who is happy and cheerful, skillful with people, and spiritual.

[37] *Question 14: Do you have exercitants copy the Exercises, and do you let them take them along when they leave the college?*

I never let anyone copy them, and they shouldn't. If I need a copy myself and the exercitant has a good hand, I have him write out for me just a few things, so as not to burden him. With the superior's permission I have sometimes openly given people a few things to take along, such as the text on Spiritual Love or the like—things which are useful throughout life.

[38] But I tell them at the beginning that they may not copy things out. I also check at the beginning how much paper they have and how much they have used up. If I suspected anyone of making copies, I would tell him jokingly about my system for catching people who secretly made copies: I would say that in their confession at the end before Communion, I asked people whether they had copied anything, and in this way catch them out, since no one was so hardened as to dare receive the Sacrament with a deliberate lie. Other times I searched their rooms while they were at Mass. Sometimes I found copies under their mattresses.

[39] *Question 15: Finally, do you have any other matters worth knowing and keeping in mind about how to give the Exercises, either as regards the director or the exercitant? And would you be willing to show and let us have the Exercises in your own possession?*

Nothing much comes to mind which I have not said in the earlier replies or which cannot be gotten from the book of the Exercises. The one warning I would give is that the director should make an effort to understand the underlying reasons of the method he determines to use and, especially at the beginning, take care to confer his procedure with someone who is prudent and wise in this matter.

[40] He should also perseveringly ask God to guide him and to assist the exercitant with his grace. On undertaking some more important task, such as an election or something equally difficult, he should urge the exercitant to pray earnestly and to forearm himself with a sound attitude.

[41] Since people usually come to the Exercises with a variety of thoughts distracting them, it is useful right at the beginning to give them some texts from Holy Scripture to help recollect and stir their spirits. But you should never give many texts at one time, whether for this or any other purpose, because they will then run through them all superficially.

[42] For the beginning, then, my practice has been to give them a text from Isaiah 1[:2]: "I have brought up children and exalted them," etc. From the New Testament: "Jerusalem, Jerusalem, you that kill the prophets," etc. [Matt 23:37]. Or else the text which depicts Christ weeping and saying, "If you also had known the time," etc. [see Luke 19:42]. It is sometimes good to add the saying of Isaiah: "Woe to the sinful nation," etc. [Isa 1:4]. But since these are all texts full of reproach and threats, some encouraging texts should be added, v.g., "Let the wicked forsake his way," etc. [Isa 55:7], or, "Come to me, all you that labor," etc. [Matt 11:28].

[43] On the method of meditating, the following remarks might also be made. In each exercise there is a definite thing aimed at which the person making the exercise is to obtain. This end is reached by the following acts. First, by reading materials suitable for aiding meditation and disposing the person for it.

[44] Next, by a process of thinking in which the person entering on the meditation focuses on the material and forms ideas about it.

[45] Thirdly, by meditation, in which he ponders and reflects upon these realities with a view to obtaining the purpose of the exercise.

[46] Fourthly, by contemplation: he dwells on what he has discovered in his reflections, feeds his spirit with it, and tries to appreciate it according to its worth. Hence, this act pertains to spiritual savoring, and it disposes the mind for spiritual movements and affections.

[47] Fifthly, by spiritual affections, whereby, depending upon the different contemplations, he breaks out in amazement at his own malice or ingratitude, or at God's mercy, goodness, majesty, beauty, etc.

[48] Sixthly, by a prayer or colloquy which concludes all this. However, this is a purely natural order for moving toward an end, and so the exercitant should be carefully warned not to trust in his own devices in this matter. Rather, since all these steps are completely ineffective without the help of God, he should form the habit of always relying on God's help. However, he should also be persuaded that God will not help him without his own efforts.

[49] The director should teach the exercitant how to implement all these acts correctly, and how to proceed in his reflection, which is the proper act of meditating. In this regard, the following should be noted. The matter for meditation either dictates something to be done, or else is of a different kind, viz., for understanding truths.

[50] In the first case, this is the order for meditating: First, we consider what is demanded of us; then we seek out reasons by which we can obtain this in our soul; then we weigh these reasons by contemplation, etc.

[51] In the second case, we first consider each point of the matter, and examine the weight of each individual element. Then we ponder what consequences this has that would be useful in ordering our life; here we reflect mainly on ourselves. This will readily happen right away if we take them as spoken to us by God. Thirdly, we should consider anything which might stir up our souls to do this, drawn from this or other exercises. Finally we should move on to contemplation and other acts.—These are just roughly expressed hints.

Praise be to God and to the Virgin Mother.

Second Directory of Father Diego Miró

Miró, already a bearer of important and difficult responsibilities under St. Ignatius, was one of the Society's most influential members under the saint's second successor, Everard Mercurian. Strict, even literal loyalty to the Ignatian heritage marks his first directory (Doc. 22 in Iparraguirre's edition), drafted sometime before 1582. Basing his work upon Polanco's (Doc. 20), whose flexibility regarding the Exercises he considered excessive, Miró stressed fidelity to the Ignatian prescriptions.

Though enjoying quasi-official status for a while, this directory of Miró's was not everywhere found adequate, as can be seen from the criticisms of Fathers Fabio de Fabi (Doc. 24.33–52) and Gil González Dávila (Doc. 31.10,31–33). Under Mercurian's successor, Claudio Aquaviva, the project of an official directory was renewed. As his contribution toward it, Miró produced an even more intransigent revision of his original directory. It is this version that we translate here, with the addition (in angle brackets) of passages found only in the earlier version. (Original in Latin.)

DIRECTORY FOR GIVING THE SPIRITUAL EXERCISES OF OUR FATHER IGNATIUS, BY FATHER DIEGO MIRÓ

The Spiritual Exercises of our Father Ignatius have been approved by the Apostolic See, and anyone with zeal for the salvation of souls should—with discretion—seize every opportunity to get people to make them. For they are extremely effective in disposing people to receive the grace of God. Wherever up to the present time their use has flourished, great fruit in the Lord has been evident, both in our own men and in externs. We have long experience of this, especially at the beginning of our Society. It was through these Exercises that the earliest fathers of our Society received the gift of their vocation. It was through the Exercises that the Society itself was founded. For our Father Ignatius first discovered this method of giving exercises, and was through him that by a special grace of God we were granted these spiritual weapons for the progress of our own and others' souls. Hence, it is through them that our men receive their first formation in the discipline of the Society. It is appropriate then that by virtue of our institute we should make every effort to acquire skill in using them well. To this end, by decree of the General Congregation, the following directory for giving the Exercises according to the mind of our Father Ignatius has been composed.

CHAPTER 1: SOME MATTERS HELPFUL FOR BOTH THE ONE WHO WILL
GIVE THE EXERCISES AND THE ONE WHO WILL RECEIVE THEM

[1] These Spiritual Exercises do not specifically envisage members of our Society but people generally, as a means by which anyone at all can be guided in overcoming himself and determining his own way of life.

[2] After having themselves made the Spiritual Exercises, our men should learn how to give them to others; and under the direction of superiors all should strive to be able to give an account of them and to be skilled in wielding this type of spiritual arms, which by God's grace so visibly contributes to his greater service.

[3] Some might be able to be trained in the Exercises by giving them to persons with whom less harm would be done by possible mistakes, and also by reporting on the procedure they follow to someone more experienced and carefully noting whatever they detect as more or less suitable.

[4] The full Exercises should be given only to a small number of persons, who either are of such a caliber that more than ordinary fruit for the glory of God may be expected from their progress, or are persons who wish to make a decision about their state of life. The exercises of the First Week, however, along with some of the examinations of conscience and Methods of Prayer (especially the first of the three listed in the book of the Exercises), can be extended to larger numbers; these exercises can be made by anyone with good will. The various ways of giving the Exercises are presented in Annotations 18–20.

[5] In explaining the Exercises to people—and they should have an explanation always ready at hand—they should aim not merely at satisfying people's curiosity, but also at arousing in them a desire to take advantage of the Exercises. They should make use of prayers and good works to obtain this grace from God.

[6] The one who is going to give the Exercises should study the entire book and have it at his fingertips, especially the twenty Annotations at the front and the material pertinent to the exercises which he is giving at the moment. He should briefly meditate beforehand the exercise he is about to give, longing and striving with great charity for the exercitant's spiritual advancement. He should pray for the exercitant and for himself, that the Lord might deign to guide them both; and he should occasionally remind the superior to have our men pray for him.

[7] The greater the desire and eagerness for spiritual progress one brings to the Exercises, the greater will be the fruit obtained. On the other hand, people pulled unwillingly into the Exercises will usually get little or nothing out of them.

[8] Great care should be taken to ensure that anyone who is going to make

the Exercises be properly disposed with this kind of desire for spiritual progress and with abandonment to God's will. However, so that people will not be frightened off or held back, this matter should not be pushed too hard at the beginning. Later, however, after they have been somewhat moved by spiritual relish, they should be brought to a more exact observance of the Exercises in accordance with the Additions.

[9] As for the place, unless the person who is going to make the Exercises is a member of the Society or has decided to enter the Society, he can be given the Exercises in some house or dwelling outside our own, where he will be away from every kind of occupation, as is indicated in Annotation 20. Alternatively, it can be in a secluded room of our house or college if this is convenient and the superior approves. To an occasional prudent woman, the Exercises can also be given in the church (but with a care to edification) so that she can then withdraw to a secluded part of her own house to make them.

<Unless the man is poor, it will suffice if we donate our spiritual assistance to him and he pays the house buyer for his food, which he will purchase for him as needed. The buyer should record the amounts received and spent in order to give him an accounting at the end, or for the superior to consider whether on a particular occasion something else should be done.>

[10] If the one who will be making the Exercises has a practice of going frequently to confession and Communion, he ought to do so before starting so that, fortified by these sacraments, he may embark on the Exercises with greater eagerness and fervor.

[11] The exercitant should be assigned a single competent director, if possible one to his liking. The director should not give the Exercises to several persons at the same time, but deal with each person individually. However, if for some reason the director who began the Exercises is unable to continue and another substitutes for him, care should be taken to ensure that the exercitant does not detect any contradiction or divergence between the two which might confuse him.

[12] The director should not bring along the book of the Exercises and read out to the other the exercise he is going to give. Instead, he should have the points he will dictate memorized and state them summarily with only the briefest comment, as is indicated in Annotation 2. To simple persons, however, and to those with little or no experience in the spiritual life, he should give the points in greater detail. All exercitants, however, can well be given the points in writing (in Latin or the vernacular, depending on the person). But the written text should be handed over only after the oral explanation.

At the beginning of the Society, however, many persons made the Exercises without ever being given written texts, and the same could occasionally be done today if the director thinks it proper. If the exercitant is illiterate, he should immediately say back the gist of the points he was given so that he will recall them better later on. This should also be done by a person who is receiving the Exercises without written texts.

[13] Written copies of the meditations and Annotations that are given one by one to the exercitant should follow the texts provided elsewhere on separate sheets. These have been accurately excerpted from the Exercises with the omission of the instructions. Thus there will be a single text for these formulae which should be used by all so that discrepancies among them will not beget confusion. These texts will also serve to indicate which elements should be given to the exercitant in writing—of course at the director's discretion.

[14] The only thing the exercitant should read is what is given to him in writing. To remove temptation, he should have no books in his room except a breviary (if he is a priest) or book of prayers of the Blessed Virgin Mary. During the First Week, however, he may read Gerson's *Imitation of Christ.* During the Second Week, he could read something from the Gospels, the *Imitation of Christ,* or the lives of the saints, as is stated in the note after the first meditation on the Temporal King [100]. However, in the Gospels he should read only the mystery being meditated that particular hour or day, as is stated in the first note after the five contemplations of the Second Week [127].

[15] All the Exercises should be given in the prescribed sequence to a person who wishes to derive the maximum benefit from them, as is stated in Annotation 20. Consequently, no one should alter either the exercises themselves or their prescribed order on his own initiative; otherwise the exercitant will make little progress, as experience sufficiently proves.[1] For it is through this order and these well calculated means that we experience that the divine Wisdom, in which alone all our trust is to be placed, has wished men to cooperate in order to receive outstanding gifts.

[16] Note that if the exercitant does not obey the director in regard to the order mentioned above, he should not continue giving him the Exercises. For in this spiritual path a person who does not act toward his master with humble docility may easily go astray. For God resists the proud and gives grace to the humble.

[17] The exercitant should be visited once a day or oftener at the discretion of the director, who is the only person who may deal with him at this time. The best time would be right after dinner or supper: this time is ill-suited for meditation, and the exercitant is then less occupied and sometimes in need of consolation.

[18] During his visit, the director should ask the exercitant about how he made the points, what insights came to him, and what consolations or desolations, if any, he has had. The director should give him clear direction and

---

[1] In Miró's earlier directory, the first clause of this sentence reads: "Moreover, our Father Ignatius frequently warned us, as a matter of great importance, to preserve this order; . . ."

instruction of every matter, with the warmest charity. He should also answer any questions he may have. He should, however, warn him against hurting his head by straining too much in his efforts to raise his mind to God or make the composition of place or application of his powers.

[19] If the exercitant's replies are satisfactory, the director should not stay long with him or say much more about the ideas of the meditations, as is stated in Annotation 2, unless he needs instruction. Instead, he should allow the Creator and the creature to deal with each other without intermediary, as is stated in Annotation 15. However, if the exercitant is not fully finding what he is seeking, the director should inquire more carefully how he is performing the exercises and their Additions, as is stated in Annotation 6.

[20] The director should be careful not to give the exercitant cause to suspect that the director harbors an unfavorable opinion of him, even if he is not behaving particularly well. Rather, he should constantly encourage him to go diligently forward on the path of God's service which he has undertaken.

[21] If the exercitant has had special consolations on any point, he should be told—if this seems advisable—to write them down for himself.

[22] The one who serves the exercitant should be told to do so in silence except for matters connected with the service or where the director has expressly instructed him to talk with the exercitant. He should also find out from the exercitant when he will be hearing Mass so that during that time he can make his bed and straighten his room (unless the exercitant does this for himself). He should take care to edify the exercitant by his humility, modesty, and diligence; and he should pray every day for him and for the director.

CHAPTER 2: MATTERS PERTAINING ESPECIALLY TO THE EXERCISES OF THE FIRST WEEK

[23] The foregoing chapter contained remarks helpful in a general way for making the Exercises. In this and the remaining chapters the remarks will apply to the individual parts of the Exercises in their proper sequence. Thus, we shall first discuss the initial meditation on the Foundation, then the Examens, then the five exercises which follow, and so forth.

[24] Just before the Foundation stands a directive which reads, "In the first place, in order that by exercises of this kind," etc. [22]. The purpose of this directive is that the exercitant may, where necessary, be admonished to put a good interpretation upon whatever is done or said.

[25] Before giving the Principle or Foundation of the Exercises, the director should explain four of the twenty Annotations which dispose a person well for embarking upon the Exercises. These are 1, 5, 17, and 20; the latter deals with withdrawing to a place where he ought to be sufficiently freed from other cares and affairs so that he can devote himself solely to God and his own salvation.

[26] The one making the Exercises should concentrate on them exclusively. He should not wish to pursue or ponder other considerations, but work solely upon these as if no others existed or had ever been the object of his thoughts.

[27] As regards the order, the first thing to be given is the Foundation, which comprises the end of man. It is called the foundation because it is the underpinning of the entire moral structure. Once the end has been set forth, the obstacles to its attainment, i.e., sins, are to be removed by grief and contrition for them. The perfect attainment of this is the purpose of the exercises of the First Week.

[28] The consideration of sins should begin the Particular Examen, so that we can first of all reflect upon and conquer the particular and principal sins and faults which are the source of others and which weigh on us most heavily. Just as people commonly suffer from one or another principal bodily malady, so also in the spiritual life there are certain particular faults or maladies in us which we need to examine and treat with special attention. Carefully made, this Examen is a great help in getting rid of these faults, for ordinarily God's grace is conferred on a person in proportion to his effort and disposition.

[29] This Examen's main use is for particular faults after one has finished the Exercises; it is for use throughout life. It is nevertheless initiated on these first two days so that he will get some practice in it and in later examens will remember especially to correct these faults; and also because he will need to use this examen on the Exercises and on their Additions, as will be explained shortly.

[30] Then, on the same or the following day, the other examens should be given as a means for attaining a knowledge of the sins of our whole past life and being helped in making the meditations of the First Week more effectively. The General Examen [32–42], however, is not given in the form of a meditation like the other Examens; its purpose is the recollection of the sins of our whole life, in whatever form this is done.

[31] Note that during the time while the examens are being given to be reflected on, the initial meditation on the Foundation is to continue; in it the exercitant should turn the reflection upon himself, asking how he has acted hitherto with regard to the end and the means, and how he proposes to act in the future.

[32] During this two-day period, hours for making this meditation and the General Examen [32–42] are not prescribed as they are for the five succeeding exercises in the directive at the end of the 5th exercise. In order to get off to an easy start, each one should take whatever time suits his strength and character, or which the director, if need be, indicates to him.

[33] The daily five-point Examen and the Particular Examen are made for a quarter of an hour after dinner and supper, and should be devoted especially to any negligence in these exercises and their Additions, as indicated in the

final note of the First Week [90], the second note on the fifth day of the Second Week [160], and the fourth note of the Third Week [207].

[34] Note that it is a great help in making the examens properly if the exercitant overcomes himself and immediately starts courageously and generously putting into effect the remedies has discovered to be needed for his faults— with the help of God's grace, which is never denied if a person does what is in his power—and if in doing so we at least realize our spirit's weakness and thus humbly implore its desired health and strength from the Lord, and with his help attain it.

[35] The valuable effects of a general confession of one's whole life [44] should be explained orally and, if need be, given in writing, depending upon the person's disposition when the making of a general confession is brought up. This should be done at the latest before the 1st exercise is given.

[36] On the evening of the second day if possible, the 1st, 2nd, and 3rd exercises should be given, so that the exercitant can begin doing the 1st one the following midnight, the 2nd immediately on arising in the morning, and the 3rd before dinner. After dinner the 4th and 5th will be given to be made at midafternoon and before supper, as indicated in the note in the Exercises after the 5th exercise of the First Week [72].

[37] If because of weakness of memory or for any other reasonable cause someone cannot be given all five exercises on a single day, they can be given to him over two days, so that by the second day he can be making them all at their prescribed hours.

[38] As indicated in Annotations 12 and 13, each exercise ought to be made for a full hour and at its prescribed time—particularly the midnight meditation in cases where the Exercises are being given in full form. Unless experience shows otherwise, no hour should be readily dropped, at least in the First Week, as our Father Ignatius indicates in the third note after the five contemplations of the Second Week [129]. Nonetheless, the Exercises should be adapted to the exercitant's character, i.e., to his strength, age, education, and intelligence, as is stated in Annotation 18 and in the note after the 5th exercise of the First Week [72].

[39] Then, on the evening of the day the exercitant has begun making all five exercises, one should give him the Additions for making the Exercises more fruitfully, or at least a good part of them. On the following days one can then give him the rest of the Additions and clearly explain to him the Rules for the Discernment of Spirits proper to the First Week.

<It is true that, according to the second Annotation, one should give the individual exercises with only a concise explanation. Nevertheless, certain clarifications can occasionally be given briefly and in passing. For example, now that the exercises of the First Week have been more or less completely given, if it seems useful one can give an explanation of how the malice and filth of sin

can be recognized (1) from the fact of God's supreme hatred of sin and his punishing it most severely even in the most excellent of creatures, such as the angels and our first parents; (2) from the gravity of the punishments inflicted for sin; and (3) from the fact of its infecting the entire soul. All these points are set forth in the exercises of the First Week.

If deemed useful, one can also give an explanation of how three elements are required for the cleansing of the soul, just as for cleaning a room. First, the dirt of the soul has to be seen and recognized. Secondly, it has to be sprinkled with the water of contrition and sorrow. Thirdly, it has to be swept with the broom of confession and satisfaction. All this can be obtained through the exercises of the First Week and a general confession. The value of the latter should be briefly explained as it is presented in the book of the Exercises [44].>

[40] The repetitions provided for in the Exercises are an important factor in the spiritual progress we aim at. For it is often the case that certain people while meditating draw a certain sustenance from curiosity and the novelty of the topics <with an activity more of the intellect than of the will>, and after a while get bored with them unless they are given something fresh to meditate on. That is why the repetitions have been provided: to forestall useless roving of the mind and ensure that the matters under consideration <, by being examined more frequently and carefully,> are retained and pondered with an efficacious will, so that we can perceive and savor them with relish and with the desired affection in the Lord. For it is not an abundance of knowledge but an interior sense and relishing of things which satisfies the desire of the soul, as is stated in Annotation 2. The purpose of the Exercises is especially to move the affections and will. This is very important. Now these repetitions should be made according to the directions of our Father Ignatius in the Exercises. Hence, during the First Week it is not right to give a single exercise to be made with its repetitions throughout the whole day, with the 2nd exercise being given on the following day, etc. This is not the procedure given in the Exercises.

[41] The directive in the 3rd exercise of the First Week—that the repetition should be on points where we had previously experienced consolation or desolation—is to be understood in the sense that it should primarily on matters where we have had more consolation. However, it is sometimes a good idea also to make it also on points where we experienced dryness, with a view to finding some consolation where we previously experienced desolation. For the Lord may later open to us the fountain of his grace at that point.

[42] The colloquy should always be made at the conclusion of each exercise, as prescribed in the book. But there is nothing to prevent a person from following his own devotion and making other colloquies and petitions at the beginning or in the middle. Indeed, this is sometimes a good thing.

[43] Greater reverence is required of us in colloquies and prayers than in meditations and speculations, since we there converse with God or his saints

and make use chiefly of acts of the will, as is stated in Annotation 3. Similarly, greater reverence should be used for the same reason in venerating and kissing places where Christ or the saints were present on earth, and so in similar cases.

[44] Besides the five exercises given for the First Week, others may be added, v.g., on death and the other penalties of sin, as well as on judgment, if this seems advisable for the exercitant's progress, as is indicated at the end of the 5th exercise of the First Week [71, Vulgate]. However, if through the five exercises he finds what he is seeking—intense sorrow for his sins—there is no need to add others. If they are added, they should be substituted for the 4th or 5th exercise of the First Week; the other three, since they are so crucial for obtaining sorrow, should not be changed.

[45] It is true that according to Addition 10 in the Exercises—on penance —we may counsel the exercitant to do penance and may suggest to him its value. Nevertheless, one should not require him to undertake all the penances mentioned there. Still, we should ask what he is doing in this regard, for a sober diet is a great help to elevation of mind. But it should be voluntary and suited to each person's constitution. Occasionally at the director's discretion a discipline or the like may be offered, depending on the exercitant's circum- stances. When the Exercises, especially the First Week, were made at the beginning of our Society, abstinence and the use of Addition 10 were vigor- ously observed, so much so that on finishing the Exercises our men were consigned to the care of the infirmarian.

With good reason was it then vigorously observed: for if on our part we dispose ourselves well by such penances, the infinite Goodness of God will enlighten and perfect our minds. <It is to be feared that through neglect of this matter nowadays the spiritual effectiveness of the Exercises is in part impeded.

In the old Rules of the Infirmarian it used to be stated that for a period of time he should have special care of those who had completed the Exercises. This shows with what diligence and exactness our men used to make the Exercises in earlier times.>

[46] From the start the director should instruct the exercitant that if he wants sometimes to cut down on his daily nourishment by way of penance, he should request after dinner what he wants for supper, and after supper what he wants for dinner the following day. The one waiting on him should bring exactly what he has requested, unless the director sees that he is carrying his abstinence to excess.

<It is quite helpful, both for relaxation from mental exercises, which cannot easily be carried on uninterruptedly, and for the benefit of humility deriving from self-abasement, if the exercitant, even if accustomed to living in luxury and being waited on by many servants, sweeps and if necessary sprinkles his own room, makes his own bed, and busies himself with the other tasks of this sort which are usually attended to by servants. However, the director

should consider whether in given cases another course might be preferable.>

[47] As regards the general confession, the exercitant should not prepare for it until after finishing the exercises of the First Week. As for the first point of the 2nd exercise of the First Week, which directs the exercitant to go through the places, offices, and persons with which he has dealt in order to ponder the multitude of his sins, this is to be done in a global rather than particularized fashion, for sorrow is fostered less by scrutinizing small points than by placing all one's serious sins together before one's eyes.

[48] While devoting himself to preparation for this general confession, he should not engage in any other exercises besides. Hence, toward the end of the First Week, when the exercitant has experienced the desired sorrow for his sins, he should be told to suspend all other meditations of the Exercises and busy himself solely with preparation for a complete general confession. The director can instruct him how to do this if he thinks it necessary. It is generally considered preferable for the exercitant to make this confession to someone else besides his director, unless his devotion or some other reason dictates otherwise.

[49] While occupied during the First Week with cleansing his soul through contrition and confession, a person reflects on his sins and sees himself as base and unworthy of divine acceptance. Unless his devotion or spiritual advancement or some other obligation dictates differently, it would be good during this time for priests making the Exercises to refrain from daily celebration of Mass out of desire for humility, so that afterwards, when they have made their general confession, they can approach the Sacrament of the Altar with greater preparation, confidence, and reverence. In the Second and following Weeks, however, priests may celebrate and others may receive Communion, in accord with each one's devotion and the advice of the director.

<Those who have finished the exercises of the First Week, even if they will not be continuing much farther, are customarily given some of the exercises of the Second Week.>

[50] Those who have finished the exercises of the First Week and will be going on to make the complete Exercises, once they have made their general confession and Communion, should be given at least a day off from the labor of the Exercises. During this time, however, it would be good for them to ponder and apply to themselves the meditation of the Prodigal Son.

[51] A person who had made the exercises of the First Week some time earlier and is returning to make the rest of the Exercises should begin afresh from the First Week, making his general confession on the second or third day, beginning from his previous confession. He should receive Holy Communion and thus, having quickly concluded the First Week, go on to the Second. Indeed, persons who have earlier made the entire Exercises and who on some occasion want to repeat a part of them, would do well to begin with the First

Week, at least in the fashion just outlined. If possible they should also be given a more experienced director, for it will help much toward receiving more abundant fruits if they have an instructor with experience in spiritual matters.

CHAPTER 3: ORDER FOR GIVING THE EXERCISES OF THE FIRST WEEK

[52] In giving the exercises of the First Week, the following order should normally be observed. It is drawn from various parts of the book of the Exercises and from early tradition, taking for granted what has been stated in the two previous chapters.

[53] Before or after dinner on the first day, a explanation should be given of four Annotations: 1, 5, 17, and 20 (on withdrawing somewhere). Then the meditation on the Foundation should be given, to be made at least twice on that same day. After supper the exercitant should be given the Particular Examen so that he can start making it the next morning along with the meditation on the Foundation, which he should then repeat at least once.

[54] After dinner on the second day, the General Examen [32–42] should be given, along with the other daily Examen, as well as the meditation on the Foundation, which he should make once in the afternoon. After supper, he should be given the 1st exercise for the midnight hour, the 2nd for the morning hour, and the 3rd for the hour before dinner. Alternatively, the latter two could be given early in the morning.

[55] After dinner on the third day, he should be given the 4th exercise for midafternoon, and the 5th for the hour before supper. After supper he should be given an explanation of the Additions for making the Exercises better, and he should repeat the same exercises the next day at midnight, in the morning, and before dinner, at the same times as today.

[56] After dinner on the fourth day he should be given some indications regarding penance. Moreover, for a quarter of an hour after dinner and supper he should always make, along with the General Examen, a Particular Examen aimed at getting rid of defects in doing the exercises and Additions. And today he should repeat the 4th and 5th exercises at their prescribed times, as on yesterday. After supper also the first seven Rules for the Discernment of Spirits of the First Week should be explained; and at midnight, in the morning, and before dinner of the following day he should repeat the exercises at the same hours as on day before.

[57] After dinner on the fifth day, he should be given the meditation on death in place of the 5th meditation on hell. After supper the remaining seven Rules for the Discernment of Spirits for the First Week should be explained; and at midnight, in the morning, and before dinner of the following day he should do the same exercises at the same hours as on the day before.

[58] After dinner on the sixth day he should be given the meditation on

judgment in place of the one on death. Then, after supper, he should be told to suspend the meditations of the Exercises and devote the following period, for as long as he needs, solely to the preparation of his confession.

[59] If the exercitant experiences boredom with these frequent repetitions of the exercises, he should be urged to overcome himself and to trust those who are experienced, with a hope for greater spiritual advance. In any case, a person who finds these things tedious would not seem to be penetrating them very deeply or to be experiencing compunction.

[60] On the seventh or eighth day, after completion of the general confession, he should be given the meditation on the Prodigal Son. This is not to be assigned to a definite hour; instead, he should ponder it throughout this time. After Holy Communion, he should be given in conclusion the Contemplation for Arousing Spiritual Love. However, if he will be going on to make the other exercises of the Second or Third Weeks, he should not be given this contemplation now; instead it will come at the end as a conclusion to his Exercises.

[61] The exercises of the First Week are ordinarily to be given in this fashion when they are being made fully according to Annotation 20. In exceptional cases, however, depending upon the exercitant's situation, a way of proceeding can be drawn from the indications in Annotations 18 and 19 given by our Father Ignatius, as was remarked above in chapter 1, paragraph 4.

<After finishing the Exercises, our own men ought to read the book and take from it what is helpful for themselves. They should also learn how to give the Exercises to others. The book of the Exercises can also be communicated to externs so that they can make further progress in the Lord by doing the exercises on their own.>

CHAPTER 4: SOME REMARKS PERTAINING ESPECIALLY TO THE EXERCISES OF THE SECOND WEEK

[62] Upon completion of the exercises of the First Week, which comprise the purgative way, the exercises of the Second Week dealing with the life of Christ should be given; these correspond to the illuminative way, as is stated in Annotation 10. When a soul has been well cleansed of its faults, it is much more capable of illumination than it was before. Likewise, once the briars of sin have been uprooted from the field of our heart by penance, the good seed of solid virtue must be sown. This is to be sought above all in the example of the life of our Lord Jesus Christ. In reflecting upon his example we see what we have to do in every kind of virtue if we are to reach Christian perfection. For assuredly the life which Christ embraced in this world is the most perfect of all, so that the most perfect state of life for a person is the one which approaches most nearly that of our Lord Jesus Christ.

<Note that during the Second Week it is a good practice on some occasions to omit rising at midnight. The four or five exercises can be made in one day, as stated in the third note after the 5th exercise on the application of the five senses, and in the note given for the second day. However, this should not be permitted during the First Week except for reasons of necessity.>

[63] The contemplation on the Temporal King is a kind of foundation for all the meditations on the life of Christ which come after it. The entire meditation has no other content than the imitation of Christ <our Lord, in which human perfection consists;> and this is of course what is to be sought in all the other meditations as well.

[64] The meditations on the Temporal King, the Two Standards, and the Three Modes of Humility can be given even to people who will not be making an election, just as was the initial meditation on the Foundation. For all these meditations treat in a general way of things which anyone can do for the greater glory of God and not specifically of a serious election needing to be made at the moment.

[65] The mysteries of the life of our Lord Jesus Christ listed toward the end of the Exercises, each divided up into three points, should be given to the exercitant in place of the history in each meditation. To those who have not read them in the Gospels, especially simpler persons, they can be given with a little more fullness, merely going through the main points of each mystery in passing and adding only a very brief explanation, as is stated in Annotation 2.

[66] In the composition of place, a person makes himself present, as it were, to the place where the event occurred, or to some other place. With the eyes of the imagination he beholds everything which is found, said, or done there, or is thought to be done there. He can also imagine that all these things are similarly present to him in the place where he is. This latter procedure is normally preferable. But he should not spend to much time on this kind of composition of place, so as not to tire his head, but should go on to meditate the event proposed.

[67] The 1st meditation, on the Incarnation, has three points: to contemplate on the person, on their words, and on their actions. Although this should ordinarily be the case with the other meditations of the Second Week also, these can nevertheless have other points added to them, as is stated in the third note after the 1st contemplation of the Fourth Week [229]; for example: the three powers of the soul and the virtues, the persons' manner and end, as well as the cause, effect, time, and other circumstances of the actions in which the persons are involved. In this way more ideas can be found in the meditation where this is needed. This method of contemplation can also be utilized for meditating the life of our Lady or any saint.

[68] At the third point in the 5th contemplation of the Second Week, where it speaks of the application of the senses of smell and taste, one should

ascend beyond the imagination to the rational level and there consider the sweetness of God's gifts in a holy soul refreshing our spiritual faculties of smell and taste. However, the imagining of corporal scents and tastes will be able to lead us into the exercise of these inward mental senses.

[69] Note especially that in the consideration of each point of the Exercises, particularly those on the life of Christ, we should always endeavor to extract some spiritual fruit for ourselves. That is, in those points especially where we are consoled we should resolve to take some action for our spiritual progress. Later, toward the end of the Exercises or after their completion, it is a good idea to recall these fruits and note what progress we have made in them.

[70] When our own men make the Exercises they should not be given the matters on the election as is done with externs, for by God's goodness they have already made a choice of the religious state and may not call it again into question. For a like reason, neither married people nor other religious should be given the election. However, our men may employ these methods of election in a case where they wish to make some decision that a superior has left to their discretion.

[71] The purpose of the meditation on the Three Classes of Men is to get us to examine and recognize our own greater or lesser attachment to worldly things, so that by removing it we might be equally ready to abandon or keep the things according as we ascertain, either by God's inspiration or by the verdict of reason, that it will be more conducive to God's service.

[72] After the meditation on the Three Classes of Men it is stated, "When we feel an affection opposed to perfect poverty, . . . it is very profitable . . . to ask God . . . to choose us to poverty of this kind, preserving, however, our liberty . . . to follow whichever way is more for the service of God" [157, Vulgate]. This is to be understood thus: our will is to be in a kind of balance, but in such a way that as far as we ourselves are concerned it inclines more toward the side of perfection should we understand this to be God's will. But if it is apparent that the will bends too much toward possessions and too little toward poverty, then the person is not properly disposed and cannot be expected to make a good election. For his affection, being adverse to the more perfect way and inclined to imperfection, would draw his intellect to think up reasons in agreement with his affection. He should be warned that stronger signs of God's will are required to remain in the ordinary way which we call the way of the commandments—since Christ says that it is hard for those who possess money to enter into life—than are required for choosing the more perfect way of the counsels, which Christ advises even though he does not enjoin, because it is without doubt the surer and more perfect way. Hence, as far as the person himself is concerned, he ought to have a greater inclination to embrace the way of the counsels than to embrace the way of the commandments.

[73] It is consequently important for the exercitant to try as hard as he can to have his will always inclined toward what is most perfect. Even if he does not actually attain it, still such a desire will do him no harm, but will in fact be extremely helpful in at least getting him to move further away from what is less perfect. That is why the Exercises always propose the more perfect thing as the principal object of our desires and earnest petitions to God.

[74] Outside the time of the election, two mysteries of the life of Christ should be meditated each day, following the pattern of the meditations on the incarnation and nativity of Christ, which are made on a single day. During the time of the election, one mystery should be meditated, as in the case of the contemplation on the Baptism given on the fifth day of the Second Week. However—although this is not prescribed—it may be thought that, depending upon the individual's degree of progress, it would be all right to meditate one or even two exercises during the time of the election,

[75] In the Second Week, in the second note before the Three Modes of Humility, it is stated [163, Vulgate]: "[Consideration of the elections is to be begun from the contemplation of the departure of Christ from Nazareth toward the Jordan,] so as to *include* that which is made on the fifth day with the rest." The reference is simply to the contemplation made on the fifth day, viz., the Baptism of Christ, and to the events *included* in it; it is with this meditation that treatment of the election begins.

[76] The Three Modes of Humility are given for the exercitant to reflect upon throughout the entire day. Nevertheless, one or two mysteries of the life of Christ should be meditated on that day as on the others; for the Three Modes are not assigned to any definite hour in place of some meditation, containing as they do only one principal point: desire to attain the third mode of humility. This point should be pondered all throughout the day, and during the meditation as well (at appropriate times), using the triple colloquy from the Two Standards, as is stated there.

[77] Election of a state of life should be proposed only to those who desire it or are willing to make it. Otherwise, being for the most part externs, they could easily become upset, as if we were trying in this way to persuade them to enter our order.

[78] If a persons wants to decide his state of life but is not indifferent toward following the counsels or the commandments, and not truly abandoned into the hands of the Lord and prepared to do whatever he wills, all treatment of the method for making a good choice should be entirely omitted. If it seems advisable, he should then continue with the Exercises, or conclude them expeditiously, or postpone them to another time.

[79] All exercitants, but especially those making an election, should be given, prior to the preamble for making an election, the Rules for the Discernment of Spirits for the Second Week, as indicated in Annotations 8, 9, and 10;

they should receive a clear explanation of these rules so as to be amply equipped in the Lord against the machinations of the enemy of human nature.

[80] During the period when the exercitant is being given considerations or procedures for making a good election, either orally or in writing, he should not spend upon them the whole time allotted for meditation. Instead, the time for treating and pondering the elections is after the conclusion of each exercise, or of some portion of it, when his mind is calm. Hence, much care should be taken that the meditations are made on schedule, for these give the soul consolation and dispose it to make a good election.

[81] A person wishing to decide his state of life normally has two distinct issues proposed to him: first, whether or not he wants to follow actual poverty, which consists of being stripped of possessions; and secondly, assuming he has decided he does, in which religious order he wishes to follow this path—since it can hardly be followed outside religious life. This summary and commonly used formulation can be given in a more elaborated form, depending upon the person's disposition: first, whether he ought to follow the counsels or the commandments; secondly, if the counsels, whether inside or outside religious life; thirdly, if inside religious life, in which order; and fourthly, the time and manner of entering it. On the other hand, if he decides for the commandments, then in what state or manner of living he wishes to observe them. If the director thinks it good to propose all these questions, the exercitant should go through each one in turn using all the modes of making an election, in each case choosing one of the alternatives.

[82] On occasion an election can also be made on an important matter a person wishes to decide even if it does not involve his state of life. Thus, <a religious might make an election on whether to go to the Indies if the superior has left the decision to him; or an extern on whether to make a pilgrimage, or to accept a responsibility, or to acquire perfection in his present state of life; or> someone might wish to make an election on reforming his life, as is indicated in the final note of the Second Week [182], or to make some similar election.

[83] Exercitants should be left to make freely whatever decision they wish regarding themselves, as is stated in Annotation 15. For what is done under constraint will not endure, especially in the matter of changing one's state. No such change or assumption of a state should be urged upon them; they should simply be given the correct way to make a good a election and urged to ponder the matter with care, and, with the help of God's grace above all and of the light of reason, to embrace what they have judged best in the Lord. This contributes greatly to their peace and perseverance. And if later they do not persevere they can blame no one but themselves.

<Even though the one making an election shows signs of a good disposition before embarking upon the this procedure for elections, the director

should nevertheless be on the lookout during the course of the elections, when inquiring about how he is making the election, either in the second or in the third time, to see if his affection is properly disposed so that he inclines to the more perfect way or at least is in a kind of equilibrium and ready for the way which better leads him to his final end and will be more pleasing to God. Otherwise he would have grounds for expecting nothing by way of a good election. There would be reason to fear that his inclination toward the less perfect comes from a spirit that is not good; yet if such a spirit is influencing him, there is clear danger of its drawing his reason and intellect to its own side. It is different if his affection leans toward what is more perfect. Such a spirit is not of flesh and blood; generally speaking, it is not likely that such an inclination would come from the evil spirit. And if it is from God it will be no obstacle to his coming to a knowledge of God's will.>

[84] When embarking upon the three times for properly making an election, a person should more than usually recollect himself, as was our Father Ignatius' opinion, so that as far as possible the one making the election neither sees nor feels anything but what is heavenly or divine.

[85] In the second time for making an election properly, it is stated that his vocation is recognized by his experience of consolations and desolations. Hence the nature of both must be fully explained to him. Consolation, then, is spiritual eagerness, love and hope for supernal realities, and every movement which leaves the soul consoled, as is stated in rule 3 for the Discernment of Spirits for the First Week. Its opposite is desolation, which is sadness, lack of trust and love, and dryness, as is stated in rule 4.

[86] When making a choice in the second time for making a good election, the person should, whether in meditation or in God's presence outside meditation, propose the matter he wishes to decide, with total abandonment of his own will and with a desire to experience what is God's will for him. He should not attend to his own reasonings but dispose himself as best he can to receive the movement of the Holy Spirit through the experience of consolations and desolations, as is stated in the same place.

[87] The method of election in the second time is superior to that in the third, so long as it is clear that the consolations and illuminations poured into the soul of the one making the election come from God, since then God shows his will more immediately by these effects of his grace than by the reasonings of the third time. Nevertheless, if the spirit which is moving him in the second time is not clearly recognized <as being from God>, and there is question whether his spiritual illuminations and consolations are from the good spirit or from the bad spirit transforming himself into an angel of light, then the election should also be made by the two methods of the third time. <For these procedures both activate a person's natural powers and at the same time dispose him to receive supernatural movements and enlightenment from God.>

Accordingly, elections should normally be made not only in the second but also in the third time. The the one making the election in this way will be able to render an excellent account to God, having done in both the second and third times what lay in his power to learn the will of God.

<The case may occur where the exercitant makes a choice in the second time and then, unsure whether the movement is from God, is given the two methods of the third time, which lead him to a contrary choice. Then the two choices made in the second and third times should be examined carefully according to the Rules for the Discernment of Spirits, right reason, and sound doctrine; and the weight of the motives in both methods should be judged. If it is clear that reason supports the election made in the third time, it is safer to follow this because of the exercitant's or the director's uncertainty as to whether the movement in the second time was from God. On the other hand, if the reasons in the third time are weak, and it becomes clearer that the movements in the second time are from the good spirit and not in conflict with right reason, then the election in the second time should be given preference. It may happen that, while originally there was some unclarity about God's will in the second time, once the matter has been further gone over and sifted, with the addition of the testimony of reason, the thing can now become clear.>

[88] In the fourth point of the first of the two methods of making a good election [181], it is stated that the exercitant should weigh the advantages and disadvantages which might derive from accepting or not accepting an office. When it is time to make this reflection, it would be good for him to list separately all the reasons on either side which occur to him, for when all the reasons on both sides are placed together they make the truth more evident and have a greater persuasive power. They should also be shown to the director so that he can direct the exercitant better.

[89] At the time of the election it is helpful to place before Almighty God on a given day one of the alternatives at issue and on the next day the other— for example, on one day the counsels and on the other the commandments. He should then observe toward which side God gives a greater sign of his will by these methods of election—as when one offers a prince various dishes and watches to see which of them he likes best.

[90] For all of the times of election, a calm mind is essential. For this, we employ the exercises of the Second Week, which should be prolonged until the election has been made. The exercises of the Third Week, however, which induce sadness and grief and so are less conducive to an election, should be given after it has been made.

[91] As is stated in Annotation 14, care should be taken to prevent the exercitant from thoughtlessly and rashly binding himself by a vow. Nevertheless, if a person with mature deliberation, and after having made his choice

with great clarity, wishes to stabilize his election by a vow in order to strengthen himself against the assaults of the devil, the world, and the flesh, the director should not stop him.

[92] The Rules for Regulating One's Diet and for Distributing Alms, the Notes on Scruples, and the Rules for Thinking Rightly with the Church are not routinely given to the exercitant. However, depending upon the person's need, they may be given, especially at the end of the Second Week when he may be dealing with a reform of his state of life. Still, they should not be given to everyone but only to those who appear to need them.

CHAPTER 5: ORDER FOR GIVING THE EXERCISES OF THE SECOND WEEK WHEN AN ELECTION IS BEING MADE

[93] After completion of the exercises of the First Week together with confession and Communion, a person beginning the Second Week—supposing the matters discussed in the preceding chapter—should, after supper on the day he has received Holy Communion and finished his contemplation of the Prodigal Son, be given the contemplation on the Temporal King. He should make this once the following morning; and after dinner on that same day he should be told to make a repetition of it before supper. After supper he should be given the 1st meditation on the Incarnation of Christ our Lord for the following midnight, and the 2nd meditation on his Nativity for the morning hour, and also the 3rd contemplation for the hour before dinner.

[94] On this first day of the meditations of the life of Christ, he should be given the 4th contemplation after dinner to be made at midafternoon, as well as the 5th contemplation on the application of the senses for the hour before supper. After supper one should explain to him the Additions for the Second Week. For the following midnight he should be given the contemplation on Christ's Presentation in the Temple, and for the morning hour the one on his Flight into Egypt, with a repetition of the two contemplations before dinner, in the same manner and form as was done with that day's first two meditations.

[95] Note that if the exercitant's fervor from the First Week seems to be abating somewhat, these meditations of the second day should be skipped, and he should go on to those of the third day so that he can get more quickly into the making of his election.

[96] After dinner on the second day, the exercitant (who by the way should, together with his quarter-hour daily Examens after dinner and supper, always be making the Particular Examen on getting rid of defects in the exercises and Additions) should make a repetition at midafternoon on the Presentation in the Temple and the Flight into Egypt, as was done in the 4th contemplation of the preceding day. In the hour before supper he should make the application of the senses to these two contemplations. After supper he

should be given points for the following midnight on how the boy Jesus was subject to his parents, and for the morning hour on how he was found in the Temple. He should make a repetition of these two contemplations in the hour before dinner, as on the preceding day.

[97] After dinner on the third day, he should be given the Preamble to Consider States, and at midafternoon should make a repetition on how the boy Jesus was subject to his parents and on how they found him in the Temple, as in the 4th contemplation of the first day. Before supper he should make the application of the senses to these two contemplations, also as on the first day. After supper he should be given the meditation on the Two Standards for the following midnight, early morning, and hour before dinner.

[98] After dinner on the fourth day, he should make a repetition of the meditation on the Two Standards. For the hour before supper he should be given the meditation on the Three Classes of Men. The note following this meditation should be given to him after supper, and he should be given the contemplation on the Baptism of the Lord for the following midnight, with repetitions in the early morning and in the hour before dinner as well.

[99] After dinner on the fifth day he should be given the Three Modes of Humility, to be pondered throughout the day. At midafternoon he should make another repetition of the contemplation on the Baptism, and before supper an application of the five senses. After supper he should be given the eight Rules for the Discernment of Spirits for the Second Week. Then, for the following midnight, he should be given the meditation on how Jesus Christ went from the River Jordan into the desert, with two repetitions in the morning hour and the hour before dinner.

[100] After dinner on the sixth day, he should be given the Preamble for Making and Election. At midafternoon he should make a repetition of the contemplation on the Desert. Before supper he should make an application of these senses on this. After supper he should be given the note on the three times for making a good election; and for the following midnight he should be given the meditation on how St. Andrew and the rest followed Christ one after another, with two repetitions in the morning hour and the hour before dinner.

[101] After dinner on the seventh day he should be given the first method of making a good election. At midafternoon he should repeat the contemplation on the Call of the Apostles, and make an application of the five senses before supper. After supper he should be given the contemplation for the following midnight on how the Lord gave his Sermon on the Mount and proclaimed Eight kinds of Beatitude. This should be repeated at the morning hour and the hour before dinner.

[102] After dinner on the eighth day he should be given the second method of making a good election. At midafternoon he should make a repetition on the Lord's Sermon on the Mount, with an application of the senses

before supper. After supper, if he has not finished the election—which can often happen—he can be given the meditation for the following (ninth) day on how the Lord appeared to his disciples in the boat walking on the waters of the sea. The procedure should be the same as on the previous days. This can continue in the same way, with a single meditation being taken each day, up to the twelfth day if necessary. The order to be followed in these meditations is that given by our Father Ignatius on the fifth day in the Second Week. If there is need to stay with the election for more than twelve days, further meditations should be taken from the Second Week, as indicated in paragraph 90 above. However, on the day after completion of the election he should with joy and gladness in the Lord make the contemplation on the events of Palm Sunday. If the exercitant ends his Exercises here, he should be given as a conclusion the Contemplation for Arousing Spiritual Love in us.

CHAPTER 6: ORDER FOR GIVING THE EXERCISES OF THE SECOND WEEK WHEN NO ELECTION IS BEING MADE[2]

[103]   After a person has completed the exercises of the First Week, at least in the brief form indicated in the final paragraph of chapter 2 above, and after he has made his confession and Communion, and presupposing the various points mentioned in chapter 4, he should, on the evening of the day when he has received Holy Communion and finished meditating on the Prodigal Son, have the contemplation on the Temporal King given to him, to be made the following morning. After dinner on that day, he should be told to repeat the meditation before supper. After supper he should be given the 1st meditation on the Incarnation of Christ our Lord for the following midnight, and the 2nd contemplation on his Nativity for the morning hour, along with the 3rd contemplation for the hour before dinner.

[104]   After dinner on the first day of the meditations of the life of Christ, the exercitant should be given the 4th contemplation for midafternoon, as well as the 5th contemplation on the application of senses for the hour before supper. After supper one should explain to him the Additions for the Second Week. For the following midnight he should be given the contemplation on Christ's Presentation in the Temple, and for the morning hour the contemplation on the Flight into Egypt, with a repetition of these two in the hour before dinner, in the same fashion as was done in that morning's first two meditations.

[105]   After dinner on the second day, the exercitant (who by the way should, together with his quarter-hour daily Examens after dinner and supper, always be making the Particular Examen on getting rid of defects in the exercises and Additions) should make a repetition at midafternoon on the Presentation in the Temple and the Flight into Egypt, as was done in the 4th contemplation of the previous day. In the hour before supper he should make an application of the senses on these two contemplations. After supper, he should be given the contemplation for the following midnight on how the

---

[2] Chapters 6 to 8 merely spell out what is said in the book of the Exercises regarding the order in which to give the exercises of the Second, Third, and Fourth Weeks.

boy Jesus was subject to his parents, and for the morning hour on how they found him in the Temple. A repetition of these two contemplations should be made in the hour before dinner, as on the previous day.

[106]　After dinner on the third day, he should make a repetition at midafternoon on how the boy Jesus was subject to his parents and on how they found him in the Temple, in the same fashion as in the 4th contemplation of the previous day. In the hour before supper he should make an application of the senses on these two contemplations, likewise as on the first day. After supper he should be given the meditation on the Two Standards for the following midnight, morning hour, and hour before dinner.

[107]　After dinner on the fourth day, he should repeat the meditation on the Two Standards at midafternoon and before supper. After supper he should be given the contemplation on the Lord's Baptism for the following midnight, and for the morning hour on how Jesus went from the River Jordan into the desert. He should repeat these two contemplations in the hour before dinner.

[108]　After dinner on the fifth day, he should be given the Three Modes of Humility, to be pondered throughout the day. At midafternoon he should repeat the contemplation on the Lord's Baptism and on the Desert. Before supper he should make an application of the senses on these contemplations. After supper he should be given the eight Rules for the Discernment of Spirits for the Second Week. For the following midnight he should be given the meditation on how St. Andrew and the rest followed Christ one by one, and for the morning hour the contemplation on how the Lord gave his Sermon on the Mount and proclaimed Eight kinds of Beatitude. A repetition of these two contemplations should be made in the hour before dinner.

[109]　After dinner on the sixth day, he should make a repetition at midafternoon on the Call of the Apostles and the Lord's Sermon on the Mount. Before supper he should apply the five senses to these two contemplations. After supper he should be given, for the following midnight, the contemplation on how the Lord appeared to his disciples in the boat walking on the waters of the sea, and or the morning hour how he taught in the Temple. A repetition of these two contemplations should be made in the hour before dinner.

[110]　After dinner on the seventh day he should repeat the contemplations on how the Lord appeared to his disciples and taught in the Temple. Before supper he should make an application of the five senses to these contemplations. After supper, he should be given the contemplation on the raising of Lazarus for the following midnight, and on the events of Palm Sunday for the morning hour. In the hour before dinner he should make a repetition on these two contemplations.

[111]　After dinner on the eighth day, he should make a repetition at midafternoon of the two meditations on the raising of Lazarus and the events of Palm Sunday. Before supper he should apply the senses to these two contemplations. After supper, if he is ending his Exercises at this point, he should be given as a conclusion the Contemplation for Arousing Spiritual Love in us.

[112]　Note that during this Second Week, as our Father Ignatius remarks, depending upon the time and needs of the exercitant, meditations can either be added—v.g., on the mysteries of the Visitation, the Shepherds, the Circumcision, and the Three Kings— or omitted from those mentioned above, since these are retained merely by way of introduction, to form the person better in contemplation.

CHAPTER 7: USUAL ORDER FOR GIVING THE EXERCISES
OF THE THIRD WEEK

[113]   A person who has made the First and Second Weeks without a break can certainly also be given those of the Third Week immediately afterwards. However, if a considerable interval has elapsed since he finished the first two Weeks, and he wishes to resume the Third Week, it would be good for him to start over with the First Week in such a way that he goes quickly through it as indicated in the final paragraph of chapter 2, and then begins the Third Week. Hence, after doing the exercises of the First Week, making his confession and Communion, and finishing his meditation on the Prodigal Son, he should be given the meditation on the Temporal King, which is a kind of foundation for all the meditations on the life of Christ our Lord, to be made once on the following morning. On that day he should be told after dinner to make a repetition before supper. After supper he should be given the 1st contemplation on the Lord's Supper and on the events before and after it for the following midnight, and for daybreak the 2nd contemplation on the events after the Supper and in the Garden. He should repeat these two contemplations in the hour before dinner.

[114]   After dinner on the first day of the meditations of Christ's Passion, he should make a repetition at midafternoon on these two contemplations of the Lord's Supper and the events in the Garden. Before supper he should apply the five senses to them. After supper one should explain to him the Additions for the Third Week. Then he should be given the events in the house of Annas for the following midnight, and the subsequent events in the house of Caiaphas for daybreak. Then in the hour before dinner he should make a repetition on these two contemplations.

[115]   After dinner on the second day the exercitant (who by the way should, together with his quarter-hour daily Examens after dinner and supper, always be making the Particular Examen on getting rid of defects in the exercises and Additions) should make a repetition at midafternoon on the contemplations of the events in the houses of Annas and Caiaphas. Before supper he should make an application of the senses to these two contemplations. After supper he should contemplate at the following midnight on how Christ our Lord was taken to Pilate and what happened there; at dawn he should contemplate what happened when Christ was sent to Herod. After this follows a repetition of these two contemplations in the hour before dinner.

[116]   After dinner on the third day, he should make a repetition at midafternoon of the contemplation on how Christ was taken to Pilate and on the events at the house of Herod. Before supper he should make an application of the senses to these two contemplations. After supper he should be given a meditation for the following midnight on Christ's return from Herod and the first half of the mysteries that took place before Pilate. He should do the second half in the contemplation at daybreak. Before dinner a repetition of these two contemplations is made.

[117]   After dinner on the fourth day, a repetition is made at midafternoon on the return from Herod through the first half of the mysteries that took place before Pilate, as also on the second half. Before supper an application of the senses should be made on these two contemplations. After supper, he should contemplate at the following midnight the events from the sentence of Pilate to the Crucifixion. At dawn he should contemplate the events from Christ's being lifted up on the cross to his breathing his last. In the

hour before dinner these two contemplations should be repeated.

[118] After dinner on the fifth day he should make a repetition at midafternoon on the contemplation from the sentence of Pilate up to the Crucifixion. In the hour before supper he should apply the senses to these two contemplations. After supper he should be given for the following midnight the contemplation on how the Lord died, was removed from the cross, and taken to the tomb. In the early morning he should meditate from the Lord's burial to the Blessed Virgin's retiring to a house somewhere. In the hour before dinner he should make a repetition on these two contemplations.

[119] After dinner on the sixth day he should make a repetition at midafternoon on how the Lord died, was removed from the cross, and taken to the tomb, as well as on the events from his burial to the Blessed Virgin's retiring to a house somewhere. In the hour before supper he should apply the five senses to these two meditations. After supper he should be given, for the following midnight, half of the mysteries of Christ's Passion; and in the morning he should continue through the other half. In this way he should ponder the entire Passion in the midnight and morning contemplations. Then, instead of the repetitions and application of the senses, he should reflect as frequently as possible throughout the whole following day on how the most holy body of Christ our Lord remained separated from his soul, and on the place and manner of his burial. He should ponder also the degree of our Blessed Mother's solitude, desolation, and affliction, as well as the bitterness of the disciples' grief.

[120] After dinner on the seventh day he should continue the considerations described above. After supper, if he is ending his Exercises at this point, he should be given as a conclusion the Contemplation for Arousing Spiritual Love in ourselves.

[121] Prescriptions for the meditations on Christ's Passion are laid down quite exactly by our Father Ignatius in the manner stated above. However, they can be given in different ways, as he himself notes at the end of the Third Week.

CHAPTER 8: USUAL ORDER FOR GIVING THE EXERCISES OF THE FOURTH WEEK

[122] After a person has done the first three Weeks of the Exercises, if he has been away from them for a long time and later wishes to pick up again with the exercises of the Fourth Week, he should start off with the First Week, finishing it quickly as stated in the final paragraph of chapter 2, and then entering the Fourth Week. Hence, after finishing the exercises of the First Week and making his confession and Holy Communion and completing his meditation on the Prodigal Son, he should be given after supper, for the following midnight, the 1st contemplation on how the Lord Jesus appeared to his holy Mother; and for daybreak the one on how Mary Magdalene and the other women went to the tomb early in the morning and how he appeared to Mary when she stayed at the tomb after the others left. At the hour before dinner he should make a repetition of these two contemplations.

[123] After dinner on the first day, he should make a repetition at midafternoon of the contemplations on how Jesus appeared to his mother and to Mary Magdalene. Before supper he should make an application of the senses to these two contemplations. After supper one should explain to him the Additions for the Fourth Week, and he should be given, for the following midnight, the contemplation on how Christ appeared on the

way to the women returning from the tomb and said to them "Hail," and they came near and fell down at his feet worshiping him. For the morning hour it should be on how when Peter heard from the women about Christ's resurrection he ran to the tomb, and as he was thinking about this Christ appeared to him, so that the apostles said, "The Lord has truly arisen and appeared to Peter." In the hour before dinner he should make a repetition of these two meditations.

[124] After dinner on the second day the exercitant (who by the way should, together with his quarter-hour daily Examens after dinner and supper, always be making the Particular Examen on getting rid of defects in the exercises and Additions) should make a repetition at midafternoon of the contemplations on how Christ appeared to the women returning from the tomb and to St. Peter. In the hour before supper he should make an application of the senses to these two meditations. After supper he should be given the contemplation on how Christ appeared to the two disciples on their way to Emmaus, for the following midnight; and for daybreak the contemplation on how he appeared to the disciples gathered in the house for fear of the Jews and said to them "Peace be with you." Then he should repeat these two meditations in the hour before dinner.

[125] After dinner on the third day he should make at midafternoon a repetition of the contemplation on how the Lord appeared to the disciples on the way to Emmaus and to the disciples assembled together. In the hour before supper he should apply his five senses to these two contemplations. After supper he should be given, for the following midnight, the contemplation on how Christ let himself be seen eight days later when the doors were closed, saying to Thomas, "Place here your finger and see, and be not unbelieving but believing." For the morning hour he should be given the contemplation on how Christ showed himself again openly to the disciples when they were fishing and how, after catching nothing all night, they cast the net at his command and were unable to pull it in because of the quantity of fish. In the hour before dinner he should make a repetition of these two contemplations.

[126] After dinner on the fourth day he should at midafternoon make a repetition of the two foregoing meditations, on how Christ appeared to the disciples after eight days, and appeared to the disciples while they were fishing. Before supper he should make an application of the senses to these meditations. After supper he should be given, for the following midnight, the contemplation on how the disciples went at the Lord's command to Mt. Tabor, where he appeared to them and said, "All power in heaven and on earth has been given to me; go, therefore, and teach all nations, baptizing them in the name of the Father and of the Son and of the Holy Spirit." For the morning hour, he should be given the meditation on how he was seen by more than five hundred brethren at once, and by James. In the hour before dinner a repetition of these two contemplations should be made.

[127] After dinner on the fifth day he should make a repetition at midafternoon on the two foregoing meditations: on how Christ appeared to the disciples saying, "All power in heaven and on heart has been given to me" and how he appeared to more than five hundred brethren at once, and to James. In the hour before supper the five senses should be applied to these two meditations. After supper he should be given, for the following midnight, the contemplation on how Christ appeared to St. Paul after the Ascension—"Last of all he appeared to me, as to one born out of due time"; and for the

morning hour the contemplation on the Ascension of Christ our Lord. These two meditations should be repeated in the hour before dinner.

[128] After dinner on the sixth day he should make a repetition of the two foregoing contemplations, on the Lord's appearance to St. Paul and on his Ascension. In the hour before supper the five senses should be applied to these two contemplations. After supper he should be given the Contemplation for Arousing Spiritual Love in us, to be made at midnight. It should also be repeated at daybreak and in the hour before dinner.

[129] After dinner on the seventh day, for midafternoon he should be given the First Method of Prayer. He should repeat this at the hour before supper. After supper he should be given the Second Method for the following midnight, and he should repeat this twice: at daybreak and also in the hour before dinner.

[130] After dinner on the eighth day, he should be given the Third Method of Prayer for midafternoon. Before supper he should repeat it. After supper, depending upon the person, he can be given some of the recommendations for those finishing the Exercises, as indicated in the concluding chapter of this directory.

CHAPTER 9: THE THREE METHODS OF PRAYER

[131] These are three particular methods of praying; they do not exclude others which are taught by the Holy Spirit and which men of spiritual experience are accustomed to give, or which any individual finds valuable for himself. But amid the others these three also—depending upon the variety and dispositions of the persons praying—are useful; they are ways by which we can prayerfully go through the commandments of God as well as holy prayers and psalms.

[132] In the First Method of Prayer it says: "In examining each commandment, it will be sufficient that the space of time should be employed in which the Lord's prayer might be said three times" [241]. This is to be understood in accordance with the fourth Addition [76], which says that wherever a person finds the devotion he seeks he ought to come to rest with no concern about going on until he has had his fill, as is also indicated in the second rule for the Second Method of Prayer [254].

[133] In the Second and Third Methods of Prayer, note that in lieu of a single word one can take a phrase, depending upon one's devotion; for example, "Father," "Our Father," "who art in heaven," "hallowed be thy name." Similarly with the remaining words or petitions of the Lord's Prayer or other prayers.

<In the Third Method of Prayer two things should be noted. One is that the interval of respiration gives the person who is praying time to let his mind penetrate more deeply into the truth signified by the words or phrases, so that his affections may be more strongly moved toward what he has understood. The other thing to be noted is that the interval of breathing should not be

taken so strictly as to prevent a person from tarrying a little more than the
length of a breath—especially since some people breathe more rapidly than
others. But one should dwell on these words or phrases for roughly the length
of a single respiration. If a person wants to understand or be moved more
deeply, and dwell on the word at greater length, he can of course follow his
devotion and do so; but then his prayer would approximate and fall under the
Second Method of Prayer rather than the Third.>

[134] The Third Method of Prayer is when we take just the length of a
single breath to consider each word of a prayer. However, if a person's devotion moves him to dwell longer on the words, he can of course do so, but
then this would be more the Second Method than the Third.

CHAPTER 10: RECOMMENDATIONS FOR AFTER THE EXERCISES

[135] Upon leaving a person after he completes the Exercises, one can give
him some of the following counsels—depending upon his age, learning,
capacity, and disposition—so that he can keep them in memory afterwards and
persevere in the spirit he has received.

[136] 1. He should often reflect upon the presence of God and upon the
fact that God always sees us, readier to pour out his gifts on us then the sun to
shed its rays, so long as we dispose ourselves, for he loves us more than we
love ourselves.

[137] 2. He should make frequent use of ejaculatory prayers to God, sometimes asking for forgiveness of his sins or for grace or help, sometimes giving
thanks, etc., since God desires more to bestow his gifts on us than we to
receive them.

[138] 3. He should endeavor to direct and perform his every interior and
exterior action for God's glory, with the pure love of charity, this being what
we were created for.

[139] 4. He should realize the greatness and multitude of the gifts God has
conferred on him, and thank God from his heart; for from God, the treasury of
every good, all goods flow as light from the sun or water from a spring. He
should also make some meditation every day on the gift of Christ's Passion, and
on what we ought to do and suffer for his sake since he suffered so much
for our sins.

[140] 5. He should reflect that we are strangers and dead men in this world;
for we have here no abiding city but seek one that is to come. It is extremely
valuable to remember the last things.

[141] 6. He should also make use every day of the Particular Examen for
removing his principal faults and sins. And he should prepare himself for
meditation by making a brief daily examen and considering himself unworthy
of converse or familiarity with God. For the prayer of a person who humbles

himself pierces heaven. After meditation he should frequently recall the points where he experienced special consolation, especially those which from habitual meditation have become clear and easy for him.

[142] 7. It is highly important that in prayer or meditation, amid the other ideas we have of God, we should reflect that he is our Father (as he himself teaches us in the Lord's Prayer) toward whom we ought to have the greatest reverential love and fear and filial trust.

[143] 8. He should endeavor frequently to bemoan his own and others' sins, and to implore the Lord for mercy, taking up every day at least some penance and accepting the tribulations he suffers as gifts of God for his own penance and progress.

[144] 9. He should frequently ponder the life of Christ our Lord, the lives of the saints, and the Holy Scriptures. Whenever he conveniently can, he should eagerly read, listen to, speak, and seek out whatever moves him more to devotion, leaving aside many other things which are useless for this.

[145] 10. Devotion to all the saints and angels is highly recommended, since they are our advocates before the Lord; with them we ought to converse so that our conversation may be in heaven. Above all, he should have a special devotion to our Lady the Blessed Virgin, to his guardian angel, to his name saint, to the saints whose relics are in the place where he lives, to those mentioned each day in the Martyrology, and to others depending upon each one's personal devotion. He can consider himself poor and beggarly in spirit and virtue, imploring the alms of spiritual goods from the citizens of paradise as his intercessors before Almighty God, before whom he is unworthy to appear. He should humbly turn now to one, now to another, now to all of them, pleading his need and indigence and their own great grace and gifts.

[146] 11. He should memorize a summary of Christian doctrine and from time to time recite part of it, meditating on it with the Three Methods of Prayer from the Exercises.

[147] 12. He should take special care to go forward in the virtues, especially in humility, patience, charity, and the others which constitute the foundations of the spiritual life. It will help him to exercise himself first in one particularly desired virtue more and with greater care, and then to go on to the others in succession. Particularly if he is a member of our Society, he ought to communicate his spiritual life and way of proceeding to the superior, spiritual prefect, or confessor, not wishing to be led by his own opinion, in accord with our *Constitutions*.

[148] 13. He should set himself some vocal prayer each day, v.g., the Little Office, the rosary of our Lady, the seven penitential psalms, the chaplet of our Lord Jesus Christ, the Litanies, or the like. On occasion he could also slowly and meditatively say and contemplate some psalm, especially the seven just mentioned, or a hymn such as the Veni Creator, the Veni Sancte Spiritus, the

Te Deum, or the Ave Maris Stella; or else the Benedictus or Magnificat or some other canticle, especially from Holy Scripture—all of which could be gone through using the Second or Third Method of Prayer.

[149] 14. If the exercitant is remaining in the world he should be told, first, to pray every day for half an hour or, if possible, for a whole hour. <He should chiefly meditate the life and passion of Christ our Lord, following the form given to him during the Exercises.> Secondly, to make an examination of conscience for a quarter hour every day. Thirdly, to go to confession and Communion once a week. Fourthly, <as God moves him,> to assist his neighbor through some spiritual or corporal work of mercy, depending upon his state of life and resources. Fifthly, to try to confer with a competent spiritual director on matters relating to his soul. Sixthly, to read religious books <from time to time and the Holy Scriptures often, so as to meditate on them and make progress in the Lord>, and to seek out good associations and avoid bad or distracting ones.

<The *Constitutions* strongly recommend to us mental prayer according to the manner of the Exercises, in which we constantly reflect upon ourselves and upon our spiritual progress. This mental prayer should of course always precede, accompany, and even follow vocal prayer, so that we may fulfil the Gospel precept to pray always and never give up.>

[150] When our men finish the Exercises they should have their own copy so that they can become intimately familiar with them and in the future observe this method of praying which belongs to our institute, as is stated in the Rules for the Novice Master and for the Spiritual Prefect. To externs who have made the Exercises the book should not be conceded, so that it will not later become public. Moreover, they do not need it since there are many other similar spiritual books they can use. They should not be allowed to keep the written texts given them during the Exercises; care should be taken to have them return these to the director when the Exercises are over.

Directory of Father Fabio de Fabi

The outstanding Roman Jesuit, Fabio de Fabi (ca. 1545–1615), held every important post in the Society of Jesus except that of superior general. This document, from about 1575, is less a directory than a proposal for organizing one, with emphasis on clarifying obscure and apparently contradictory passages in the Exercises. On the way, de Fabi has occasion to criticize Miró's directory (in an earlier version than the one given above). (Original in Latin.)

A Directory to the Exercises Will Be More Useful If Divided into Definite Headings.

[1] The term "directory" itself suggests some organization of the materials contained in it, and this is also demanded by the variety of topics to be explained. Thus the reader will have what he is looking for available under its proper heading. It will be easier to understand and retain material if it is organized so that each topic is treated separately, and this will prevent tiresomeness at frequent rereading.

A Directory Could Be Divided into Seven Chapters.

[2] Since the memory of our Father Ignatius is still fresh, and there is hardly anyone among us who perfectly masters the art of giving the Exercises, there is justifiable concern that with time everything may be forgotten. Hence it would worthwhile, for the sake of those who come after us, to assemble in this directory any guidelines, however few, that survive from recollections of our holy Father, either given directly by himself or handed on to us by the reports of others. It should include the remarks on this special instrument of our institute that are scattered throughout the Society's *Examen* and *Constitutions*. It will be equally important that it explain and clarify obscure passages in the book of the Exercises, as well as answer a number of questions which regularly arise regarding the Exercises.

[3] Finally, a satisfactory execution of this whole business will require some discussion of the highly essential point of the purpose and connection among themselves of the various exercises, individually and in general. Ignorance of the goal and purpose of individual elements (Examen, Foundation, exercise,

etc.), even when the text is read and dictated as it stands and in the same order as in the book, can lead to numerous blunders. Forsaking the mind of Father Ignatius, the individual director can think up for himself some new sense and meaning, thus failing to give people a satisfactory or authentic instruction. We must assume that Father Ignatius had a particular aim in view for each exercise, and that the order in which he presents them is neither casual nor unconsidered—as he himself indicates in Annotation 10 of the book of the Exercises.

[4] *Seven chapters for the directory.*—In my view, the directory could be divided into seven chapters.

CHAPTER 1 would present everything said in the *Constitutions* and *Examen* on the fruit, manner, and duty of making the Exercises.

CHAPTER 2 would give directives on the preparation, sequence, and order to be observed in giving the Exercises, both for the director and for the exercitant.

CHAPTER 3, after a brief treatment of the Exercises in general, would detail the particular purpose and aim of the individual elements, or at least of the more important of them, explaining the reason behind their sequence.

CHAPTER 4 would give brief explanatory notes on the more difficult passages in the book of the Exercises.

CHAPTER 5 would solve a number of uncertainties in order to reap more benefits from this practice; some of these uncertainties are indicated below.

CHAPTER 6 would comprise any surviving directives, either expressly given by Father Ignatius or noted down by others during his lifetime with his consent, regarding both spiritual and physical matters pertinent to either exercitants or directors.

CHAPTER 7 would furnish means and counsels for the help and perseverance of persons once they have finished the Exercises.

EXPLANATION OF THE INDIVIDUAL CHAPTERS

[5] Lest this division appear arbitrary, the following grounds for it are given.

[6] CHAPTER 1: Regarding the first chapter, there is no doubt that our men will be more favorably disposed toward the Exercises if they realize the importance and high dignity attributed to them in our *Constitutions;* they will thus embrace them more eagerly as a special and indispensable means for the end of our specific vocation.

[7] CHAPTER 2: *First remark.*—Regarding the second chapter: in order for our men not to trip up when reading or practicing what is given in the book of the Exercises, they need to be forewarned about certain matters essential to the proper and authentic understanding of the Exercises. A religious, for instance (to come to particular cases), could run into difficulty if he wanted to

take everything in the book literally. For example, it says in the first of the twenty Annotations that these Exercises are for seeking the will of God as regards one's state of life. This could lead a religious to call into question his own vocation, whereas this passage should actually be applied to persons who do not yet have a definite state of life.

[8] The same would be true for what is said about indifference to poverty or wealth at the end of the Foundation, and what is said about voluntary poverty in the contemplation on the Kingdom of Christ or in the colloquy of the Two Standards. These and any similar passages should be explained as applying to persons who need to choose their state in life, not to those who are already religious.

[9] *Second remark.*—Similarly, Father Ignatius could not give particularized directions and annotations in the book of the Exercise for individual cases. He set down only the main and essential points, leaving it to the director's prudence and judgment to provide differently as occasion demanded, so long as he did not depart from the purpose and aim of the Exercises. See Annotation 17, which says, "He should prescribe some exercises adapted to the present needs of the soul."

[10] An imaginary example: Annotation 6 says that if the exercitant experiences no consolations, etc., he should be asked whether he is making all the exercises at their proper times and observing the Additions, etc. Yet it can happen that even with while faithfully following all the prescriptions the person fails to experience these affections for other reasons, one of which, mentioned in Annotation 20, arises frequently with extern retreatants, viz., failure to withdraw their minds from all concern about human affairs.

[11] *Third remark.*—The third remark would be to avoid being so bound to the letter and sequence in the book of the Exercises as to exclude any alternation for better results through freedom of spirit and the light of God's grace. For example, each exercise ends with a colloquy and begins with a petition. It can happen, and often does, that one's spirit is moved to a colloquy at the very beginning of a meditation; or, conversely, that something that should be done at the start of the meditation actually comes at the end. It does not seem against the intent of the Exercises, but rather in accordance with both the Exercises and good sense, that the parts of an exercise should follow the order of one's devotion and spiritual impulse, each being placed wherever there is promise of greater fruit.

[12] CHAPTER 3: Light on this third chapter can be had from what was said above before giving the division into chapters, as well as from a single argument. If a person does not understand the purpose of the Foundation, or the meaning of the 1st and 2nd exercises and the difference between them, or the point of the Examens and Additions, he will fail to focus his mind properly on getting the fruit aimed at in these exercises. Instead, he will drift confusedly

among all the exercises, getting stuck on individual points. However, if he sees the purpose of the individual elements, their interconnections with each other, and other reasons for them, he will be able to work more intelligently at obtaining the end proper to each exercise.

[13] CHAPTER 4: 1. Annotation 18 says to prescribe a method for more frequent confession. What is this method? Should it be taken from the book of the Exercises, or from some examination of conscience, or from some other source?

[14] 2. Annotation 19 speaks of "the Particular and General Examen for a half hour." Should this half hour be taken as continuous? Should the two examens be made at the same time and in the same way? They are quite different from each other, both in purpose and in practice.

[15] 3. Annotation 19 also says that the same procedure should be followed in the mysteries of Christ's life as in the exercises of the First Week. However, the Second Week gives a method of meditation that differs from that of the First. Clarification is needed on how this is possible.

[16] 4. Annotation 20 [Vulgate] speaks of "also having the main points written down." This seems to imply that the points of the Exercises should not be given in writing to everybody but only to those making them in full form.

[17] 5. The composition of the 1st exercise of three powers says: "If the meditation is on something incorporeal, as in the consideration on sins, the construction of the place should be such that we imagine souls shut up in prison," etc. [47]. Should the composition be made in this way in all spiritual meditations or only in the consideration on sins?

[18] 6. In Addition 5 after the exercises of the First Week [77], it says, "if the contemplation succeeded." Some wonder if they are supposed to consider a prayer successful when they were not plagued by bothersome thoughts while praying and not assailed by evil spirits, or when they battle strenuously and courageously against such evil movements. For the latter seems to betoken greater success and progress in prayer than if they underwent no struggle or opposition.

[19] 7. In the points of the 1st and following meditations of the Second Week, how is the consideration supposed to be "reflected upon ourselves" so as to derive fruit therefrom, as is prescribed there?

[20] 8. In the Second Week, how does the application of the senses in the 5th exercise differ from or agree with the preceding exercises? It seems indistinguishable from the from the 1st and 2nd exercises, since what takes place in the consideration of the persons, words, and actions is nothing other than the application of one's senses or sensitive faculties. There is need for a clearer explanation, such as that in the second note of the Fourth Week [227].

[21] 9. The fifth note of the Second Week [131] seems to contradict itself. It says to use an equivalent of the second and third Additions in all other

meditations except in the 1st and 2nd exercises, whereas the immediately preceding fourth note [130] seems to say otherwise.

[22] 10. What is the difference between the first and second classes of persons in the meditation which follows upon the Two Standards [153, 154]? They seem to come down to the same thing.

[23] CHAPTER 5: 1. Some ask why a repetition is supposed to be made on contrary movements that may have occurred, and indifferently whether accompanied by consolation or desolation [62]. An explanation should be given why the repetition should be suitably made on these contraries and with what results.

[24] 2. A person who needs to prepare for a general confession cannot be satisfied with just the General Examen [32–42], since the confession requires giving the circumstances and species of one's sins. In fact, the General Examen is not placed in the book of the Exercises for a general confession but rather for a particular or daily confession, and hence immediately precedes the treatment of the daily Examen. Moreover, the things listed there are by and large common, everyday sins, and for the reason indicated this seems insufficient for a general confession.

[25] 3. May prayer be extended to two hours or longer? Father Ignatius' mind seem to be that it should last a little longer than an hour [12, 13]; otherwise fatigue and distaste for prayer may set in.

[26] 4. May an exercise be made at any hour after dinner or supper? It would seem that there should be a rest of three, or at least two, hours after a meal.

[27] 5. Must all the exercises be done mentally or not? While the first Annotation, the Additions, and the exercises themselves indicate that the prayer should be mental, still there is nothing against bursting into vocal prayer out of the overflow of the heart, as is expressly stated regarding the colloquy in Annotation 3.

[28] 6. A reading of the book of the Exercises seems to suggest they are aimed entirely at persons in the world. In the treatment of indifference toward poverty or wealth [23], in the preparation for the choice of a state of life, in Annotation 14 on not making vows, it is clear that only persons in the world are envisaged. The opposite is the case in the Society's *General Examen*, where the Exercises are listed as the first of the Society's probations; and in the *Constitutions,* where this salutary ministry of the Society is frequently mentioned.

[29] 7. Should persons not making an election be given the note on reformation of life from the end of the Second Week [189]? If so, should it be given generically, as it stands, or specified to the duties of the particular person's state of life?

[30] CHAPTER 6: This is already present at several places in the directory.[1]

[31] CHAPTER 7: See the last three chapters of the directory.

[32] If it is preferred to reduce the matter to five chapters, the contents of chapter 5 above can be divided up between chapters 2 and 4, and those of chapter 6 wherever they fit in. Chapter 1 could also be divided up among the other four, if that is preferred.

NOTES ON SOME POINTS IN THE DIRECTORY

[33] In paragraph 39,[2] it says "after supper" (similarly in the third note): the time immediately after dinner or supper does not seem suitable for serious conversation, when both director and exercitant need to be fully concentrated and intent upon the matter they are discussing. It could be harmful to health and prejudicial to the seriousness of the discussion. Hence, the time for giving exercises or asking an account of what of has been done would rather seem to be before meals. The time after supper should be given over to relaxation, even by way of a familiar conversation with the exercitant should charity and the exercitant's condition so require.

[34] In the same paragraph, where it speaks of "presenting the Particular Examen": one should perhaps add, "with an explanation of the examen itself and its fruits, which can be obtained both during the Exercises and throughout life." For normally things presented at the very beginning are taken in more readily and attentively and retained for a longer time.

[35] In the same paragraph, on giving the Rules for Spirits: it would perhaps be better not to give all of them to everyone, but all or some of them as the situation arises and the person needs them.

[36] Paragraph 40: Many can lose the fruits which can be obtained from prayer unless they are given an explanation of these repetitions, especially with the same exercises along with their repetitions being repeated over several days. Hence it would be good if the explanation presented here regarding the importance and value of the repetitions were passed on to the exercitant.

[37] Paragraph 47: Since persons preparing for a general confession do not find in the General Examen of the Exercises [32–42] the species of sins and the circumstances they need to mention in confession, they commonly request a confession manual, and they should be given one.

[38] Paragraph 50 speaks of the priest's saying Mass, implying that he should not celebrate before this. But many priests' devotion moves them to celebrate Mass rather than refrain from doing so, even during the First Week. They should perhaps be let free to follow their own devotion in this matter.

---

[1] Of Father Diego Miró, document 23.

[2] Of the earlier version of Miró's directory upon which de Fabi is commenting.

[39] In the same paragraph, the suggested meditation on the observance of the commandments does not seem "light" or appropriate to that time, when, having confessed his sins and grieved over the recollection of them, the exercitant rather needs to rest from such matters and turn to more pleasant ones, meditating either on the favor he has been granted (using the Prodigal Son, for instance) or the Raising of Lazarus, etc.

[40] Paragraph 92: The Rules for Regulating one's Eating go together with the Addition on Christian practice [82–85] given in the First Week, which deals with penance, particularly in regulating one's eating.

[41] In addition, some further points are mentioned in the previous section regarding further clarification of this directory.

[42] *Another directory.*—There is a different way of structuring the directory which might be easier and more helpful. A first chapter could deal with the value of the Exercises both for the person making them and for others: it could show how our own men are able through the Exercises to pursue and obtain the end of the Society, which consists in their own and others' salvation and perfection.

[43] For, as it says in paragraph 13 of the directory, confessors have an opportunity to suggest the Exercises to their penitents; and at the beginning of the Society the Exercises produced great fruits, both in our own men, many of whom received the gift of their vocation through them, and in other persons. However, at this point there could also be a general treatment of how confessors can make use of the Exercises for directing souls in the way of the Lord by pointing out the end and giving advice on the means for attaining it appropriate to the state and vocation of the penitents; likewise a discussion of what preachers, teachers, and those engaged in other ministries of the Society should be aiming at for themselves and for others. For, in view of the fact that large numbers of outstanding persons have been won for God through the Exercises, either in religious or in Christian lay life, there can be no doubt that they contain a hidden power, grounded as they are in the teaching of the saints, the truth of Scripture, and long experience. Will not this power, if exercised with God's favor, burst into rich fruit?

[44] CHAPTER 2: Here could be added the matter mentioned just above.

[45] CHAPTER 3: on the end and interconnections of the Exercises, in general and in particular.

[46] CHAPTER 4: answers to questions.

[47] CHAPTER 5: a treatment of obscure passages.

[48] Paragraph 39: Where it says, "The ten Additions should be given together with the Particular Examen," etc., it would not be inappropriate, particularly for persons coming to the Exercises without previous experience, to present some of the Additions together with the Foundation; v.g., Addition 3 on preserving the presence of Christ in meditation, Addition 4 on posture

during meditation, etc. This could be very helpful for these persons.

[49] In the same paragraph, on giving the Rules for Spirits, at the end: there are times when necessity requires dictating some of these on the very first day, when the person is meditating the Foundation and practicing the Examens. In this way, when either assailed by some incursion of the evil spirit or led by the promptings of the good spirit, he will more readily be able to be on the lookout for the good of his own soul, repelling the evil spirits and welcoming the good. However, this should not be explained unless, as mentioned, a real need appears in the one being directed, and he gives occasion for or requests it. For, unless given help against its initial temptations, the soul often falls into discouragement.

[50] In paragraph 6, it says that "anyone wanting to be a competent director needs to read the book of the Exercises thoroughly." Here it seems necessary that he should also have a complete familiarity with the mysteries of our Lord's life in the Second, Third, and Fourth Weeks, drawn from frequent reading of the Gospels themselves, so that he can resolve on the spot any difficulties the one being directed may have. A mere reading of the book of the Exercises is often insufficient in this regard.

[51] For the same reason, it is not sufficient simply to have acquired a literal understanding of the text of the Exercises on the topic of sins and various other kinds of exercises. A broader knowledge and careful study of these matters is required, both from consultation of other books and especially from frequent meditation on these matters, as is stated in Annotations 2 and 8.

[52] Paragraph 75: In the explanation about the second note before the Three Degrees of Humility [163] on when the process of the election should begin, it says that the words should be taken to mean that it ought to begin during the meditation on the Baptism of Christ, which comes on the fifth day. But third note immediately following [164] seems to say the opposite, viz., that before embarking upon the election the persons should spend an entire day pondering the Three Degrees of Humility, which also takes place on the fifth day. This seems to indicate that the Three Degrees should be pondered before any of the election is done, so that the election should apparently be entered into not that day but the following one.

How to Give the Exercises, by Father Fabio de Fabi

The following observations were taken down around 1580–1590 by Girolamo Bencio, doubtless while making the Exercises under de Fabi's direction. They represent a kind of supplement to the preceding document. We have changed the original page references to the Exercises to the modern paragraph numbers. (Original in Latin.)

HOW TO GIVE THE EXERCISES

[1] I will discuss five points: the number of the Exercises; their order; the place for making them; the disposition of the exercitant; and the preparation of the director. In general, the Exercises should be given just as described in the book when being given in full form, as indicated in Annotation 20.

[2] However, when the Exercises are made only in part, the procedure given in Annotations 18 and 19 should be followed.

1. NUMBER OF EXERCISES

[3] They contain four Weeks, not of days but of exercises, running to about thirty days (Annotation 4), and divided among the three spiritual ways (as alluded to in Annotation 10).

[4] For particular reasons indicated in the book of the Exercises, other exercises may be employed (see *Constitutions*, IV, 1.R) for motivating the exercitant to the fear and love of God and to the love and acquirement of the virtues. Thus, in the First Week something on death and judgment may be given to strike fear; likewise in the Second and Third Weeks something on humility, patience, chastity, poverty, and the other virtues; and in the Fourth Week considerably more on God's benefits than is found in the meditation on Divine Love.

[5] The three Methods of Prayer belong to the Fourth Week, as indicated in Annotation 4.

[6] Account should be taken of the exercitant's intention, constitution, age, capacity, and success—the number of days both overall and within each Week

being increased or diminished accordingly, as indicated in Annotations 4, 18, and 19, and in the first note after the Second Week [162].

2. ORDER

[7] Like nature, the order of the Exercises proceeds from the imperfect to the perfect, i.e., from penitence to perfection. They imitate the operations of natural agents, which constantly strive toward some goal which they have set before them.

[8] Thus, the first consideration, in the Foundation of the Exercises, is of the final end of man; also presented there are the general means for attaining it, i.e., the proper use of creatures. Then the person undertakes to remove the obstacles to the goal—one's own passions and disordered affections—by means of the Particular Examen and of interior and exterior penance. Next his efforts are turned to exercises on the virtues. Finally, the person enters into union with God through love.

[9] This is the order followed. In dividing up the Exercises the first thing to be given is the Foundation, preceded by Annotations 5, 13, and 20, which deal with committing ourselves to God, disclosing our conscience and thoughts, and entering into retreat and recollection of mind. Annotation 4, on the number and length of the Exercises in general, could also be added. However, for giving the Foundation no definite length of time or fixed hours for meditation are assigned.

[10] On the evening of the first day, the Particular Examen can be given (to be started the following day) on some particular fault, passion, natural inclination, or disordered affection. This is to help the person recognize his malady and begin plucking it from the field of his soul where he must sow the good seed of the Exercises, uprooting the weeds and thorns which would inhibit its fruition.

[11] The General Examen [32–42] is also given, to be read over frequently until the exercitant fully understands the meaning of all the points and is thus prepared for making the general confession. For the following day no other meditation is given but the Foundation, which is continued until then for deeper consideration.

[12] On the evening of the second day, Annotations 3, 11, 12, and 17 should be given. Then something on the advantages of general confession and Communion should be presented, as found in the book of the Exercises after the daily General Examen (see [44]). The use and practice of this examen, which should be succinctly and clearly explained, can be recommended either on the first day along with the other examens or at this point.

[13] Then the first three exercises of the First Week should be presented, each for its designated hour, along with Additions 1–3 [73–75]. After dinner on

the third day, the 4th and the 5th exercise on hell should be assigned for midafternoon and before supper.

[14] On the evening of the third day the same exercises should be given for the following day, together with some or all of the seven remaining Additions; the use of the Particular Examen on the ten Additions and the preludes should be recommended.

[15] See the fourth note attached to the end of Addition 10 in [90]; this examination should be made throughout the following Weeks.

[16] Any meditation on death, judgment, etc., when substituted for the meditation on hell as indicated in [71, Vulgate], should be made in fifth place. There should always be five hours of meditation, even if the exercitant does not get up at midnight (see [72], before the ten Additions, and the third note after the 5th meditation in the Second Week (see [129]).

[17] The frequent repetitions in the First, Second, and remaining Weeks, far from being useless or fostering boredom, are actually indispensable for obtaining the purpose of the exercises and meditations, i.e., sorrow for sins in the First Week, imitation of Christ in the Second, etc. For through these repetitions the will is in the highest degree affected and moved through complete knowledge of the subject matter. Moreover, the repetitions keep the mind from roaming about and indulging its natural appetite for novelties.

[18] The Second Week with the method of election should not be given to anyone who is not indifferent with regard to the counsels. A person who is going to make the election should be given something to make a good meditation on, v.g., the Prodigal Son, after the general confession and before Communion.

[19] The time of the election, which begins on the fifth day (see the second note in [163]) demands the greatest recollection and union with God. However, one or two mysteries of the life of Christ should be given each day during the election—although the election itself should not be pondered during the meditation but after it is over, when the mind is tranquil and free from interior motions.

[20] To this Week belong the Rules of Spirits for the Second Week, as do those of the First Week for the First. The Rules for Food, Alms, Scruples, and Thinking with the Church are only given when the person is engaged in reforming his state of life.

3. THE PLACE FOR THE EXERCITANT TO STAY

[21] Unless the exercitant belongs to our Society, the place for him to stay could be a secluded room in a separate house; this would be more suitable than in our college.

4. The Exercitant's Disposition

[22] He should not begin his preparation for the general confession until after completing the exercises of the First Week. During the time of preparation he should refrain from doing the exercises.

[23] While meditating the second point of the 2nd Exercise [57], the exercitant should not dwell on the individual details of his sins but only upon all of them in a general way; he should be forewarned about this.

[24] First and foremost he must be carefully questioned about what he hopes to get out of the Exercises, the better to direct him, as is indicated in Annotation 18; similarly, his own willingness to dispose himself is what should determine what exercises and help he is given.

[25] The exercitant should observe Annotations 5, 17, and 20; likewise the Additions for the individual Weeks and the Particular Examen to be made upon these; likewise Annotations 12 and 13 about extending rather than cutting short his hour of meditation.

[26] During the First Week, he should have no books to read except his breviary or office of the Blessed Virgin and Gerson [*The Imitation of Christ*]. During the Second Week he should also have the book of the Gospels.

[27] He should write down his insights and significant meditations. It helps for him to engage in humble occupations like sweeping his room.

[28] He can make the election on the counsels and precepts. If he chooses the counsels, he should be asked whether in or outside religious life; if the former, in which institute and when. If he chooses the commandments, in what state of life.

5. The Preparation of the One Who Gives the Exercises

[29] (1) He should read the entire book of the Exercises. (2) He should commend himself to God. (3) He should note each point in his reading. (4) Before giving each meditation he should spend some time pondering it himself. (5) There should only be a single director, to avoid causing confusion. (6) When giving the exercises, he should not bring the book with him but dictate the points from memory. (7) He should not coerce the exercitant into observing Addition 10 on penances, but merely bring the topic up, leaving him free and asking where he stands on the matter. (8) He should find out from the one serving the exercitant how he is behaving with regard to food. (9) If the exercitant replies well at the visits and is making progress, he should not stay for any length of time with him; if the opposite is the case, he should carefully question him about the points, his observance of the Additions, his consolations, desolations, movements of spirits, etc., as indicated in Annotation 6—particularly as regards the grace that is being sought. (10) He should instruct the

one serving the exercitant how to behave with him; i.e., that he should treat him with courtesy, preserve silence except where necessary, show him love and kindness, pray for him, edify him, etc.

Short Directory

This anonymous directory, preserved in the archives of the Belgian Province and dating probably from the 1580s, it was apparently not used in preparing the official Directory. It is notable for its strong stress on the priority of the affections over mere ideas in prayer and on the importance of the director's care for the exercitant. The author also shows a certain concern to ground his statements in spiritual theology. (Original in Latin.)

SHORT DIRECTORY
FOR GIVING THE SOCIETY'S EXERCISES EFFECTIVELY

PRELIMINARY PREPARATIONS

[1] It is important first of all that a person about to give the Exercises should not only have made them seriously once himself, but also have studied and become familiar with the entire book.

[2] He should have the first twenty Annotations at his fingertips, and he should have carefully pondered, prepared, and organized into points or sections the matter for the exercises prior to giving them.

[3] It is a great help to this if on the day just before giving an exercise he meditates it himself with due care.

[4] Finally, he should also have at hand additional exercises—on death, the effects of sin, judgment, heavenly glory, the Prodigal Son, etc.—by means of which, together with other instructions and teachings gotten up for this purpose, he can give the exercitant opportune assistance and direction, particularly as regards the Week currently being made.

PROCEDURE WHEN VISITING THE EXERCITANT

[5] The exercitant should be visited once or twice each day, preferably just after dinner or supper; this is a time in which he less engaged, which is less suitable for meditation, and when he may need advice and consolation.

[6] Moreover, when he is visited he should be asked in a general way about how he is doing, and then in detail about each individual point, particularly those where he has experienced stronger affections or movements in his spirit;

and in detail about whatever was being especially sought in the exercise, v.g., contrition, tears, and confusion when the exercise had been given on sin, death, judgment, hell, etc.; or faith, trust, joy, consolation, etc., when the meditation had been given on the Incarnation, Resurrection, eternal glory, etc.

[7] If he has done well and as desired, he should be congratulated, and one should expend less time and fewer words with him. One should not ask or explain much else, as indicated in the second of the twenty Annotations mentioned above.

[8] However, if the he sees the exercitant being swept away by excessive consolation and fervor, he should intervene in good time to keep him from binding himself hastily and unadvisedly by any promise or vow; he should restrain him by means of timely and wholesome advice, according to Annotations 14 and 15.

[9] If he has not succeeded satisfactorily, one should examine the causes, as stated in Annotation 6, and as far as possible remove them: for example, failure to keep the full time assigned, disregard of the schedule for the hours, failure in properly observing the sequence of exercises or the directives and instructions that were given. The exercitant should be gently instructed and encouraged to carry out the prescriptions more carefully and energetically.

[10] One should also carefully explain to him the method of meditation and, briefly, the elements that could be considered in that mystery, such as the causes, manner, effects, advantages, or virtues set forth there for our imitation. If it appears worthwhile, he should be given some easier exercises which will lead him on to more substantial ones.

[11] The director should above all take care that, when he finds his novice barren and dry at the beginning, never to display the slightest sign of discouragement or annoyance, but to encourage and stiffen the exercitant to perseverance, telling him to keep his hopes up since it often happens (divine providence so disposing) that persons who appear weak, barren, and dry at first receive enormous spiritual illuminations and spiritual consolation during the course of the Exercises.

[12] For at the beginning God sometimes abandons his elect to their own powers, seeming to desert them, so that they will come to know their own frailty and poverty and will abase themselves more deeply; once they have become humble, keeping their eyes upon God as servants do upon the hands of their masters, he enriches them with more abundant graces.

[13] The director should also see whether he lacks light, paper and ink, or anything he needs by way of food. He should also ascertain whether he is getting sufficient sleep, is going to excess in any matter, or is omitting any of the Additions.

[14] He should also ascertain whether he had given exercitant enough time beforehand to tell him confidentially all about himself, and whether it would

be a good idea to have him write down his thoughts and spiritual movements.

[15] Whether he is doing well or poorly, he should be advised that even though a definite number of points—three, four, or five—is prescribed, he is still free to structure the meditation with more or fewer as he sees most helpful for his own progress. Hence, before launching on a given exercise he ought to go over the points carefully and arrange them as he sees fit.

[16] The director should also carefully observe and later reflect back upon what the exercitant tells him about the course and end of his meditation, so as to learn the movements of the good angel, good desires, holy inspirations, and spiritual consolations which he has experienced; or, on the other hand, the temptations, maneuvers, and wiles of the devil, dejection, etc.; so that by studying these he can better guide himself and his novice and provide opportune assistance where needed.

[17] Note also that, while any affection can be elicited from any mystery, some are more suited for producing a given affection than are others. Thus, the meditations or mysteries of the Transfiguration, Resurrection, or glory of paradise engender joy and hope rather than sadness and fear; whereas death, judgment and hell instill sadness and fear more than joy or trust.

[18] However, a spiritually advanced person with much experience in prayer has no difficulty in eliciting great joy, love, and trust from meditation on judgment and hell—as also fear and confusion from paradise. For example, he can reflect that he actually deserved the pains of hell: the very person whom Judas betrayed as a mortal and sold a single time for thirty coins, he himself has over and over again despised and sold, immortal, for some insignificant trifle or pleasure; yet despite his ingratitude God has not only not sentenced him to the same sufferings, but has heaped him with graces and walled him about with divine protection. Recognition of God's enormous mercy toward him fills him with joy, engendering deep hope and love of God.

[19] However, the director should be very careful that the exercitant does not push himself too hard. While he should not be sluggish or lazy but should exert himself, still the primary role belongs to the Holy Spirit; it is the Holy Spirit who stirs the will, draws the soul to himself, and inflames it with the sweet fire of his charity. Sometimes he does this for specially chosen persons more quickly and lavishly, so that the soul is borne Godward in a sudden surge of love, remaining fixed in him, mentally and spiritually beholding him, drawn onward by an inexpressible delight, speaking and dealing with him wordlessly and voicelessly in the silence and privacy of the heart—so much so that, pierced by his appearance and sight as by rays or arrows of love, it faints like the bride of whom it is said: "Prop me with flowers, strengthen me with apples, for I faint with love" [Song 2:5].

[20] However, those to whom the divine Goodness thus suckles with milk from the breasts of charity are few indeed. Meanwhile, those who are not

drawn in this way must be prevented from attempting to raise themselves up in prayer by straining their heads, breasts, or sides, or by excessive abstinence or deprivation of sleep to the point where they seriously jeopardize their health, and also endanger their souls inasmuch as this appears to stem from a certain hidden pride and trust in self that leads a person to think that he is capable of bringing himself through his own effort and initiative to the same point in meditation reached by those other persons through the bestowal of a special privilege. Consequently, they should be taught humbly to restrain themselves, and to get rid of what prevents greater illuminations, i.e., their own faults; for the rest, they should wait upon God's goodness and be content with whatever bestowal of divine favors he vouchsafes them.

THE FIRST WEEK

[21] First he should consider what Annotation 4 says about the character of the Weeks. Then the Presupposition placed just before the Foundation [22] should be tactfully explained first so that the exercitant may be forewarned to take in good part whatever is subsequently done or said; also that he should try never to conceal anything suggested to him by either the good or the evil spirit but tell everything to the director freely and willingly so as not to be led astray by the devil's cunning (see Annotation 17).

[22] This done, he should be given an explanation of what is meant by spiritual exercises (see Annotation 1), and of the value of the Exercises when made and followed properly and perseveringly: knowledge of self, sorrow and confusion for sins, a method for making a good confession, the pursuit of virtue, the amendment of one's life, proper guidance in one's actions, reform of the inward and outward person through the example and imitation of Christ the Lord.

[23] The exercitant should be given an explanation of the part of Annotation 20 that specifically applies to him.

[24] Then he should be given Annotation 3, which explains that the Exercises aim not so much at knowledge and theory as at the affections and activity of the will, i.e., charity and a love, desire, and enthusiasm for virtue—in other words, at the soul's experiencing a more ardent desire to please and serve God.

[25] Indeed, if the exercitant aims not at affections and the moving of the will but at theory and ideas or reasonings, we should deem that he is not praying or meditating but studying. Given that meditation and spiritual exercises are means for obtaining the virtues and God's grace, and that the way virtues are acquired is by acts emanating from the dictate of the will, achievement of the Exercises' purpose requires that the will be enkindled with longing for virtue once the intellect has come to know it, so that, inflamed with a desire to obtain it, it will labor effectively and steadily until it does so, or least

obtains help and grace from God for attaining it.

[26] Once this has been adequately explained, Annotation 5 should be given; and then, finally, the Foundation. For ease in handling and pondering it, it can be divided into three points: (1) the presentation of the end for which God created us; (2) the means he has given for achieving this end; and (3) the difficulty commonly encountered in properly using and employing these means. To this may be added an explanation of the harm which ensues from not taking up the means in the proper order and way.

[27] With this foundation laid, the hindrances which call us back or hamper us from the achievement of this end—all our sins—must be removed by contrition and confusion. Doing this well is the special goal of the exercises of the First Week. The Particular Examen is placed first, to focus the exercitant's first attention on the specific sins that weigh most heavily on him—just as is done with bodily sicknesses—so that, with greater clarity about the enemy's action against him, he will try to fight back by means of frequent acts of contrary justice and virtue until he routs him.

[28] The director should frequently investigate and note how vigorously or feebly the exercitant makes this resistance, supplying him with timely measures and instructions and giving him encouragement and guidance to wage the struggle better.

[29] Then come the four Additions immediately following the Examen in the book of the Exercises [27–31] for more easily uprooting a given fault.

[30] To this is added the more general daily Examen in five points [43].

[31] Finally, to pull out all the weeds infesting the conscience, together with every fiber of their roots, there is the broad General Examen [32–42]. Here one should carefully explain in how many different ways we can sin or merit by thought, word, and deed, as a means for reaching a knowledge of the sins of our entire past life. This is extremely important for making the subsequent exercises of the First Week better and more effectively, and for making a general confession of one's entire life, should the Lord grant the desire to do so.

[32] To encourage this, it will be worthwhile giving the three points just before the 1st exercise [44]. However, this confession should not be prepared or made until near the end of the First Week; there is a single remark to this effect at the end of the three points [44 end].

[33] Note, however, that while these examens are being given the first meditation on the Foundation should still be retained and made. Thus these exercises will last approximately two days—without, however, using the schedule of hours for meditation that will be prescribed for the exercises that follow.

[34] Toward the end of the second day, one should explain Annotations 12 and 13 to help the exercitant understand how he ought to behave with regard

to the prescribed amount of time; also Annotation 16.

[35] To aid in carrying out these Annotations, it will be worthwhile handing him at least of summary of them, adapted to his own person and capacity, for frequent rereading and pondering. This applies to other Annotations and Additions as well.

[36] Then (following the schedule given after the colloquy of the 5th exercise [72]) one should give in the evening, if possible, the 1st, 2nd, and 3rd exercises to be made at midnight, at daybreak, and before dinner respectively. After dinner the 4th and 5th exercises should be given, to be made at mid-afternoon and before supper.

[37] The exercitant should be instructed that, upon completion of each exercise, he should spend a quarter of an hour thinking it over and reviewing it, as indicated in the fifth Addition after the 5th exercise [77].

[38] He should also be instructed that whenever he resolves upon something in prayer, he should never let it go (that would be ingratitude) but carry it out with great eagerness and love of God. In prayer we bring our plans before God in order to learn his own will and preference in the matter; once we have learned it, it us up to us (with the help of his grace, which is never lacking to a good will) to spare ourselves no effort in afterwards putting it consistently into practice.

[39] Note also that each exercise is made up of two and often three preludes followed by several points and one or more colloquies.

[40] The preludes should not be bare acts of looking or imagining; they should be coupled with a longing to make the meditation, and to make it fruitfully.

[41] Many people find it quite hard to make the composition of place, straining their heads in the attempt. Those who have difficulty with it should be told to recall a painting of the history they have seen on an altar or elsewhere, v.g., a painting of the judgment or of hell, or of Christ's Passion. Thus, when beginning a meditation on the mystery of Christ's prayer in the Garden and arrest, they should try to visualize some painting they have seen that depicted Christ praying apart from his apostles, the apostles in a different place asleep, the betrayer coming into the Garden from the other side with the soldiers, torches, and weapons, the betrayer kissing Christ in a different part of the picture, Peter cutting off Malchus's ear and Christ restoring it, the soldiers falling backwards, Christ being seized and bound, etc. This procedure will make it easier for them to construct the imaginary composition of place, from which then to draw themes for the meditation.

[42] The points supply the actual material and substance for the meditation that will be made.

[43] Colloquies are employed. Since all the activities of meditation culminate in prayer, this prayer comes at the end of our exercises; it is carried out in

the form of a conversation. Everything that precedes it—mental reasoning or knowledge of the truth; affections of fear, hope, love, trust, zeal, etc.; holy desires and resolutions—is a kind of preparation for this act of prayer. Prayer begs and implores from God whatever it is that the exercitant has come to awareness of, or else grace and assistance for attaining it.

[44] Thus, meditation gives light and stirs up the affections and warmth, moving and enkindling the soul to pray. For while movements prompting us to prayer cannot be had without a special help from God, they should also come from ourselves; hence we perform meditations and exercises to help stir and dispose ourselves to prayer.

[45] After supper on the following day, the ten Additions should be given that occur in the book of the Exercises immediately after the 5th exercise [73–90].

[46] At this point the Particular Examen should be recalled and employed—not just here but twice every day, before dinner and after the evening exercise, for detecting any faults committed in doing the meditation, as is indicated in the last paragraph of the tenth Addition [90].

[47] Finally, an explanation should be given of the rules of the First Week for discerning the movements caused in the soul by different spirits (these are found right after the meditation on the Passion [sic]). These may even be given in writing—in full or in summary form as the director deems best—so as to fix them in the exercitant's memory and make him familiar with them.

[48] It is up to the director's prudence to give the exercitant instructions accommodated to his capacity, and carefully to investigate which fault principally assails him so as to equip him with salutary weapons against the enemy and urge him to the frequent practice of the contrary virtue.

[49] If, besides the exercises given, the director thinks it worthwhile to furnish others on death, judgment, etc., he should do so, as indicated in the second paragraph following the explanation of the colloquy for the 5th exercise [72, Vulgate], and in Annotation 17. The First Week can be prolonged by adding further exercises of this sort, according to the needs, capacity, and condition of the exercitant.

[50] The repetitions of the exercises, which some may find excessive, are of great importance for the spiritual progress we aim at. It not infrequently happens that persons are so attracted and fed by mental curiosity and the novelty of the topics that they remain content with largely sterile intellectual trains of thought and ideas unaccompanied by affections of the will. This is why persons soon find meditations and spiritual exercises tiresome and get little or no benefit from them. The repetitions are envisaged as a remedy against this.

[51] For the principal purpose and fruit of the Exercises consists in movements of the will's affections toward detestation of sin and love of God. Meditation is like wood fueling a fire. For by meditation on a point from the

mysteries of the life or passion of Christ the Lord, or on heavenly glory, God's love for us, reformation of life, etc., a certain forceful movement of the will stirs in us if we have penetrated the points of the meditation through careful and persistent mental cogitation; this movement stimulates and inflames us to acts of the virtues—love, fear, hope, trust, compassion, sorrow, imitation, etc. And this, as we have indicated, constitutes the purpose and aim of meditation. However, I do not mean that we should stop just with the affections and delights, but that, under the lure and stimulation of these pleasures and delights, we should move onward toward the actions which arise from these affections, i.e., the pursuing of virtue.

[52] To foster this enkindling of the affections, it is worthwhile to ponder and carefully estimate whatever in the assigned mystery the intellect represents to the will as having been done for us by almighty God. This estimation will give rise to love. For example, when we weigh our own vileness and offenses against the will of God, and all that God's goodness has nevertheless done for us, and constantly does for us, we are certainly stimulated to love him. How could we fail to have a burning love for one who we see has spontaneously given to us, so utterly unworthy of even a kind thought from him, both himself and so many other enormous goods?

[53] What the ninth Addition says about not looking at anybody, etc. [81], needs to be applied to all created things. We should not only restrain our eyes from looking at persons, but also from looking curiously and unnecessarily at anything whatever for sensual enjoyment during the time when we are engaged in meditating topics aimed particularly at fear, sorrow, and confusion. Moreover, while meditating sacred things we should keep our eyes shut so as to bridle our appetites; for "out of sight, out of mind."

[54] The directives on penance in the tenth Addition [82–87] should be adapted to the exercitant's situation and degree of progress. Great care must be taken here that excessive fervor does not lead to extremes; the sagacious director and teacher should prudently moderate in all these matters.

[55] Note, however, that one should never impose any penance—the exercitant must be free to perform them or not according to his own wishes or devotion. However, one may suggest that it would be helpful for him to undertake some penance voluntarily (but with the director's knowledge) in order to obtain remission for his sins and to share in the pains and sorrows of Christ crucified.

[56] For this purpose, and in token of greater humility, it could also be helpful if mental exercises, which cannot be sustained indefinitely without prejudice to one health, are occasionally set aside and, during the time of the retreat, even persons accustomed to living in comfort and being waited on by numerous servants sweep their own rooms, set the table, fold up the table linens after meals, make their beds, etc. Such acts of humility for religious

motives are very pleasing to God and marvelously dispose the soul for an increase of grace and virtue.

[57] Further, what is stated in the first point of the 2nd Exercise [56] about reviewing places, duties, etc., in order to consider the full extent of one's sins should be understood to mean doing this in a general rather than particularized way. Arousing sorrow is fostered less by fine and detailed examination of individual sins than by an overall view of the more serious sins of one's entire life; for when a person who is still weak and unsteady goes into great detail on his past sins he risks finding distraction or pleasure rather than confusion, or at least some sort of disturbance.

[58] Upon completion of the 5th exercise [65] and any others that may have been added to arouse increased sorrow and contrition, if the exercitant had brought up the general confession earlier he should be told that now is the time to prepare for it; if it had not, he should invited to make it and told to review the advantages of this confession that had earlier been presented to him [44]. However, it will help in making the confession more fruitfully, and in being able afterwards to deal with the director with the same freedom and less shame, if he makes use of someone other than the director to hear his confession. But if he strongly urges the director to hear it, he should not be refused.

[59] While preparing this confession, the exercitant should do no other exercises; suspending all meditations and other occupations for the time being, he should devote himself exclusively to this preparation for an entire day, or even two if necessary, so that he can make the confession more fully and completely.

[60] An exercitant desiring to continue the Exercises past the general confession should, after he receives holy Communion or, if a priest, says Mass, take a rest from his exertions until evening—unless perhaps it seems advisable, in order to prevent his having nothing to do at all, that he be given some something to meditate that is easy and pleasant, v.g., the Prodigal Son or the observing of God's commandments authentically and out of perfect love.

THE SECOND WEEK

[61] An hour and a half before the evening meal on the day of the general confession, the exercise of the Second Week on the Kingdom of Jesus Christ should be given, to be made during the hour before supper. Afterwards (or, should the exercitant be so weak or worn out from his past labors as to require it, on the evening of the following day) he should be given the meditation on the Incarnation, to be made at midnight; the 2nd meditation, on the Nativity, for daybreak; and the 3rd to be made at nine o'clock or a little earlier.

[62] Then, after dinner, he should be given the 4th meditation—a repeti-

tion of the earlier ones—to be made at about two o'clock; and finally, an hour and a half before supper, the 5th meditation—as indicated in the second of the five notes following the 5th meditation for this day [128]. The director should carefully read and observe these notes before launching into the Second Week, especially the fourth [130], about the changes in the ten Additions that are supposed to be made for different exercises. Basing himself on these, a skilled director will be able to devise and apply special Additions for the individual exercises.

[63] The director should also study the three notes found in the book of the Exercises just after the contemplation for the twelfth day on the events of Palm Sunday, and just before the Three Modes of Humility [162–164]. These will instruct him which exercises to present and explain at the appropriate time, and shed light on how to give these exercises well. Together, these materials provide a full treatment of how to give the exercises of the Second and following Weeks.

[64] Note also that, as in the First Week, one should in this and the following Weeks urge the exercitant to use the Particular Examen for detecting faults committed in the practice of the exercises, Annotations, and Additions, as is remarked just before the Second Week [90] and in the fourth note just after the 2nd contemplation of the Third Week [207].

[65] Throughout this Week the individual contemplations or exercises should comprise a preparatory prayer, three preludes to be varied according to the subject matter (see the note attached to the third prelude of the exercise for the first day of the Second Week [105]), and three colloquies in which I feelingly address either the individual Persons of the holy Trinity (the Word, however, under his human nature), or, instead of a divine Person, the blessed Virgin or some other important personage in the mystery, asking them, in accord with whatever affection I feel at the time, for help in reaching true imitation of my Lord Jesus Christ. At the conclusion, an Our Father.

[66] Note further that, in meditations for which no preludes or colloquies are assigned in the book, one should use those of the first day, adapting them to the requirements of the particular mystery as indicated in the note after the meditation for the fifth day [159]; this note outlines the procedure for making and repeating the meditations of the sixth, seventh, eighth, and remaining days.

[67] The director should make sure that the Particular Examen is made twice a day on defects in the day's meditation and in observance of the Additions.

[68] Note also that a repetition of any of the following exercises is possible, especially where the exercitant has experienced much consolation or some other good affection. If it has been little, a repetition of two or more exercises at once should be made, depending upon the likelihood of greater or less fruit. However, these contemplations or exercises can also be transferred or changed

for others as the director thinks worthwhile, just as they can sometimes be omitted for the same purpose, as indicated in Annotations 18 and 19 and in the first note after the twelfth day of this Week [162].

[69] Regarding the election, note that the directives for making a good election should not be given to anyone who does not want to decide his state of life, nor to anyone who is not indifferent as regards following the counsels or the commandments and not fully resigned in the hands of the Lord and ready to do whatever he concludes is most pleasing to him.

[70] Thus, the methods for making an election should not be given to religious of our own or another order, since these already have, at God's call, obtained their state of life. These persons should be given the remaining exercises, however, so that, by meditating on how God has been so good to them and has snatched them from the dangers of secular life, they can find greater joy in their vocation, being more and more confirmed in it and rendering constant thanks to God.

[71] Moreover, both these and all other persons should have the Three Degrees of Humility and the three Methods of Prayer carefully explained to them, along with the eight Rules of the Second Week for the Discernment of Spirits.

[72] Even while engaged in his election, a person about to make an election could still be given one or another mystery from Christ's life to meditate and to repeat on the same day; however, it ought to be one that will help guide him in the business of the election.

[73] The issues to lay before a person deciding his state can be the following: (1) whether to follow the counsels or the commandments only; (2) if he chooses the counsels, whether he should observe them outside or inside religious life; (3) if the decision is for religious life, the religious order in which he thinks he will observe them most readily; (4) when and how he will enter the order. On the other hand, if his decision is to observe the commandments only, in what state of life he should observe them, with what manner of living, etc.

[74] It was stated above that on the day when he is engaged in the election the exercitant might meditate one or another mystery from the life of Christ or the like. However, the exercitant should not ponder the methods for making an election during the time of the meditation. Rather, it is after the exercise is over, and when the mind is altogether quiet and tranquil, that the right time has come for taking up and pondering the methods of election. Hence it is important to ensure that the meditations are made at their proper times and that they are such as will bring the exercitant consolation and dispose and strengthen him for the election, as indicated in the note to the three times suitable for making a correct election [177], located in the book of the Exercises just before the first of the two methods for making a good election.

[75] Since it is stated in the second paragraph on the time for making an election [176] that a vocation is recognized through the experience of consolation and desolation, it will not be inappropriate to give the exercitant a good explanation of what these consist in. Consolation, then, is a spiritual eagerness, a love and hope of supernal realities, fervent desire to serve God, great trust in God's goodness, and, in fine, any interior movement that leaves the soul tranquil, serene, consoled, and so fired with love for its Creator that it will love nothing except for his sake, as indicated in rule 3 of the First Week for the Discernment of Spirits.

[76] Desolation, on the other hand, is a sadness infesting the soul, lack of trust, disquiet, lethargy, lack of love, dryness in the affections, and darkness in the mind, as is stated in rule 4.

[77] During the election, a good procedure is to lay before almighty God one side of the issue under consideration on one day, and the other side on the next, conferring intensely with him to see on which side God gives clearer signs of his divine will through these methods of election—the way a butler will present different foods and dishes to a prince, noting which he prefers so as to have the same prepared for him in the future.

[78] The Rules of the Second Week for the Discernment of Spirits should be given to the exercitant immediately after the first method for making a good election, to assist him in making the election well and to equip him adequately against the other difficulties that can occasionally arise.

[79] The Rules for Regulating one's Eating, for Distributing Alms, for dealing with Scruples, and for Thinking Correctly with the Church should not be given to the exercitant as a matter of course; however, they can be given, if needed, toward the end of the Second Week in cases especially where a person is engaged in a reform of his state of life, since that is their purpose. Hence the director should be familiar with these rules and notes so as to give better advice on individual situations as they arise.

THE THIRD WEEK

[80] During the Third Week, the same procedure as in the Second should be preserved in visiting the exercitant, giving the exercises, and meditating them. That is, the 1st contemplation should be made at midnight, the 2nd at daybreak, a first repetition about the time of Mass and a second at mid-afternoon, and finally the application of the senses at supper time, always with the preparatory prayer, three preludes adapted to the subject matter, and one or more colloquies, as indicated in the note following the 2nd contemplation of the Third Week [204], which should be carefully considered before beginning this Week.

[81] In addition, one should ponder the two notes in the book just after the seventh day [209], about shortening or lengthening this Week.

THE FOURTH WEEK

[82] In this Week the director and exercitant should follow the same procedure as in the Third, making the appropriate changes in the preludes, points, and colloquies. I.e., the first three points are a consideration of the persons, their words, and their actions, as indicated for the first point of the 1st contemplation [222] and the note that follows it [226]—the procedure for the two remaining points being given in the fourth and fifth points of the 1st exercise. The director should carefully read and think all this through before embarking on the Fourth Week.

[83] The meditations for the individual days should be taken from the series of Christ's appearances after the Resurrection; these can be found in the section of the book containing the mysteries of the life of Christ the Lord, just after the mystery of the burial [299–311]. To them can be added a final meditation on the Ascension.

[84] As for the Contemplation for Arousing Spiritual Love in us, it may be given during this Week, or in the Third or even the Second, depending on the exercitant's needs and the director's judgment—as also the Methods of Prayer with their rules and notes.

Let this suffice for the guidance of the one who gives the Exercises.

For the greater glory of God.

Jesus.

Method and Order for Giving the Spiritual Exercises

The following are two separate anonymous documents transcribed by the Jesuit historian Orazio Torsellini, one a set of directives (nos. 1–15) and the other specification of the benefits and aims of the Exercises (nos. 16–18). (Original in Latin.)

METHOD FOR GIVING THE SPIRITUAL EXERCISES

[1] First, the benefits of the Exercises should be given, along with the Principle and Foundation.

2nd. The Additions, which should be read after dinner and supper until fixed in the memory.

3rd. The 1st exercise, with the Additions at the same time or somewhat later.

4th. The 2nd exercise.

5th. The 3rd exercise, i.e., a repetition of the 1st and 2nd.

6th. The method for discerning sins.

7th. The 4th exercise, i.e., a repetition of the 3rd.

8th. The fifth exercise, on death.

9th. The sixth exercise, on particular judgment.

10th. The seventh exercise, on the universal judgment.

11th. The eighth exercise, on hell.

[2] Note that during this Week, when the exercises are being given on death, judgment, and hell, Denis the Carthusian's book on the Four Last Things[1] should be read during free time.

[3] During the Second Week, since Christ's mortal life is being meditated, the New Testament should be read.

[4] During the Third Week, when the Passion is being meditated, Tauler or someone else on the Passion should be read.

[5] Those who will be meditating the First Week only, or just a little from the Second, may be given the second and third Methods of Prayer found at the end of the Week in the printed Exercises, etc.

---

[1] For the readings mentioned here and in par. 4, see Doc. 21.23 and footnotes.

[6] As a preparatory prayer, the less educated can recite the Our Father, Hail Mary, Creed, and the prayer "Direct, we beseech you."[2]

[7] The individual exercises should be given to the exercitant to write out, but without confusion, so that none is given until the preceding one has been completed. Thus, he will write them out in the evening; but the director should then come as well and explain all the points and individual words, giving him a little instruction anywhere he gets stuck, leading him by the hand as it were and pointing out areas where he would be able to derive more fruit, with advice to dwell more on these, etc.

[8] Upon completing an hour's meditation, they should gather the spiritual fruit briefly in writing, v.g., their consolations, desolations, tears in the First Week, joy in the Second, compassion in the Third, etc., as well as the areas or points where these movements were most intense. For the repetitions, however, unless stronger movements were experienced, etc., there is no need to write these again.

[9] Young people in particular should be carefully examined on how they did in their meditation, where they experienced greater spiritual feelings and what they were, so as to determine if they were meditating for the full hour, etc.

[10] If they do not request them, penances should be suggested to them (with discretion and taking the person into account) when they are particularly moved, etc.

[11] Before meditating they should get the individual preludes and points by memory, in substance if not verbatim. If it is needed because they cannot remember, some may use written texts.

[12] Along with the Preamble on Making an Election the exercise on the Call of the Apostles should be given.

[13] When the matter on the three times of making a good election is presented, the exercise on the Miracle at the Wedding should be given.

[14] Along with the first method for a good election [178–183] the exercise on the expulsion of the merchants from the Temple should be given.

[15] With the second method for a good election [184–188] the exercise on the Eight Beatitudes should be given.

Benefits of the Exercises

[16] Union with God (according to St. Bonaventure, this is had through love; love is had through knowledge about God; and this knowledge is had through assiduous meditation).

Understanding of God.

Illumination of the mind and soul of man.

---

[2] The prayer *Actiones nostras:* "Direct, we beseech you, O Lord, our actions by your holy inspirations, and carry them on by your gracious assistance, so that every prayer and work of ours may always begin from you and through you be successfully completed."

Clear knowledge of one's entire life and past sins.

Method for serving God.

Discernment of good and evil spirits.

Care in living unto God for the future and avoiding sins.

Knowledge of Christian living.

Acquirement of virtues.

Knowledge of self.

Recollection of spirit and of our life.

Sorrow for sins if the Exercises are made well

Groundwork for a genuine amendment of life.

Gratitude to God.

Contempt for worldly vanity.

Fear and trembling before the Lord

Acquirement of humility, the foundation of all the virtues.

Reformation of the interior man.

Longing for Christian perfection.

Way of following Christ in this life.

Thing to be sought and asked from God in the Exercises

[17] Perfect knowledge of sins, so far as is possible.

[18] Perfect loathing for sins, so that we loathe nothing in the whole world so deeply as sins.

[18] Perfect contrition for sins, penitence, weeping, tears welling up from filial fear and love—from consideration of their number, gravity, heinousness, and filthiness; from consideration of the enormous offense to God; from consideration of the bitter passion of Jesus, which I have trod underfoot and set at nought by my sins; from consideration also of the infinite goodness of the holy Trinity, which has lavished so many benefits upon me while I have despised them all because of my sins and rendered myself unworthy of them; and from consideration of my own great loss in losing through my sins eternal life, God's grace, the angels' love for me, the saints' intercession, and divine sonship—becoming a slave of everlasting gehenna.

[20] An abiding holy and firm resolve to live a new life and truly to amend all my sins.

[21] The acquirement of all the virtues, since we have sinned by the contrary vices.

DOCUMENT 28

Notes of Father Giuseppe Blondo

The Sicilian Giuseppe Blondo (1537–1598), one of the great preachers of the early Society and twice provincial in Italy, published in 1587 a book of meditations for use by Jesuits when making the Ignatian Exercises. His free adaptation and creation of new meditations for the use of religious (see footnote 1 below) provoked a vigorous plea by Father Diego Miró for strict fidelity to the Ignatian tradition. The following is Blondo's introduction to his meditations. (Original in Italian.)

[1] The Exercises of Father Ignatius, while fully comprising the perfect method of prayer and interior formation for everyone, remain for the most part on the general level, being normally used for seculars who are in sin or who need to change their state or reform their lives. Hence, experience has shown that for them to be of use to our own men in the Society it is essential to adapt and apply them to the latters' state, following the mind and thought of Father Ignatius. This has been done in the Exercises that follow (this, however, does not exclude giving them in their original form to anyone having a need or inclination for it).

[2] Hence, the following exercises have been drawn up, keeping to Father Ignatius' own order and adding certain special elements for our men. Moreover, since he says that other exercises may be added where needed, we have created some new exercises special to our institute, which may be given in accord with each individual's needs.[1]

---

[1] The following are the meditations given by Blondo:
The Foundation of the Exercises.
1st exercise: the nobility and excellence of the soul.
2nd: vocation
Remarks on the General Examen, for our men.
Examen for the general confession, for our men.
Examen for the amendment of a particular fault.
3rd exercise: ingratitude and lukewarmness in the service of God.
4th: sins committed in religious life.
5th: first repetition.
6th: second repetition.
7th: examen on the evil habits of one's past life.
8th: death.
9th: particular judgment.

The Form and Order of These Exercises

[3] These exercises have been structured according to the three ways—

10th: universal judgment.
11th: hell.
12th: the love of God.
13th: paradise.
14th: annihilation.
15th: expropriation.
16th: perfect expropriation.
17th: oblation.
19th [sic]: dedication or consecration.
20th: the benefits of God.
Exercise on the Kingdom of Christ.
Repetition of the exercise on the Kingdom of Christ.
Exercise on the Incarnation.
Exercise on the birth of Christ
Exercise repeating the two previous meditations.
Contemplation by applying the senses to the previous meditations.
Exercise on the Two Standards.
Exercise on the Three Classes of Religious.
Three degrees of religious perfection.
Preamble to Making an Election for a member of the Society.
Three times for making a good election, for members of the Society.
Exercise on the endeavor to move toward greater perfection.
On having an internal attachment to our institute.
On the various grades and states within the Society.
On esteeming solid virtues more highly than learning or other talents.
1st exercise on obedience.
2nd exercise on obedience.
3rd exercise on obedience and its degrees.
4th exercise on the conditions of obedience.
Exercise on having one's conscience disclosed.
On eagerness to have one's faults disclosed to the superior and to manifest one another's faults, with due love.
On accepting penances with good will, even without fault.
On zeal for souls.
On recognizing the image of God in everyone.
On fraternal love between members of the Society.
On each one's laboring with good will at his own task.
On modesty for the edification of one's neighbor.
On poverty.
On the Blessed Sacrament.
On the Washing of the Apostles' Feet.
On the Christ's entrance into the Garden and Agony.
First method of prayer for our men, on the Rules.
The end.

purgative, illuminative, and unitive—which are envisaged and indicated by Father Ignatius. Hence, starting with the purgative way, which for our own men must differ considerably from what it is for seculars, we have added to the Foundation the end of our own institute, together with the means that are peculiar to it and the indifference required in our men.

[4] The 1st and 2nd exercises to be given if it seems advisable are by way of being corollaries to the Foundation: the first on the nobility of the soul as to its creation, and the second on vocation as regards the end of our institute.

[5] The third exercise, on tepidity and ingratitude, etc., corresponds to Father Ignatius' 1st exercise on the sin of the angels. Similarly, the fourth, fifth, and sixth correspond to the 2nd, 3rd, and 4th.

[6] The seventh, on evil habits, etc., aims at our men's perfect interior cleansing and preparation for general confession. For this there is also a General Examen [32–42], with some remarks for those who might need them, to be given along with the third exercise or whenever seems best. This examen is modeled on that of Father Ignatius in the book of the Exercises.

[7] Then follow exercises on the last things: death, particular and universal judgment, and hell. These are followed by a pair on paradise and the love of God for purifying any excessive servile fear the previous exercises might have engendered.

[8] Since for members of the Society perfect interior purgation has to be more than from sins and evil habits, we have added the fourteenth exercise on annihilation and perfect subjection, in order to remove from the soul every blemish of self-esteem, bringing it to enter into the lowest opinion of itself before God. The fifteenth and sixteenth, on expropriation and abnegation, are to detach it from every disordered affection for created things.

[9] For the same purpose, i.e., the soul's perfect abnegation and detachment from self, there are exercises on oblation, donation, consecration.

[10] Finally, as a complement to the purgative way, so that one may no longer abuse God's benefits as before, and as a preparation for the illuminative way, there follows the concluding exercise on the benefits of God.

[11] The exercises on the election have been adapted . . . with a view to the full amendment and interior reform of one of our men in accord with the spirit of our institute, as can be seen in these adapted Exercises.

[12] The matter for this interior reform—to be made, as has been stated, by way of an election—are: evil inclinations, passions, evil habits, principal faults, temptations (especially violent ones), the virtues, divine inspirations, ministries of our Society such as preaching, hearing confessions, praying, etc., and any other actions which may need reforming, v.g., eating, sleeping, studying, etc.

[13] This material will be provided mainly by the seventh exercise of the purgative way on evil habits, by the exercises on the Kingdom of Christ (with its repetition), on the Two Standards, and on the three degrees of perfection.

[14] The way to approach an election on these matters is as follows. For evil inclinations, passions, habits, and faults: where a person has available a variety of means for amending them, in or outside of prayer, he should choose the most suitable and effective, just as, for bodily health, a good physician will choose the best of the several treatments that occur to him; for temptations, the best means for resisting and mastering them; for the virtues, the best means to acquire them; for ministries, the most fruitful method of exercising them; for other actions, the most perfect way of performing them.

More Particular Remarks on Giving These Exercises

[15] The procedure for giving these exercises fruitfully should be drawn from the Annotations, Additions, notes, and other rules of Father Ignatius' exercises, these being applied and adapted to our own men as is done with the exercises themselves.

[16] Although it is quite a task to synthesize this fully, the following are the most widely applicable and important points.

[17] First, one should endeavor to prepare the exercitant to the extent of his capacity, urging him to have a great desire for the perfection to which he is called, and to remove whatever hinders and embrace effectively whatever helps toward it, under the guidance of the one giving the exercises.

[18] Secondly, the exercitant should realize that the seclusion in his room, the silence, and everything else prescribed in the Additions and other notes must be observed not just to the letter outwardly but also and above all inwardly and with a view to what Father Ignatius aims at in each of them; v.g., spiritual recollection in the seclusion in one's room; and so with the others.

[19] Thirdly, he needs a thorough knowledge of all the elements of prayer, i.e., the preliminary preparations indicated in the Additions, the preparatory prayer, preludes, points, colloquies, acts of intellect and will exercised in prayer and how to perform them properly—with special stress on one's going to prayer stripped of any disordered attachment to feelings, illuminations, and spiritual delights, with total resignation to God's will.

[20] While following the order and rules of Father Ignatius' Exercises exactly, the one giving them should take care not to be so bound to these that he cannot, when he deems it right in the Lord, vary and adapt them according to the disposition and capacity of individual persons; likewise, he can drop or add points in the exercises, and abbreviate or expand them, with a view to the purpose of the Exercises, just as an intelligent physician does in dosing his medicines.

[21] There are different grades of persons: the quite capable, the average, the uninventive, the slow-witted. The average need some brief additional explanation, as suggested in Annotation 2. The unimaginative need more am-

plification by way of examples. The slow-witted should be given just a few points with a simple but short explanation. In each case the aim is to guide the soul toward being able on its own, with greater enjoyment and interior profit, to think over the points proposed using its own powers of discovery and to deal with God directly—as can be seen in Annotations 2 and 15 of the Exercises.

[22] With regard to the rules and other directives for praying well that are found in the Annotations, Additions, and other texts of Father Ignatius' Exercises, one should, when dealing with the first grade of persons, neither urge upon them things they already know nor hold them to such fixed procedures, since they are already experienced in praying well. The second group has greater need of them, since they aid them be more recollected and serve to strengthen their mediocre powers. The third grade need to observe them more exactly, since they provide them an effective stimulus. With the last group, incapable of such exactness, there is probably no use trying to bind them to all these rules.

[23] Experience has shown that it is important that the directives that are to be given to everyone not be presented all at once (see Annotation 19) but little by little, according to the occasion and the disposition seen in the exercitant when receiving the account of his prayer. This will be seen to constitute a good part of the fruit aimed at, if it is done well.

[24] The one giving the Exercises needs to be quite skilled in detecting the various movements of grace, so that he can second and foster them the way a physician does the movements of nature in his patient. For God leads some persons by love and others by fear; v.g., if during the meditation on death a person is helped more by the way of hope than of fear, the director should second this movement and not worry about the fear that the exercise seems to be geared for; similarly with other matters.

[25] Regarding the purgative way, it has been remarked that there are three sorts of souls needing spiritual purgation: some need much, some less, some little. Those in great need of it (like persons who have lived dissolutely and grown hardened in their passions and evil habits) can successfully be given all the exercises of the purgative way, as their need demands. Those with less considerable faults, after the Foundation and the first two exercises, should be given the third and fourth lightly and then the seventh, with the eighth, ninth, tenth, and eleventh being dropped. Then they should be given the remaining exercises in order. The third group, for example those fresh out of the novitiate or those endowed with a good or timid nature, etc., should jump from the second to the seventh exercise on evil habits, and from thence to the one on paradise, and so forth.

[26] As for this exercise on evil habits, experience has shown that it should be emphasized, and be repeated as often as required. Besides its usefulness for

the general confession, it also suggests particular subjects for the election, as said above. At this time also, if any strong passions are detected in the exercitant, or any deep-rooted and dangerous defects, he can be given the Particular Examen adapted for our men, either for his morning prayer in the form of an exercise or for the time of the two examens, rather than waiting until the last minute at the time for the election.

[27] As for the exercise on annihilation, which is of great importance for the purgative way: in meditating on his miseries and on the sins he has recognized in the other exercises, the person must aim not so much at sorrow and compunction as at forming a low idea and sense of himself, drawing from this light and love for the divine Majesty.

[28] Care must be taken not to give the second exercise, on expropriation, to persons who are not capable of it; it might encourage tepidity.

[29] With persons who are not ready for these exercises, one might prepare them by giving the first Method of Prayer adapted for our men, getting them to prepare in this way for the general confession, and trying to help them with all or some of the above-mentioned exercises, as was indicated for those who are not capable.

[30] As regards the illuminative way: when the exercise on the Kingdom of Christ is given, it is quite helpful have the exercitant at that point, rather than reading Gerson [*The Imitation of Christ*] or the New Testament, read instead the Summary of the Constitutions and the Common Rules with fresh spirit, reflection, and observation of whatever the Lord may send by way of inspirations, special interior insights into the Institute, and light on how he may have failed against his vocation in the past—taking these rules as the law and manual of discipline of the army of Christ's Kingdom to which he is called.

[31] Regarding the above-mentioned interior reform by using the election, note first that, unless the exercitant is determined genuinely to aspire to the third of the three degrees of perfection mentioned in the corresponding exercise,[2] there is little use in pursuing his reform by means of the election, as one incapable of this for the present. He either needs additional preparation, or efforts have to be made to bring about his full amendment by some other means such as the Particular Examen on a fault, instructions, admonitions, etc.

[32] Secondly, persons who are ready to make the election, but fall within the above-mentioned fourth class of persons with poor intelligence, can be helped through use of the four points of the second method of election [184–187].

[33] Thirdly, for persons who do better at affective than at highly discursive prayer, it is more helpful to make the election by way of the second time.

---

[2] This exercise of Blondo's (see the list in note 1) is an adaptation of the Three Degrees of Humility.

[34] Fourthly, quite often all three of the times concur and reinforce each other for a better election.

[35] For clarity in the second time of election, and for the profit of the exercitant, it is very important to have a full knowledge of the movements of the different spirits in members of the Society. For, just as is done with the rest of the Exercises, it is quite helpful to make an application of Father Ignatius' Rules for the Discernment of different Spirits in the purgative and illuminative ways; for just as Father Ignatius first lays bare in the purgative way the movements of the good and evil spirit, and then proceeds to explain how to deal with each, so it is likewise suitable to explain for our own men the movements of different spirits which customarily occur in them.

[36] Thus, as Father Ignatius in the first rule for the purgative way sets forth the effects produced by the devil and the good angel in sinners, so in our own men we see the two spirits producing similar movements in the tepid and imperfect: the devil arouses satisfaction with their insincere life and evil liberty, as well as darkness and confusion, discontent, and boredom. The good spirit produces the opposite sentiments.

[37] And just as Father Ignatius sets forth the different movements of these spirits in persons who are resolved to abandon sin and go from good to better, so also with those of our own men who are beginning, going forward, and perfect: the evil spirit exaggerates the difficulty of the way of God, instills doubts about being able to last it out, misgivings about one's own imperfections, inordinate desires for spiritual delights and sentiments, for a change of occupation or for retirement, immoderate zeal for souls, etc.

[38] Here the deceits of the devil should be clearly exposed, and the means for overcoming them should be given. The same should be said of the various illusions of the intellect that can occur in the way of God.

[39] Finally, we have experienced that the procedure outlined by Father Ignatius in Annotation 19 for giving the Exercises to busy persons, using an hour of prayer with the two examens, is quite successful in giving Exercises of this sort, particularly for men who have no special need or inclination to make them in seclusion with more hours of prayer. For in this way, besides their being easier, they are willingly embraced by everyone, prayer and one's regular duties not interfering with each other. In fact, our men can learn to unite to their activities devotion as well; moreover, because of the longer duration of these exercises, the men have more frequent contact with their superior and spiritual father, obtaining full instruction in prayer and virtue for a lifetime.

[40] These persons, in lieu of seclusion in their room, can be advised to cultivate special interior recollection; to make use of darkness, light, etc.; to habituate themselves to seeing God in all creature and raise themselves to him by means of them; to refrain from laughter, etc.; to observe with care the Rules of Modesty and custody of the senses; to spend more time in prayer; to

acquire the habit of ejaculatory prayers and of recalling frequently throughout the day the sentiments had during the morning's prayer; the use of external mortifications and penances; frequent acts of solid virtues and of interior mortification, not excluding exterior mortification under the direction of the one giving the Exercises.

[41] With persons who have weak heads and cannot manage an hour of prayer, it has proved quite successful to give them the same points for them to think over during the day as often as they can—in the same way that Father Ignatius describes for making the meditation on the Three Degrees of Humility and on the seventh day of the Third Week [208, end], or as a person does with any matter that he has deeply at heart.

Notes of Father Jerónimo Ripalda

The noted spiritual director and writer, Jerónimo Ripalda (ca. 1537–1618), has left us one of the clearest and most succinct syntheses of the directives on prayer scattered throughout the Exercises. (Original in Spanish.)

PRENOTE TO THE REMARKS OR COMMENTS MADE
BY FATHER JERÓNIMO DE RIPALDA
ON THE BOOK OF THE EXERCISES OF
OUR FATHER IGNATIUS OF BLESSED MEMORY

(This was placed here separately because it was copied much later than the points.)

[1] There are two elements in the book of Exercises and ways of mental prayer given us by our Father Ignatius. One might be called the form, the other the matter. Thus, the book of the Exercises contains formal and material elements. The material elements comprise the topics for meditation—the exercises of the First Week on sins, death, etc.; those of the Second and Third on the life and death of Jesus our Lord; and those of the Fourth on the Resurrection, the benefits of God, the articles of the Creed and commandments.

[2] The form, or formal aspect, are the activities, directives, and methods to be observed while meditating. These are taught by our blessed Father Ignatius in the Annotations placed at the front of the exercises; in the Additions; in the numerous Rules for the Discernment of Spirits, Scruples, Temperance in Eating, and Giving Alms; as well as in other directives within the exercises themselves.

[3] However, these directives or instructions can be systematized into a method or practical guide for meditating, all the instructions or Additions being categorized into one of four groups: some for before the exercise or meditation, others for the time when the exercise or meditation is being made, others for after its completion, and others outside but connected with the exercises themselves. All this is briefly summarized below.

INSTRUCTIONS ON THE SPIRITUAL EXERCISES DRAWN
FROM THE EXERCISES THEMSELVES BY FATHER JERÓNIMO DE RIPALDA
(IN THE 1574 BURGOS EDITION OF FELIPE DE JUNTA[1])

1. For before beginning the exercises:

[4] 1. The generous spirit with which they should be entered upon, with freedom from all other occupations, offering oneself wholly to the Lord for his Majesty to do with as he wills (Annotation 5).

[5] 2. Selection of the exercise and concentration upon it from the night before, as the director's may judge, letting nothing extraneous come in (Annotations 17–19; note [127]; first Addition [73]).

[6] 3. To recall the meditation first thing in the morning (Addition 2 [74]), and the method for imagining oneself before a judge (note 5 [131]).

[7] 4. To raise the mind a pace or two in front of the place of the exercise, considering that the Lord is present and rendering him interior and exterior reverence (Addition 3 [75]; note 5 [131]).

[8] 5. Preparatory prayer asking the Lord for grace to direct all things, and all our powers and actions, to the greater glory of God (1st exercise on sins [46]).

[9] 6. To picture with the imagination the places, actions, and persons in the exercises (ibid. [47]; exercise on Incarnation [103]).

[10] 7. Petition for the affection of sorrow or joy, depending on the exercise (1st exercise [48]).

[11] 8. Warning against admitting any different sort of affections, even if ordinarily good (Addition 6 [78]; note 1 [127]; Annotation 11).

[12] Note that in this first set of directives, the first three are for just prior to entering the prayer, while the remainder are for after entering it but before starting on the points of the exercise to be meditated; hence we say they are preliminary to the prayer.

[13] *2. For the actual time of the prayer or exercise:*

[14] 1. To think through the points of the planned exercise (1st exercise on sins [50] with the application of the three powers).

[15] 2. To exercise the memory, recalling the history or the matters contained in the points (ibid.).

[16] 3. Then the intellect—thinking over, penetrating, weighing, comparing, synthesizing, or inferring one thing from another (ibid.)

[17] 4. Then the will—spurring myself, moving myself, employing different affections (ibid.)

---

[1] We have replaced the text's page references to this edition with the modern paragraph numbers of the *Exercises*.

[18] 5. Application of the interior senses of spiritually hearing, smelling, seeing, tasting, and touching (1st [sic] exercise of the Second Week [121–126]; 5th of the First Week [66–70]).

[19] 6. To reflect upon myself and make frequent application in each point so as to draw some fruit of teaching, consolation, or movement (exercise on the Incarnation, in the individual points [106–108]).

[20] 7. To dwell on the point or event where I feel devotion, without going ahead (fourth Addition [76]).

[21] 8. Always to end the exercise with a colloquy, speaking to our Lord as in a conversation, like one friend to another (first exercise [54]).

[22] 9. To remember to have greater reverence in the operations of the will, when we speak, mentally or vocally, with the Lord or with his saints (Annotation 3).

[23] 10. To endeavor constantly to incline ourselves to affections opposed to those toward which we find ourselves viciously inclined (Annotation 16).

[24] 11. To spend a full hour on the exercise—rather more than less—whether devotion is present or not (Annotations 12, 13).

[25] 12. To make a repetition of the same exercises, pondering more deeply the points which impressed or consoled one more (3rd and 4th exercises of the First Week [62, 64]).

[26] 13. The method for pondering the individual commandments, sins, powers, and senses ([238]).

[27] 14. The method for Arousing Spiritual Love in us ([230]).

[28] 15. To maintain in the exercise whichever physical posture helps me most (fourth Addition [76]).

[29] *3. For after completing the exercise:*

[30] 1. To reflect upon how one did during the exercise, well or badly, giving thanks for the good, confounding myself and asking pardon for the bad, with a resolution to amend (fifth Addition [77]).

[31] 2. To give an account of whatever is going on inside me to the person giving the Exercises, and making use of his directions (Annotations 6–8; rule 13 for discerning spirits [326]).

[32] 3. When I feel in myself no spiritual movements, to examine in detail how I observe the time and all the Additions (Annotation 6).

[33] 4. Throughout the period of the Exercises, to apply the Particular Examen to them (final addition [90]; [160], [207]).

[34] 5. To remember not to make in the rush of fervor any rash vow without consultation, nor any extraordinary penance (Annotation 14).

[35] 6. To remember also not to make during a time of desolation any change in the resolutions or state of life I had settled on in the time of consolation (rule 5 for spirits [318]); instead to increase my prayer and meditation

against whatever the desolation dictates to me (rule 6 [319]).

[36] *4. Things outside but connected with the exercises:*

[37] 1. To keep the distribution of Weeks, days, and hours for the exercises, for meals, sleeping, and all activities (Annotations 4, 12; 5th exercise [72]), with the procedure for shortening or lengthening the Exercises ([209]).

[38] 2. To obtain a quiet and secluded place, with freedom from all occupations and friends (Annotation 20).

[39] 3. To deprive myself of light (seventh Addition [79]) and refrain from conversations (ninth Addition [81]).

[40] 4. It is most appropriate to avoid words that might arouse laughter (eighth Addition [80]).

[41] 5. To make use of exterior penances in eating, dress, disciplines, staying awake at night (tenth Addition [82–87]).

[42] 6. When one does not find the movement he is seeking, to make a change in his penances ([89]) or remit exercises ([133]).

[43] 7. Make use of the reading of devout books ([100]).

[44] 8. The Methods for praying vocally ([249–260]).

[45] 9. The method for Dealing with Scruples ([345–351]).

[46] 10. The Rules for Discerning Various Spirits ([313–336]).

[47] 11. For Thinking and Speaking Properly ([352–370]).

[48] 12. For Regulating One's Eating ([210–217]).

[49] (All four parts have been carefully corrected.)

DOCUMENT 30

Remarks on the Exercises

In these brief but incisive anonymous notes (ca. 1585–1590), we have replaced the author's page references to 1576 Roman edition of the Exercises with the modern paragraph numbers of the Exercises.

VARIOUS REMARKS ON THE EXERCISES

[1] The Presupposition before the Foundation was placed there, either to ensure a good construction being placed upon what is presented by both disciple (according to Annotations 12 and 17 and rule 13 for the Discernment of Spirits) and master; or else, given the suspicion of holding the heresy of the *alumbrados* that arose against our men in Father Ignatius' time, to ensure that this idea would not be immediately aroused in the hearer by what our men taught according to the Exercises.

[2] The colloquies can be made both vocally and mentally, as is apparently indicated in the first rule after the second Method of Prayer (see [253]) and in Annotation 3.

[3] The points do not all have to be meditated as they are given in the book, as is stated in [76] and [228] (the third note after the 1st meditation of the Fourth Week). The person meditating may reduce or increase the points as he sees fit, provided he has them laid down precisely and definitely from the start.

[4] Neither is it always necessary to do five hours of prayer, or five exercises. In the second note of the Fourth Week ([227]) it says that in that Week it is more appropriate than in the others to make four exercises; it follows that four exercises may be made in the other Weeks also, albeit less appropriately. Hence it is said explicitly in the second note for the Third Week ([205]) that five or fewer exercises may be given, taking into account the exercitant's age, constitution, and disposition. Likewise in [72], just before the ten Additions.

[5] The 5th exercise in the Second and Third Weeks, on the application of the senses, has as its purpose impressing the day's meditations more strongly upon the soul by recourse to the action of the senses. This is clearly stated in the second note for the Fourth Week ([227]).

[6] The exercises of the First Week apparently require a considerable number of days, as is made clear by the third note following the ten Additions

([89]), which mentions doing a given penance for three days, then interrupting it for the same number of days, and taking up different penances at different times.

[7] The first two exercises of the First Week—on the three sins and the review of one's own sins—can apparently be divided up so that a single exercise on each point can be assigned to a single hour. See Annotation 19 and the second rule of the Second Week for spirits ([330]).

Directory of Father Gil González Dávila

A prominent sixteenth-century Spanish Jesuit, serving several times as provincial and for two periods as assistant to the general in Rome, Father Gil González Dávila was one of those chiefly responsible for the composing of the official Directory to the Exercises. In the document below (ca. 1587) he first comments on the earlier directories at his disposal, including those of St. Ignatius, Mercurian, and Polanco. He then describes what he thinks a directory should contain, in effect presenting his own draft of one. His outline is notable for its completeness but also for its theological grounding. Much of this document passed straight into the official Directory of 1599. His reserves about the "spiritual senses" probably influenced the treatment of the application of the senses in the final directory. (González Dávila's references to earlier directories have been adapted to the numbering in this volume. Original in Latin [nos. 1–82] and Spanish.)

NOTES FOR THE DIRECTORY, SENT FROM THE ANDALUSIAN PROVINCE BY REVEREND FATHER GIL GONZÁLEZ

[1] THE REMARKS ON THE DIRECTORIES TO THE EXERCISES WILL BE MADE IN THE FOLLOWING ORDER

I will begin by giving my overall opinion of these directories. I will then make particular remarks on points to be noted or corrected in each one. Finally I will give a brief indication of how I think a directory to the Exercises should be drawn up if it is to provide a full and complete treatment of the matter. I will indicate which materials can be selected from these directories where one or another author handles a topic more fully.

[2] I prefer Directory A by Father Polanco [Doc. 20] to all the others for its clarity of style and its organization, and because it is a fuller and far richer presentation of the essential teaching in this matter. In comparison with this directory, the others are defective and truncated. The outlines of the exercises at the end of this directory I would by all means retain for the use of our men who will be giving the Exercises. In this summary the author furnishes what is prescribed in Annotation 2 but has hitherto not been implemented: that the

director should have written texts available to leave with the exercitant. Up till now our men have been leaving the written exercises in our Father's own wording as circulated in the book of the Exercises.

[3] The anonymous Directory B which follows[1] contains much noteworthy material of considerable value for our men in ministerial work. However, it appears to be incomplete. As the author himself acknowledges in nos. *488* and *489*, he has omitted discussion of the methods of praying and meditating and of the exercises of the First, Second, and Third Weeks. What follows, down to no. *493*, has no connection with what precedes. Again, nos. *493* to *504*, from an earlier directory have been stuck in here with no regard to order. In no. *495* there begins a chapter 7, whereas there are no preceding chapter divisions. At no. *505* the entire treatment of the election breaks off suddenly, almost in mid-sentence; compare this with no. *83* of the previous directory. I conclude that someone else tacked this on, and that the author of this directory had omitted these topics altogether.

[4] No. *506* seems to begin another directory by a different author. Since it quotes Father General Mercurian in no. *518*, it must be fairly recent. It gives quite brief summaries of matters treated much more fully elsewhere.

[5] No. *539* begins yet another directory, as the title itself indicates. A few points could be excerpted from it for our purpose; the rest is given more fully elsewhere.

[6] At no. *570* we have the points dictated by our Father of holy memory, apparently received and then written up in a fuller style by Father Vitoria [Doc. 4]. I would insert them at the appropriate place, viz., in the treatment of ways to attract people to the Exercises and of the dispositions needed in the exercitant.

[7] Our Father's letter[2] at no. *579* I would preserve in the directory (preferably entire, or at least abridged) as a witness to our men of how highly they should esteem the Exercises.

[8] The sections certainly by our Father Ignatius, nos. *581–604* [Docs. 1, 2, 3], should be inserted at the appropriate points in the directory under his name and preserving as much as possible the gravity of his style. As is only right, these pages will always enjoy special weight and esteem among us.

[9] Nos. *605–635* [Doc. 4.10–30] are not by Father Ignatius himself, as is clear from no. *623* However, the were drawn up from his dictation by Father Vitoria, and will be quite useful for our purpose.

[10] Directory C, by Father Miró [Doc. 23] was put out some years ago. I have always thought its instructions insufficient for a future directory for the use of our men—even though it has been widely received, and approved by

---

[1] No longer extant. It contained materials from Docs. 1, 4, 18, 19, 20.
[2] This is the letter to Manual Miona; see Appendix 1.

almost daily use on the part of our men.

[11] Directory D,[3] which comes last, seems to be patched together from the previous ones, but it does give a quite useful treatment, brief and rather well organized.

[12] This will suffice for an overall estimate of these directories. I will now discuss each individually, as I indicated above.

REMARKS ON DIRECTORY A [FATHER POLANCO, DOC. 20]

[13] A few criticism and remarks:

No. 54. I would note that more sluggish or negligent persons ought to be urged to do some exterior penance. This kind of penance not only is important as a penalty and satisfaction for sins, but is also remarkably effective in disposing a person to obtain contrition and sorrow for the offenses of one's previous life.

[14] No. 66. The ideas here on the application of the senses from St. Bonaventure are pretty remote from ordinary human sense and too subtle to be given to simple and unexperienced persons like the general run of those who come to the Exercises. For those who are trained in these senses it will suffice to give the reference to Bonaventure. Inasmuch as many persons are altogether ignorant of this practice of applying the senses in meditation, or do it ineffectually, it will be worthwhile giving an explanation which is clearer and more adapted to the ordinary person.

[15] No. 76. He calls the ordinary and common way the "way of the commandments." I agree with the idea but not with the expression, inasmuch as the keeping of the commandments comprises the complete perfection of the Christian life.

[16] Ibid.: "If that should be what God prefers," etc. This refers to following the counsels of Christ, which are without any doubt what God prefers, since they are better and more perfect. St. Paul says that whoever does not marry does the better thing [1 Cor 7:38.] However, many people have obstacles which hold them back from following the counsels even though they would be otherwise ready to.

[17] No. 78. I would not say "in an even balance," but rather that the soul should be more inclined toward the counsels, as our Father Ignatius himself taught.

[18] No. 82: "What is the better thing considered abstractly is not the better thing for every individual." In the very last article of the *Secunda Secundae* St. Thomas teaches the contrary. Hence this probably should be corrected according to his teaching.

[19] No. 91: "To have a thorough awareness (*persentiscere*)," etc. This word

---

[3] No longer extant.

has been much criticized. Explained according to sound doctrine it is not dangerous, but since such expressions are abused in Spain by the *alumbrados* and *dejados*, I would prefer to make clear the mind of our Father Ignatius, rather than use this word without distinction.

REMARKS ON DIRECTORY B [FATHER MERCURIAN, DOCS. 18 AND 19]

[20] Doc. 19.9. The remark here in commendation of the Exercises, to the effect that the treatment of the election contains unprecedented and amazing teaching, as well as those in Doc. 18.2–3, about Christ having given the Exercises to our Father Ignatius in their precise order, and their being much like the sacred Scriptures, I would drop altogether, lest some persons be constrained to find us lacking in modesty in our commendation of these things.

[21] Doc. 18.13,18. I like what is said here about the division of the Exercises according to the threefold way: purgative, illuminative, and unitive. It is in close agreement with what our Father Ignatius teaches in the Annotations. Nevertheless, I would like a clearer and fuller explanation of this so that our men can be better equipped to approach giving the Exercises.

[22] Doc. 18.47. I would correct what is said here about instructing religious. Even if they have sometimes have not been given to mental prayer they still need to be instructed and treated in a particular way, differently from seculars.

[23] Doc. 18.52. The method of election is highly commendable for handling and deciding actions to be carried out. But I would not advise using so much deliberation for choosing between two virtues, or two degrees of humility.

[24] Doc. 18.54. The book of the Exercises should be given out only very rarely, and only to those who have completed the Exercises in the fullest form and appear able to make use of the book for further progress.

[25] Doc. 18.56–61. I would omit these paragraphs on forming our own men in the Spiritual Exercises. I would relegate these matters to the Constitutions and the Rules of the Novice Master.

[26] Doc. 18.107. While it is very important to recommend living one's entire life in the Lord's sight, I am not much in favor of what is taught here about the presence of God under some physical image. This type of meditation is extremely damaging to the head and on that account is disapproved of by masters of the spiritual life. It also gives ready access to delusion and the devils' sleights.

[27] Doc. 20.73ff. As noted above, these paragraphs are from Father Polanco, transposed here out of order for no good reason.

[28] Doc. 4.8. Such visits, even by our own men, should be allowed only with great circumspection and very rarely.

[29] Doc. 4.17. All the other directories prescribe more frequent visits to the exercitant, and this is confirmed by the old and longstanding custom of the fathers and by our men's almost daily practice.

[30] Doc. 4.21. The assertion that the words "He that can take, let him take it" sometimes imply an absolutely obligatory command I consider errone- ous and in need of correction. In general, what is here given on the election is handled much better in other directories.

REMARKS ON DIRECTORY C [FATHER MIRÓ, DOC. 23]

[31] Doc. 23.2. I am not in favor of lumping together all the statements on the Spiritual Exercises from the Constitutions. They should be inserted methodically in their proper places.

[32] Doc. 23.48. I would advise having the exercitant make some repeti- tions of earlier exercises during the time he is preparing his general confession, especially if he takes a long time on it, for fear it may turn into a dry and barren scrutiny of his past life and sins.

[33] Doc. 23.50. The meditation on the Prodigal Son, if used at all, is far more useful and appropriate for the time preceding his confession of sins.

REMARKS ON DIRECTORY D [NO LONGER EXTANT].

[34] A person who appears altogether unfit for religious life because of natural infirmity or other apparently insuperable impediments should by no means be urged to the religious state. Experience shows how their fervor later cools and the natural impediments and difficulties create great problems for the persons. The result is that they eventually abandon religious life or remain in it to their own and others' harm. For while "it is easy in the eyes of God on a sudden to make the poor man rich" [Ecclus 11:23], we nevertheless see that the above-mentioned things do happen quite frequently—unless the calling from God is such that we can expect a particularly abundant assistance of grace to overcome all difficulties.

[35] These directories ought to explain those passages in our Father's book of the Exercises which are somewhat obscure and have been called into question by some not overly impartial critics, so that our men can give an account of them if needed. Of itself, the testimony of the Holy See that the Exercises as a whole and in all their parts are highly recommended to every Christian is sufficient. However, we are "debtors to all, wise and unwise" [see Rom 1:14].

[36] Now We Must Address Our Final Point: the Order and Topics for Drawing up a Directory Adequate to Provide Our Men with a Full and Comprehensive Treatment of This Matter

[37] The preface ought to deal with why a directory for the Exercises is needed for our men. The main reasons are the following.

[38] Among the other aids it judged necessary for our men in ministerial work, the First Congregation proposed the drawing up of a directory (title 6, decr. 28). The superior general was charged with this.

[39] For this directory we have a certain number of directives handed down from our Father Ignatius, partly written in his own hand and partly taken down from his dictation. Although he was unable to complete a directory, he left attestation of his opinion about the need for one.

[40] In some places the practice of giving the Exercises is extremely rare. Where it has been kept up, the results have diminished. This type of spiritual instrument, which did so much good at the beginning of the Society, has become less effective and less fruitful because of our own men's lack of skill in handling it. See *Constitutions*, IV, 8.5.

[41] How many of our men are able to give an account of these Exercises? Most do not even have a nodding acquaintance with the rules or Annotations. Methods of praying and meditating from other sources than the directives of the Exercises have crept in—methods which are unsafe and ill-suited to the Society's special vocation.

[42] Our men in the ministries experience less success in aiding the salvation of their neighbor—the Society's sole aim—for no other reason than that, deprived of this spiritual formation, they approach the ministry with unwashed hands, so to speak. Hence I would recommend putting out this directory not merely as for the use of those of our men who will be giving the Exercises but also as a help for our men in any ministry whatever, whether preaching, hearing confessions, or teaching the unlettered and ignorant. See Doc. 20.2; and Doc. 19.3–4.

[43] After the Preface, There Follow Certain Preliminaries to the Rest

1. There should be a statement of what the Spiritual Exercises are and what the term means, as is found in the first Annotation and in the directories. See Doc. 18.12; Doc. 12.2. The term Spiritual Exercises refers to spiritual activities of our mind for the purpose of removing inordinate affections and seeking and embracing God's will—activities not sporadic but sustained so that they deserve the name of exercises. In the Church histories and decrees of councils we find

persons who led a spiritual life withdrawn from ordinary human life called "exercisers," or leaders of a "life of exercise."[4] Scripture also frequently uses the word in this sense, for example in the Psalm [77:7]: "I was exercised, and I swept my spirit."

[44] 2. The usefulness and high value of the Exercises should be demonstrated first of all from the testimonies of the Holy See, in the approbation of Paul III placed at the front of the book. Further, Father Ignatius' own estimation of them, from his letter to Father Miona[5]; and how much he himself was benefited by them at the beginning of his conversion. They are also one of the instruments of the Society for the salvation of souls (*Constitutions*, IV, 8.5, and VII, 4.8). Indeed, proof that from this single instrument all the others derive special effectiveness—their life and spirit—can be witnessed to by the first fathers of the Society as well as by nearly all of our men, who received both the spirit of the Lord and the gift of their vocation through the Spiritual Exercises. Witnesses also are the persons of all orders and states—ecclesiastics, religious and seculars—who through the help of the Exercises achieved outstanding reform and change of life. See Doc. 20.2; Doc. 19.4; Doc. 18.2–10; Doc. 12.4–6; Doc. 23, preface.

[45] 3. As for the particular reason why persons experience so much progress in the Spiritual Exercises, see Doc. 20.4–8: in the Exercises the soul is with the divine grace excellently disposed to receive the gifts of God. It is purged of sins by a confession of one's entire previous life. It is given light to know the benefits of Christ the mediator and is stirred up to imitate the pattern of his life and to undertake the way of life which it believes will be most pleasing to God. Moreover, the person strives to achieve all this by means which are highly suitable and have been established by God for obtaining this end: prayer and meditation, proper use of the sacraments, castigation of the body, and other religious acts. Finally, he cooperates strenuously with divine providence, setting aside completely whatever might distract his spirit and concentrating exclusively on the salvation of his soul. Add to this the exercitant's humility and self-abandonment together with the director's care and foresight. See three reasons for this effectiveness in Annotation 20. In the directories see Doc. 19.4; Doc. 18.7; Doc. 19.9–10; Doc. 12.10–14.

[46] 4. Ways to invite and attract people to the Exercises can be found in the notes taken down by Father Vitoria from our Father Ignatius' dictation, Doc. 4.1–3. In general it is important to make sure that exercitants come spontaneously, not reluctantly; and that their intention is so they can please God more and concentrate better on the salvation of their soul. People need to be

---

[4] This the meaning of the Greek words *askêtês* and *askêsis*, from which we get our words 'ascetic' and 'ascesis'.

[5] See Appendix 1.

led to this stance gradually, partly in familiar conversations and partly in the sacrament of confession. In this way each one will be able to invest his efforts more effectively and with hope of better success.

[47] 5. The attitude a person ought to bring to the making of the Exercises can be found in the book of the Exercises in Annotation 5. It should be a large, generous, and liberal attitude, such that the person offers and hands over himself and all he possesses to our Lord and Creator; that he is free and unimpeded by any other business and concentrates entirely and solely on this one; that he strives by alms and other works of piety and prayers, and by confession and Communion if he is used to them, to prepare himself for this work and "appease the face of the Lord" [1 Sam 13:12] so as to have the Deity's favor in so vital a matter; that he has a high estimate of the Exercises and is eager to be helped by them; that he is obedient to his director and instructor and does not fail to do anything he is told; that he keeps his heart open and conceals nothing, for he will thus be guided more surely and unerringly. Finally, he should be mentally strong and stable.

[48] 6. There should be a treatment of the various types of people who may be given the Exercises (this is closely connected with the previous heading), for they should not be given indiscriminately to all. See *Constitutions*, IV 8.5 and E. The person should be a mature adult of sound judgment and intelligence lest we waste our oil and our toil. Great selectivity must be exercised if we are to keep the Exercises from falling into disrepute; we must use the gift of discretion so as not to build our house on sand. See Doc. 20.10–19. For all of this, Directory B (Doc. 18.20–52,63–73) gives a very thorough discussion and treatment; it should be strongly recommended to all our men in the ministry: it gives handy instruction on how to lead each individual—according to his capacity, age, condition, and talent—toward greater progress in Christian living. See also Doc. 12.17–22 and nos. *745–744* [sic].

[49] 7. The character and preparation needed in the director: according to *Constitutions*, IV, 8.5, he should have previous personal experience of the Exercises; and (IV 8.E) confer his method of proceeding with someone of greater experience, giving the Exercises at first to persons with whom less is at risk. See also Annotations 2, 6, 7, 15, 17, and 20 in the Exercises themselves. He should have acquired a thorough acquaintance with Father Ignatius' entire book of the Exercises, with all the rules and Annotations. He should be kindly rather than severe. He should never give an exercitant cause to suspect that he thinks poorly of him, even should he not have behaved very well; instead, he should encourage him and pray for him, getting the superior to have others pray and offer Mass for him. He should have gotten insight into the exercitant's character, mentality, and situation, so that he can adapt himself to him and fully answer his problems. His entire effort must be to cooperate with God's movement and providence by clearing out of the way, as far as he can, every pos-

sible hindrance. In the directories see Doc. 20.27–33; and Doc. 18.80–93,90–93.

[50] 108. There should be treatment of the place for giving the Exercises and the duties of the one who does the serving. As far as possible, the place should be secluded: see Annotation 20 in the book of the Exercises and our Father's instructions in Doc. 4.4–5. The exercitant should be served nothing at dinner or supper that he has not ordered after being explicitly questioned. Our Father gives quite strict directions for this in Doc. 4.6–7. The one who serves should not talk with the exercitant except about matters connected with the service. Unless the director tells him otherwise, he should keep the room clean and everything else in order. Once each day he should report to the director how much the exercitant has eaten and anything else he has noticed that the director ought to know. He should edify the exercitant by his humility, modesty, and mature behavior. He should pray for him each day. If the exercitant tries to ask him any questions, he should modestly refer him to the director. See Doc. 23.22,45–46.

[51] 9. Indications about the division of the Exercises into four Weeks, and about the correspondence of these Weeks to the threefold purgative, illuminative, and unitive way, will be found in Annotation 14.

[52] The First Week corresponds to the purgative way, the aim of which is scrutiny of one's past life and purgation of sins, along with appropriate satisfaction. The Second and Third Weeks correspond to the illuminative way: they contain imitation of our Lord's life and teaching, and the choice of a life which will be most pleasing to God—all of which is strongly confirmed through the mysteries of the Passion. The Fourth Week, on the Resurrection and other topics presented there, corresponds to the unitive way: meditation of these realities powerfully inflames the human spirit with love for the eternal fatherland, so that it desires "to be dissolved and to be with Christ" [Phil 1:23]. See Doc. 20.41; Doc. 18.13–18; Doc. 12.10; Doc. 23.39,62.

[53] These four Weeks should ordinarily be completed in thirty days, more or less. There is no superstitious value in this length of thirty days, as some have wrongly inferred: it may be shortened or lengthened at the instructor's discretion. Moreover, regarding the Exercises in general and the individual parts we call Weeks, we make the exercitant no promise of finished sanctity in such a short period, as if during these days he is supposed to reach the peak of Christian perfection. All we do is open a way for him to know himself and, with the help of God's grace, embark upon a life that will lead him straight to the eternal blessedness for the attainment of which he was created.

[54] 10. There should be a treatment of how to give the individual exercises when given according to their own nature and in full form. On the other procedures enough is said in the book of the Exercises in Annotations 18 and 19. When the Exercises are being given in full form, the director should visit the exercitant at least once a day—during the First Week twice a day, rarely

oftener—and at any time he thinks necessary.

[55] The best time for this seems to be after dinner and supper. The person is then more agitated by movements; he is free then and not suited for meditating or praying. See Doc. 4.16.

[56] During the visit the director should present a cheerful countenance yet be not unmindful of a fatherly seriousness. He should not bring along the book of the Exercises but should faithfully recount from memory the history of the meditation, going briefly through the main points, and then leave in writing the outline from Father Polanco's summary, as indicated in Annotation 2. The exercitant may prefer to write the points out for himself, but this should be rarely done and should be permitted only for serious reasons. Nevertheless with inexperienced persons and at the beginning of the Exercises some developments ought to be indicated and a path into the meditation opened, lest some uneducated persons might hurt their heads. See Doc. 23.12; Doc. 4.11,14,18; Doc. 18.83,60.

[57] Moreover, the director should be told to keep his speech serious, brief, and suited to the material, meditating beforehand what he will say and commending it to God in prayer. In this way the hearer's mind will be fired and better disposed for prayer. The opposite will happen if the instructor's speech is diffuse and he just talks on without forethought or spirit.

[58] The exercitant should be asked how he behaved, what he experienced, what problems arose, whether he is following all the prescriptions of Annotations 6 and 7. The instructor should always aim at encouraging him to keep hard at it in the future. See Doc. 20.35; Doc. 18.82,93; Doc. 1.5; Doc. 23.17,18.

[59] For his part, the exercitant should, with great candor and concealing nothing in his soul, be completely open with the director so that he can better direct and instruct him, as stated in Annotation 17 and Rule 13 for the Discernment of Spirits [326]. He should be convinced of the great importance of this one point. He needs, however, to be patient. Even if he suffers distractions and dryness, he should "wait for the Lord, and do manfully" [Ps 27:14]. During the First Week reading a devotional book like the *Imitation of Christ* or St. Augustine's *Confessions* may occasionally be helpful. See the final note after the 2nd meditation of the Second Week [100], and in the directories Doc. 20.34; Doc. 18.89; and Doc. 23.14.

[60] It should be said in general that the Annotations, rules, and entire order for giving the Exercises as presented in the book of the Exercises should be followed with the greatest exactness. Our Father Ignatius taught that if these are implemented correctly, the meditations will be very productive; if neglected, the fruit and benefits will be slight.

[61] For the daily schedule of meditations, see the notes after the 5th exercise [72], and the first directory, Doc. 20.51–52. I am not in favor of

always doing the full five exercises on one and the same day; the mass of materials can easily be overwhelming. It will also frequently happen that the meditation will be dry and barren if the mind is engaged in nothing but repetitions for so many days in a row. Add to this the practice of many of the most distinguished fathers who had Father Ignatius as their teacher in giving the Exercises: they would give one or two exercises to be gone through in four or five hours on a single day, depending on the exercitants' various dispositions. Some more fertile minds are scarcely able to get through all the points of a single meditation in one or two hours. Some are slower, some quicker, at obtaining what they seek. Hence this must be left to the director's prudence; and this seems to be in harmony with our Father's remarks in the book of the Exercises.

This Suffices for the Preliminaries to the Exercises; Now We Will Indicate Points Deemed Worthy of Comment or Explanation

[62] The note placed toward the beginning of the Exercises [22] before any of the meditations should nowadays be omitted altogether, or at least for the most part. It was deemed necessary in the Society's early days when neither our fathers nor the Exercises enjoyed such authority and esteem that people could easily be expected to place complete trust in them. This admonition was useful in creating a proper attitude in the exercitant and also in getting him not to hold back anything suggested to him by either the good or evil spirit but to disclose everything confidently. But now that by Christ's grace the Exercises have acquired such authority, the only effect of our baldly presenting this text as it stands would be to fill the minds of those approaching the Exercises with suspicion and fear. See Doc. 20.31 and Doc. 23.24.

[63] In the first meeting, the Foundation should be presented as divided up into points in Father Polanco's summary [Doc. 20 bis.1]. Some amplifications may be added as an aid for meditation. Thus, in the first and second points, after the end for which man was created has been presented, the exercitant can meditate on how much he has strayed from this goal in his life so far, what was the direction of his endeavors, and how many creatures he has abused which were supposed to help him in attaining his final end. In this way he can begin right away to recognize the shamefulness and deformity of his life and, having recognized it, to hate it; to long for that righteousness which consists in charity; and to rid himself of his evil desires and master his disordered affections. In this manner he will prepare the way for the indifference and resignation of self that will be presented in the third and fourth points. Now this single meditation constitutes the foundation of the spiritual structure. For here we are presented with the end of the law, i.e., "charity from a pure heart and an unfeigned

conscience" [1 Tim 1:5]—a charity such that we place nothing ahead of love for God and have nothing in our spirit which could retard or impede it; a charity such that the measure of our love for God should be to have no measure, the law of charity itself laying down the measure and mode for every other; a charity such that we "cast all our care upon him, for he has care of us" [1 Pet 5:7], without ever wavering, in the enjoyment of true peace and calm of soul. However, since hostile critics have wrongly interpreted what is said here about indifference as being derived by us from the Pyrrhonian school, this doctrine should be explained, especially to learned persons, in the light of St. Thomas' teaching in the *Prima Secundae*, q. 13, a. 3; and *Secunda Secundae*, q. 83, a. 5 and 6. The exercitant should be told that the deeper he lays this foundation the firmer will be the structure built on it. Father Ignatius explained how important this is in Annotations 15 and 16.

[64] The Particular Examen is given in the second meeting. During the Exercises this examen is used to remove defects that creep in regarding the Additions and rules of the Exercises, as you will find in the final Addition for the First Week [90]. However, this examen is to be used constantly throughout the exercitant's life. It is extremely valuable, and among all the means for obtaining purity of soul it is uniquely effective and quick-working. Cassian teaches this in Conference v [ch. 14], as well as Bernard on many occasions and other writers on the spiritual life. Indeed, even the philosophers, guided solely by reason, discovered the great advantages of this examen for breaking and taming the lusts of the soul. Hence, although during the Exercises it is not a good idea to spend too much time explaining this examen, at the end, when the exercitant is given guidelines for living well, a fuller and ampler treatment of it can be presented. Note, finally, that the lines which you watch getting shorter as the week goes by are not some superstitious practice but merely indices of mindfulness and care in uprooting each fault. See Doc. 20.46–47.

[65] Note also that the General Examen [32–42] is for daily use, and was composed only for those who have already begun a spiritual life: the types of sins by thought and word which are fully discussed there are the ones more frequently found in such persons, as instanced merely in the manner of swearing by creatures. These matters will be very helpful for one's monthly or weekly confessions.

[66] However, to make a proper preparation for a general confession of one's whole past life it will be necessary to seek instruction from other sources, since what is given in the Exercises is too scanty for the purpose and not as well organized or brought down to specifics as it would need to be. Thus in dealing with sins of thought it passes over almost entirely what the moral theologians say about dwelling on pleasurable thoughts. On sins of deed, it gives the commandments only in a general way. In such a brief treatment it was obviously not the writer's aim to furnish a comprehensive presentation of

everything one needs to know about sins throughout one's life but only to remind devout persons of those which are of everyday occurrence.

[67] A further confirmation of this is that the writer devotes so much care and earnestness to calling for obedience to the directives of superiors when bulls or directives of the popes are promulgated. As with the Particular Examen above, I would advise explaining the value of this General Examen, along with its use for purging the soul and confessing one's sins, at the conclusion of the Exercises.

[68] While being given these matters, which call for explanation but not meditation, the exercitant should continue meditating the Foundation.

[69] The matter on general confession and preparation for Communion is most valuable; however, it should not be given at this point, but at the end of the First Week when the director provides instruction on how to prepare for a general confession.

[70] At this point, before beginning the 1st meditation, the exercitant should be told the purpose of the First Week, i.e., the purgation of sins, with genuine contrition and sorrow, along with a resolve to live a better life and make due satisfaction—so that a person may recognize and grieve that he has strayed from the true purpose and end for which he was created and may strive with all his might to return to the path that leads straight to God.

[71] In this 1st exercise, where one meditates with the three powers of the soul, the exercitant should be given a detailed explanation of all the elements he will be using in the succeeding meditations. For here we are given the method for meditating and praying which we must always follow if we are to make the Exercises fruitfully and without damaging our heads. It is a method highly adapted to our human nature: it makes use of discursive reasoning, which then arouses our spirit and affections—as Scripture says: "In my meditation a fire shall flame out" [Ps 39:4].

First of all, then, he should be taught why this is called "meditation of the three powers," how he is always to use these three powers in the remaining Exercises, and how he must be more concerned with affections and interior relish than with an abundance of knowledge, as is stated in Annotations 2 and 3, for fear that by indulging too much in our own trains of thought our affections may dry up and the heat kindled in the meditation be cooled.

Secondly, he should be instructed how to recollect himself for prayer and prepare himself for dealing with God.

Thirdly, he should be taught the nature and correct use of the composition of place, i.e., to prevent the mind from wandering aimlessly by giving it something to focus its scattered faculties upon so that the prayer will be attentive—and so that if the mind later wanders off, it has a base to which it can easily return. However, many persons spend a lot of time uselessly dwelling on this, and the violent effort damages their head and renders them unfit to go on to the other things for which the composition of place was devised.

Fourthly, they should be taught about the petition in which we place before our eyes the specific aim of the meditation.

And fifthly, they should be taught about meditation itself: about how to use the reason therein, how and when to make the colloquies, and any other relevant matters. This should not all be explained in a single meeting but imparted gradually over a period of time. Some additional thoughts on the ugliness and gravity of sin are usually given for persons who are less quick or experienced in these matters.

[72] In the first point of the 2nd exercise, it is important to warn the exercitant against going into an overly detailed and exact examination of conscience as he reviews the various places, occupations, and persons. This will be done later when he prepares for the general confession. At this point it suffices to focus on those sins which are more serious and can cause him greater shame— in a general way only, for fear that by dwelling too long on particular details he may be infected by the memory of past pleasure.

[73] The practice of the repetitions in the 3rd and 4th exercises is highly to be commended. For it often happens that at first the understanding alone is nourished by the novelty and interest of the topics and there is only very slight interior relish in the will. But later, when the understanding's speculation and interest is largely stilled, there is freer room for spiritual and interior affections. Hence, in these repetitions one should avoid pursuing new trains of thought in the intellect. Instead, once the exercitant has gone over and ruminated his earlier meditations he ought to dwell rather on the internal relish which feeds the will. For this reason you find more frequent colloquies here than in the earlier exercises. Again, it often happens that, where we had at first experienced dryness on certain points, in these repetitions we find a rich and lavish source of divine consolation. For to him who perseveres and knocks, the Lord opens the door of his mercy. See Doc. 19.6; and Doc 23.40–41.

[74] The second colloquy to Christ as mediator, asking him to intercede with the Father, needs to be explained to simpler and less educated persons: he is our mediator and advocate with the Father, and so we do not hesitate to pray that he intercede for us. See Doc. 20.51.

[75] The application of the senses in the 5th exercise is easy, and a great help in meditating the torments of hell. From this meditation the mind conceives a horror of sin. To this meditation can be added the considerations on eternal punishment found in Father Polanco's summary [Doc. 20 bis].

[76] In my opinion the meditations on judgment and death should be omitted only very rarely. The are very important for recalling the mind from an inordinate love of visible things: it is easy for someone who thinks he is going to die to despise all things. Moreover, in these meditations a person conceives a holy fear of the Lord in order to beget a spirit of salvation—

as Scripture says: "Remember your last end, and you will never sin" [Ecclus 7:40].

[77] The best time to explain the Additions is indicated in the directories. Regarding the tenth Addition, I have already stated above how important external penance is and how much it contributes to obtaining sorrow for sins. The degree to which penance was formerly practiced is indicated by the examples of the first fathers who made these Exercises, and by our old rule that men just finishing the Exercises should be listed among the infirm and placed under the person in charge of the sick. See Doc. 23.45.

[78] Once having completed the meditations, the exercitant begins to prepare for his general confession. The advantages of doing this properly are listed in the book of the Exercises after the General Examen [44]. Apart from any other, it would surely suffice that we have such repeated experience of people going to confession either without a careful examination beforehand, or without proper sorrow, or with little or no resolution to amend their lives. Hence, for peace of conscience it is most helpful for a person to prepare himself as carefully as he can at least once for this general confession, so as to "recount in the bitterness of his soul" [Isa 38:15] the crimes and evil deeds of his previous life.

[79] Care must be taken, however, during this examination to keep the exercitant from falling into such excessive or troublesome scruples and mental anxiety that the recollection of his past sins and the aftereffects of the confession permanently deprive him of calm and peace of soul. On the other hand, he should not examine his life so carelessly that he will forever be deprived of peace of soul because he failed to satisfy himself in such an essential matter. Consequently the exercitant should be instructed on the degree of care he should exercise in this matter if he is to enjoy later on the conviction that he did this with all requisite care, for on this alone true peace of soul and tranquillity of conscience depend. A way and method for examining all our actions should be given, lest the person be overwhelmed and confused by their multiplicity; the number of sins generally causes much trouble and the exercitant needs help in figuring out how to get an overview of them.

[80] For this, the director can obtain instructions from Father Polanco's *Directory*,[6] or from other authors.

[81] Included among the recommendations handed on to us by our Father Ignatius was that, if feasible, it is better for the general confession to be heard by someone other than the director himself.

[82] The exercitant should be prepared for Communion so that he will approach it with reverence, fear, faith, and joy. He should be furnished beforehand with some devout meditation.

---

[6] See the note on Doc. 4.29.

The Second Week

[83] The aim of the First Week was acknowledgment that we have gone astray and missed the way that was to lead us to the end for which we were created, along with consequent sorrow for this abuse and a strong desire to follow the way of justice and truth. The aim of the Second Week is to set before us Christ our Lord, the true way, as he himself says: "I am the way, the truth, and the life; no one comes to the Father except through me" [John 14:6]. For he is the sole model given to humanity by the eternal Father and it is by imitating him that we are to amend and set in order our corrupted habits, and direct our steps on the way of peace [see Luke 1:79]. Since, then, the life of Christ is our perfect pattern for all the virtues, we must endeavor to dispose ourselves to imitate him. The nearer we come to this the nearer we will be to our final end and the happier we will be. The more our life conforms to his the more perfect it will be.

[84] For this reason the Second Week corresponds to the illuminative way, for Christ is the sun of justice, "who enlightens every man who comes into this world" [John 1:9]. He came "to enlighten those that sit in darkness and in the shadow of death" [Luke 1:79]. The word and law of God, whose practical embodiment is Christ, is a light and lamp: "The command of the Lord is lightsome, enlightening the eyes" [Ps 19:9]. And so that there will be nothing to blind us or make us close our eyes, we need to have gotten rid of the excesses of our attachments so that they will not keep us from recognizing what is best and will not cool or retard our following and imitating it.

[85] The disposition looked for by our Father in those who are to make the Exercises of this Week exactly is that they show great fervor and desire to go forward to a decision about their state of life. And if we see them somewhat lukewarm about this we should not allow them to go ahead even if they want to. It is better to put them off for a month or two. For if this business is undertaken without fervor of spirit it will not succeed and will have poor and illusory results. It demands great resources and courage stemming from intensified devotion. Of course, in the case of some persons from whom nothing further can be expected, either because they have already made an unchangeable election or for some other reason, we can help them with some meditations of the Second and Third Weeks by way of guidance toward a life more pleasing to the Lord in their present circumstances. With others, however, it is better to leave them hungry and with the awareness that they still have more to do, rather than launch them into something for which they are still ill-prepared. And it sometimes happens that their experience during the time of delay makes them see their need more clearly so that they come then to this work at a riper moment.

[86] The Rules for the Discernment of Spirits at the end are helpful for this

Week when the time comes for the election. The changes to be made in the Additions are indicated at the end of the 5th exercise [130]. At the end of the 1st exercise [100] there is a note that we can make use of religious books, such as lives of the saints, the *Imitation of Christ*, or the Gospel—with the reminder not to go beyond the exercise I am presently meditating.

[87] Once the exercitant, then, has finished his general confession, he should rest on the day of his Communion without being given the usual load of exercises. He may, however, occupy himself with some easy meditation suited to this time. The order and distribution of the exercises of this Week is given in the book of the Exercises, and so there is nothing to remark about it here.

[88] The first meditation is on the Kingdom of Christ. It is the foundation of this entire phase and a summary of the Lord's life and works and of the enterprise he has received from the eternal Father—"his work before him" [Isa 62:11]; "the work which you gave me to do: I have glorified you on earth; I have manifested your name to men" [John 17:4,6]. And he calls men to help him in this task, each in his own degree—which points up the variety of degrees and ways of life in the imitation of Christ. The disposition asked of our exercitant is that on his part he ought to prefer that which is more perfect should the Lord give him strength for it. Hence it is clear that even at this point the exercitant is being prepared for the election, toward which this and the following meditations are all directed.

[89] Note that, as prologue, the meditation on the Kingdom of Christ is not numbered with the rest. Thus the meditation assigned for the first day is that on the Incarnation, followed by the Nativity, two repetitions, and the special meditation of this Second Week on the senses.

[90] Secondly, our Father counts twelve days from the meditation on the Incarnation to Palm Sunday, for once the election is begun fewer mysteries are given for meditation and the exercise on the Standards and other preliminaries to the election take up time. Of course, some mysteries, v.g., the Shepherds, the Circumcision, and the Visitation, are left to the director's discretion, as was said in the First Week regarding the exercises on death and judgment.

[91] Thirdly, five hours of prayer are assigned for each day: two mysteries and three repetitions. However, if one gives the exercitant only four hours to avoid tiring him, there should be only one repetition; the application of the senses should never be omitted.

[92] The meditations on the Incarnation and Nativity should be explained in detail because the rest follow the same pattern. What is taught here is an easy way of thinking about these mysteries by persons, words, and actions, going into the causes and circumstances of the event, etc. Simpler persons need to be given some suggestions for them to take hold of wherever they find sustenance.

[93] In the composition of place the exercitant should act as if present to the entire event. St. Bonaventure says in the prologue to his life of Christ: "If you wish to gather fruit from these matters, make yourself as present to what is recounted about the sayings and actions of the Lord Jesus Christ, as if you were seeing them with your own eyes and hearing them with your own ears. Do this with all the affection of your spirit, carefully, lovingly, and slowly, leaving aside all your other concerns and cares."[7]

[94] The 5th exercise on the application of the senses is highly valuable and appropriate for this, provided that it is carried out plainly and simply. Subtleties in this regard are usually much tainted with mere curiosity and this causes dryness. The more attention given to these anagogical senses the more the fruit of the meditation tends to be lost.

[95] This use of the senses is easy: hearing the words and sounds, touching and kissing the feet of Christ our Lord and the places where he stood. This should be done reverently, without discourteous boldness; emotional people particularly need to avoid mixing in human affections in place of spiritual. Our Father applies the sense of smell to smelling the fragrance of God's gifts in the soul and the sense of taste to tasting their sweetness. In his commentary on Philippians 2:18, St. Thomas applies these senses to intercourse with the Word made flesh: seeing his light, hearing his wisdom, smelling the graces of his meekness ("Draw me after you" etc. [Song 1:3]), tasting the sweetness of his compassion, touching his power in order to be saved.

[96] In chapter 4 of his *Journey of the Mind to God*,[8] St. Bonaventure gives a loftier treatment of this. He says that seeing is the act of faith which makes supernatural things present to us. Hearing is the proper act of faith, which is believing: "At the hearing of the ear he has obeyed me" [Ps 18:45]; this is understanding and believing with the affective power, for these are the two ears of the soul: the understanding and will. Smelling refers to hope. Touching is the union effected by love: "Let him kiss me with the kiss of his mouth" [Song 1:1]; "What we have heard, what we have seen, and our hands have handled— of the Word of life" (1 John 1[:1]). Tasting is of charity: "Taste and see" [Ps 34:9]; "they tasted and were illuminated" [Heb 6:4]—one savors the relish of the eternal tastes, "lest we savor earthly things" [see Phil 3:19]. Employment of the spiritual senses is a sign of spiritual life. See also St. Bonaventure's *De septem itineribus*, iter 4, dist. 1; and iter 6.[9]

[97] The outline of the mysteries of the life of Christ our Lord given at the end should be very helpful—if one attends to the words of Scripture inter-

---

[7] Quoted from the Pseudo-Bonaventuran *Meditations on the Life of Christ* (see note on Doc. 21.23).

[8] See note on Doc. 21.23.

[9] *De septem itineribus aeternitatis*, not by St. Bonaventure but by a sixteenth-century Franciscan named Rudolph of Biberach; edited in Quaracchi, *Opera omnia* 10, p. 23, n. 29.

woven there—not only as material for prayer but also as reminders throughout the day. The person making this Second Week should try to achieve familiarity with the eternal Word made flesh: bearing him company, listening to him, serving him, revering him as his lord, his elder brother, and his entire good.

[98] It will suffice to visit the exercitant once [a day], except during the election when there are often desolations and spells of sadness which call for more frequent visits.

Class 8   ⟶   [99] THE ELECTION.   ⟶ ℱ 156

[100] Nothing in the whole of the Exercises is harder than knowing how to manage this matter of the election properly. Nowhere is more skill or spiritual discretion needed, for this time is subject to various interior movements, and at times deceptions, when a person can seize upon evil under the appearance of good. It is the time of bringing to birth, when there are involuntary sadnesses which can be overwhelming. Without light from heaven and prudence from above there is danger that, unless the midwifery is expert, out of all the labor nothing may come to light and everything turn out disastrously.

[101] Out Father was so convinced of the importance of this matter that he not only provided a long explanation in the Exercises of what can be said on the subject but gave it serious treatment in his own directory [Doc. 1], contenting himself with only brief comment on other topics. It is wholly aimed at showing us the preparation needed in the person who will make an election. The election must be made with deliberation and at the right moment; the exercitant must have the right dispositions and be free from all evil affections— as is indicated by the words in our Father's directory: "Upon entering . . . the times of election, he should particularly seclude himself, not wanting to see or hear anything that is not from above" [Doc. 1.6].

[102] In order to handle this all-important topic systematically, we shall discuss (1) who should be admitted to an election, (2) how he should behave during the election, (3) on what matters an election can be made, (4) how the director should behave, (4) what are the times of the election, and finally (6) the details of this matter, the order, and other guidelines.

[103] Obviously the election of a state of life is not for everyone, since persons such as married people or religious, who already have a definite state, cannot make it. They have to be helped in seeking what is most perfect and in pleasing our Lord more in their own state of life, which they neither can nor should change.

[104] Persons who do not yet have a definite state should not all be given the election indiscriminately, as can be seen in the *Constitutions,* VII, 4.F. They must be persons from whom much can be hoped by way of service to our Lord and who will not bring the way of virtue into discredit. Hence, persons

with unruly passions or evil habits, as well as inconstant and soft, effeminate persons from whom not much improvement can expected, should ordinarily not be admitted—for even the *Apostolic Constitutions* [viii.22] teach that such people should not be admitted to baptism without long and serious testing, for "it is not easy for a human being to change his life." Daily experience teaches the same. This is why we see that St. Gregory would not admit military men to religious profession without three years of previous probation. Of course, there can be such tokens of a particular vocation as to substitute for all this.

[105] Moreover, it should be a general rule that no one is admitted to the election unless he requests and desires it and is convinced that he ought to deal with this issue. Hence, the election should not be given to anyone who does not have a desire for it, for even where there is a will the difficulties are considerable—how much more where the will is lacking! Thus by overeagerness to obtain the less we lose the greater and the already achieved.

[106] We should also note that the person entering upon the election should bring along no other concerns or affairs to distract him. For the voice of the Lord is subtle and needs complete attention to be heard.

[107] We must try to get the exercitant (as our Father says) to reach the third, or at least the second, degree of humility. The exercises on the Standards and the Classes of Men are geared to this. A person who has not reached the second degree of humility is not fitted for the election and it is better for him to wait and mature through other means and meditations. See Annotation 16.

[108] This, then, is the conclusion: the person undertaking an election must bring a soul free of all disordered desires and inclined solely to what God wants. If possible, as far as he is concerned he should be readier to follow the counsels than the commandments, noting what our Father says [Doc. 1.9] about more signs being needed for the commandments alone than for the counsels because in themselves the latter are more secure. This is enough on the first point.

[109] On the second point—how the one making the election must behave throughout this period—we can say nothing more emphatic than the words of our Father just referred to [Doc. 1.17–23]. Moreover, it is clear that we are here not out for revelations or "illuminations," and that the *experience* referred to there is not evidential certitude. This is a term used by Scripture and the saints signifying an experiential but not evidential knowledge in this matter, grounded on the analogy between natural acts and those of grace, as St. Thomas indicates in the *Prima Secundae*, q. 112, a. 5 ad 1.

[110] What is required here, then, is (1) that he one making the election be totally concentrated on this task with his whole soul focused on it, without going off on anything else; (2) that in his deliberation he admit no grounds or motives except those from above, i.e., none that smack of flesh and blood. Everything must spring from one principle: desire for God's glory alone. This

is the true resource for building the tower of the Gospel parable [Luke 14:28–30]. This is the satisfaction possessed by the soul enabling it to trust much in God, who will not let it be deceived; for since it is seeking him with all its heart it will find him. And we can believe nothing else of this divine goodness than that he will welcome whoever so truly seeks him, since he goes out to meet even to those who do not seek him.

[111] And if candor is required at other moments in the Exercises, how much more so here, where the exercitant must give a frank account of the representations of the good or evil spirit. It is easy to be deceived in one's own affairs and where self-love is so sophistical and comes up with such plausible arguments that it carries conviction. With this candor we proceed in the election with peace and contentment, making use of all available means and utilizing the principles of faith and those taught us by the Church as well as human reason and consultation, sincerely entrusting the matter to God—so that clearly nothing that could be asked from our side is left undone.

[112] Let us now come to the third point: the matter for the election. Obviously it has to be something that is good and bears the testimony and warranty of the Church for this, whether it is a state of life or some enterprise. With a state of life, the first decision to be made is whether to follow the path of the commandments alone—which St. Dionysius the Areopagite calls the middle and ordinary way—or that of the counsels. The second decision is: if the counsels, then outside or within religious life? For while religious life is the state of the counsels, a person can be chaste, poor, etc., outside religious life—if, say, he is ill-suited for living in community. The third decision is: if inside religious life, then in what congregation—does the Lord invite me more to retirement or to imitate him in gaining souls? The final decision is when to put this into execution. Our Father emphasizes that the election has to follow this sequence step by step and not be made all at once or we will be overwhelmed. If you lay too much at once on a pusillanimous spirit it will fall to the ground under the load. So the exercitant should progressively offer himself to God as he makes the decisions, one day for the counsels, the next for religious life, the next for the particular order, and the next for the time.

[113] Note that in choosing a religious order, one should not go for a corrupt one; we know what Cajetan left written in this regard on the *Secunda Secundae*. To know which order is best, one should follow the teaching of St. Thomas [*Secunda Secundae*, q. 188, a. 6]. We should also take account of the qualities and talents of the one making the election, for the greater service of our Lord.

[114] In other matters, such as choosing this or that office, which are mutable, the same rules should be employed, selecting what is sufficient for the nature of the matter. The criterion is to look to the honor of God, leaving out of account one's own advantage. The intention must be right—"a right heart

before the Lord" [Acts 8:21], as the Scripture so often urges. One must look to God alone, not stoop to things here below.

[115] Now for the fourth point. It is the director's duty in this business to cooperate with the movement from God, to follow behind it and prepare the way for it, clearing away the obstacles of deceptions, mistakes, and disordered affections. The exercitant must go straight ahead; the director must not motivate him to one side or the other, as is stated in Annotation 15, where it says that although this is lawful in itself it is much better in the Exercises to let God act alone with his creature and the business be concluded without a third party.

[116] The reason for this is that in the choice of something so important as a state of life one should not rely upon human persuasion or inducement but on the will of God. The soul must be convinced that God has willed to make use of it in this state. "Every plant which my heavenly Father has not planted shall be rooted up" [Matt 15:13]. In the trials and difficulties which will inevitably come in that state, one will not find much help in the friend who brought him to it unless the soul can look to heaven and recall: God is the one who brought me here, he holds and will hold me in his hand.

[117] From this it can be seen that the director in his own way must also be indifferent, in order to carry out faithfully the task entrusted to him. He must look only to God and to what God desires and not intrude anything of his own spirit. He must be convinced that what he achieves through the rules for a sound election will be safe and without danger; it is his part to be diligent in helping and supporting the person whom our Lord has entrusted to his care and loyalty.

[118] He must be alert to uncover the deceits and fallacies of the devil, for from false premises only false conclusions can come. He must realize that the exercitant sometimes enters the election with the proper dispositions and is thwarted at the moment of concluding it by some disordered affection which drags him along and makes him seize on what is less good for him.

[119] The next point is the fifth: to explain the three times and manners of a sound election as found in the book of the Exercises. There is little to say about the first time because it is extraordinary and falls under no rule; nor should one ask God for this type of election. Of course we do sometimes read about and see vocations with such signs of God and such contentment of soul that there seem no remaining grounds to doubt it.

[120] The second type is commoner. It is by interior inspirations and movements through which our Lord unchains persons from the world and draws them to himself. The first thing needed is an explanation of the nature of consolation and desolation as found in the first set of Rules for the Discernment of Spirits, rules 3 to 11, and in the directories Doc. 1.11,18. This visitation by our Lord is when the soul finds itself buoyed up and energetic, feeling ease for dealing with God and for coming forward with arduous and difficult

works out of love of him, finding itself as it were relieved of the weight of this body. See Cassian, *Conferences*, iv.2.

[121] This consolation is not an abiding quality but is kind of supernaturally bestowed spiritual experience. Its nature is that, when it is present, acts of virtue are performed with savor, relish, and inflaming of the heart, which is unable to adhere to any other thing. "No one knows it but he who receives it" [Rev 2:17]. The Scripture is full of this, and so there is no need to cite testimonies. This consolation also brings it about that works of the flesh become disagreeable, with much more power than is the case with one's habits. See St. Bonaventure's book on progress in religion, ch. 18.[10]

[122] Now let us look at the use and practice of this for knowing which of the choices about which one is consulting God pleases him more. During the time of the meditations, when the soul is consoled it should propose the choices it is deliberating, and examine which of them the consolation and ensuing peace of soul inclines him to—and, on the contrary, at the time of desolation, which of them the desolation moves him to more, what perturbation and faintheartedness it causes him.

[123] In these opposed periods, when the soul is moved to opposed effects, he must be convinced that these are and spring from opposed principles and spirits. It is characteristic of the evil spirit to attack in time of desolation with faintheartedness, and of the good spirit with eagerness—each one giving what is its own—as can be seen in the second set of Rules for the Discernment of Spirits, which are useful for this time and without which the director will be groping in the dark.

[124] The second way of practicing this can be understood by the image given by our Father in his directory [Doc. 1.21]—that of a person who presents to his lord a particular food to see how he likes it. In the same way, the soul, with deep humility and ardent love, should offer to the Lord first one thing and then the other at different times to see how the Lord receives the offering and how he likes it: "Lord, what would you have me do?" [Acts 9:6].

[125] The soul should also examine whether the Holy Spirit is assuring him of sufficient spiritual capital to erect this tower of gospel perfection [see Luke 14:28–30]; whether he is making difficult things easy for him, as Augustine said regarding chastity [*Confessions*, x.30].

[126] The difference between these two procedures which we have outlined is that in the first we enter as though indifferent, to see what the different movements incline us to, whereas in the second we enter as though with our decision made, looking to see what our Lord receives with best countenance and signs of greater satisfaction.

---

[10] *De processu religionis* or *De septem processibus religionis*, not by Bonaventure but by his contemporary David of Augsburg; published as part three of his *De exterioris et interioris hominis compositione* (Paris, 1899.)

[127] The signs that can be present for our own satisfaction are furnished us in the same second set of our Father's rules: they are also given extensive treatment by St. Bonaventure in the book alluded to and by [Jean] Gerson in his book *On the Testing of Spirits*.

[128] We should examine the aftereffects of these movements of the soul, to see where they leave our hearts inclined, for that will reveal what their sources were. We should also examine whether they continue indefinitely to move us to the good; for the devil, though he may play his fraudulent game at the beginning, cannot continue very long without betraying his aims. There is a little more about this examination below.

[129] When the soul reaches complete peace and satisfaction by this procedure, one can move on. If it this satisfaction falls short, there follows the third mode of election, which, while not as excellent as the preceding one since not deriving from so high a source, is nevertheless ordinarily more secure; it preserves and consolidates the second mode just described, and is in fact often confirmed by it, as we shall see.

[130] This third mode demands calm in the soul; one should not make a choice in time of perturbation. It is written in Ecclesiasticus 2[:2], "Make not haste in the time of clouds." Lacking this calm, it would be better to continue with the meditations until the weather clears and the storm abates. Nothing can be seen clearly in troubled waters. It is taken for granted that the soul is purged of sins in order to find and know the will of God, and that the words of the prophet Isaiah do not apply: "They desire to know me and my ways as if they were a nation that does justice," etc. [Isa 58:2].

[131] Given this calm, then, the advantages and disadvantages of the alternatives between which the choice is being made should be set down; it is good to do it in writing to ponder them more adequately. Note that all the reasons or advantages which are envisaged and move to a given choice ought to derive from the already mentioned principle of the love of God.

[132] Then one should proceed with the four methods in the Exercises [184–187], first calling upon the Lord's grace, placing myself in his hands with the desire of finding his holy will. The more important the matter the more deliberately one should proceed.

[133] A few final remarks should be made on these two methods of election for further clarification. As for the second method, it is clear that if the soul has reached certainty that the thing is an inspiration or movement from God it should not wait for further consultation, for even Aristotle said (as quoted by St. Thomas, *Prima Secundae*, q. 68, a. 1): "Those who are moved by a divine impulse should not take counsel with human reason, for they are moved by a principle higher than human reason."

[134] He calls it a movement from God when there is no foregoing disposition on man's part. Our Father teaches us this same sign of a movement from

God in the second set of Rules for the Discernment of Spirits, rules 2 and 8. But because the angel of Satan transforms himself into an angel of light, passing counterfeit money for good, we need to move with great caution and careful scrutiny.

[135] It ought to be a very important premise in this matter that for a person to be guided unquestioningly by interior movements and sentiments is highly dangerous and the source of all the illusions and "illuminations" by which the devil has been waging a mighty war against the Church of God. Even though such people were deceived when they entered in, afterwards, even when the wickedness has been uncovered, they have become so deeply committed that they cannot retreat. And since they take these things under the cloak of God, they are so stubborn that they hold the door shut against being undeceived.

[136] St. John tells us in his canonical epistle: "Believe not every spirit but try the spirits, to see if they are from God" [1 John 4:1]. All that glitters is not gold. St. Paul says to the Thessalonians: "Extinguish not the spirit; despise not prophecies; but prove all things; hold fast that which is good" [1 Thess 5:19–21]. We should not condemn everything; do not roundly approve or disapprove anything; examine it first.

[137] On this point Pope Gelasius quotes this text of St. Paul in *Sancta Romana Ecclesia*, dist. 15, ch. 3. See Cassian, *Conferences,* i.20, who quotes the saying of Christ our Lord which is not found in the Gospels but is cited by many ancient fathers: "Be reliable money-changers," i.e., persons whose profession is to tell good coin from counterfeit. We must avoid being deceived as to the quality of the metal, its weight, or the minting. We must scrutinize the beginning, middle, and end of the interior movement in order to know which author to ascribe it to. Hence we see the numerous rules which our Father left in writing for this purpose.

[138] This testing and scrutiny must be done with light, for "all that is made manifest is light, but all things that are reproved are made manifest by light" [see Eph 5:13]. St. Paul was speaking of the Gnostics, who were the *alumbrados* of ancient times. This light is the word of God, the Church and the public magisterium of God in the Church, together with human reason; all these are from God and cannot be mutually contradictory, "for he is not the God of dissension but of peace" [1 Cor 14:33]. So the inspiration should be examined by means of the three above-mentioned principles.

[139] It is a very certain sign of the evil spirit when he does not want to be revealed and loves the darkness, "and does not come to the light, that his works may not be reproved" [John 3:20]. And it is a sign of the spirit of God to want to be revealed, as our Father teaches in his rules; for God is light and loves the light [see 1 John 1:5].

[140] For this reason it is said that the third mode of election is surer

because in it reason, supported by the faith and teaching of the Church, performs its office and contributes to the person all that it can and applies all its resources to learning what God wills. And if, along with these considerations of reason, the person also has an awareness of his own weakness and of how much danger and risk to his salvation he runs in the world, the matter will go more solidly and surely.

[141] And when these reasonings are confirmed by some tokens of which we spoke in the second method—peace, calm, consolation and relish—then the soul remains entirely satisfied. In conclusion, it is very important to examine a person's motive for entering religious life to see whether it is perfect renunciation, which is the sole form of capital for this construction, as St. Thomas teach in the last article of the *Secunda Secundae.*

[142] If there is a conflict between the second and third methods of making an election, so that he inclines to something different in the one than in the other, we should examine which is more weighty, which motive is more on track, which is more or less weak; and in this way we should reach a decision. For this time of elections St. Augustine's *Confessions* are quite helpful.

[143] But now let us take a look at how important it is to choose a state of life. First of all, if a rational person is bound to have an appropriate end in all his actions, if a Christian must examine how to direct all he does to a supernatural end, and this individually for every action, how much more does he need to examine how to do this in his choice of a state of life, from which a great many other actions will ensue, so that, if the end of his state of life is wrong, everything that ensues from it will also be wrong.

[144] Secondly, it is clear that in God's Church there are various degrees and various vocations. There are not all eyes or hands in the body, not all prophets [see 1 Cor 12]. It befits the greatness of the household of God it should have many different officials, and this variety renders it beautiful. This distribution and division belongs to the Spirit of God: "The same Spirit, the same Lord" [1 Cor 12:28]; and it says, "To some he gave," etc. [Eph 4:11]. And St. Paul says of David in the Acts of the Apostles [13:36] that after having accomplished what God had wished to employ him for he died, indicating that God gives to each person a task in which to be employed. This shows how important it is for a person not to block God's doing with him whatever will be for his greater service; for while God never denies anyone what is needed for his salvation, he gives special morsels, precious helps, and particular favors to those who garner his good will by choosing a state of life pleasing to him.

[145] The same can be seen in the punishment deserved by those who resist God's will. "Because I called, and you refused, etc., I will also laugh in your destruction" [Prov 1:24–26]. See also the evils which Christ our Lord said were to come upon Jerusalem "because she has not known the time of her visitation" [Luke 19:44]. It is impossible for these souls to have peace while

fleeing from God, as it is written: "Who has resisted him and has had peace?" [Job 9:4]. Whenever they turn into their hearts, they will be smitten—and woe betide them when they loose these feelings of remorse, for that is the mark of a hardened heart and reprobate mind.

[146] What is more suited to a creature, and to the homage which it owes, than to receive its state in life from the hand of its lord and father, as a good son does? After all, we say, "So and so was not for this state in life; in another he would have had fewer difficulties in being saved." And our Father says in the *Constitutions*, II, 1.1, "It is expedient to dismiss those . . . who as time passes make it evident that this is not their vocation." For while one cannot conclude with certainty, "He failed, therefore he did not have a vocation from God," since Judas failed even though personally chosen by Christ, what our Father means is that the passing of time makes it evident that this person did not enter by the gate but through some human impression or motive, and that he entered without calculating his strength and so failed.

[147] The other things which need to be decided—which institute to enter and when—should be handled in the same order and by means of the same testing. There is commonly a special difficulty with the time, because the person keeps delaying the time in order to avoid this bitter draught, looking for reasons to put God off—something God does not want from his own, "for the grace of the Holy Spirit knows no tardy efforts" [St. Ambrose]. We see the alacrity of the patriarchs: "Here I am; I am ready" [Gen 22:1, etc.]. The Gospel says of our Lady that she went in haste [Luke 1:39] and of the apostles that they ran [John 20:4].

[148] The question St. Augustine tells us in book 8 of his *Confessions* that he went about with for a long time is a decisive argument: "If ever, why not now? And if not now, perhaps never." Now, while God's movement in me is fresh and I have courage and momentum from him, is the time to leap this ravine. Later, if I grow cold and torpid, I'll stand there trying to screw up my courage with nobody to give me the push I need for this leap. There are two letters of St. Bernard for persons who put off carrying out their decisions and their vocation [Letters 105, 107, 412].

[149] Note that at these critical moments we should not overwhelm the person who is making the election, and should not be constantly pushing him. He needs to catch his breath sometimes and not constantly be under such pressure that "such a one may be swallowed up with sorrow" [2 Cor 2:6]. For if his heart once fails it is hard to restore his courage.

[150] Now for the final point. In presenting these elections the order of the Exercises ought to be followed. From the start of the Second Week an effort should be made to spur the person on to what is more perfect in imitating the life of Christ our Lord and to having his soul inflamed with gratitude toward him who has done so much for us.

[151] The election begins on the fourth or fifth day with the exercise on the Temple, where our Lord began to give us a model of obedience: "And he was subject to them" [Luke 2:51]. Along with the election, some points on the life of Christ our Lord should be given which will be most appropriate to the spiritual state of the person making the election. The number of days and exercises will depend upon the person's progress.

[152] The soul is readied for the election by the exercises on the Two Standards, the Classes of Men, and the Three Degrees of Humility. If the director detects in the exercitant an attachment to anything, he should get him to incline to the contrary affection so as to be able to steer straighter; and he should explain to him the Preamble to the election [169], which is practically the same as the Foundation at the beginning of the Exercises.

[153] Note that the exercitant should not make any vows in a moment of fervor, as is indicated in Annotation 14. However, if his age and character are such that there is no reason for suspecting him of lack of prudence, and if the election has proceeded with great deliberation, he should not be prevented from making a vow.

[154] Our Father's teaching at the end of his treatment of elections [189] is extremely important for persons who already have a state of life or who it is deemed should not change their plans; it is a means for reforming many abuses which, if not themselves sins, are at least the source of much evil.

[155] This teaching makes it possible for married men and fathers of families, while remaining in the world, to pursue in their own way that perfection to which we are to invite them according to our vocation.

[156] If our ministries were accompanied by the teaching and instruction that we have in this book, we would see much more progress in the people who deal with us. Let this suffice for the Second Week.

THE THIRD WEEK.

[157] The Third Week confirms and consolidates the previous Week's choice of a good life and the resolve to serve our Lord more genuinely, based on the pattern of the life of Christ our Lord. For in this final phase his virtues shine forth and display themselves with greater excellence and invite us more forcefully to imitate him.

[158] There is enclosed here a great treasure of Christian life, and that why we see the saints were so versed in the practice of this; everything can be found in it. All the books they left written for our instruction invite us to this.

[159] And so it is important to ensure that the exercitant is well grounded in dealing fruitfully with these mysteries, which should be the ordinary sustenance of the soul throughout life.

[160] The procedure in these meditations is the same as previously: to consider the persons, words, and actions. For some people with less experience it will be well to open up this matter further for them by means of the points which are commonly taught here, i.e., seeing who it is who suffers, what he suffers, at whose hands and for whom he suffers.

[161] In the composition of place, the one meditating should make himself present to the mystery as though it being done for him alone, as St. Paul says speaking of Christ our Lord: "He loved me and gave himself up for me" [Gal 2:20]; and as Dionysius the Areopagite relates at the end of his eighth letter, at the conclusion of the vision of the apostle's disciple Carpus: "I am ready to die for them again"—which shows the infinity charity of the Lord.

[162] The soul must enter into this consideration looking upon itself as the cause of so much pain, shame, and torment, and seeing how every good that it possesses, and its having been shielded and delivered from evil, flow from those merits, and because "with a strong cry and tears offering up prayers . . . he was heard for his reverence" [Heb 5:7]. There our sins and ungratefulness were present to the Lord.

[163] Although the affection of compassion is very precious and should be asked, desired, sought, and when granted received with gratitude, one should at the same time seek other affections which are much more important for the spiritual life, as can be gathered from the third point of the 1st meditation.

[164] The first thing we should seek is a deep appreciation of what an offense to God is and of what it means for a sinner to be made friends with God, seeing that in order to bring about this reconciliation God's wisdom saw fit to employ the means set before us in the Passion.

[165] Secondly, here we see how much God abhors and punishes sin, since if the sins of others placed on the shoulders of Christ, the spotless lamb of God, produce such a feeling and impression, what will they do on our own shoulders, who are children of traitorous fathers and who drag behind us our own sentence? "If in the green wood they do these things, what shall be done in the dry?" [Luke 23:31].

[166] From this we derive indignation against sin, and the attitude expressed by the prophet: "I have hated and abhorred iniquity" [Ps 119:163]; we derive zeal for souls whose cost was so high; and we conceive a horror-filled pity toward sin (as Basil said) and take on the heart of David: "I beheld the transgressors and I pined away; a fainting has taken hold of me," etc. [Ps 119:158, 53].

[167] The third consideration is the goodness and wisdom of God, who was able to find this means of softening the hard hearts of men: "God commends his charity toward us, because when as yet we were sinners," etc. [Rom 5:8]; and St. John: "God so loved the world," etc. [John 3:16].

[168] Fourthly, our hope is here stirred up and the faintheartedness of mean

and pusillanimous persons is removed: "He that spared not even his own Son," etc. [Rom 8:32]. Finally, we draw courage for imitating him: God has done so much for me, at so great a price to himself; what shall I do for him? Especially if this is accompanied by the further awareness: Have I done so much against God until now? Here is what St. Paul proposes for our imitation of Christ: "He emptied himself, humbled himself, became obedient," etc. [Phil 2:7–8].

[169] A few texts from Scripture—such as Psalms and Isaiah speaking about Christ our Lord in this mystery, and the evangelists recounting this history— in which we behold the Lord's heart in the midst of the storm of his most holy Passion will serve as reminders throughout the day to keep close to Christ crucified, so that we can say, "My love is crucified."

[170] The other matters concerning this Week are presented clearly and distinctly in the book of the Exercises where it gives the number and sequence of the meditations and the changes that should be made for this Week in the Additions; hence nothing further need be repeated or added here.

The Fourth Week

[171] The Fourth Week corresponds to the unitive way of love and longing for eternity, where the reward of the risen Christ is set before us. Some considerations may be added for meditating the glory and reward that await the just, the pledges of which we see in these mysteries of the glorious Resurrection: "He has raised us up with him and made us sit together with him," says the Apostle [Eph 2:6].

[172] Some people place the exercise on the Love of God at the beginning of the Second Week, deeming it helpful for the election. But its place is the one it has in this Week, which is all joy and love and considerations that awaken a relish for heavenly things: "If you are risen with Christ, think the things which are above" [Col 3:1]; "our conversation is in heaven; we mind no earthly things" [Phil 3:20, 19].

[173] The Methods of Prayer are little taught, despite their great value. Our Father strongly recommends the first method in *Constitutions*, VII, 4.F, and he wishes it, along with the examens, to be very widely used—"for anyone who has good will seems to be capable of these exercises." In Annotation 18 our Father proposes it for the instruction and help of unlettered people, and our men ought to be very familiar with it. Father Francis Xavier used to use it with his penitents with remarkable results and help to their souls; he would give people as a penance to make this prayer once in the morning and once in the evening.

[174] This method of prayer is easy. It contains intercourse with God and the meditation of his law which is so commended by Scripture, along with help for fulfilling it. The prayer here can be vocal or mental, whichever most

helps the person who makes use of it. It can also be used by more advanced persons, as is seen in the directories, Doc. 20.104–105.

[175] The other two methods are very helpful for making vocal prayer with attention and devotion, so as to fulfill the Apostle's words: "I will pray with the spirit, I will pray also with the understanding" [1 Cor 14:15]. This teaching is very valuable for those bound to the canonical hours and other vocal prayers.

[176] The Rules for Regulating Oneself in Eating and for Distributing Alms are useful depending on the exercitant's disposition, need, and desire to take advantage of them. The Rules for Thinking with the Church are very much needed nowadays for those who are engaged in ministerial work and who deal with the word of God, since they all run straight counter to the thinking and speaking of the heretics of these times, when it is clear how essential it is to speak soberly and to obey the St. Paul's precept to his disciple: "Hold the form of sound words" [2 Tim 1:13].

[177] When the Exercises are completed, we should instruct the exercitant on how carry forward what has been begun and continue in the path upon which he has now set foot. We should urge the use of prayer, the Examen, reception of the sacraments, and the profitable reading of spiritual books. Matters regarding these means should be explained in more detail than was done at the beginning of the Exercises, as was noted in its place. See the directories, Doc. 23.135–141. Above all, they should endeavor to engage in good works, according to each one's state of life.

DOCUMENT 32

Directory of Father Antonio Cordeses

Antonio Cordeses (1518–1601) repeatedly held the highest offices in the Spanish Society of Jesus. He nevertheless became a focus of controversy by urging upon his subjects his own somewhat idiosyncratic teachings on prayer and the spiritual life, a practice from which he was commanded to desist by Father General Mercurian. His directory to the Exercises sandwiches expositions of his personal spiritual doctrine between sections of practical directives borrowed, largely without change, from Polanco's directory (Doc. 20).

DIRECTORY FOR THE SPIRITUAL EXERCISES
OF THE SOCIETY OF JESUS, FOR THE GUIDANCE OF BOTH
THE ONE WHO GIVES AND THE ONE WHO MAKES THEM.

CHAPTER 1: ON THOSE WHO GIVE THE EXERCISES
AND ON WHO CAN MAKE THEM

[1] By the Spiritual Exercises of the Society we mean the spiritual meditations that were composed by Father Master Ignatius of Loyola, the Society's first founder, and which are employed by the Society's members for their own spiritual advancement and communicated to others outside for the same purpose. For being taught them, a master and guide is essential—so much so that some saints even say that it is better for a person not to enter the way of the spirit than to do so without a guide.

[2] Anyone giving the Exercises to others ought to have the anointing of the Holy Spirit, i.e., the Holy Spirit's instruction in the Exercises for himself and for others. He also needs discernment of spirits or experience with them, i.e., long experience in meditating on them and in dealing with souls. Lacking this gift, he should at least have studied and carefully worked out his method for giving them, with some degree of experience in them, entrusting the rest to God, who is the chief master in this work; and he should pray God from the heart to make up for his own lacks.

[3] The Exercises should not be given in the same way to everyone. Those who request them fall into four groups. The first are those who have no suitability for mental prayer, either because they have poor judgment or poor

health, or are so busy that their occupations leave them no time for it.

[4] Also included here are persons who, although enjoying sound judgment, health, and freedom from occupations, are unwilling to give themselves
to mental prayer but nevertheless wish to reform their lives and get some
instruction in the spiritual life so as the more surely to be saved.

[5] The instruction given to such persons can consist of four points. (1)
They should be instructed to make a general confession of their entire past life,
not as though it were necessary for someone who has been making good
confessions, but for their well-being and the considerable advantages afforded
by this practice. (2) They should be taught how to make a daily examination of
conscience. (3) They should be shown how to make a general examination of
conscience preparatory to confession by using the Method of Prayer on the
commandments of God and the five senses. (4) They should be instructed to
receive the holy sacraments of confession and Communion every week or
every other week. It is good to give these persons an explanation of the
commandments, deadly sins, and works of mercy.

[6] The second group is of those who possess adequate understanding and
judgment to receive the Exercises, so that if they made them in full much fruit
might be anticipated from them, but who desire from them only what help
they need for purifying their souls and reforming their lives. For these persons
it suffices (1) to give them the First Week as far as the general confession—but
in full form, with the Additions and the Rules for the Discernment of Spirits
for the First Week, just as when giving the full Exercises. (2) They can have
the three Methods of Prayer explained and taught to them. (3) They can be
urged to receive the sacraments. (4) Where appropriate, they can be instructed
in the method for distributing alms, and also for discerning scruples should they
need them.

[7] The third group are those who, while having aptitude for prayer, are
unable, because of occupations or poor health, to make them in full form but
only in part, yet wish to make them as well as they can. These can be given
the Exercises to spend an hour on each morning, as follows. (1) They should
first be given the Foundation to ponder for a day. (2) They should be taught
the examinations of conscience. (3) They should be given the 1st exercise of
the First Week to meditate for three days, along with an explanation of the first
six Additions.

[8] Then they should be given the 2nd exercise for a further three days,
along with an explanation of the remaining Additions; then the meditation on
hell for three days; and if the one giving the Exercises judges that the exercises
on death and judgment would be helpful, these meditations should be given in
the same manner as the previous three. The 3rd and 4th exercises should not
be given; as mere repetitions of the first two, their place is taken by the
meditating of each exercise for two or three days. As for the Rules of the First

Week for the Discernment of various Spirits, that is left up to the judgment of the one giving the Exercises.

[9] He will make his general confession, and then go on to the exercises of the Second Week, which will be given in the same way as those of the First Week, with an explanation of their Additions and other pertinent matters. These persons should meditate each exercise for two or three days, then going on do the same with the Third and Fourth Weeks. If the person desires and is suitably disposed to make the elections, these will be given during the course of the Second Week. If the person is willing to spend more than an hour a day on meditation he will be able to finish the Exercises sooner.

[10] The fourth group consists of those who are able and willing to make the Exercises in full form, for the greatest possible benefit. They will be given the Exercises as described below.

[11] To induce people to make the Exercises, they can be told of their fruits or effects, to wit: (1) reform of one's life, the reformation consisting in penance for one's sins, the mortification of one's vices—particularly disordered affection toward earthly things—and the implanting of the virtues in the soul; (2) reception of instruction in mental prayer and in dealing with God, which is the substance of the spiritual life; (3) they can be told that countless persons have received extraordinary help from the Exercises and become great ministers of God's service; and also (4) that the Exercises have received the approval of the Apostolic See.

[12] CHAPTER 2: THE FIRST THING THAT NEEDS TO BE DONE WITH PERSONS WISHING TO MAKE THE EXERCISES.

[13] Once a person has decided to make the Exercises, provision should be made for him to withdraw to a secluded cell, remaining secluded throughout the Exercises from any conversation or dealings with others that might distract him from them. The more secluded he is from disturbances and concerns the freer and readier he will be to devote himself to God and the salvation of his soul and the greater will be his progress. This cell should be such that he can leave it to hear Mass (or say Mass if he is a priest) without running into persons who might disturb him.

[14] Once he has gone into seclusion, he should first be reminded of the fruits which he will reap from making the Exercises.

[15] Second, he should be informed that the Exercises will last four Weeks, more or less. Note here, however, that while these Exercises are divided into four Weeks, the Weeks should not be taken to mean exactly seven or eight days. Each Week ends when, and only when, the exercitant has found what he was aiming at during that Week. Thus, the First Week ends when he has achieved a deep understanding and contrition regarding his sins, and the

Second when he has derived substantial fruit from the meditations on the life of Christ and has assimilated the method for meditating well on the life of Christ in the future. In this way, depending on the aim of each Week (and taking other circumstances into account as well), more or fewer exercises will be given and more or fewer days will be spent on each Week.

[16] Third, he should be instructed on the recollection he ought to maintain throughout the Exercises, and the difficulties that he will experience in the course of them. This is to instill steadfastness in him and so that he will not cry foul when difficulties come—as has been done by some persons who then broke off the Exercises. He should also have what is said in Annotation 5 brought strongly to his attention.

[17] Fourth, he should be told that he must report everything happening in his soul during this time of the Exercises—ideas, illuminations, inflammations of spirit, consolations, desolations, penances, temptations—so that he will not fall into any error through keeping silent about these things, and may receive suitable instruction.

[18] Fifth, he should be told that during the First Week he must not have any spiritual books to read: he requires the entire time for the exercises and the other things he will be doing, and should apply himself exclusively to the cleansing of his conscience. Thus, he should be allowed to have only his breviary or book of hours and the rosary that he will recite. He should have paper, pen, and ink on the table, along with a devout picture, of the Passion if possible. If a priest, he can say Mass, or else hear it if it is available; he might also attend some other offices, as indicated in Annotation 20.

CHAPTER 3: REMARKS ON THE FIRST WEEK

[19] On the first day, the final end of human life should be explained to him, to spend some periods of time thinking about. It should be given to him in short points to make it easier to remember and think about.

[20] The points are as follows: (1) Man has been created to know, love, and serve God, and in this way eventually to possess and enjoy him. (2) All things have been created to help him in reaching this end. (3) He must therefore desire and make use of them to the extent that they help him to this end, and abstain from them to the extent that they hinder him. (4) He must make himself indifferent to things which are in themselves indifferent, not desiring health more than sickness, wealth more than poverty, honor more than contempt, or a long life rather than a short one, but only whatever will help us more.

[21] He should be told to extend his consideration to an examination of his own behavior up to now regarding this end and the means, and how he rightly ought to behave in this regard in the future; and he should try to root this indifference in his soul.

[22] On the second day the director should explain the Particular and General Examens to him, making sure to have him learn this well and practice it that same day, for these are matters of great importance which must last throughout his life.

[23] The advantages of a general confession should be explained orally when the time comes for him to prepare for this confession.

[24] All of the five exercises should be made on the same day, each day of this Week. However, they should be given not all together but one at a time, so as not to overwhelm the memory. The procedure should be as follows.

[25] On the evening of the second day, the 1st exercise, on the three powers, should be explained along with the first five Additions. If necessary, the director should faithfully narrate the history in the three points, repeat it, and then have the exercitant repeat it after him so as to fix it in the memory; he should also leave it in writing. This exercise will then be made the following (third) day, not at midnight but upon arising in the morning.

[26] After this meditation he should visit him and give and explain the 2nd meditation, on sins, in the same fashion, along with the four remaining Additions (6–9), for him to make before dinner; he should also leave this in writing.

[27] He should tell him that in meditating he should not go into too much detail on the first point regarding his own sins, since he will be doing this when he prepares for his general confession, but that for meditation it suffices to form an a general and global idea of their number and gravity. If he does go into detail, he should do so on the sins that will cause him the greatest confusion and sorrow.

[28] Then he should visit him again after dinner between 2:00 and 3:00 and give him the 3rd exercise, which is a repetition of the first two, to be made from 3:00 to 4:00.

[29] After this he should visit him once more and give and explain the exercise on hell in the same way, to be made before supper. In this way the meditations will be fixed clearly and distinctly in his mind, so that he will master them and be able to make them perfectly on the following days.

[30] On the fourth day he will make these same exercises for five hours: the powers at midnight, the sins upon arising, the first repetition before dinner, the second at midafternoon, and the meditation on hell before supper; similarly with all the remaining days of this Week.

[31] The one giving the exercises should remember that God is the principal author of mental prayer; it is he who enlightens the mind, moves the will, and gives an inward sense of one's sins, compunction of soul, and shame for one's sins. Hence, the director should not imagine that he is supposed to instill these things in the exercitant through his own skill or efforts; he must be a mere collaborator of divine grace. He should therefore give the exercises

simply, not enlarging on the points or going any more deeply into them than is needed to get the meditation started. In this way he will leave more room for God's instruction than if he gave them in detail or in depth; moreover, the exercitant gets greater enjoyment from any new insights that come to him.

[32] However, in this matter of how fully to explain the points he should adapt himself to the exercitant, to his talent and habits. With the intelligent he can speak concisely and learnedly; with those not so bright and lacking spiritual experience he needs to expand somewhat, even suggesting ideas for them to follow out if this is deemed advisable. With all he should speak in an organized fashion.

[33] Beginning on the fourth day, he should visit him once daily. On this occasion he should question him in detail about how he proceeds in meditating, whether he is straining his head or breast, and how he makes the Additions; also about whatever illuminations, movements, penances, etc., he has had. If he sees that the exercitant is proceeding well, he should commend him; if badly, he should try to discover the causes so as to give him proper direction.

[34] He should try to bring him something fresh each day, from the four notes at the end of the ten Additions, from the fourteen Rules of the First Week for the Discernment of Movements, or from the Rules on Scruples should he need them. However he should leave in writing only the exercises and Additions.

[35] If the exercitant is inclined to perform external penance, the director should commend him, even suggest this to him. Thus, he should be given no more food or drink than he requests—unless he is already going to extremes either way, in which case he should be handled as discreet charity dictates. If he requests a hairshirt or discipline, it should be given to him; if he does not, he should be asked if he wants them, for there will be some who want them but are too bashful to ask.

[36] If the exercitant is extremely devout and fervent, he should be warned against making any vows during this time, particularly if the person is impetuous or inconstant. It should be explained to him that, while vows are good and holy, they need to be made with great forethought to ensure that they will be more pleasing to God and will be more faithfully kept later on.

[37] If the exercitant finds what he is seeking, i.e., contrition, there is no reason to change the five exercises; he should stick with them as long as he derives good from them. However, if he is in great aridity and finds the repetition of the same exercises tiresome, but still clearly needs further work on contrition, then the meditation on hell can be replaced with one on death or judgment. In fact, even the 1st exercise can be replaced by that given below, using the same preludes and colloquies as in the 1st exercise, with the appropriate adaptations.

[38] *Meditation on sins*

1. God punished David severely for the adultery and murder that he committed (2 Kings 12).

2. Because of sins God destroyed the world with the universal flood.

3. He mysteriously punished his only-begotten Son for the sins of the world.

[39] The second meditation as well can be replaced with the following, retaining the same preludes, with the appropriate changes.

[40] *Second meditation on sins*

1. Reflect on the enormous harm sin has done you: through it you lost friendship with God, grace, the virtues, the gifts, and the right to everlasting blessedness; you have merited hell.

2. Reflect on your ingratitude to God after all his favors to you.

3. Reflect that through sin you turned into an irrational beast, inasmuch as you abandoned reason and were ruled by your sensual appetite.

[41] *Meditation on death*

[42] The preparation, i.e., the preparatory prayer, will be the usual one.

[43] The first prelude is the composition of place: here it is to place myself at the hour of my death, imagining myself lying in bed, given up for lost and with no hope of life.

[44] The second will be to ask our Lord for the grace to feel and taste while still alive what one feels at that moment, so that I will act and live as I would wish at the hour of death to have acted and lived.

[45] First point: Reflect on the agony and stress a person undergoes at the moment when the soul has to part from the body, and on the great fear a person then feels of being eternally condemned and of appearing before one whom he has served so badly.

[46] Second point: Reflect that the demons, who in this world kept emphasizing for the soul the mercy of God, will now straiten the soul, presenting thoughts that God is just and will leave nothing unpunished.

[47] Third point: Reflect on what you will wish at that moment that you had done, and on how little you can do then, when your senses are too disoriented and your mind too darkened to turn to God and ask mercy; and how at that moment you will yearn for a single hour of life in which to do penance.

[48] Fourth point: Reflect on what your body will look like after you die, and how it will be buried and soon after that rot.

[49] Fifth point: Reflect on the strict judgment of God that you will have to endure; as St. Peter says, "If the just man can scarcely be saved, how shall

the ungodly and sinner appear before God" [1 Pet 4:18]. After this judgment your soul must be consigned either to eternal glory or to the everlasting pains of hell.

[50] The colloquy will be to ask our Lord for the grace to consider everything in this world except his service as nothing, and to live always in this world so well prepared that my soul will be saved. End with an Our Father and a Hail Mary.

[51] *Meditation on judgment*

[52] The usual preparatory prayer.

[53] The first prelude is the composition of place: here it is the valley of Jehoshaphat, where all the good and the evil are assembled together with Christ and his entire court.

[54] The second prelude is to ask for the grace.

[55] First point: Reflect upon the general resurrection, in which all the good will arise with bodies endowed with the glorious gifts, and all the evil with bodies that are heavy, ugly, and loathsome. Reflect on their fear upon finding themselves at the judgment and realizing how badly they will fare in it.

[56] Second point: At the judgment the evil will be separated from the good, never to be with them again; after this everyone's book will be opened and everyone will see everyone else's actions—in St. Jerome's words: "All will see all the secrets of all." Think of the confusion and shame in which the evil will then find themselves. And then the sentence will be passed on both the good and the evil.

[57] Reflect that the sentence will be executed immediately: the earth will open and swallow up the evil to suffer forever in hell in body and soul; the good will ascend to heaven, there to possess everlasting glory.

[58] The colloquy will be the same as in the meditation on death.

[59] Having five exercises each day is not so essential that four will not suffice in some cases where the exercitant is older or weak. The midnight meditation can be dropped, so that the 1st will be made upon arising; the 2nd, on sins, before dinner; the 3rd, a repetition of both, at midafternoon; and the 4th, on hell, before supper. However, if the exercitant is in robust health he should not be dispensed from making all five, at least during the First Week.

[60] During the Second and Third Weeks there can be a relaxation on some days, with the exercitant making only four exercises and not getting up at midnight, so as to keep him from getting exhausted.

[61] During the Fourth Week all should normally make only four exercises, just as during the First Week they should normally make five.

[62] Beginning on the third day, preparation for the general confession can be made during the periods between meditations, or else toward the end of the First Week—without abandoning the meditations but continuing with them, or

at least a part of them, until the person is fully prepared.

[63] Confession should normally be made to a person other than the one giving the Exercises; however, if the exercitant is very inclined toward him or no one else is available, he may make his confession to him.

CHAPTER 4: FURTHER REMARKS ON THE EXERCISES OF THE FIRST WEEK.

[65] For a fuller understanding of these exercises, you should know that the matter meditated in all of them is the fact that sin an enormous evil. This conclusion is proved in the 1st exercise by means of three points, i.e., three means or effects or evils which sin has caused or causes: one in the angels, who for a single sin were lost and relegated to hell; the second in the entire human race, which through the sin of our first parents Adam and Eve became God's enemy and subject to countless miseries and evils; and the third in the individual persons who because of a single sin are condemned eternally to hell.

[66] In the 2nd exercise the same conclusion is proved by three means: one in the second point, another in the third, and a third in the fourth.

In the 3rd exercise, on hell, the same conclusion is proved by five means or effects, in the five points.

[67] The work of meditation is not in the speculative understanding, which aims only at knowing, but in the practical understanding, which has as its aim moving the will to an affection of either fear or sorrow, grief or hope, love or some other similar affection.

[68] And thus in this First Week the principal aim sought by the exercitant in the meditations is to move the will to grief and affliction over its sins, or, in other words, compunction of soul, dwelling in this compunction for several days in order to purify and cleanse the soul from sins and thus prepare it for the following Weeks. Hence, when it finds this compunction, it should stop there and not pass on to the meditation of the remaining points, so as not to interfere with the compunction.

[69] From what has been said you will see that this meditation with the understanding is not mere consideration, but a considering, weighing, estimating, and judging of the malice and gravity of sins so as to obtain compunction for them. With this sort of consideration the exercitant's mind is illuminated and his will inflamed in the good.

[70] And thus the aim of the Exercises, of all mental prayer, and indeed of the whole spiritual life, is for a person to have his understanding enlightened in the things of faith and the will inflamed. Thus the enlightenment of the understanding is the proximate aim of the meditations, while the inflaming of the will is the higher and hence more important aim.

[71] These aims are achieved in the Exercises in one of two ways. The first is by divine infusion. This is the vivid sense of the gravity and loathesomeness

of sin which God is accustomed to give. This sense is nothing else than an experiential and affective knowledge of deeply weighing, estimating, and judging the gravity of sin, accompanied by great amazement and giving rise to deep compunction of will, with much relish and consolation. This sense is not in our power to have. Indeed, at times, when we desire and strive for it, it is denied us and we are left in much dryness. At other times, when we are neither thinking of it nor striving for it, it is lavished upon us by God, sometimes for long periods, sometimes for short ones. It is, then, infused by the hand of God. The way to obtain it is to ask it of God very humbly; this is the purpose of the second prelude.

[72] The second way of obtaining these aims is by our own effort and labor. When God will not give us this sense, we ourselves endeavor to consider, weigh, estimate, and judge the gravity of sin by employing the points, so as to move our will to contrition.

[73] This labor is not accompanied by amazement, sweetness, and consolation, nor is it as fruitful as the first. But it is still profitable, and so we must persevere in it. Its profitableness is like the growth of a nursing baby: the mother gives it her breast every day, laboring on with it; she does not see it growing on any particular day, but at the end of the year she sees to her joy that it has grown bigger.

[74] Although this work proceeds from our own striving and effort, you should not think that the striving should be physical or that the meditation should involve any straining of the head or breast, like squeezing an orange. They should be efforts in the mind, of attention and thinking, which require bodily calm and tranquillity: "Our soul becomes wise by sitting and keeping calm," says the Philosopher.

[75] Nobody should imagine that seven or eight days of contrition will suffice to purify and sanctify his soul, or expel from it all the aftereffects of sin. This may have happened to some persons because of the intensity of their contrition or love of God, as with Mary Madgalen, but this is rare. Hence many persons persevered for long periods in contrition—St. Mary of Egypt for forty-seven years, St. Jerome for four years, St. Hilarion and many others for long periods.

[76] Hence, whoever wishes to reach perfection must, after finishing the complete Exercises, return to those of the First Week, continuing to work on contrition of heart and exterior works of penance. In this way, while God infuses in him a deep sense of his sins and gives him compunction, he should persevere in penitence as long as this influence lasts, even though it be for many years. For when God lays such a deep foundation of penitence in the person, it is a sign that he wishes to raise in him the edifice of the spiritual life.

[77] The outcome of this penitence is customarily great peace and serenity of conscience and extraordinary confidence in the forgiveness of one's sins.

Persons like this, when God moves their spirit and feeling to something else, can safely follow God's call.

[78] However, if God does not infuse such a feeling in them but does give it occasionally by means of these or other exercises while denying it to them on other occasions, they should follow St. Bonaventure's opinion and keep at their penitence for two or three months before going on to the illuminative way through the exercises of the Second and Third Weeks.

[79] St Augustine advises the servant of God to do some penance for his sins every day of his life. He himself did this: in his final illness he had the seven penitential psalms put on the wall before him so he could pray and meditate them.

[80] CHAPTER 5: REMARKS ON THE EXERCISES OF THE SECOND WEEK

[81] After the general confession, when it is time to go on, the exercitant should be given, as he catches his breath for a bit, the meditation on the Kingdom of Christ, to be made twice during the day, once in the morning and once in the afternoon.

[82] That same evening he should be given the meditation on the Incarnation to be made at midnight and that on the Nativity to be made upon arising in the morning. He should make the 3rd meditation before dinner, the 4th after dinner at midafternoon, and the 5th, the application of the senses, before supper. He should follow this procedure on the following days, carefully observing the Additions and notes laid down for the Second Week.

[83] In meditations on the life of Christ, those on the Incarnation and Nativity which are given on the first day of the Second Week are models for all the others. Thus, for all the mysteries and actions of Christ the first point is to see the persons in the mystery, the second to hear what they are saying, and the third to see what they are doing.

[84] Do not be confused by the fact that in the dividing up of the life of Christ the points seem structured differently, i.e., by segments of the history. This division was made only to facilitate the review of the history in the first prelude. The meditation itself should be made using the points indicated in the first two [meditations], as has been said. However, if God visits the exercitant and inspires in him an inward understanding of the matters being meditated, he need not force himself to go through the points of seeing, hearing, etc., but may follow the lead of the Holy Spirit.

[85] In meditating the life of Christ, if the one meditating is doing well and getting good results, nothing should be added to or subtracted from the meditations. But if he is short of insight and needs additional guidance, he should be instructed that after meditating the third point, on what the persons in the history are doing, he should turn his eyes to a consideration of the

grounds of these actions, such as God's or Christ's goodness and charity, or our own salvation. This will get him started on a broader and more fruitful meditation.

[86] Regarding the application of the five senses to the matter that has been meditated, note that this can be understood in two ways. One way refers to the senses of the imagination; this is suitable for persons inexperienced in meditation and contemplation such as those being given the Exercises commonly are. There is no difficulty with this method, for there is no difficulty in imagining oneself seeing the persons in the history, hearing what they are saying or might well say, kissing and reverencing Christ's feet, footsteps, or clothing. Smell and taste can here be left aside as not being applicable to this like the other senses.

[87] The second way refers to the spiritual senses of the mind; this is for persons experienced in contemplation. According to St. Bonaventure in his *Journey of the Mind to God*, chapter 4, these senses are the mind itself when with it we contemplate Christ's spiritual rather than physical splendor. Hearing is the mind being used to listen to his inspirations. Smell is the mind when with it we smell Christ's renown, virtues, and gifts ("We are the good odor of Christ" [2 Cor 2.15]). Taste is the mind when used to taste the sweetness of God ("Taste and see how sweet is the Lord" [Ps 34:9]). Touch is the mind when with it we unite ourselves with God ("It is good for me to cling to God" [Ps 83:28]).

[88] During this Week he need be visited only once a day, unless the time for the elections has come, when he should be visited twice a day.

[89] The Rules for Temperance, although located in the Third Week, can be practiced during the Second Week or at any time that they seems appropriate. Similarly with the Rules on Scruples, the Distribution of Property, and Thinking with the Catholic Church. It is pointed out that, in general, these four matters are not to be given to everyone but only to those who need them or at least will derive considerable help from them.

[90] CHAPTER 6: REMARKS ON THE EXERCISES OF THE SECOND WEEK

[91] Just as the First Week instructs and exercises us in the purgative way, which aims at our cleansing and purification from the filth of our sins, so the Second and Third Weeks instruct and exercise us in the illuminative way.

[92] To enter upon the exercises of the illuminative way in the Second Week means aiming at the enlightenment of our minds with the light of estimation and judgment regarding the realities of faith—i.e., as is appropriate for each of them—and the inflaming of our will by situating it in the appropriate affection toward these same realities of faith—i.e., loving the good ones and loathing the evil ones, each in its due degree.

[93] This knowledge and affection aimed at in the Second and Third

Weeks regarding the things of faith is not on the same level for all of them. It regards first and primordially God, our creator, savior, and glorifier, so as to love, glorify and serve him; secondarily, the means by which we go to God: Jesus Christ, true God and man, the virtues and gifts of the Holy Spirit, the sacraments, the Scriptures, etc.

[94] The experiential knowledge of God sought in the Second Week includes three matters. The first is his attributes: his power, wisdom, goodness, justice, mercy, charity, etc.

[95] The second is the personal properties: their being threefold and one; Father, Son, and Holy Spirit; person sending or person sent.

[96] The third is how God communicates himself to creatures: how he is the first cause of all things; how he created this entire world; how he governs and preserves it; how he predestined the elect; how he is savior; how he is glorifier; how through the Scriptures and the Church he reveals to us what is his and promises us his good things, threatens us with punishments, and guides us toward the good.

[97] Regarding Jesus Christ we need to know chiefly four things. First, that he is true God, altogether equal to the eternal Father in every way.

[98] The second is that as man he possesses six preeminences or excellences. He is savior, high priest, mediator between God and mankind; king and lord of the whole universe and head of the Church; lawgiver and universal judge; spouse of the Church, full of grace, virtues, and wisdom, from whose fullness we have all received, grace upon grace; our justice and sanctification; the lamb of God, etc.

[99] The third is the great and astounding favors that we have received from him: his redeeming us; his purchasing eternal blessedness for us; his instituting the seven sacraments through which he imparts spiritual life to us; his giving us such great examples of virtue; his giving us the light of the gospel law, etc.

[100] The fourth is the perfection of his most holy life for us to imitate: i.e., his purity from all sin, his heroic virtues, and in fine his sublime perfection.

[101] From his virtues and gifts we must come to a knowledge of his works: their sublimity and value, how much they please God, etc.

[102] Regarding the sacraments: their holiness, their power and worth, their effects, etc.

[103] Regarding the Scriptures: their truth, holiness, splendor, etc.

[104] CHAPTER 7: HOW MEDITATION ON THE LIFE OF CHRIST LEADS
TO KNOWLEDGE OF GOD AND OF THE OTHER REALITIES OF FAITH

[105] While knowledge of God can be obtained by meditation on creatures, on the lives of the saints, and on the divine Scriptures, nevertheless the first and chief means of all is meditation on the life, death, and passion of Jesus Christ, for he is the way and the truth and the life.

[106] In him and through him—i.e., through his mysteries, life, and miracles—we understand especially all supernatural realities: the mystery of the most Holy Trinity; the fact that God is savior and has such charity toward human beings that he gave his only-begotten Son to redeem them from the power of the devil by his death and passion; that he will give them whatever they ask through Jesus Christ. Through Christ we also understand whatever is naturally knowable about God, i.e., his attributes: his power, wisdom, goodness, charity, mercy, justice, etc.

[107] While knowledge of Jesus Christ, true God and true man, can be obtained through the Scriptures and the thinking of the Roman Catholic Church, it is nevertheless obtained chiefly through the words and actions of Christ.

[108] While knowledge of the virtues and gifts can be obtained through the teaching of the theologians and through their own effects, it is had chiefly by meditation upon the life, teaching, death, and passion of Christ.

[109] While knowledge of the seven sacraments can be had from theology, the authors, and the determinations of the Church, it is obtained chiefly through meditation on the teaching, life, and death of Christ.

[110] While knowledge of the Scriptures can be had from the teaching of the saints and the declarations of the Church, it is had chiefly by meditation on the life, death, and passion of Christ; for he "opened the book sealed with seven seals" [Rev 5:1; 8:1].

[111] Thus you can see that in the meditations on the life, death, and passion of Christ—whether we meditate his words or his actions—Christ is always the means by which we reach knowledge of these five things: God, Christ himself, the virtues and gifts, the sacraments, and the Scriptures. Consequently in every meditation we are to keep our eyes open for these five things.

[112] Moreover, I remind you, as I did above in my remarks on the First Week, that the practical knowledge obtained in these meditations is of two kinds. The first is infused by the hand of God; it is a strong interior perception of the matters meditated, accompanied by much consolation—in other words an experiential and affective knowledge which God imparts at whatever time he wills to those who are prepared. The second is acquired: a weighing, estimating, and judgment regarding the things meditated.

[113] The former is what we should chiefly aim at. But if God does not

give it, one must keep working hard, with God's help, at the second: weighing, estimating, and judging the matters meditated so as to hold, appreciate, and love them as is appropriate.

[114] CHAPTER 8: REMARKS ON THE ELECTIONS

[115] The first and primary election a person can make is whether to serve God and attend to his own salvation in the common state of the observance of God's commandments or in the way of perfection which is only for a few and consists in embracing Christ's counsels.

[116] Next, after choosing the way of perfection, whether to pursue this way of perfection in religious life or outside it, i.e., in the celibate or clerical life.

[117] If the choice is for religious life, whether in the contemplative or the mixed life.

[118] If he chooses the common state of the observance of the commandments, then he must decide whether to do so as a married man or as a cleric. If as a married man, then whether with a given office or responsibility or not; if as a cleric, whether with a benefice or not.

[119] This breakdown is for the guidance of the one giving the Exercises; it is not intended to be given right off to the exercitant all at one time.

[120] Third day. The time to begin dealing with the elections is the third day, when the 1st meditation is about how the boy Jesus was subject to his parents, Joseph and Mary, and the 2nd about how he left his parents and went to the Temple. For in the first Christ gave an example of ordinary life in being subject to his parents; in the second an example of the other state, that of the evangelical counsels, by leaving his parents and going to the Temple. Hence, the one giving the Exercises should find out from the exercitant whether he wants to make the elections; if he does not, or ought not because he is unsuited for the state of perfection, he should have him continue with the exercises, giving him the meditation on the Baptism and those which follow.

[121] Fourth day. However, if he is desirous and capable of making the elections, he should be instructed that as he meditates on Christ's life he should begin reflecting about which type of life God will want to make use of him in, without coming to any conclusion. Then there follow for the fourth day the meditations on the Standards and Three Classes of Men, which are geared to this and enable anyone to learn the attitude that he ought to have in order to reach perfection in whatever state God calls him to.

[122] To make a good election, a person must, first, be free of disordered affections of love, hatred, sadness, joy, hope, fear, anger, or any other. A good election is impossible unless one is free of passions and in a calm, tranquil, and composed state of mind.

[123] Secondly, it is essential, as indicated in the note after the Three Classes of Men, that he have made himself quite indifferent as regards embracing whichever state God may call him to. Because of its extreme importance, he must beg God most earnestly for this indifference.

[124] Fifth day. On the fifth day, after he has meditated Christ's departure to the Jordan from Nazareth and his Baptism, he should be given the Three Modes of Humility to meditate upon two or three times; at the end he should make the colloquy of the Two Standards, constantly striving to reach perfect indifference.

[125] Sixth day. First, besides the exercises of the day, the Preamble for Making a Good Election [169] should be explained to him: first, that man has been created to know, love and serve God and thereby to save his soul.

Second, that he must therefore chose only what will help him to this end, since the means must be conformed to the end, not the end to the means.

[126] Third, that this shows what a great mistake it is when one first marries or accepts a benefice and then decides to serve God in this state, thus making the means the end and the end the means, wishing not to go straight to God but to have God come to him; whereas what he ought to do is the opposite, i.e., first resolve to serve God and only then choose marriage, a benefice, or whatever else he understands will help him serve God.

[127] The one giving the Exercises should take care not to incline him in one direction rather than another. His job is not this; it is to prepare the creature by bringing it to indifference so that it may be taught by the Creator, either through inspiration and movement in the affections or through reasoning in the mind. The director must leave the entire business of a vocation to God, who will be able to preserve and perfect the person therein.

[128] If he sees that the exercitant has not placed himself in the required indifference, and is not doing all he can to achieve it, there is no basis for proceeding with the elections; he will not make a good election in this state. He should go on with the exercises of the Second and—if he holds out that long—Third Week, until he obtains this from our Lord.

[129] When he has made himself indifferent and is going on with the exercises, the first time of election should be explained to him, just in passing; then a detailed explanation should be given of the second time, stating that it consists in the exercitant's seeking the God's will through the experience of consolations and desolations. The meaning of consolation, however, should be explained carefully—and all of this should be given orally, not in writing.

[130] The method of election in the second time is as follows. Where it is an election of a state of life, he puts himself in the presence of God in prayer, places before his eyes the way of Christ's counsels—without trying to reason about it either way—and waits to see if he feels any movements of consolation or desolation in its regard. For God is accustomed at times to illuminate such

a person and give an interior realization that this and no other is the state for him, enkindling his will toward this state, or giving him consolation when he pictures himself taking it up; or, on the contrary, to give desolation and confusion. After this, he should do the same with the common state of the commandments of God.

[131] No special exercise is needed for this; he can do it during the time of his exercises or in any other prayer. Even if outside the time of the exercises he experiences any movements, the one giving the Exercises should examine him using the Rules for the Discernment of various Spirits for the Second Week. He should have him repeat the procedure several times to see whether the same movements persist or different ones come. If it becomes clear that they are from the good spirit, and that they persist, and he chooses the way of perfection, then the director has grounds for approving the election. Then he can go on in the same fashion to the second election, on whether to follow the counsels in religious life or outside it; and from there to the third, on whether in the contemplative or mixed life, etc.

[132] If the exercitant concludes the business of the election well in the second time, he can conclude here without going on to the elections in the third time, for he is being guided by a better light than that of human understanding.

[133] If he chooses the common way of the commandments, it should be explained to him that a decision for this way requires greater signs of God's will than does the way of the counsels, since Christ himself said that it would be hard for the rich to be saved, and because the life of the counsels is without doubt more perfect and secure.

[134] If he failed to make the election as described above, because he either felt no significant movements or was unsure whether those he did feel were from God, he should move on to the third time. The methods of this time dispose a person for enlightenment from God. In fact, I would say that even if he did make an election in the second time he may, if he wishes, test it by means of the third time for greater certainty.

[135] In the third time, the starting point is to place before himself his final end, which must be the basis for his inquiring and deciding which means will be best for attaining that end, either the common state or the way of perfection. Both the first and second procedures of this time should be explained to him. If he concludes the election in one hour using the first procedure, he should test it in a second hour using the other; if the same conclusion emerges in both, this is a strong indication of a good election.

[136] When the exercitant is engaged in making an election in the third time, one meditation on Christ's life, with a repetition, is plenty. The remaining time is needed for the elections.

[137] He should be advised to write down his arguments on both sides to

compare with each other in the fifth point [182], so that he can see which of them are weightier, i.e., which of the things he is choosing between presents more advantages for reaching his end and which more disadvantages.

[138] If the election in the third time turns out the same as in the second, this is a strong argument for the election's being from God.

If no election emerged in the second time, yet after making the election in the third time the exercitant experiences the same sort of enlightenments and movements and consolations confirming his election—assuming that these movements are from God—this strongly argues for the election's having been made in accord with God's will.

[139] If the outcome of the third time contradicts that of the second, a careful examination should be made—having recourse to the Rules for the Discernment of Spirits, to right reason, and to sound doctrine—of the elections made in either time and the weight of the motives. If it is seen that reason favors the election made in the third time, it should be followed as more secure. If, on the other hand, it is seen that the reasons in the third time are weak and that the motives in the second time are from the good spirit and not in conflict with right reason, then the election in the second time should be preferred to that in the third. If the issue remains doubtful, the election should be made over again.

[140] No matter what he chooses, either in the second or in the third time, he should be warned against making any vows in the matter during the time of the Exercises, particularly if he is an impulsive and possibly inconstant person.

[141] However, if he is an older person, mature and constant, and wishes to confirm his election by a vow in order to defend himself against the assaults of the devil, the world, and the flesh, then the one giving the Exercises neither may nor should forbid him—just as he should never for any reason urge him to make a vow.

[142] CHAPTER 9: REMARKS ON THE EXERCISES OF THE THIRD WEEK

[143] While it is true that the third prelude describes the purpose of these meditations as seeking sorrow for one's sins and confusion over the supreme Lord's submitting himself to such torments because of them, this does not mean to exclude other holy affections that arise from these meditations, v.g., compassion for Christ; resolutions of obedience, courage, patience, humility, meekness, and other virtues which shine forth in the Passion; longing to imitate Christ in suffering for the honor and glory of God and for the salvation of one's neighbor; hope, charity, and other similar affections.

[144] Of the four Additions after the 2nd exercise [204–207], only the third should be given in writing; the rest should be explained orally.

[145] The Rules of Temperance at the end of this Week should not be given in writing but explained orally, and not all at once but a few one day and others the next, as discretion dictates. Not everyone has the same capacity for abstinence: some are physically more robust and need more to eat than others, so that the one giving the Exercises needs to reflect carefully to whom and in what way he gives the fourth rule, and how the person uses it, to avoid any extremes.

[146] The time for explaining these rules is not exclusively the Third Week; some of them can be given even in the First or Second Week if the one giving the Exercises sees that the exercitant needs them.

However, they should all be explained during this Week if they have not been earlier; there are fewer bits of instruction to give during this Week than in the previous ones and it is good always to bring something new at each visit.

[147] CHAPTER 10: REMARKS ON THE EXERCISES OF THE FOURTH WEEK

[148] The exercises on the Resurrection include also those on the Ascension and the coming of the Holy Spirit.

[149] All the exercises of the life, death, passion, and resurrection belong to the illuminative life. The fruit gathered from the exercises of the illuminative life is that anyone persevering in them daily obtains new light of practical knowledge for weighing, estimating, and judging all the realities of faith, both primary and secondary; but chiefly the primary realities. Through this light he progressively comes to give each of them its rightful degree of estimation, and through this estimation to accord each its proper degree of love or detestation. He thereby grows more perfect in faith, hope, and charity, both intensively and extensively: intensively, by advancing daily in a limited number of things; and extensively, by progressively broadening out to other realities of faith regarding which he had not yet acquired a practical awareness.

[150] And while this actual awareness does not last continuously but is frequently interrupted by eating, sleeping, or other distractions, the soul nevertheless retains a habitual illumination, and this habit later frequently inclines and motivates him to similar acts, especially if he makes an effort to motivate himself often with these acts, so that eventually he is acting most of the time out of this knowledge, and in acting even finds almost always or regularly that he has a greater light in weighing and estimating these realities. Thus, if his thoughts turn to his sins, he has a deeper knowledge of their gravity and a greater detestation for them; if to hell or death, he experiences deeper sorrow or fear; if to earthly things, a greater contempt for them; if to the virtues, gifts, or good works, a greater appreciation of them; if to divine things, a loftier judgment in their regard; if to God, he finds him occupying a

higher place in his soul. This is the enlightenment or illumination of the soul, growing from day to day like the morning light.

[151] The exercise on Love belongs to the Fourth Week. It can be given a day or so after it has begun and may be made contemporaneously with those on the Resurrection. Thus, one hour could be given to the Resurrection and the others to the exercise on Love. If it is preferred to make it by itself, the exercises on the Resurrection should first be concluded in two or three days, and then the exercise on Love begun.

[152] Since the four points of the exercise on Love are extremely fertile, a person who finds one of them sufficient for an hour of meditation can do the others in the following hours, although the colloquy should be made at the end of each meditation. As much time as seems good can be spent on this exercise, provided that time is left for the three Methods of Prayer.

[153] The exercise on Love pertains to the unitive life, for while we do unite ourselves to God through faith ("I will espouse you to myself in faith" [Hos 2:20]) and hope, we achieve union with God directly through love and charity, whereby we embrace him in our hearts and are transformed into him; as John says, "God is love, and he who abides in love abides in God and God in him" [1 John 4:16]—although we need to aspire toward perfect union through a charity that is perfect, i.e., burning and vehement.

[154] CHAPTER 11: REMARKS ON THE THREE METHODS OF PRAYER

[155] The third method is the easiest and the most suitable for simple persons.

[156] The first is a method of examining one's conscience on the commandments of God and the Church, the deadly sins, the works of mercy, etc., so as to confess one's sins better afterwards. Do not think that this whole examination has to be completed in an hour. When the hour is up you can stop where you are, adding the colloquy at the end, and in the next prayer take it up again where you left off.

[157] If someone is so experienced and gifted at meditating that he can go deeper into this prayer, he can, after the Addition and the preparatory prayer, consider in the case of each commandment (1) how holy and good it is, (2) how beneficial it is for those who keep it, and (3) how he himself has kept it— proceeding in this way from commandment to commandment, ending with a colloquy in which he asks God's pardon for his faults, etc.

Chapter 12: Remark on the Rules for Thinking with the Catholic Church

[158] These rules are framed for thinking with the Roman Catholic Church against the heretics of our time; they are more needed by those who live and deal with heretics than by those who deal only with Catholics.

End

Let all this be submitted to the judgment of the Roman Catholic Church.

PART III

THE OFFICIAL DIRECTORY OF 1599

The Official Directory of 1599

This, the fullest of all the directories, is essentially a compilation drawn up by a special commission from what was judged, after extensive consultation, as most valuable in the earlier Jesuit directories. It was published with official status by Father General Claudio Aquaviva and thereafter, together with the book of the Exercises itself, formed part of the Jesuit order's "Institute," or corpus of fundamental documents.

For a more detailed account of its genesis, see the introduction to this volume. (Original in Latin).

DIRECTORY TO THE SPIRITUAL EXERCISES

SOME YEARS AGO, printed copies of a *Directory to the Spiritual Exercises* were sent to the provinces, so that before the work was given its final touches practice and experience might indicate whether anything might advantageously be added, removed, or better expressed. To this end we instructed that if such improvements occurred to anyone he should send them through his superiors to our Reverend Father General in Rome. Accordingly, now that observations by several persons have been sent to Rome and all points have been fully and exactly discussed in the Fifth General Congregation by the fathers deputed for the revision of the Directory, and have been once more carefully weighed by our Reverend Father General and the Fathers Assistant, it has been judged that the Directory could finally be edited in its present form. We hope that this labor will not only meet with approval but also be of great use to those who will give the Spiritual Exercises. It only remains for our fathers to take advantage of this occasion (as is more fully stated in a circular letter to the provincials) by applying themselves with increased zeal to the practice of the Exercises and endeavoring to give them to others also with greater profit.

Given at Rome, October 1, 1599, by order of our Reverend Father General.

JACOPO DOMINICI
Secretary

INTRODUCTION: EXCELLENCE AND UTILITY OF THE EXERCISES,
AND THE NEED FOR A DIRECTORY

[1] 1. **A means of salvation.**—Among other instruments which God in his goodness and clemency has deigned to bestow upon our Society of Jesus for procuring both our own and our neighbors' salvation and perfection, not the least is the Spiritual Exercises.

[2] 2. **Taught by the anointing of the Holy Spirit.**—These Exercises consist of spiritual instructions which, as the preface to the book states, our Father in Christ Ignatius composed not so much from books as from the anointing of the Holy Spirit and his own inward experience and practice. They are the lights which God gave him in the first fervor of his conversion and afterwards constantly confirmed to him throughout his growth in virtue and holiness.

[3] 3. **Direction needed for prayer.**—God our Lord communicated to him as head and founder the entire idea of our Society in both its outward form and its special type of interior virtues. Hence, seeing that prayer and communion with God are of such paramount importance that religious observance and spiritual progress in great measure depend upon them, it was of the greatest importance to have from our founder also this method and guidance for prayer for all of us to follow and strive to keep continually before our eyes.

[4] 4. **Strongly recommended by Father Ignatius.**—This is why our Father Ignatius himself used to commend these Exercises to our men so highly —not only constantly in his conversation, as tradition tells us, but also by his personal example. He frequently mentions them in the Constitutions also, especially IV, 8.5, where he says that all should strive to acquire skill in the use of these spiritual arms which so manifestly conduce to the service of God. There is also extant a letter of his to a priest named Miona[1] who had been his confessor in Paris, in which he indicates very plainly what he thought of the Exercises: he advises and even earnestly begs him to make them with all diligence, promising that if he does so he will find great spiritual profit both for himself and for helping many others. This he states in quite weighty and pregnant terms.

[5] 5. **Recommendations by others.**—Similar testimony has come from many others. Among them are men distinguished for their learning, virtue, and experience in human affairs, and above all for their skill in spiritual matters— persons who after actually experiencing the Exercises formed so high an opinion of them that they willingly declared both in word and writing that by using them they had reaped more fruit for their souls than they had dared to hope for.

---

[1] For this letter, see Appendix 1.

[6] 6. **Approved by the pope.**—But above all there is the sanction of the Apostolic See. After submitting the Exercises to careful scrutiny by learned men, it approved them in 1548 as being "replete with piety and holiness, and most conducive to the edification and spiritual advancement of the faithful."

[7] 7. **Their great value confirmed by the experience of many.**— Lastly, there is the experience of the huge and almost unbelievable benefit which commonly follows upon the use of the Exercises. First of all, large numbers of our own men, especially in the early days, received through the Exercises the spirit of their vocation; so that it can be truly said that it was through the Exercises that our Society came together in the beginning and afterwards received its increase. Secondly, many others also have left the world and entered other religious orders, or else, being already religious, have been remarkably reformed—not only individuals, but often whole communities. Numbers of people, too, living in the world and so given up to vices that they could not be drawn from their sinful ways by either exhortations or sermons, have by this means alone been converted and permanently brought back to a better life. In short, there is no denying that immense fruits have been produced among people of every kind, state, and condition; or that the more the use of these Exercises prevails anywhere, there is also seen a correspondingly greater reformation of morals.

[8] 8. **Main fruits of the Exercises.**—It should cause no surprise that such great results are obtained—and in relatively little time and even with relatively little labor. Given that "the will of God is our sanctification," as St. Paul says [1 Thess 4:3], so that his boundless goodness is always ready to pour out his gifts upon his creatures, there can be no doubt that a creature that throws up no impediment but instead brings the right dispositions will easily and in a short time obtain great graces from God. This is what the Exercises accomplish, and with great effectiveness: they dispose the soul for the reception of these gifts. First, they withdraw the person from all occupation with other things and business and lead him into a kind of desert where God may speak to his heart [Hos 2:14], and he on his part may obey the words of the psalm: "Be still, and see that I am God" [Ps 46:11]. Then, placing at the outset before the retreatant's eyes the ultimate end of a human being, viz., eternal blessedness, they show him first how far he has strayed from it up until now, and thus engender in him sorrow and hatred for sin. Next, they reveal the beauty of virtue, and by the example of Christ our Lord kindle the desire of imitating him. Finally, they furnish a method for reforming one's whole life according to the rule and will of God—whether the state of life itself is to be altered, or not altered but corrected for the better.

[9] 9. **The Exercises commended to our men.**—Seeing how great are the utility and fruits of the Exercises it, is evident how earnestly their use should be commended to all of our men. And this is more clearly seen when

we add—as in all humility we can and ought to know—that this whole work, namely this special instruction and method of meditation, and all this special teaching, at once so useful and so solid, is a truly remarkable gift and bestowal of God on our Society. With God having given it to us, and given it to be used, this very fact undoubtedly ought to stimulate us all to use it more eagerly and not keep such a treasure hidden and buried in the earth unused.

[10] 10. **Method needed for giving the Exercises.**—But great as is the value of this use of the Exercises which we have described, great also is the need to have a method for imparting them. This is partly because all cannot have the same expertise and skill; partly also because not everything could be included in the book of the Spiritual Exercises, so that some points in its practical application remain obscure; and finally in order that uniformity may be observed by all our men, and that the Exercises may not be interpreted by each according to his own bent and preference, which would result in the progressive introduction of new and divergent methods.

[11] 11. **Directory commissioned by the First General Congregation.**—For these reasons, among the other things which the First General Congregation deemed necessary for the guidance of our men in the ministry and for the help of their neighbor, they decreed in title 6, decr. 28, the drawing up of a directory for giving the Exercises. This task was entrusted to the superior general.

[12] 12. **Senior fathers consulted.**—After certain of the fathers, at either their own prompting or the command of superiors, had spent much labor on the matter, our Father Claudio Aquaviva decided to transmit their work, along with some suggestions from other persons, to certain of the senior fathers of the Society for them to examine and give their own opinion about, putting in writing whatever they thought might be added. From these opinions and criticisms what seemed most suitable to our purpose has been selected and put together under its proper headings in this directory—to the glory of God and the spiritual profit of our Society and of our neighbors.

CHAPTER 1: HOW PEOPLE ARE TO BE INDUCED TO MAKE
THE EXERCISES

[13] 1. **A desire should be stimulated in people.**—Our Constitutions say that when giving an explanation of the Exercises to people our aim ought to be not only to satisfy their inquiries but also to awaken in them a desire to be themselves helped thereby. Hence it is plain that it should be the purpose of our fathers gently to persuade as many as possible to make the Exercises. For inasmuch as charity and zeal for souls ought to move us to desire and labor for others' salvation and perfection, they should also impel us to make use of this means which is so well fitted and so powerful to effect these ends.

[14] 2. **To be done discretely and modestly.**—Prudence, however, is required for doing this with discretion and moderation, that is to say, at the proper time and occasion, without being troublesome or offensive; and especially with care not to arouse any suspicion that we are trying to draw people into the religious state. Good sense and the anointing of the Holy Spirit, who in this and in all else is ready to direct and help those who work along with him, will suggest to each one the judicious and cautious way of inviting others to make the Exercises.

[15] 3. **How to proceed.**—Our blessed Father Ignatius thought and often advised that it was best to do this in confession, not unseasonably or abruptly but on some suitable occasion either naturally presenting itself or skillfully contrived; or even outside confession, when a person is seen to be not altogether content with his present state, either on account of some inward uncertainty or outward trouble, as for instance reverses in his affairs or unkindness on the part of his friends or some other similar cause. Sometimes a person's very vices or falls may afford the best opportunity, especially when he is enlightened by God to recognize them, grieves over them, and desires to amend. This is often a good occasion for suggesting the Exercises as a remedy for his malady.

[16] 4. **Indicate the fruits of the Exercises.**—Whatever occasion is made use of, one should point out the great fruits which customarily follow from the Exercises: peace and quiet of soul, interior light, knowledge of how to order one's whole life aright, whatever one's state.

[17] 5. **Examples of persons who have made them.**—It is also helpful to cite examples of persons who made the Exercises with fruit and were afterwards quite satisfied, testifying by the reformation of their lives to the great good they have gained thereby. In this regard, it is useful to point out the spiritual consolations and sweetness these persons experienced, so that people will not be frightened off by the labor entailed. However, in relating such examples we should refrain from instancing persons who have entered religious life—or at least omit mentioning this fact. We should speak instead of those who reformed their lives while remaining in the world. Otherwise the person we are trying to encourage may easily fear that he too will be drawn into religious life, and on that account shrink from the Exercises.

[18] 6. **The Exercises needed by all.**—On the contrary, we ought to rid people of the idea that the Exercises are only for religious or for persons who wish to become religious. Everyone is in need of God's grace: not religious only but all people in the world as well, given the dangers in the midst of which they constantly live. And so they too ought to seek the helps by which they may be best disposed to receive this grace.

[19] 7. **To whom should they be given? Father Ignatius' mind.**—When it comes to the full and complete Exercises, however, it should be noted

that Father Ignatius considered that these should not be given to everyone indiscriminately but only to a select few who appear fit for greater things. That this is so may be plainly gathered from an instruction said to have been written at his dictation which runs as follows (cf. Doc. 4.1):

"I do not think it advisable to encourage a person to make the Exercises unless he possesses the following qualifications, or at least the more important of them. Firstly, he should be a person who may be expected to be very useful in the Lord's household if called to his service. Secondly, even if he lacks such superior endowments by way of acquired arts and sciences as to give assurance of this, he should at least be of an age and sufficient intelligence to reach it eventually. Thirdly, he should be free to make a decision regarding his own life, even for embracing the state of perfection should God will to call him. Fourthly, he should be spiritually inclined, and have a decent and presentable appearance. Fifthly, he should not be so strongly attached to anything that it would be difficult to withdraw him from it and bring him to that state of even balance which is necessary for rightly transacting this business of the soul with God. The more unsure he is about his way of life, and the more desirous he is of knowing what he ought to do with himself, and the apter he is for helping the Church, the more suitable he will be—other things being equal—for making the Exercises. Persons who lack these dispositions or who are married or otherwise unqualified should not be given the full Exercises, particularly when other more suitable persons ask for them or when our men are occupied with other work. Nevertheless, such persons could be given some meditations of the First Week, in their own homes if possible, with the recommendation to withdraw to a secluded part of the house and not go out except for Mass and vespers or when they go to receive the meditations. In addition, they can also be given some other exercises if this seems good, v.g., the three Methods of Prayer and the like."

These same ideas of Father Ignatius can be found in somewhat briefer form in the *Constitutions*, VII, 4.F.

CHAPTER 2: DISPOSITIONS WHICH THE EXERCITANT SHOULD BRING TO THE EXERCISES

[20] 1. **He should understand their importance.**—In the first place, the person who comes to make the Exercises should endeavor to realize the importance of what he is undertaking. It concerns his soul—and in such a way that, provided he is diligent in doing his part, he will lay foundations for his spiritual advancement which will be of value throughout the rest of his life. From this he can understand the eagerness, diligence, and courage that he ought to bring to so great a work and enterprise. He should therefore make up his mind to act manfully, to throw aside all hindrances to God's grace, and to

bend all the power of his soul to cooperate with this grace and to dispose himself as fully as he can for receiving it.

[21] 2. **Severance from affairs and responsibilities.**—For this purpose, he should first disencumber himself from all his domestic affairs, or at least hand them over for a time to others. For the whole time he should cut off all contact with friends and relations, even all messages and letters. These things frequently fill the mind with a lot of distracting thoughts, and chill whatever fervor a person may have gained. Indeed, his endeavor should be to shut out every other consideration, no matter what it may be, just as if he had no other business in the world.

[22] 3. **Entering with hopefulness.**—Next, he should have a great hope in God's goodness and generosity. God seeks out even those who go astray, and pursues those who flee from him; how much more will he receive and welcome those who come to him with a good will. The exercitant should therefore put his trust in that infinite clemency which has given him this good desire and so will give him also grace and strength to follow it through well and fruitfully. For "his will is our sanctification" [1 Thess 4:3].

[23] 4. **The aim he should have.**—Furthermore, his attitude ought to be such that he is willing and eager to undertake these Exercises not so much in order to enjoy spiritual sweetness as to learn God's will for him and, withdrawing his affections from all earthly things, to fix them on his Creator. Above all, in addition to this desire for spiritual progress, it is essential that he be wholly resigned to the will of God in all matters where he is still free, and be fully resolved to do whatever he discovers God wants of him.

[24] 5. **How he should enter the Exercises.**—Therefore no one ought to bring with him any settled decision from which he is unwilling to be moved. He should avoid setting any measure or bounds to God's grace, i.e., being ready to receive light and help only within certain limits and no farther. Apart from the inappropriateness of a creature acting in this way toward his Creator, such a course is extremely harmful to the persons himself. Firstly, he deprives himself of the greater graces which God was perhaps going to give him. Secondly, his lack of generosity and his grudging and ungrateful stance toward God deserve that he should be denied even the graces he was willing to receive. He ought to open wide his heart, desiring to unite himself as closely as possible with God and to be enriched and filled to his utmost capacity with heavenly treasures. This describes the attitude he should have with regard to God.

[25] 6. **His behavior toward the director.**—Toward the one giving him the Exercises he ought to behave as a pupil toward his master and guide in this difficult and dangerous journey. For this reason, even if in other respects the exercitant is a man of prudence, learning, and wide experience in affairs, nevertheless during this time he should not trust to his own prudence or

learning but surrender himself wholly to his guide. As St. Paul says, "'Let him become a fool, that he may be wise" [1 Cor 3:18]. He should follow St. Peter's admonition: "As newborn babes, desire milk without guile, that thereby you may grow unto salvation" [1 Pet 2:2]. Accordingly, he should look upon his director as an instrument of God sent to him to direct and conduct him along the way that leads to eternal life. He should receive the director's instructions to him with all reverence, eagerness, and trust.

[26] 7. **He should conceal nothing.**—Furthermore, he should not conceal anything from his director, and not make any pretence. He should sincerely bare his whole heart to him, telling him candidly how each meditation went, and what consolations, desolations, lights, or good desires he experienced during the meditations or at other times. Finally, he should be completely obedient to the director in all things. He should make no other meditations, follow no other order, and undertake no other penances or bodily mortification than those prescribed by the director. In short, he should convince himself that the more carefully and exactly he follows the director's guidance the fitter he will be to receive a larger measure of grace; for such humility and simplicity are very pleasing to God, and it is with such persons that he will hold converse. These, then, are indispensable conditions for gaining more abundant fruit.

[27] 8. **What exercises to suggest to the exercitant.**—But if the one giving the Exercises has reason to fear that proposing the complete Exercises might frighten the exercitant off and hold him back, it would be better either to offer only some of them at first, or make them sound less demanding. Afterwards, if he sees the exercitant to be filled with spiritual sweetness and more capable of bearing it, he can gradually urge him to make the Exercises in the fullest and most perfect way.

CHAPTER 3: INSTRUCTIONS TO BE GIVEN THE EXERCITANT AT THE OUTSET, AND THE TIME TO BE SPENT IN MEDITATING

[28] 1. **Exact observance.**—Other instructions which the exercitant needs to be given are contained in the Annotations and rules printed in the book of the Exercises and so there is no reason for repeating them here. This much, however, should be said about them: the exercitant must devote the greatest diligence to observing these instructions, for the more fully he does so the sooner and the more abundantly will he find the spiritual fruit which he seeks.

[29] 2. **Which books to have and read.**—In particular, the exercitant ought to be told not to read anything except the written texts handed to him and that, to remove the occasion for reading, he should have no books in his room except the breviary (if he is a priest) or the office of the Blessed Virgin. However, if the director thinks it advisable, he can read Gerson's *Imitation of*

Christ during the First Week, and parts of the Gospels and the lives of the saints during the Second, as is said in the note at the end of the meditation on the Kingdom of Christ [100]. However, any lives of the saints ought to be carefully selected and matched to the exercitant's circumstances. Thus, if he is a married man it should be the life of one who has lived devoutly in the world, and so with religious and other such cases. The director must therefore take pains to pick out suitable materials.

[30] 3. **Which mysteries to read.**—In reading the Gospels, also, the exercitant should only read the mystery upon which he is to meditate in the same hour or day, as is laid down in the first note after the 5th contemplation of the Second Week [127].

[31] 4. **Books to relieve boredom.**—However, if after making his meditation the exercitant seems to be bored and wasting his time, some other reading, as has been said above, may be added, v.g., during the First Week, Denis the Carthusian on the four last things, St. Augustine's *Confessions*, and the like. Care should be taken that this reading is not only good and useful in itself but also calculated to produce the affection which the exercitant is seeking at that point in the Exercises, v.g., contrition, fear, or love of God. The exercitant should also be warned and instructed to read with a view to meditation, i.e., not superficially out of an appetite to know and see something new, but dwelling upon and carefully weighing what he reads, and entering into the affections which it suggests.

[32] 5. **What the exercitant should write.**—The same applies to writing. The exercitant should write only what is connected with prayer, i.e., points which God may communicate to him in meditation, or even outside of meditation. These should be noted very briefly, not diffusely after the manner of a discourse. These points can be of two kinds: either practical, pertaining to action, as for example desires or resolutions to do something; or pertaining to knowledge, as truths or lights bearing on a topic such as a virtue like humility, contempt of the world, patience, etc., or bearing on some matter of the meditation, such as the Incarnation, the Passion, or the like—particularly truths that serve as fundamental principles opening the way to a good understanding and meditation of these subjects.

[33] 6. **Moderation in reading and writing.**—But care must be taken not to let the pleasure of reading or writing encroach upon the time for meditation, or upon that of preparation for meditation. Prior to each meditation the exercitant should set everything aside for a while and turn his whole mind to the points of the upcoming exercise. Care must also be taken not to weary the mind or drain its strength by excessive reading or writing. The meditation must always be safeguarded, and everything else subordinated to it.

[34] 7. **Number of hours for prayer.**—Those who wish to make the Exercises in full form and who have the strength for it will generally spend five

hours each day in meditation: the 1st about midnight (a time most helpful for meditation because of its quiet and deep silence), the 2nd at daybreak, the 3rd a little before dinner, the 4th in the afternoon, and the 5th in the later afternoon. After each hour's meditation a further quarter hour should be devoted to examining the meditation just made.

[35] 8. **Who should be dispensed.**—Others who are not in strong health, or who cannot observe such a demanding program, may be dispensed from making the meditation at midnight, yet still retaining the five hours—or fewer if the director thinks it desirable. It will rarely be a good idea to have more than five hours. When these mental exercises are prolonged too much, the result is apt to be a dulling of the mind and debilitation of the will.

CHAPTER 4: THE PLACE FOR THE EXERCISES, AND OTHER DETAILS

[36] 1. **Place.**—There is no doubt that the place where the Exercises are made ought to be secluded from all social contact and even the sight of others, especially family and friends. This is what Father Ignatius advises in Annotation 20, where he also points out three advantages of this. Hence, if the person about to begin the Exercises is unable to find so convenient and suitable a place elsewhere, he may with the superior's approval be received into one of our houses. However his room should be as removed as possible from the other rooms and domestic offices so that he will see and hear as little as possible of our men's doings.

[37] 2. **Payment of expenses.**—As regards expenses, when the guest arrives at our house the superior ought to be consulted. It should be his responsibility to arrange matters so as not to overburden the house, but also not to let concern for the house cut down the number of those who can make the Exercises. Generally speaking, if payment of expenses is offered, especially by wealthier people, it should not be refused—nor, if not offered, should it be demanded. At all times we should avoid anything in this respect which might appear mean or unbecoming.

[38] 3. **The person who waits on the exercitant.**—In this place, besides a director, the exercitant should also have someone to wait on him and bring him his meals. This should be a trustworthy person, discreet, silent, and one who will give edification by the example of his modesty, humility, and devotion. He should talk only about things connected with the retreatant's food, room, or service—and that in the fewest possible words, always referring everything to the director, to whom he shall report every detail. He should not bring the exercitant anything, even if requested to do so, without consulting the director.

[39] 4. **He should make up the bed, etc.**—He should make up the bed and sweep the room at a convenient time, which will usually be during Mass.

Whatever else is needed he should bring clean and fit for use, always showing the greatest charity and attention. At the same time, he should remember to pray daily for his charge.

[40] 5. **May be an acquaintance.**—Sometimes it is good to assign to this service a person who is known to the exercitant or on friendly terms with him, not only for his consolation but also for his spiritual profit. Sometimes persons will open their hearts to such friends more freely than to a director they have not previously known. But it is altogether up to the director to decide how far such a friend should go, what he ought to say, and in what manner. The director ought to make use of him as his instrument in whatever way he thinks will be most helpful to the exercitant.

[41] 6. **Food.**—With regard to food, the exercitant should be asked what he wishes to be prepared for him, and he should be brought what he has asked for.

[42] 7. **Visitors.**—With the exception of the person waiting on him, the exercitant should normally not have visits from anyone else—certainly not from seculars, unless an emergency requires it. However, one or other of our fathers might be sent to him if he asks this of the director—or even if without his asking the director judges it would be a help and comfort to him.

[43] 8. **Conversations.**—But whoever visits him should take care that only useful conversation is held, and that it is confined to spiritual matters—without, however, any indication of a wish to urge him to a particular state of life, least of all to entering the Society. For besides the fact that a vocation ought to be free and come from God, people who are deliberating about this matter are usually put off if they observe or suspect any such intention. On the other hand, experience often shows that they are urged on when they detect no such desire on the part of our men.

CHAPTER 5: QUALITIES AND DUTIES OF THE DIRECTOR

[44] 1. **Qualities of the director.**—Regarding the person who gives the Exercises, the main advice given by Father Ignatius (*Constitutions*, IV, 8.5), is that he should first have experience of them himself, so as to be able to give an account of them and possess skill in giving them. The better to obtain this, he should at the beginning (as is stated in the declaration on the same passage) give them to persons with whom the loss would be less considerable if he makes mistakes, such as young persons or those who will not be making an election about their state of life. It will also be good for him to confer his own method of procedure with that of someone more experienced, noting carefully anything he may find useful or counterproductive. The main thing, then, is for the director to possess experience in spiritual things, and specifically in these Exercises.

[45] 2. **His character.**—He should be prudent and discreet. His speech

should be spare, moderate, and well thought out. He should be kindly rather than austere, especially toward persons suffering from temptations, desolation, aridity, or weariness. These he ought to console, inspire, and encourage with suitable counsel and advice, as well as by his own and others' prayers. It is good if he is liked by the exercitant, who will then trust him more fully and open himself more freely.

[46] 3. **Authority combined with gravity.**—Further, in dealing with the exercitant he should take care always to preserve a certain authority, as a person of maturity and gravity, especially with an exercitant of higher rank or station than his own. For it is very conducive to the exercitant's spiritual profit that the director preserve the position and character of a master, as in truth he is. But this authority should always be tempered with a religious humility shining forth in his words and acts, so that not the least trace of vanity is observed in him. In this he should imitate Christ our Lord, who, though the model of all modesty, nevertheless, as it is written, "taught as one having authority" [Matt 7:29]. Thus the director should carry out his office with all freedom, whether in giving instruction, admonition, or direction—wherever he sees anything that needs to be set right or corrected.

[47] 4. **He should ascribe any results to God.**—When he sees any good results in those making the Exercises, he should take care not to attribute anything to his own efforts or skill, since all these effects of grace are from God alone. Advice from without (which itself, if good, derives from God) is helpful and effective only insofar as God concurs and cooperates with it. On the other hand, the director should put great trust in God, and confidently hope in his help both for himself and for the exercitant.

[48] 5. **He should let God deal with his creature.**—He should be most careful not to intrude anything merely his own. Seeing that such counsels ought to be received from God's inspiration, he needs to beware of urging anything upon the exercitant with indiscreet zeal, but should leave it to God to deal with his creature as his own goodness sees fit. The better and more easily to do this, he should preserve in himself an attitude of complete indifference, desiring only that the most holy will of God to be fully and perfectly accomplished in the exercitant's soul. His only effort should be to get the exercitant to know how to seek the will of God and how to free himself from the snares which the devil employs to hold people back.

[49] 6. **Insight into the exercitant's character.**—He should also study the exercitant carefully: not only his state and condition—whether noble or commoner, learned or unlearned, etc.—but also his special capacities—whether simple or astute, spiritually advanced or still unskilled and a novice, intelligent and capable or duller and slower. Persons of different characters will have to be handled in different ways: to persons who are uneducated things will have to explained more fully, to other persons more succinctly, etc.

[50] 7. **He must know the book of the Exercises.**—Above all the director has to have thoroughly studied the book of the Exercises and have it at his fingertips, especially the Annotations and rules. It is not enough to look through these cursorily. He needs to weigh every matter—indeed almost every word—with care, for some points of the highest importance are expressed quite briefly and serious loss could occur if these were to be passed over unnoticed. So the director will need careful study of the Exercises beforehand, as well as a careful rereading while giving them, especially of the part the exercitant is currently making.

[51] 8. **He should meditate the exercise beforehand.**—It will also help if before giving each exercise the director himself meditates it somewhat, so far as possible, in order to impress it better upon the exercitant.

CHAPTER 6: VISITING THE EXERCITANT

[52] 1. **How often.**—Once the Exercises have begun, the director should be careful to make his scheduled visits to the exercitant. It seems a good practice to visit him once a day, and no oftener unless some need arises, as sometimes happens during the First Week because of the newness of the matter or in the Second because of difficulty in the election.

[53] 2. **When not to visit.**—On the other hand, with mature persons who are well initiated in spirit and devotion, it may be a good idea occasionally to omit a day. As for the time of the visit, the director should pick that which is most convenient and suitable. In itself the best time would seem to be the early morning; the exercitant's mind is then more apt for perceiving and penetrating things. Toward evening, however, is usually when he needs the visit most, for that can be a time when temptations and desolations are intensified, the mind being then less fit for contemplation so that it sometimes becomes depressed and more vulnerable to temptation.

[54] 3. **Assigning someone for recreation.**—The director should also consider whether for special reasons it may not sometimes be a good idea for either himself or some other mature and discreet person assigned by him to spend time with the exercitant immediately after dinner or supper for suitable recreation.

CHAPTER 7: ASKING AN ACCOUNT OF THE MEDITATION

[55] 1. **How to ask.**—Whatever the time the director may choose for his visit, when he comes he will ask the exercitant how he has been doing since he saw him last, particularly in his meditations. He will ask what method he has followed in them, what trains of thought and movements of the will he has had, what consolations he has experienced, and in which points.

[56] 2. **If consolations are plentiful.**—If it has gone well with him and he has an abundance of consolations, the director should not praise him too much lest he become pleased with himself. Instead, he should first of all instruct him how to reap solid fruit from these consolations. For if nothing further is done, the sweet affection, which usually does not last long, will die away and leave no fruit. Hence, the exercitant should be taught how to direct these consolations to the amendment of his conduct and the ordering of his whole life, as it is written: "Not the hearers of the law are just before God, but the doers of the law shall be justified" [Rom 2:13]. At the same time, the exercitant should be told to put down briefly in writing the principal consolations and lights that come to him, as well as his good desires and resolutions. These will be very useful to him at another time when he no longer experiences these lights.

[57] 3. **Preparation against time of desolation.**—The director should also prepare him for the period of desolation and aridity which often ensues, so that he will not be unprepared when it comes. Moreover, when all is going well the director should not stay long with the exercitant but instead allow God to deal with his creature and the creature with God—unless it seems necessary to give him some direction, or even some recreation if he is overly caught up in these thoughts.

[58] 4. **In time of desolation.**—On the other hand, if the exercitant is suffering from aridity, desolation, or distractions while meditating, the director should question him about his behavior during the meditation, especially his observance of the Additions. If he finds he has been remiss in any of these things, he should give him advice and instruction.

[59] 5. **Opening a way to meditation.**—He should also open up a way for him in his meditation, suggesting and pointing in the direction of ideas that he can follow up on his own.

[60] 6. **Encouragement.**—He should urge the exercitant to be patient and persevering and not to let himself be overcome by weariness or be deflected from prayer because of the difficulty and toil he is experiencing. If he courageously perseveres in knocking with hope and confidence at the door of divine mercy, it will surely be opened to him, as it is written: "If he delays wait for him, for he will surely come and will not be late" [Hab 2:3].

[61] 7. **Means of obtaining devotion.**—He should also remind the exercitant that the best way to obtain devotion from God is to humble himself under his mighty hand, subjecting and resigning himself to his divine will. Often the despondency and bitterness he feels comes not so much from fervor as from an unspoken pride by which he places reliance on his own efforts, or from ambition to excel, or from a self-love that is avid for consolation. Hence it is important to remember that when a person has done his best he should leave everything else to the will and charity of God, trusting that the very

aridity from which he suffers is permitted by God for his best. This affection of humility and subjection of oneself to God often the surest way to win the grace of praying well.

[62] 8. **Give no occasion for suspicion.**—Above all, the director should take care never to give the exercitant any cause to suspect that he has a poor opinion of him, even when he has not behaved as well as he might. He should always show that he has good hope for him, and by his own hope instill hope and courage in his pupil.

CHAPTER 8: GIVING THE MEDITATIONS

[63] 1. **How to give the points.**—In giving the points of the meditations, the director should not expand them much or develop them so fully that the one meditating is unable, or scarcely able, to discover anything new for himself. Experience shows that in all cases people find more pleasure in, and are more deeply moved by, things they find out for themselves. Hence, it is enough for the director to point out a vein which the exercitant can then mine for himself. Still, with exercitants who may not be capable of this a slightly fuller explanation can be given.

[64] 2. **Should be given in writing.**—Usually the meditations are given in writing to avoid straining the exercitant's memory and so hindering his devotion. All his strength and powers should be reserved unimpaired for the exercise of the understanding and will.

[65] 3. **Avoidance of mental strain.**—Another duty of the director is to make sure the exercitant does not strain his head by excessive application to prayer. This is a considerable danger, both in time of desolation when the soul works harder rowing against the current, so to speak, as well as in time of consolation when it runs unrestrainedly before the wind. Hence, it is not enough merely to warn the exercitant about the need for moderation. Those who make the Exercises are generally inexperienced and novices in meditating, incapable of recognizing what might be harmful for them. And so they need to be questioned about the method they are using to raise their minds to God and hold them there, particularly about the composition of place. If it appears they are doing violence to themselves, they must be taught a manner and method for thinking gently about divine realities, because otherwise they will not be able to continue meditating for very long; also because all true and solid fruit consists in knowledge of truths and movements of the will deriving from an interior light, and not in this strained attention or in the forced tears which Cassian deservedly derides [*Conferences* ix.29]; and finally because, while this work of prayer demands our own cooperation, it nevertheless depends far more upon God and is his gift. Hence a soul should dispose itself for this work by humility and purity of heart rather than trust to its own preparation and efforts.

[66] 4. **General admonitions for the director.**—Any further instructions the director may need are found for the most part in the book of the Exercises, partly in the meditations themselves, partly in the Annotations, and partly also in the Rules for the Discernment of Spirits. The latter are most helpful, shedding light over the entire spiritual journey, in both the First and the succeeding Weeks. And so, to repeat a remark made earlier, the director must be thoroughly familiar with the book, and refresh his memory of it while he is giving the Exercises. Each time he reads it he will derive fresh light and insight.

[67] 5. **Modifying the order and method.**—A further observation for the director is this. On the one hand, he is supposed keep exactly to the order, method, and detailed instructions found in the book, and the more strictly he does this the more God will work together with him. On the other hand, he is allowed considerable discretion, in view of the differences among persons who make the Exercises or of the spirits by which they are moved, to alter the exercises or prescribe others appropriate for individual needs. This is stated plainly in Annotations 17 and 18, and elsewhere.

CHAPTER 9: TYPES OF PERSONS TO WHOM THE EXERCISES
CAN BE GIVEN

[68] 1. **Two classes of exercitants; first class.**—Persons to whom the Exercises may be given can be broadly divided into two classes. The first comprises those who have all the conditions described in chapter 1 as requisite for making the complete Exercises. Regarding these persons nothing special needs to be said, since the whole of this directory will apply to them, particularly if they wish to consider the question of a state of life.

[69] 2. **Second class.**—But there are others who ought not to be given the complete Exercises. They may be persons whose state of life is already fixed, such as those bound by matrimony and others who for various reasons ought not to be given the election. Or they may be persons who, because of public business or other occupations, lack time or opportunity, as is the case with public functionaries and sometimes with persons of the nobility, heads of families, and the like. There are also persons who only want some help from the Exercises in preparing a general confession and drawing up a plan for the good ordering of their life in the future. Finally, there are those of insufficient ability, such as ignorant and illiterate people, who still ought to be helped according to their capacity.

[70] 3. **Religious.**—Religious (apart from members of our own Society, who will be treated separately in the following chapter) with no previous experience of mental prayer should be instructed in the same way as any secular person, especially if they have previously led a lax and careless life. In that case they should be well exercised in the First Week, so as to come to know and

have contrition for their sins, whether committed in the world or in religious life, for this is the foundation of all reformation and amendment of one's whole life. If they have previously been given to mental prayer and devotion, the First Week can be gone through more briefly so that they can dwell with greater intensity on meditating the life of Christ.

[71] 4. **Their aim in the Exercises.**—Special care should be taken, both in the First Week and afterwards, that religious be confirmed in their vocation and fully convinced that for them the way to reach eternal happiness is to give the highest importance to the rules of their order, to observe them with great care, and to have the deepest possible attachment to their own institute. They need to discover the reasons why they have hitherto made so little progress, and should direct their meditations and examinations to this goal. All this should be set forth at the start and pursued thereafter throughout their retreat.

[72] 5. **Zeal for souls.**—Finally, religious need to be stirred up to zeal for helping others by their good example and works—whether their neighbors, as specified by their institute, or their own religious brethren.

[73] 6. **The election.**—Religious should not be given the election of a state of life. However, it will be helpful to give them the rules and instructions for the election so that later they can assist themselves or others in deliberating about issues which may arise, as will be explained below when speaking of members of the Society.

[74] 7. **Whether to give them the book.**—Upon completion of the Exercises, where there is good hope that this may be fruitful—and with much discrimination—religious may be given a copy of the book if they themselves desire it and seem likely to make good use of it. However, this should be done only with the provincial's permission. Finally, religious may also be taught how to give the Exercises to others.

[75] 8. **Value of giving the Exercises to religious.**—In conclusion, our men should be convinced that hardly any effort they expend will be more fruitful than that on religious. The results produced will not be restricted to the exercitants but will commonly spread out to others. Beneficiaries will be, first, their fellow religious who will be helped by their example, and then people in the world with whose souls they deal. Hence, while the Exercises are always useful to all religious, they will be especially valuable for those who by reason of their office or some similar cause are in a position to help others, v.g., novice-masters, superiors, professors, preachers, and the like. In this way the reformation of a single person will often bring about the reform of many others; and this is preferable to our performing this function ourselves, lest we appear eager to be reformers of other religious—generally an invidious role.

[76] 9. **Married persons.**—With married persons or fathers of families, the Exercises should be directed toward helping them govern their families and instruct their children and servants according to God's commandments. They

also need to make a just, religious, and responsible use of their incomes and resources, giving alms according to their means, not going to excess in their expenses, etc., as is discussed in the book of the Exercises at the end of the Second Week. These goals are usually produced in the soul by the meditations themselves, even when on other subjects. Once the fear and love of God are truly implanted, a person's whole life is easily reformed. However, if the director thinks it good to give special instructions on these matters, either apart from prayer or in prayer by means of an appropriate meditation, he can do so. The same applies to other classes of persons about whom we shall speak immediately.

[77] 10. **Ecclesiastics.**—For ecclesiastics the Exercises should be aimed at teaching them how much virtue is demanded by their state and arousing in them a desire to acquire it, along with sorrow if they have not hitherto possessed it. Hence, they should be directed in a way that will lead them to resolve to put away their sins and evil affections and to furnish themselves with the contrary virtues which are so necessary for a churchman. They must always remember that they are dedicated and consecrated to the service of God and his Church, and must therefore do their utmost to fulfil their duty. They must also make a right use of the income from their benefices and spend it upon appropriate objects. Finally, they must have zeal for God and must labor for the salvation of souls according to their strength and talents, as demanded by their office.

[78] 11. **Persons of high rank.**—Persons of rank or governmental officials should also be given their own appropriate guidelines and instructions. They need to administer justice, avoid avarice and pride, assist the poor, realize that they are God's ministers in this work, and always set the fear and honor of God before all other things. The director's own prudence may suggest other points to which he should call such persons' attention.

[79] 12. **Very busy persons.**—If because of public responsibilities or any other good reason persons of this class cannot devote full time to the Exercises, we must accept what they can devote, viz., at least a few hours for meditation each day. In this case they can even remain in their own home, with the director visiting them at the scheduled times. Sometimes, especially in the case of more illustrious persons, this will preferable to their coming to our house for direction, as it makes it easier to preserve secrecy.

[80] 13. **Secluded place of retreat.**—Nevertheless, it would be much better if they could make a retreat in some country place or monastery, as in the case of our Father Ignatius at Monte Cassino. But in the Exercises themselves we must adapt to the circumstances and time available. If exercitants cannot spend much time on meditation each day, then proportionally more time will have to be given to the First Week, the general confession, etc. If they are able to spend several hours, these things can be gotten through more quickly—thus

approximating to a greater or lesser degree the standard form of the Exercises.

[81] 14. **When to give them the election.**—Such persons, however, should not be given the methods of election, unless perhaps they wish to deliberate about accepting or resigning an office or dignity, or about a state of life in cases where they are free to choose. But they should be instructed to rid themselves as far as possible of all thoughts about other matters, at least during the hours which they give to meditation.

[82] 15. **Ignorant and unlettered persons.**—Not much time should be spent on ignorant and unlettered persons, and they should not be given the complete Exercises. Instead, the method outlined in Annotation 18 should be followed.

[83] 16. **Women.**—This applies also to women, who occasionally ask to make the Exercises. The same method should be followed with them as with persons of little education. However there may be cases of women who possess such good judgment and capacity for spiritual things, and sufficient leisure at home, that they can make all or most of the Exercises in full form. There is nothing to prevent this. However, prudence demands that women should come to receive the meditations in our church. Every caution should be taken so that there will be no room for suspicion or scandal. For the same reason it may be best to give the meditations orally and not in written form, so that no one will think they are letters. If they are given in writing, great discretion must be observed.

CHAPTER 10: GIVING THE EXERCISES TO OUR OWN MEN

[84] 1. **Those entering the Society.**—In the first place, to men just entering the Society the Exercises should be given integrally and according to the form laid down in the book. This is one of the trials which our Father Ignatius requires and so they must be given exactly as they stand, with the exception of the election. Each meditation should be brought to them daily written on a separate sheet; on this first occasion they should not be given the book.

[85] 2. **Those more advanced.**—When later in the course of time they recollect themselves to make the Exercises, they should go over the same ground several times, i.e., two or three times—if not completely, at least the exercises of the First Week and some meditations from the following Weeks, v.g., those on the Kingdom of Christ, the Incarnation, the Temptation of our Lord, the institution of the Blessed Sacrament, the Passion, and the Contemplation for Obtaining Love—as seems expedient and as time allows.

[86] 3. **Reason for our men making the Exercises.**—This should be done also because they will later have to give the Exercises to others and certainly ought themselves first to have acquired a thorough knowledge of

them. For the same reason, in addition to the meditations, they should thoroughly understand and have practical experience of various rules and Annotations: the twenty Annotations at the front of the book, the methods of examination of conscience, the ten Additions at the end of the First Week, the rules for the election, the Rules for the Discernment of Spirits, and the like. Hence they should study and thoroughly understand the book, bringing any questions they may have to the one directing their Exercises.

[87] 4. **After having repeated them.**—Even after having made the Exercises once in this way, and repeated them several times, for as long as they are still not too experienced in meditation, while it is all right in their daily meditations for each one to follow his own devotion or needs and meditate on anything suggested by the Lord from the Gospels, Scripture, or other sources (always conferring this with the spiritual prefect or superior for their safer direction and greater profit), nevertheless during the special time set apart for meditation and retreat which we commonly call "the Exercises," inasmuch as it is practically always good to begin with a certain amount of purgation, it is best to include some exercises on this, v.g., on death and on sins—with special attention being given to sins committed inside religious life.

[88] 5. **Other written exercises not to be given.**—It is not good, however, to give in writing these "Exercises adapted to the religious state." The Exercises of Father Ignatius should always be preserved in their integrity just as they stand, with no additions or changes.[2] And in any case, exercitants will doubtless experience greater spiritual relish and emotion from what they discover for themselves than from ideas minutely laid out for them by someone else. Nevertheless, the director may give some brief instruction or explanation to get them started, instructing exercitants to make a habit of applying things to themselves. For example, in the Foundation, after considering the end of man, they should actualize this end in their present state: since they may now no longer be indifferent to riches and poverty, they should apply this indifference to matters which arise within the Society, and similarly in other cases.

[89] 6. **Length of First Week with our men.**—Our men who have once made the Exercises completely should ordinarily go through the First Week in a fairly short time—sometimes less than three or even two days where appropriate—so that they can go on to the Second Week, where much more time should usually be spent. This will depend mainly on the judgment of the director. If he sees that anyone needs further purgation he can and should keep him for a longer time in the First Week, endeavoring principally to lead him to desire his complete reformation.

[90] 7. **Matters for reform.**—The matter for this reformation will gener-

---

[2] The official Directory thus discountenances Giuseppe Blondo's argument (Doc. 28) that the Exercises as they stand are aimed at seculars and therefore require considerable adaptation and supplementing for use by Jesuits.

ally be passions not well under command, evil habits, or wrong inclinations, such as desire for honor and esteem, doing one's own will, physical comforts, and so on. They can also be temptations coming from without, especially if violent and frequent. They can be ministries of the Society such as preaching, hearing confessions, and teaching school—or any other activity which a person may desire to order and set aright, v.g., eating, sleeping, studying, dealing with externs or with our own men, etc.

[91] 8. **Self-knowledge most needful.**—Hence it should be the chief concern of the one making the Exercises to get as complete a knowledge of himself as possible. He should review the period gone by, along with his occupations and duties. He should weigh both the number of his defects and their seriousness by reason of his state and obligations. Finally, he should consider also the causes, origins, and roots of his faults.

[92] 9. **General confession helpful.**—A considerable help for this reformation will be to make at the end of the First Week a general confession covering the entire duration of his religious life—not every time that he repeats the Exercises but at the moment when he is especially moved by God to a desire to inaugurate a new life and reform himself more perfectly. Experience shows that this has been very profitable for many men and has aided them toward self-knowledge and amendment.

[93] 10. **Additional meditations.**—However, if the director thinks it will help the exercitant in attaining the end in view, he may give some meditations appropriate to the individual's state and present needs, v.g., on the gift of vocation, the three vows, the reasons for renewing one's vows, our vow formula itself, the benefits bestowed on us by God, the dangers of tepidity, and the like. Meditations may sometimes be added from the *Summary of the Constitutions*, especially on the chief rules which sum up religious perfection, such as rules 11 and 12,[3] and the like. In general, any subjects may be used which are apt to increase fear and love of God, hatred of self, zeal for virtues, contempt for visible things, desire for eternal things, and the ardor of charity.

[94] 11. **Meditation for persons with little instruction.**—As a way of easing entry for those who lack the ability or time to find it for themselves, a way might be opened for their meditations on the mysteries of the life and passion of our Lord if some theological truths are presented to them. For example, in the meditation on the Incarnation the reasons and fruits of this mystery could be explained; or in the case of the Passion the causes of its bitterness. Ways of meditating on the mystery could also be suggested, v.g., for arousing compassion, imitation, wonder, etc.

---

[3] The *Summary* was a selection of mainly ascetical passages from the *Constitutions of the Society of Jesus* that was read aloud monthly in Jesuit refectories down until the Vatican II era. The "rules" alluded to here correspond to numbers [101] and [103] of the *Constitutions*.

[95]　12. **For the more advanced.**—Finally, those who have made considerable spiritual progress and are more experienced in meditation (concerning
whom see *Constitutions*, VI, 3.1) may sometimes come into retreat to seek
spiritual recollection and an increase of fervor, or with a view to undertaking
a work such as a mission or the like. For these men it does not seem well to
prescribe any particular subjects of meditation, for they have different dispositions and are subject to different standards. They can meditate on anything they
think will be useful and conducive to the end they seek. We may well believe
that the knowledge they have already gained from the Exercises of our Father
Ignatius, together with the anointing of the Holy Spirit, will enable them to
run this path without stumbling, indeed with great profit.

[96]　13. **The election not to be given.**—Our men who make the Exercises should not be given the election of a state of life. On the other hand,
deliberating and making an election on undertakings and actions is not confined to the Exercises and can be done apart from them at any time and on any
occasion. Hence, our men need to be carefully trained in making good use of
the rules of election for ascertaining the will and good pleasure of God—such
as when superiors need to decide some difficult matter, especially if they are
unable to get the advice of their consultors (see rule 16 of the provincial). In
any matter which needs to be settled and determined in the presence of God,
the method of election which we shall discuss at length below will always
prove most helpful. In it our men can find the resource they need for knowing
what is the will of God in all such questions of various kinds.

CHAPTER 11: THE FIRST WEEK IN GENERAL

[97]　1. **The Exercises divided into four Weeks.**—The Exercises are
divided by our Father Ignatius into four Weeks. These Weeks, however, are
differentiated not so much by the number of days in each as by the nature of
their subject matter. Hence, it is not necessary for each Week to last seven or
eight days. All that is needed is for the affections or fruits aimed at in each
Week to be attained.

[98]　2. **Contents of each Week.**—The content of the First Week is reflection upon sins with a view to reaching knowledge and genuine detestation
of their foulness, along with appropriate sorrow and satisfaction. The Second
Week sets before us the life of Christ with a view to arousing within us
eagerness and desire to imitate him. The better to realize this imitation, we are
given also the method of making an election of the state of life which will be
most in accordance with God's will. If such a choice is no longer possible, we
are given instruction on reforming our life in the state we are in. The Third
Week contains Christ's passion, which engenders pity, sorrow, and shame, and
greatly inflames our desire for imitating him, along with love of God. Finally,

the Fourth Week is concerned with Christ's resurrection and glorious appearances, as well as with the benefits bestowed on us by God and similar matters calculated to arouse love for God in our hearts.

[99] 3. **First Week: the soul's purgation.**—The First Week, then, furnishes us with means for cleansing the soul by contrition and confession and for engendering true penitence therein. Hence, the exercitant should bend all his efforts to the goal of coming to know the malice of sin and his own degradation and baseness, and of having a deep realization of this. Consequently, it would be well for a priest, out of this spirit of humility, to refrain during this time from daily celebration of Mass (unless devotion, spiritual advantage, or some obligation impels him), so that after a general confession he may return to the Sacrifice of the altar with greater preparation, assurance, and reverence.

[100] 4. **The First Week basic, and never to be omitted.**—The First Week is the groundwork and basis of all the others and should therefore never be omitted. Hence, even someone who has already made the First Week or even the full Exercises in an earlier retreat and now wishes to come back to the Exercises must still begin with the First Week, although he may go through it more briefly.

[101] 5. **Preliminaries to the retreat.**—When the exercitant arrives in the place for his retreat, the director should visit him that same day. Before giving him the Foundation, he should explain to him some of the Annotations: 1, 5, the admonition in 17 about opening his heart, and in 20 about the importance of retirement to a secluded place. This will afford the director an opportunity to give the exercitant the instruction which we said above in chapter 2 ought to be given him. He should do this, however, with the tact also mentioned there, and not say everything to the exercitant at once but only as much as prudence dictates.

[102] 6. **The note preceding the Foundation.**—Nowadays the note preceding the Foundation [22] is better not given in such general terms at the outset of the Exercises. However, should some doubt or difficulty arise during the Exercises, or some lack of trust on the exercitant's part seem to warrant it, it may then be explained.

CHAPTER 12: THE FOUNDATION

[103] 1. **Consideration of one's last end.**—The consideration of our last end forms the entrance into the First Week. This consideration is therefore called the Foundation, because it is the groundwork of the whole moral and spiritual edifice.

[104] 2. **May be divided into three parts.**—It may be divided into three parts: (1) the end for which man was created, (2) the means for attaining this end, and (3) the difficulty of choosing the right means, given that what is most

conducive to the attainment of this end is unknown to us, yet any error here cannot help being harmful and perilous. This gives rise to a final point: (4) that a person must place himself in a state of entire indifference and equilibrium.

[105] 3. **Importance of indifference.**—This indifference is extremely important. The exercitant should be instructed that the deeper he lays this foundation the firmer will be his edifice. Father Ignatius points this out also in Annotations 15 and 16.

[106] 4. **Helps against dryness in this meditation.**—In giving this meditation, especially to persons unused to mental prayer who may find it rather dry and barren, some developments may be added to assist meditation. For instance, where it is said that man was created, we may also consider how God created him out of nothing, how numerous and great were the endowments man possessed at creation, and how God continually preserves him in being.

[107] 5. **Aim of this meditation.**—However, these points should be reflected on not so much for exciting gratitude—as in the meditation on God's benefits to us—but rather as they bear on the aim of the Foundation, which is that all these things have been given to us by God in order for us to attain our final end. Hence, in this meditation a person can also reflect upon himself and on how he has hitherto acted with regard to the end and the means, and the degree to which he has gone astray by making a wrong use of creatures which were supposed to be a help to him—so as to lay at this point in a general way a foundation for the knowledge of the deformity of our lives which we will afterwards ponder with more fullness and detail in the meditation on sins.

[108] 6. **Time for this meditation.**—The book of the Exercises does not prescribe fixed hours for meditating on the Foundation as it does for the subsequent exercises. To make the beginning easier, each person may devote time to it in accord with his strength and devotion. If necessary, however, the director may set him a time.

[109] 7. **This meditation must sink in.**—However, he should make sure that realization of the truth contained in the Foundation sinks as deeply as possible into his mind. Just as a building's foundation bears its entire weight, this truth influences the whole of the Exercises. It is especially important for the election of a state of life, which depends almost entirely upon it. Hence, the better this meditation is made, the better will be the outcome of all the rest.

CHAPTER 13: THE TWOFOLD EXAMEN

[110] 1. **Director's duties at the time of the Foundation.**—During the meditation on the Foundation the director should visit the exercitant several times, bringing something new in writing each time. This will help relieve tedium, and matters will be grasped better if presented piece by piece.

[111] 2. **When to explain the Particular Examen.**—Hence, in the first meeting after giving the Foundation, the director should give the Particular Examen. Here he should explain that every person usually has one or two principal faults or sins which are the source or root of the others.

[112] 3. **The uprooting of vices.**—And even if a person should have several main faults, it is still good to select one and focus all our efforts on uprooting it. Once it has been overcome, we then concentrate this special effort on a different one, and so on in succession.

[113] 4. **Great value of the Particular Examen.**—The Particular Examen will be of service here. Even though it is to be used throughout one's life after the Exercises, it should be begun now, both to so as acquire skill in it and because it must be used on the exercises themselves and the Additions.

[114] 5. **Its practice should be urged.**—The practice of this examen should be strongly urged in view of its great value, particularly for obtaining purity of soul, as we learn from Cassian, *Conferences*, v.14, and from many passages in St. Bernard. Accordingly, at the close of the Exercises when the departing exercitant is given guidelines for the good ordering of his life, this practice should be specially inculcated. Whether to dictate the four notes given at the end of the Particular Examen or just explain them orally will be left up to the judgment of the director.

[115] 6. **When and how to give the General Examen.**—Next, on the same day and the following, the General Examen [32–42] should be given together with the daily Examen [43]—not as a meditation but as an instruction, so that the person will begin to open his eyes to know the sins of his past life.

[116] 7. **Catalogues of sins to be sought elsewhere.**—Regarding the General Examen [32–42], there are of course many other kinds of sin which are not listed there. Only those are mentioned which occur with greater frequency; the remaining kinds of sins can be found in other authors who treat the subject professedly. Or else this Examen was composed only for somewhat more spiritual persons who fall more often into these sins and not into other more serious ones. Thus it was not our Father Ignatius' intention to include all sins in such a brief treatment but only—as indicated—to remind devout persons of those which are more frequent.

[117] 8. **The daily Examen.**—The daily five-point Examen should be dictated just as it stands. A help in making it is the light afforded by the General Examen with its distinction of sins into those of thought, word, and deed.

CHAPTER 14: THE FIRST EXERCISE OF THE FIRST WEEK

[118] 1. **Order for giving the exercises.**—In presenting the exercises the order laid down in the book should be followed. In the first hour the exercises of the three powers should be made; in the second, the exercise on sins; in the third and fourth, two repetitions of each of these; and if a fifth hour is added,

it should be on hell. If only four hours are made, this exercise on hell should
be postponed until the following day. On that day also can be given further
exercises on death and judgment, with their own repetitions. On the third day
the same matter should be given, but with some fresh points. For example, in
the meditation on sins the effects of sin in the soul or some similar matter can
be given. This will forestall tedium and bring about a deeper penetration of the
matter.

[119] 2. **The 1st exercise, that of the three powers.**—The 1st exercise
is the one called the exercise of the three powers. This is not because the three
powers are not used in the other exercises, but because our Father Ignatius
wished in this beginning and approach to the entire Exercises to lay out the
method to be followed in meditation, viz, that with the support of the memory
the intellect should engage in a reasoning process and through this process the
will and affections be stirred up. He wished this to be applied to the matter of
sin, which was the first subject that came up for meditation.

[120] 3. **Explanations for the 1st exercise.**—Accordingly, in this 1st
exercise the exercitant should have explained to him in detail all the elements
he will need to make use of in the subsequent exercises: the method to follow
so that he will be able to persevere in meditation attentively and without
straining his head; the way to concentrate his thoughts and keep them concentrated; how, while using his intellect for thinking, he should be more
concerned with the affections and interior relish than with a multiplicity of
ideas, no matter how beautiful and ingenious; and other such instructions.

[121] 4. **Preludes to be explained.**—This is also the moment to explain
the preludes prescribed for all the exercises. The first is the composition of
place. This is simply imagining or visualizing the scene of the mystery we are
meditating, v.g., the stable where Christ was born, or the large furnished dining
room where he washed the apostles' feet, or the mount on which he suffered.

[122] 5. **Value of the composition of place.**—This composition of place
is a great help toward concentrating and moving the soul. With the imagination tied down to some definite matter, the soul itself is tied down and prevented from straying. If it does stray, it has a ready means of refocusing and
calling itself back to the spot where it originally imagined itself. Hence, St.
Bonaventure writes in the preface to his life of Christ: "If you wish to gather
fruit from these matters, make yourself as present to what is recounted about
the sayings and actions of the Lord Jesus Christ as if you were seeing them
with your own eyes and hearing them with your own ears; do this with all the
affection of your spirit, carefully, lovingly, and slowly, leaving aside all your
other concerns and cares."[4]

[123] 6. **Where applicable.**—This procedure is applicable to the medita-

---

[4] Pseudo-Bonaventure. See note on Doc. 31.93.

tion of corporeal realities. Incorporeal topics such as sin require a different sort of composition of place, which is explained clearly enough in the book of the Exercises, in the exercise of the three powers.

[124] 7. **Dangers to be avoided.**—Lastly, care should be taken not to dwell excessively on constructing this representation of the place and not to strain the head. The composition of place is not the primary fruit of the meditation but only a way and an instrument toward it. There is no denying that some have greater facility in this, viz., persons with a more vivid imagination. Others who find it harder should not labor at it to the point of dulling their minds and becoming unable to make the meditation itself.

CHAPTER 15: THE REMAINING EXERCISES OF THE FIRST WEEK

[125] 1. **Directions for the exercitant regarding the 2nd exercise.**—In first point of the 2nd exercise [56] the exercitant should be told not to descend to particulars in examining his sins, as is done when preparing for confession. He will do this later outside of meditation. At this point he should only set before himself his sins in a general way, together with their great number and gravity, for purposes of arousing shame and contrition. For this, it will be helpful to make a review of places, occupations, and persons, as is indicated there.

[126] 2. **The repetitions.**—The 3rd and 4th exercises consist in repetitions of the 1st and 2nd. These repetitions are of great value. It often happens that in an initial meditation upon such matters the understanding is stimulated by their novelty and a certain curiosity. Afterwards, when we abate the activity of the understanding, the way is more open for interior affections, in which the fruit principally consists. In these repetitions, then, we must avoid lengthy processes of thought. We should merely call to mind and briefly run over the matter of our previous meditation, and then dwell upon it with our will and affections. This is why there are more colloquies here than in the earlier exercises.

[127] 3. **Understanding the 3rd exercise of the First Week.**—In the 3rd exercise of the First Week it is stated that we should dwell especially on the points where we felt greater consolation or desolation. This is to be understood to mean that we should repeat especially those points which have brought us light and fervor. However, it is also good to repeat the points where we felt dryness, because it often happens that we later find in these very points a greater abundance of consolation. Indeed, the same matter can be repeated twice if one feels consolation or any other good and spiritual affection, especially in the First Week.

[128] 4. **Other meditations may be added to the five.**—Besides the five exercises given by our Father Ignatius, others may be added, as is stated at the

end of the 5th meditation.⁵ They can be on further punishments for sin, on death, on judgment, or on other torments of hell. In fact, these topics should seldom be omitted, for they are very important in withdrawing the soul from an inordinate love of the visible things of this world. In these meditations the soul "conceives a holy fear of the Lord so as to bring forth a spirit of salvation."⁶

[129] 5. **When to make the colloquies.**—A colloquy should always be made at the end of each exercise, as indicated in the book of the Exercises. However, there is nothing against making other colloquies and petitions, in accord with each person's devotion, even at the beginning or in the middle of the meditation. In fact, it is often a good idea to do this. But the most appropriate place is at the end, when the soul feels itself more elevated by its meditation—for the best colloquies are those which spring variously from one's interior affection, as the affection itself varies.

[130] 6. **Various modes of dealing with God.**—Thus, at one time a person deals with God as a son with his father; at another, as a slave with his master; at another, as a friend with his friend; at another, as a culprit with his judge—sometimes begging a gift, sometimes giving thanks for benefits received, sometimes accusing himself before God, sometimes conversing familiarly with him.

[131] 7. **Understanding the third Annotation.**—Note here the remark in Annotation 3 that in colloquies with God or the saints greater reverence is required than in the meditations or reflections themselves. In particular, with regard to the second colloquy where we ask Christ to intercede for us with the Father, one should explain to uneducated persons that this refers to Christ not as he is God but as he is man, our mediator and advocate, so that he may intercede for us.

[132] 8. **When to give the Additions of the First Week.**—The Additions in the book of Exercises at the end of the First Week should be given on the day prior to beginning these exercises (i.e., before the meditation of the three powers and the others) since they deal with many matters helpful in meditating. The tenth Addition may be put off till the following day, for there is less need to give it on that day. Then, on the following days the remaining Additions can be given along with the Rules for the Discernment of Spirits that are appropriate to the First Week and to the exercitant's condition. These need not always be given in writing; this is left to the director's judgment.

[133] 9. **Exact observance of the Additions.**—Care should be taken that these Additions are observed exactly, for the spiritual fruit of the exercises depends in great measure upon them. On the other hand, all excess should be

⁵ In the Vulgate edition, after number 72.
⁶ A reminiscence of St. Augustine on Ps 48:6.

avoided. Account should be taken of each individual's character and temperament. Thus, persons melancholy by nature should not be too much constrained: the endeavor should rather be to enlarge their spirits. The same holds for
persons in weak health and unaccustomed to this kind of labor. Thus discretion
and prudence are needed. Experience has shown that in some cases it is good
to relax these rules somewhat, while in others strictness and rigor is best—
always tempered, of course, with kindness.

CHAPTER 16: THE GENERAL CONFESSION

[134] 1. **When to encourage the exercitant to make it.**—When the
exercitant making the first five or other additional exercises appears to have
sufficiently attained the end set for this Week, viz. deep interior knowledge of
his sins and genuine contrition, having made serious efforts at this and
cooperated with God's grace both in the exercises and in the Additions, he
should be advised to prepare himself for a general confession. Unless the
director finds him too fatigued, he may still continue making one or two
hours' meditation on subjects suited to produce contrition for sins, or, if it
seem preferable, he may read something for the same purpose.

[135] 2. **Value of the general confession.**—So that he may do this more
carefully and thoroughly, the great benefits of this general confession should be
pointed out to him. These are discussed in the book of the Exercises itself, after
the General Examen [44]. Even were there no other reason, the following
ought at all events to suffice: experience shows that persons often approach
confession without sufficient examination, or without due sorrow, and with
little or no purpose of amendment. Consequently, in order for a person to set
his conscience at rest and dispel the scruples which, at least at the moment of
death if not earlier, often torment the soul and imperil its eternal salvation, it is
well worthwhile to cleanse himself once and for all from all the sins of his
past life.

[136] 3. **Method to be used for this confession.**—For this reason, while
it is important in making this confession to avoid excessive anxiety which
could beget permanent scruples and aftereffects, as sometimes happens, still the
exercitant should earnestly endeavor to make the confession carefully and
accurately so that he will later have the assurance that he did his best.
Otherwise he will never enjoy this peace of mind and serenity of conscience of
which we have spoken. Hence, besides the exercitant's own effort and care, he
should be assisted with some kind of method or procedure, i.e., some
guidebook for making a good confession. If needed, many such excellent and
suitable works can be found, fitted to various individuals' needs.

[137] 4. **Who ought to read Navarrus' Manual.**—It will sometimes be
helpful, especially for persons of high station, to be given the section of

Navarrus' *Manual*[7] to read where he deals with states of life, so that the exercitants may carefully ponder the duties of their own state. In this way they will
see more clearly where they fail, whereas if our own men brought up these
matters with such persons they might place no credence in them and think
they were pressing consciences too hard.

[138] 5. **Who should hear the confession.**—In most cases it is better that
the director not be the one to hear this general confession. However, if the
exercitant prefers it or no other priest is available or any other reason requires,
there is nothing to prevent the director's doing it.

CHAPTER 17: THE CONCLUSION OF THE FIRST WEEK

[139] 1. **When to shorten or lengthen the First Week.**—Since, as has
been said above, the Weeks of the Exercises are determined not by days but by
the results aimed at in each Week, the First Week may be shortened or
lengthened depending on how quickly or slowly the exercitant attains
contrition, devotion, and skill in meditation. For some this comes sooner, for
others later. Note, however, that persons who are making great progress in the
way of the spirit and who have been receiving the sacraments for some time,
or who are very eager to reach a decision about the state of life in which best
to serve God our Lord, should not be kept for any great length of time in the
First Week. In fact, they should finish it in four or five days if possible. The
opposite should be done persons who are not so well disposed. They need to
grieve for their own sins and come to recognize the turpitude and filthiness of
sin, and so ought to spend a longer time in the First Week. Changes should
also be made from time to time in their pattern of eating and sleeping and
other kinds of penance, as indicated in the third note after the Additions of the
First Week [129].

[140] 2. After their general confession and Communion, those planning to
continue the Exercises beyond the First Week should take at least a day's rest
from the intense labor of meditation. However, in the meantime they can
think over and apply to themselves the parable of the Prodigal Son or something similar. Moreover, they should be given a preparation for their Communion so that they will approach it with reverence, faith, and spiritual relish.
They should be given some suitable meditation for this.

---

[7] Martín de Azpilcueta ("Navarrus"), *Enchiridium sive Manualis confessariorum et
poenitentium*, Rome, 1588.

CHAPTER 18: THE SECOND WEEK: ITS GOAL

[141] 1. **Goal of the First Week.**—The primary end and purpose of all the exercises of the First Week is to recognize that we have strayed from the way that should have brought us to the final end for which we were created, and consequently to grieve for this enormous error and to conceive an intense desire of returning to the way and persevering in it forever.

[142] 2. **Goal of the Second Week.**—In the Second Week the end is to place before ourselves Christ our Lord and savior as the true way, as he himself has said: "I am the way and the truth and the life; no one comes to the Father except by me" [John 14:6].

For he is the pattern given to humanity by God. By imitating him we are to correct and regulate our corrupt ways and guide our feet into the way of peace [see Luke 1:79]. Hence, since Christ's is the most perfect of all lives and the very pattern of virtue and holiness, it follows that the more closely our own lives imitate his, the more perfect they will be and the more nearly they will approach their final goal, and in consequence the happier they will also be.

[143] 3. **The Second Week corresponds to the illuminative way.**— This is why the Second Week corresponds to the illuminative way, for Christ is the sun of righteousness "who enlightens everyone who comes into the world" [John 1:9]. He has come to "enlighten those who sit in darkness and in the shadow of death" [Luke 1:79]. It is because sins and wrong affections darken the soul, hindering and withdrawing it from the imitation of Christ, that sins had to be first rooted out of the heart by means of the previous exercises and meditations.

[144] 4. **Dispositions looked for by our Father in persons making these exercises.**—The disposition looked for by our Father Ignatius in those about to make the exercises of this Week is that they should demonstrate fervor and a longing to go on to a deliberation about their state of life. A person not interested in doing this, or only mildly interested, should be put off for a month or two, even if he is eager to continue the meditations. The nature of this task is such that unless undertaken with fervor of spirit it cannot turn out well. It demands a large, courageous, and persevering spirit arising from heightened devotion.

[145] 5. **When the person is less suitable.**—However, a person from whom little can be hoped, either for want of capacity or because barred by matrimony, can be given some further meditations from the other Weeks suited to his powers to guide him in living a good life in his present state.

[146] 6. **Leave with an appetite for more.**—Other persons, however, are better left with a hunger and the realization that they still have more to do. It often happens that thanks to this postponement experience itself reveals to them more clearly their needs and weaknesses, so that they return with better and more fervent dispositions.

CHAPTER 19: THE FIRST FOUR EXERCISES OF THE SECOND WEEK

[147] 1. **Nature of the 1st exercise of the Second Week.**—The 1st exercise of the Second Week is on the Kingdom of Christ. It is not numbered among the meditations, however, the 1st meditation being on the Incarnation. The exercise on the Kingdom, then, is a kind of foundation or prologue to the whole of the following Exercises, and a summary or compendium of the life and deeds of Christ the Lord in the work which the Father gave him—of which Isaiah said: "His work is before him" [Isa 62:11]. The Lord himself spoke of "the work which you gave me to do" [John 17:4], immediately adding what that work was: "I have glorified you on earth; . . . I have manifested your name to those you have given me" [John 17:4, 6]. And he calls all to share this great and glorious work, each person according to his own degree. Thus, even at this point it already begins to emerge that there are various degrees in the imitation of Christ.

[148] 2. **Necessary disposition.**—The disposition required in the exercitant's soul is that so far as it depends upon himself he is inclined to whatever is more perfect should God give him the grace and strength for it. Hence it is already evident at this point that the soul is being initially prepared and disposed for the choice of a state of life which will be brought up explicitly later on. Thus with remarkable dexterity the Holy Spirit is already here urging the soul to perfection so that it may later focus upon and investigate this same perfection in all the following meditations on the Incarnation, Nativity, etc. In this way the seeds of perfection sown here will secretly grow and advance through the subsequent meditations until they bear fruit at the moment of the election. The director should take note of this for his own guidance, not so that he may speak of it to the exercitant; rather he should leave the realities themselves to work in his soul and exert their own power.

[149] 3. **Who should be given this meditation.**—This is not to say that this meditation and the subsequent mediation on the Two Standards cannot be given even to persons who will not be making an election. Even such persons can be helped by these exercises, which merely deal in a general way with things such as every person, according to his capacity, can do for the greater glory of God in his service.

[150] 4. **Why the additional prelude in the Second Week.**—Note that in the Second Week there is an additional prelude. While in the First Week the first prelude was the composition of place, here, before the composition of place, we have a sort of outline of the history or mystery which will be meditated on. This does not mean that we should stop to meditate the mystery at this point; otherwise the prelude would be identical with the meditation. What is intended in this first prelude is an overall and global view of the mystery in order to know the matter which will subsequently be reflected

upon, so that the soul can begin to engage with it and be raised toward to it. Later, in the meditation itself, it will begin spending time on its individual parts, weighing and penetrating them. It is like when a person casts his eyes upon a painting which contains a great variety of objects: he first gets a hazy impression of the whole in a single glance, and then afterwards focuses on the individual details of the painting, inspecting them more fully and accurately one by one.

[151] 5. **Where to get the points for these meditations.**—The points for these meditations will be taken from the back of the book of the Exercises where the mysteries of Christ's life are listed in order, usually divided into three points. (With less educated persons who have never read or cannot read them in the Gospels, the points should be given more fully, with a short explanation, as is stated in Annotation 2.) Hence, what is said in the meditations on the Incarnation and Nativity about contemplating the persons and their words and actions should be understood to refer to the above-mentioned distribution of points at the end of the book. That is, the persons, words, and actions should be contemplated in each point as it occurs in its own order. There is no need to meditate separately first on all the persons of the entire mystery, then all the words, and then all the actions. This would beget confusion, particularly in some meditations.

[152] 6. **Reason for meditation by points.**—Hence, all Father Ignatius wanted was to give a rule for the guidance of the exercitant in meditating upon each point, viz., that he should first turn his attention to the persons found in that point, and then to their words or their actions, whichever occur first. In this way, when he has exhausted one point the exercitant will go on to the next, following the same procedure.

[153] 7. **Other points can be added.**—However, while only these three points are mentioned, there is nothing wrong with adding other points, v.g., the thoughts and interior affections of the persons, their virtues, the manner and purpose of the various mysteries, the cause, effect, time, and other circumstances—so as to enrich the meditation and produce more abundant fruit.

CHAPTER 20: FIFTH EXERCISE OF THE SECOND WEEK:
APPLICATION OF THE SENSES

[154] 1. **Fifth exercise: application of the senses.**—The 5th exercise, the application of the senses, is quite easy and beneficial. It consists in using our imagination to see the persons, to hear their words or any other sounds, to touch or kiss places or persons (this latter should be done with due reverence, modesty and fear). The sense of smell is applied by our Father Ignatius to smelling the soul's fragrance from God's gifts, and the sense of taste to tasting its sweetness; both of these betoken a kind of presence of the reality or person

we are meditating, joined with a relish and heartfelt love for them.[8]

[155] 2. **Meaning of the note on the application of the senses which follows the meditations on the Incarnation and the Nativity.**—The note about making a separate application of the senses after the meditations on the Incarnation and the Nativity should be taken to apply to the subsequent meditations on the life of Christ as well. However, it does not mean that the application of the senses has to prescind from all matter of meditation, but only that the main thing being sought in this consideration of the mystery is the application of the senses.

[156] 3. **How the application of the senses differs from meditation.**— The application of the senses differs from meditation in that meditation is more a matter of the intellect, involves more reasoning, and is altogether higher. Meditation reasons about the causes and effects of the mysteries and traces out the attributes of God in them, v.g., his goodness, wisdom, love, and the like. The application of the senses, on the other hand, is not discursive, but merely rests in the sensible qualities of things: sights, sounds, and the like; these it enjoys and takes delight in, to its spiritual profit.

[157] 4. **Its twofold value.**—It is valuable in two ways. It sometimes happens that when a soul is unable to penetrate higher realities by reasoning it is gradually disposed and lifted up to them while dwelling upon these sensible things. Sometimes, on the other hand, when the soul is already enriched and filled with devotion from its knowledge of higher mysteries and then descends from there to the contemplation of these sensible things, it finds in each one of them nourishment, consolation, and fruit because of the abundance of its love,

---

[8] In the 1591 preliminary edition of the official directory, this paragraph continued as follows: "There are also persons who apply this to the senses of the mind, following the teaching of St. Bonaventure in chapter 4 of his *Journey of the Mind to God*. Thus, seeing is the act of faith which makes spiritual realities present to us. Hearing is a further act of faith which makes us believe and assent, according to the words 'At the hearing of the ears he has obeyed me' [see Ps 18:45]; i.e., an understanding and believing with the affections— the understanding and will being the two ears of the soul. The sense of smell is referred to hope, and touch is the union produced by love, according to the words: 'Let him kiss me with the kiss of his mouth' [Song 1:1]. The sense of taste is referred to charity, which makes us care not for earthly things but for those which are above, as St. Paul says [Col 3:2]. This use and practice of the spiritual senses is a sign of a spiritual life. However, while this kind of application of the senses may be practiced and is approved by spiritual men, it is nevertheless preferable to use the previous method, which is simpler and clearer. These subtleties in this matter smack of curiosity and do not produce solid effects in the soul. Indeed, they produce aridity, and the more effort is put into them the more the fruit of meditation is lost. The same should be said of all spiritualizing interpretations, which are more appropriate to preaching than to meditation. Hence it is better to leave them aside; and this is more in the spirit of our Father Ignatius' Exercises, which, as we see, always dwell upon more tangible realities such as actions, persons, and the like."

which makes even the slightest detail and tiniest gesture assume great importance and afford matter for love and consolation.

[158] 5. **Where the mysteries of Christ are to be found.**—In giving the mysteries of Christ's life, the director should take them from the back of the book of the Exercises itself. There, as was indicated above, they are set forth divided into points. With an exercitant experienced in meditation, it will suffice to dictate or give in writing the points just as found there, with instructions to follow the same method as on the first day. With less experienced persons, it will be necessary to go into greater detail, adapting the preludes to the subject matter and leading them into the method of representing to themselves the persons and their circumstances, and then their words, their actions, etc.

CHAPTER 21: HOURS OF MEDITATION, SPIRITUAL READING, AND VISITS TO THE EXERCITANT

[159] 1. **When to allow the exercitant relaxation.**—Should the exercitant appear fatigued, even if not excessively so, it will help him hold out longer if he is given some relaxation in the number of hours of meditation. The midnight meditation could be dropped, keeping the other four.

[160] 2. **Reading during the Second Week.**—In this and the following Weeks the exercitant can read a book during the time left after the meditations. However, it should be a book calculated to nourish piety rather than busy the intellect with novelties. Such are some works of St. Bernard, or Gerson's *Imitation of Christ*, or the works of Luis de Granada.[9] If the book treats mysteries of Christ's life, the exercitant should avoid reading about mysteries he has yet to meditate on, and should read only ones he has already meditated or will be meditating that same day.

[161] 3. **When to visit the exercitant.**—The exercitant should be visited at least once a day, except during the election, when desolations and perplexities are usually more common, making more frequent visits necessary.

CHAPTER 22: THE ELECTION: ITS IMPORTANCE AND THE PROCEDURE TO BE FOLLOWED

[162] 1. **Difficulty of the election.**—In the whole of the Exercises no subject is more difficult or demands greater skill and spiritual discretion than the election. This phase of the Exercises is exposed to a variety of spiritual movements, and often to errors as well, in which a person may be not only overcome by evil, but quite often deceived by what appears to be good and right.

---

[9] See note on Doc. 18.114.

[163] 2. **Attention to the need and seriousness of the election.**—The main thing to understand and keep in mind in this matter is the great importance of one's choice of a state of life. For if a human being, as rational, ought to have in all his actions an end that is consonant with reason; and if a Christian ought to direct all his actions to an end that is supernatural—if this ought to be done in every single action, how much more so in taking on a state of life, upon which almost every action of our life will depend, so that if the end is faulty all that depends upon it will of necessity be faulty as well.

[164] 3. **Indifference in the election.**—Furthermore, just as in the living body there are many members, yet, as St. Paul says, not all the members are eyes and not all are feet, so in the body of the Church there must be various grades and states. And the originator of this division and distribution is the Holy Spirit, to whom it belongs to assign to each person his proper place. Hence, the Apostle says in the same place: "There are diversities of graces, but the same Spirit; and there are diversities of ministries, but the same Lord; and there are diversities of operations, but the same God, who works all in all" [1 Cor 12:4–6]. From this it is clear that just as servants are assigned by their master to their individual tasks and responsibilities, so human beings are assigned by God. And so a person should not place any obstacle within himself to what God wishes to do in and with him, but should instead render faithful service in whichever way his Majesty wills.

[165] 4. **Value of this election.**—There is another special advantage to this election, one of great importance because having to do with eternal salvation. For while God refuses no one the help needed for his salvation, he unquestionably imparts his grace, light, and help far more abundantly when a person has not thrust himself into a state of life following his own inclination but has instead chosen the state which he deems, after careful consideration, to be God's will for him.

[166] 5. **Not our will but God's must be followed.**—Lastly, if in such an important matter we chose to be guided by our own judgment and will, we shall easily fall into great and extremely harmful errors. But if we have followed the will of God, he, as our Father and Creator, will ordain nothing for us except what is good and salutary, indeed suited and adapted to ourselves, for he knows what we are made of.

[167] 6. **The exercitant to be told these things.**—All these considerations, and others along the same lines, will be helpful not only for the director, to ensure that he takes the greatest care with the election, but even more for the exercitant as well, to let him see what attitude he ought to bring to such a crucial matter as this.

[168] 7. **Division of the following chapters.**—In order to put some order in our treatment of this matter, we shall delineate (1) the qualities needed in the person admitted to an election, (2) those needed in the director, (3) the

matter for an election, (4) the guidelines to be followed in the course of it, and (5) the order and procedure to be employed in making it.

CHAPTER 23: QUALITIES NEEDED IN SOMEONE ADMITTED TO THE ELECTION

[169] 1. **Who should be admitted to an election.**—Obviously not everyone is to be admitted to the election of a state of life. Those whose state is already fixed, such as married persons or religious, should not deliberate on this matter but should only be aided to strive after perfection, each in his own state, according to the measure of grace which God our Lord may give him. Even in the case of those whose state is not fixed, the election is not to be given indiscriminately to everyone. See *Constitutions*, VII, 4.F, where it is stated that the election is to be given only to a few, and those of such a character that there is good hope that their spiritual progress will bring a more than ordinary measure of fruit for the glory of God. Hence, persons incapable of this high perfection (such as fickle and inconstant persons, who must be detected with care and on no account allowed to make an election), or those with unmastered passions or apparently incorrigible bad habits, should not be admitted unless there happen to be such clear signs of special grace as to make up for all these deficiencies.

[170] 2. **The exercitant must desire and request it.**—Secondly, over and above having good natural endowments and character, the person to whom the election is given must also himself desire and request it. This is an altogether indispensable condition, and under no circumstances should the election be given without it, much less urged or forced upon a person who has no desire for it. Not only will such a person receive with suspicion whatever is said to him and therefore not be helped by it, but in addition the numerous great difficulties which occur in making an election even when the will is good and fervent will be far greater when the will is reluctant; it will then never be able to surmount them.

[171] 3. **Freedom from all attachments needed.**—Thirdly, it is very important that a person entering upon the election endeavor to be free from every inordinate affection and absolutely indifferent to all things, desiring solely to follow God's holy will, whatever he may discover it to be. Hence, if he shows himself too much inclined to riches and too little to poverty, he would not be properly disposed and there would be no hope of his making a successful election. His attitude of aversion from the more perfect way and inclination toward the more imperfect would influence his intellect to come up with reasons in agreement with his inclination. And since, as the maxim goes, whatever is received is received according to the measure of the one receiving, he could easily take to be God's will what is in fact his own. He needs,

therefore, to attain the third degree of humility described in the book of the Exercises, or at least the second degree. The meditations on the Two Standards and Three Classes, together with others discussed below, will help such an exercitant to attain this. He should accordingly be kept in these meditations for a longer time so that, partly by his own efforts and partly by asking it of God with fervent prayers, he may gradually be brought to this equilibrium of mind. But unless he reaches this resignation and indifference, all discussion of making an election must be forgone. If it seems advisable, he should continue with the rest of the Exercises in hope of their possibly bringing him to greater readiness; otherwise he should end them after a brief interval.

[172] 4. **The best dispositions for an election.**—Fourthly, the best of all dispositions is that in which a person does not incline to the retention of earthly possessions but as far as possible constantly endeavors to incline his will to that which is more perfect. Even if this may not be what he ends up choosing, because God perhaps does not call him to such a state, it will do him no harm to desire it and in fact it will do him much good. That is why the Exercises always present the more perfect way as what we should most desire and ask of God. Our Father Ignatius has a very noteworthy remark on this point in one of his writings [Doc. 1.8–9]. He says that the director ought to endeavor to bring the exercitant to a frame of mind where he will be quite as ready to follow the counsels as the commandments—indeed, on his part he should rather be more inclined to the counsels in case that should be more pleasing to God. He adds that it takes stronger signs to decide that it is God's will for someone to remain in the state where it suffices to keep the commandments than for him to enter upon the way of the counsels, seeing that our Lord has so plainly urged us to embrace the counsels and shown how perilous is the other state.

[173] 5. **Final disposition for the election.**—The final disposition for an election, as indicated by Father Ignatius in the same text [Doc. 1.6], is that anyone engaged in making an election should enter a state of total inward recollection. During the whole time of deliberation he should close the doors of his senses and mind to everything else, desiring to see and hear nothing which is not from above. There are two points here. The first is that the soul must not let itself be drawn away to other considerations but turn its whole effort and attention exclusively to this task, setting all other affairs aside. Second, in the course of the deliberation the soul must admit no considerations which are not from heaven, i.e., none which savor of flesh and blood, or anything human and worldly, since everything ought to emanate from the single source of desire for the glory of God and the fulfilling of his will. This is that true cost of building the tower spoken of in the Gospel [Luke 14:28], and it gives the soul great confidence that God will not let it be deceived. For whenever anyone seeks God truthfully and wholeheartedly, God will never

turn away from him, seeing that his goodness and love for his creatures are so great that he often comes forth to meet even those who do not seek him. But although this is the case, and a perfect election is one motivated solely by love for God, nevertheless so long as God is the chief motive, even if the person is moved in the same direction by other reasons compatible with God's law and will and good in themselves, such as spiritual consolation and peace of soul, considerations of health, or the like, the person's election should not on that account be condemned. But these additional motives should always be subordinate and have less weight in the decision, and should themselves always be referred to the love of God.

CHAPTER 24: QUALITIES NEEDED IN THE DIRECTOR OF AN ELECTION

[174] 1. **Responsibilities of the director.**—As regards the second point, the responsibility of the director in this particular business is to cooperate with God's movement, not anticipating but following it, and disposing the exercitant's soul for this by clearing away impediments, i.e., errors, deceptions, and inordinate affections and inclinations. As Annotation 15 warns, he should not urge the exercitant to one side or the other. For although of itself it is lawful and even meritorious to exhort a person to what is more perfect, nevertheless, in order that a deliberation of this kind may made more solidly and apart from human influence, it is much better to allow God to deal alone with his creature with no intervention from a third party—particularly during the Exercises, when the soul disposes itself precisely for this. The reason for this is that an election in so crucial a matter as one's state of life should not be based upon human persuasion or influence but solely on the will of God; otherwise there would be grounds for fearing what our Lord has said: "Every plant which my heavenly Father has not planted shall be rooted up" [Matt 15:13]. And since on a path of this kind, which is difficult in itself and in addition exposed to the devils' malice, numerous temptations and difficulties are sure to follow, we can look for no help or support from the human being who led us there unless we lift our eyes heavenward and can say, "The Lord alone was my guide" [Deut 32:12]. For St. Paul tells us that we may hope that he who has granted us to will a thing will also grant us to accomplish it, and will confirm it to the end [see Phil 2:13; 1 Cor 1:8].

[175] 2. **Indifference in the director as well.**—From this it follows that, if the director is to execute faithfully the responsibility entrusted to him, he himself must be indifferent in his own way. He must have no other concern or wish than that God's will be done; he must interject nothing of his own spirit, for that would be thrusting his own sickle into God's harvest. Besides, it could later become a cause of temptation for the exercitant, for the door would

always be open for the devil to insinuate that the exercitant had been drawn into religious life at human instigation. On the other hand, the director should be confident that a decision which he has scrutinized by the rules of a sound election will be secure and without danger. He needs only to be diligent in supporting and directing the person God has committed to his care.

[176] 3. **The director's vigilance.**—The director must be vigilant in unmasking the devil's deceits and sophistries, for from false principles such as the devil suggests nothing but false conclusions can follow.

[177] 4. **How he should enter the election.**—The director should also be aware that a person often enters upon an election with excellent dispositions, yet at the actual moment of the election some untoward affection arises in him which upsets everything and chokes the good seed. The director must be circumspect and careful to foresee and head off things of this sort.

CHAPTER 25: MATTER FOR THE ELECTION

[178] 1. **The thing must be good.**—As regards the third point, it is evident that any matter falling under an election needs to be something good, whether it is a particular undertaking or the choice of a state of life.

[179] 2. **Election of a state of life.**—The election of a state of life turns upon two alternatives: remaining in the way of the commandments or going on to that of the counsels.

[180] 3. **What to do if the counsels are to be followed.**—If the counsels are to be followed, the question is then whether inside or outside religious life. For though the counsels can nowadays hardly be followed outside religious life, a person's character can be such that he is not suited for community life and obedience yet is able to observe poverty and chastity.

[181] 4. **Decisions in case of entry into religious life.**—Thirdly, if it is to be religious life, there remains the question of which order it should be. God calls some to greater solitude and others to the help of their neighbors; and different kinds of natural constitutions, whether of body or soul, are suited for different institutes.

[182] 5. **Choice of the time.**—Fourthly, once the particular order has been selected, there is the question of the timing and manner of carrying out the decision.

[183] 6. **Cautions in choosing an order.**—In choosing a particular religious order, care must be taken first not to pick one which has become corrupted, or in which strict observance does not flourish. Secondly, among those in which observance does flourish, the order whose institute is more perfect should be preferred. For determining this, St. Thomas gives excellent teaching (*Secunda Secundae*, q. 188, a. 6). The individual's personality needs to be taken carefully into consideration—not just his strength and propensities but also the

gifts and talents which he possesses for the greater service of God.

[184] 7. **Difficulty of implementing one's vocation.**—When the moment comes to carry out God's vocation, there is sometimes a special difficulty. In matters repugnant to our sensitive nature, human weakness tends to procrastinate as long as it can and to delude itself, thinking up grounds and reasons for delay. It is best to rout this particular difficulty during the Exercises themselves, and to reflect on St. Ambrose's words: "The grace of the Holy Spirit knows no tardy efforts." We should imitate the eagerness of the apostles, who left their nets and their father immediately. One should also reflect: "If ever, why not now? And if not now, maybe never." God's inspiration and help are fresh now, but later it can easily happen—and does happen daily—that this spirit may cool, and then it will be far harder to resist the assaults of the flesh and the devil. Thus much concerning the election of the counsels.

[185] 8. **If the commandments are chosen.**—On the other hand, if a person chooses the way of the commandments, he will still need to deliberate on the state or style of life in which he will keep them. These points will need to be examined one by one, so that his life may be ordered better and with clearer light.

[186] 9. **The same rules to be used for other matters.**—Lastly, in other particular matters, such as undertaking or not undertaking a work or office, these same rules should be used insofar as applicable. The method or criterion in all such particular actions is to weigh everything from the point of view of God's honor, taking no account of one's own advantage, especially temporal, so that one's intention is always directed straight to God and not deflected to any earthly object.

CHAPTER 26: THE THREE TIMES FOR MAKING A GOOD ELECTION

[187] 1. **The three times of election.**—As for the fourth point, only the three times for making an election which are mentioned in the book of the Exercises should be explained. If these are thoroughly understood, nothing further seems needed. They are called "times" because when the soul experiences movements described in them, it is then the right and proper time for making the election. Regarding the first time little needs to be said. In it the will of God is so abundantly clear and certain that there can be no doubt about it, as in the case of the vocations of Matthew and Paul. Even though such miraculous vocations may no longer occur, we both read and see some cases which in a way come close to them: cases where there is such spiritual clarity and contentment, and such evident illumination regarding God's will, that these vocations seem to admit no doubt. But this type of calling is quite out of the ordinary and is not subject to any rule. Hence it should not be asked or expected from God. Because of the rarity of such cases, not much time should

be spent discussing this first time; it should merely be indicated to the exercitant in passing.

[188] 2. **The second time more common.**—More common is the second time, i.e., when the soul is inwardly stirred by such powerful inspirations and movements of grace that with little or no reasoning of the intellect the will is borne onward toward the service of God and toward perfection.

[189] 3. **The third time.**—The third time is when by considering and weighing the reasons on either side the intellect comes to see the truth more clearly and provides a light for the will, so that the will finally chooses what, all things considered, it judges the best course.

Chapter 27: Comparison of the Second and Third Times of Election

[190] 1. **Difference between intellect and will in the election.**—Although these two powers of the soul are so bound together that the one cannot operate without the other in making a choice, they nevertheless differ in that during the first and second times of election it is the will that takes the lead, with the intellect following and being led by the will without any reasoning of its own or hesitation. In the third time, on the other hand, the intellect takes the lead, proposing numerous reasons to the will in order to arouse and impel it to the side it judges to be better. Moreover, provided the movement comes directly from God, there is no doubt that the higher and more excellent way is when it is the will which, under God's illumination, takes the lead and draws the intellect after it. Aristotle himself, as cited by St. Thomas, says that it is not good to counsel with human reasoning persons who are moved by divine inspiration, for they are moved by a principle higher than human reason [*Eudemean Ethics*, vii.14]. On the other hand, the third way by means of reflection and reasoning is safer and more secure.

[191] 2. **Elements of the first and second times.**—For an understanding of the first and second times—i.e., when the soul is moved by inspiration from God—the exercitant ought to have explained to him what is meant by consolation and desolation. Both of these are treated in rules 3 and 4 for the Discernment of Spirits.

[192] 3. **What consolation is.**—This consolation, however, is not a stable condition of the soul. It is rather a supernaturally bestowed spiritual experience of such a nature that when it is present acts of virtue are performed easily, even with delight, relish, and ardor. Consolation makes the works of the flesh, on the other hand, lose their attractiveness and seem distasteful. Consolation has various elements or forms: peace and inward tranquillity, spiritual joy, light, a clearer knowledge of the things of God, tears, elevation of the mind to God,

steadfast hope in God, perception of eternal realities, heavenly-mindedness, warmth of holy love, and other similar workings or affections, all of which proceed from the good spirit.

[193] 4. **What desolation is.**—Desolation, on the contrary, is sadness, disquiet of mind, hope in human realities or persons, love of baser realities, dryness, low spirits, and wandering of the mind after things of this world. All of these proceed from the evil spirit.

[194] 5. **Directions for an election in these times.**—In order, therefore, for a person to discover which of two alternatives on which he is deliberating is more pleasing to God, he should note in times of consolation to which side consolation and tranquillity of soul incline him more; and on the contrary, when he experiences desolation, to which side that inclines him more. When he sees himself moved in opposite directions in these contrary times, he should take it as certain that the movements stem from contrary sources. For it is characteristic of the evil spirit to invade the soul in times of desolation and to overwhelm it with cowardice, sadness, and torpor. On the other hand, it is characteristic of the good spirit to bring the soul joy, and in periods of joy to deal with it and influence it. Each spirit gives what is its own and what it abounds in. This is clear from the Rules for the Discernment of Spirits, especially those of the Second Week. During this time, these rules are highly useful; without them one is practically walking in the dark.

[195] 6. **Image used by our Father Ignatius.**—There is another procedure for doing this given by our Father Ignatius under his image of a person who offers a certain kind of food to his prince to see how he likes it. In a similar way, the soul, with deep humility and fervent love and a desire to please God, may offer him at different moments first one thing and then the other, watching to see which of them is more acceptable and pleasing to him, saying always, "Lord, what would you have me do?" [Acts 9:6]. The person should say and feel this not just with his lips or only a slight affection of his mind, but with his whole heart, indeed with many hearts if he had them.

[196] 7. **The best sign of a call to perfection from God.**—Among all indications that God's will is calling a person to the state of perfection, the following is the best: if the soul feels that God promises it all the spiritual capital it needs to build the tower of evangelical perfection. That is, the soul feels that the hardships of this life which appear so heavy to others, and once appeared so to itself, are now made light and easy. Voluntary poverty, the abnegation of one's own will, the observance of chastity, and the practice of other virtues no longer seem so burdensome, as St. Augustine writes of himself in his *Confessions* [xii.30]. A second indication is if these thoughts continue moving the soul to what is good. For although Satan may disguise himself at first, he cannot hid his real character for long and is sure in the course of time to begin spewing his venom.

[197] 8. **Signs of the good and evil spirits.**—Lastly, there is a fine and quite clear discussion of the good and bad spirits in the second series of Rules for the Discernment of Spirits in the book of the Exercises. Gerson treats the same subject in his work *De probatione spirituum*; also St. Bonaventure[10] in his *De processione religionis*, ch. 18.

[198] 9. **When to move on to the third time.**—What has been said will suffice for the first and second times of election. The exercitant can stop here if the will of God is so manifest that his soul is firmly established and settled and has no desire for further certitude. But if it is not sufficient, he may move on to the third time.

CHAPTER 28: THE FIRST AND SECOND METHODS OF MAKING
A GOOD ELECTION

[199] 1. **Two methods in the third time.**—The third time in the book of the Exercises is divided into two methods, called the first and second methods for making a good election. The first comprises six points, the second four rules. Thus, if an election is not concluded by the first method we must go on to the second, which is the final method which can be presented in this matter.

[200] 2. **Requirements for these methods.**—A requirement for these two methods of making a good election, as throughout the entire time of election, is tranquillity of soul. In a time of perturbation there is no place for an election: "Make not haste in the time of clouds" (Ecclus 2 [:2]). Hence, unless person experiences this tranquillity it would be better to continue with the meditations until the storm dies down and the calm returns, for nothing can be made out in turbid waters.

[201] 3. **Given tranquillity, what should be done?**—Assuming, then, the presence of this tranquillity, the advantages and disadvantages of the course under deliberation should be set forth separately, each point then being carefully weighed and examined to see toward which side the balance inclines.

[202] 4. **Where to seek the reasons.**—The one thing to be observed and practiced here is, as we indicated above, that the reasons adduced in the deliberation must all proceed from the principle of the divine service. No considerations of human respect or worldly advantage should be admitted here.

[203] 5. **The third time as confirmation of the others.**—Note also that these two methods of the third time are not only for use in cases where no conclusion has been reached in the second time. Even if an election has already been concluded in the second time, the third time contributes to its further confirmation and settling. Of course, if the soul were completely certain that

---

[10] Actually, David of Augsburg.

the movement in the second time was from God, it would doubtless have no need to look further. But since Satan's angel at times transforms himself into an angel of light [2 Cor. 11:14], it is generally rather dangerous for a person to wish to be guided solely by the movements of the will and certain interior feelings, without adding appropriate reflection. Hence there should be a testing and examination by means of the light, for, as St. Paul says, "all that is made manifest is light" [Eph. 5:13]. Now this light, after that of faith, is human reason (helped and enlightened of, course, by the light of faith), which is itself from God. The two cannot contradict each other, for truth must necessarily agree with truth.

[204] 6. **Another sign of the evil spirit.**—It is a further sign of the evil spirit when he shuns this examination, for he loves darkness and is unwilling to come to the light for fear his works should be reproved [John 3:20]. On these grounds, therefore, this method of election is safer, because in it reason, illuminated by faith and instructed by the teaching of the Catholic Church, performs its proper function and, by exerting all its strength and capacity in seeking to know God's will, faithfully does what it can.

[205] 7. **Experience of one's weakness.**—And if to these reasons were added the experience everyone has of his own weakness, so that he had a clear realization of how imperiled his salvation is in the world, there is no doubt that the election would proceed with greater security.

[206] 8. **Greater light in the soul.**—Further, if these reasons should be confirmed by some signs from the second time spoken of above, viz., peace, consolation, or relish, then the soul receives even greater satisfaction and clarity.

[207] 9. **If the two times conflict.**—The question might arise as to what should be done if we happen to incline to one thing in the second time and something different or opposed in the third. We reply that the matter would need to be carefully examined by the Rules for the Discernment of Spirits and by right reason, and the motives on either side carefully weighed. If it is quite clear that reason supports the election made in the third time, it is safer to follow this one, since we have no certitude that the movement experienced in the second time really was from God, especially with reason pointing in another direction. On the other hand, if the reasons moving us in the third time are weak, while the movements in the second time appear after thorough examination according to the rules to be from God and compatible with right reason, then we should prefer the entire election made in the second time. For while God's will was not at first entirely clear by means of it, yet once the matter has been more fully turned over and considered, and the confirmation of reason added, it may become clear.

CHAPTER 29: THE PROCEDURE AND ORDER FOR THE ELECTION

[208] 1. **Procedure of the election.**—Now we come to the final point: the overall procedure and order for presenting the election and guiding the exercitant through it. First of all, it should be carefully noted, as we have pointed out above, that already at the beginning of the Second Week the meditation on the Kingdom of Christ begins to dispose the soul for the election by raising the mind from earthly and transitory things to a desire of imitating the Savior. Of course, this disposition needs to be continuously nourished in the exercitant afterwards through his being spurred on and directed to what is more perfect by means of the subsequent meditations— those on the Nativity, Circumcision, etc.—in which he should be instructed in such a way that he conceives a desire of conforming himself to the Son of God, along with the deepest gratitude toward him who has given us so much and done so much for us. (In the contemplation on the Kingdom of God, the words "testifying that I desire," etc. [98] are not to be taken as having the force of a vow, given that Annotation 14 expressly warns against the exercitant's binding himself hastily by a vow.)

[209] 2. **Meditation on the election begins on the fourth or fifth day.**—Then on the fourth or fifth day the meditations of the election begin with the exercise on the boy Jesus remaining in the Temple, where, as the book of the Exercises states [135], he first gave us an example of this evangelical perfection by leaving his putative father and natural mother and choosing to be occupied solely with his eternal Father's business.

[210] 3. **Disposing the exercitant for the election.**—And so, to prepare the soul for the election, this meditation is followed by the exercise on the Two Standards, and then on the same day by the meditation about the Three Classes of Men. The purpose of the latter is to have the exercitant examine himself in the light of these classes and determine what is his own attitude toward things of the world. If he finds he is in the first or the second class, he should make an effort to overcome himself in order to move into the third.

[211] 4. **Understanding the Three Classes.**—For a clearer understanding of these Three Classes, note that it is taken for granted in all three cases that the person has acquired the money legitimately and is under no obligation to restitution. Otherwise the person could not be indifferent to keeping it or giving it up, as he is stated to be in the third class.

[212] 5. **Further notes.**—His way of acquiring it, then, would have been, say, by doing business with an excessive love of gain or some other human and faulty affection. Note, secondly, that the first and second classes differ in that, although both have a will that is weak and lax in ridding itself of attachment to the thing, persons of the first class never take or even envision any steps toward doing so, while those of the second class do more inasmuch as they take some

steps—but only such as suit themselves, not such as are in accord with God's will and good pleasure. And so they consider themselves ready to do anything else except actually part with the thing they love. Persons of the third class are ready to do even this should God will it, and their only question is whether he does so will.

[213] 6. **Purpose of the meditation on the Three Classes.**—Thus, it is clear that the whole purpose of this meditation is to show the soul how disgraceful and perverse it is not only to refuse to get rid of disordered desires, but also to be willing to get rid of them only on one's own terms, not abandoning oneself in God's hands. This shows a very weak will indeed, for it really both wills and does not will.

[214] 7. **Further examples should be thought up.**—Because of the great importance of this point, especially for readying the soul as the moment of election draws near, the exercitant can try to come to greater clarity by thinking up for himself other examples along the same line besides this example of the three businessmen. One might take three sick persons. They all want to get better, but the first refuses to take the medicines because of their bitter taste, or to let himself be operated on because of the pain. The second would be willing to use some treatments, but only the ones he himself approves and judges fit, not the ones really indicated for his malady. For instance, he might refuse to give up wine, etc. The third will place himself unreservedly in the physician's hands, allowing him to prescribe him a diet, a cauterization, or even an amputation if need be.

[215] 8. **When to give the Three Degrees of Humility.**—Along with the pair of meditations on the Two Standards and the Three Classes, or on the day following if it seems preferable, after the meditation on Christ's departure from Nazareth and his Baptism, the exercitant should be given the Three Degrees of Humility. As indicated in the book of the Exercises, he should ponder them throughout the day. However, he should at the same time meditate one or two mysteries of Christ's life on that day just as on the others, for the Three Degrees are not given for a definite hour of meditation, having as they do only a single point, viz., desire to reach the third degree of humility. This should be pondered throughout the day outside of meditation, or even at suitable times during the meditations, using the triple colloquy from the Two Standards, as indicated there [168].

CHAPTER 30: THE ACTUAL ELECTION ACCORDING TO
THE SECOND TIME

[216] 1. **Explaining the Preamble to the election.**—With the completion of these exercises, we now approach the election itself. First of all the Preamble to the election [169] should be explained. It is practically the same as

the Foundation at the beginning of the Exercises, so that anyone who meditated the Foundation well should have no difficulty with it.

[217] 2. **Sounding the exercitant's will.**—Meanwhile the director should sound the exercitant's will to see if he possesses indifference, the necessity of which we described earlier. Should the director see that he is inclined rather to the less perfect state, he ought to explain the note which follows the Three Classes [157] to the effect that when we feel repugnance for actual poverty we should ask God to incline our will more strongly to that side. The reason is that if you want to straighten a crooked stick you must bend it to the opposite side so that it will end up midway between the two and thus straight. This principle is particularly applicable here since the opposite side would actually be the safer one, and acting in this way would put no limitations on God's will or our own freedom. Assuming that this is done, the exercitant should continue meditating on the mysteries of Christ as found in the book of the Exercises, while at the same time devoting himself to the election. To guide him in this, the director should give him the three times of election, either orally or in writing as may seem better.

[218] 3. **Procedure for the election.**—In making his election, however, the exercitant should not meditate the three times throughout his whole time of meditation. The period after each meditation, or a point during the medita- tion when his mind is calm, is the proper time for acting and reasoning about the matter in question. Hence, great care should be taken that the meditations on Christ's life are diligently made at their proper times, as we have already said. Wishing to drop these meditations altogether and concentrate exclusively on the election of a state would be a mistake; in fact, it would be harmful. These meditations strengthen and illuminate the mind, lifting it from earthly things and making it fitter to perceive and embrace God's will and to overcome all obstacles. To cease from meditation, on the other hand, would weaken and becloud the soul.

[219] 4. **Blending meditation with the election.**—That is why, as has been said, due time must be given to meditating divine realities as presented in the various mysteries, as well as due time to the election. Otherwise, if the mind is exclusively occupied with the thoughts of the election, its juice and flower of devotion might easily be sucked dry and exhausted and the soul enfeebled.

[220] 5. **Details of making the election.**—As for the details of the elec- tion, it can be said that when engaged in the second time the exercitant should avoid any cogitation or reasoning of his own; while making his meditation or colloquies, or in general while in God's presence, he should place before his mind's eyes the way of the counsels and watch to see if he feels in his soul any movements of consolation or desolation. Then he should set before himself the way of the commandments and watch for the same.

[221] 6. **No special meditation necessary.**—As we said earlier, no special meditation is needed for this. It suffices to do it during the time of meditation and prayer. Moreover, the exercitant should do the same thing outside the time of meditation, setting the matter before himself as described above and watching to observe the movements. He should engage in no reasoning of his own but simply listen to the voice of the Lord and dispose himself as best he can to hear that voice and receive the movements. He should especially make a frequent renewal of his resignation into God's hands and of his desire to know God's good pleasure, and he should be constantly striving to set aside any will or inclination of his own.

[222] 7. **An account of the movements to be asked.**—During his visits, the director should ask an account of these movements. If he detects signs of the good or evil spirit he should have recourse to the Rules for the Discernment of Spirits, particularly those of the Second Week, explaining to the exercitant anything he judges needful for his guidance or, if necessary, encouragement. If he sees the exercitant is coming along well, he should give him a further meditation and urge him to keep up the same procedure regarding the election in question, in order to test whether the same movements continue or are succeeded by contrary ones. If contrary movements occur, the director should try to discern by means of the rules which movements are good and which are evil.

CHAPTER 31: ELECTION ACCORDING TO
THE FIRST AND SECOND METHODS

[223] 1. **If no election is reached in the second time.**—If no election is reached in the second time because the exercitant has experienced no significant interior movements, or because he feels moved in both directions, recourse should be had to the two methods of the third time. These should be explained to the exercitant; he should be told that once having come to a decision by use of the first method, he should then weigh his conclusion by means of the second. Getting the same result from both methods is an excellent sign of a good election.

[224] 2. **One meditation should be given during the third time.**— During this third time the exercitant may be given only a single meditation from the Second Week, together with its repetition, so that he can devote the rest of his time to the election. This seems to be intimated in the book of the Exercises in the case of the contemplation of the Baptism on the fifth day [158]. However, while no directions are given for this, we may suppose that the director is free to give one or two meditations a day, depending on what he sees will best help the exercitant, taking into account the difficulty the latter is experiencing and the time he needs for carrying out this deliberation.

[225] 3. **Writing down the reasons.**—The exercitant should also be told to write down in separate columns the reasons which occur to him on either side. When all the reasons on either side are lined up together, they make the truth more evident and have stronger motivating force. The exercitant should lay these reasons before the director so that he can guide him better.

[226] 4. **Do not overburden the exercitant.**—The director must also be careful not to overburden the exercitant in this matter—it is already difficult and laborious enough of itself. He must not be continually pushing and fatiguing him. Rather, he should occasionally allow him breathing space, for fear that he will be under continual strain, or overwhelmed by sadness or disgust, and so plunge into despair. This is especially to be feared when over and above the exercitant's own weakness and the repugnance of the flesh there are additional attacks from the devils. It is difficult to restore the courage of such a person once it has collapsed.

[227] 5. **Bearing with an exercitant who is not prompt in responding to God's call.**—Even if the exercitant seems not to respond to God's will with much readiness, or to overcome himself as he ought, he should still be patiently borne with in hopes that gradually and step by step he will overcome the obstacles in his way. In this we ought to imitate the way of acting of God's own goodness, of which we are collaborators, for he disposes all things sweetly, and perseveringly waits out the soul's delays in coming to him.

[228] 6. **No vows to be made during this time.**—A final note is that, whatever he may decide in the second or third time, the exercitant should make no vows, as indicated in Annotation 14. This applies especially to the second time. In moments of ardor or consolation vows are often made which are regretted later. This precaution needs to be taken especially with persons of ardent, hasty, or unstable character. Nevertheless, in a case where the election has been made after mature consideration and with great clarity and unmistakable tokens of a calling from God, particularly if the person's age or character give no warrant for suspicion and he wishes to confirm his election with a vow the better to forestall the assaults of the flesh, the world, and Satan, then the instructor neither may nor should oppose what his devotion impels him to—just as he should in no way encourage it.

CHAPTER 32: PRAYER AFTER THE ELECTION

[229] 1. **What to do after the election.**—The last phase in the election is what the book of the Exercises mentions in the concluding point [183], viz., that after completing his election the exercitant should betake himself to prayer. If in prayer he feels himself confirmed in the election he has made, experiencing inward movements and lights from above that indicate that God approves what he has done and promises him strength to carry it out, it is an excellent sign and should be taken as a seal put upon the whole election.

[230] 2. **If the election is tried by the evil spirit.**—But if the movements, affections, or illuminations of the intellect are of such a nature as to weaken the election that has been made, and if under examination by the guidelines given above they appear to be from the evil spirit, or at least doubtful, the election should not be altered.

[231] 3. **If by the good spirit.**—But if it is clearly evident that these movements are from the good spirit, it is a sign that the deliberation was flawed and that the election needs to be made over again.

[232] 4. **If nothing noteworthy occurs in prayer.**—But if during this prayer there occurs nothing notable either in the affections or in the intellect inclining in one direction or the other, and the exercitant's will perseveres in its resolve, the election should not be called into doubt. Instead, we should conclude from this that it was through the reasoning process that God wanted his will to be discovered.

CHAPTER 33: WHAT THE DIRECTOR SHOULD DO WHEN HE SEES
THAT THE EXERCITANT IS SUBJECT TO DELUSIONS

[233] 1. **If the exercitant suffers from delusions.**—However, it sometimes happens that an exercitant making an election can suffer from delusions: even though God may be calling him to a more perfect life, he himself may— either through the devil's deceit or through his own infirmity—choose the less perfect and be immovably convinced that this is from the Holy Spirit.

[234] 2. **He needs encouragement.**—A wise director will not oppose him too strongly—it would do no good. On the other hand, he should not confirm the election that has been made. Instead he should show that he is somewhat dissatisfied with it but hopes that in the course of time the Lord will manifest his will more clearly to the exercitant. Thus he should leave him in some doubt and uncertainty about his election, and then instruct him how to dispose himself properly so as not to shut the door to God's light.

[235] 3. **Many recognize the truth after the Exercises.**—For experience has often shown that there are persons who cave in under the struggle during the Exercises but then afterwards come to see the truth more readily—in the light of the very principles which they got while making the Exercises. This may be because the devil's attacks are fiercer at the moment of election, or because nature itself (especially in the case of the timid and faint-hearted) is overwhelmed and suffocated in this deadly struggle, whereas afterwards, when they have caught their breath, such persons are in a better condition to reflect and to perceive God's light. Or it may be that experience later shows them that they are unable to live the life in the world which they had perhaps imagined for themselves, or been persuaded to by the devil, while they were making the Exercises.

CHAPTER 34: THOSE WHO ALREADY HAVE A STATE OF LIFE

[236] 1. **Method for reformation of life.**—After his treatment of the election, our Father gives a method for amending or reforming one's life. This instruction is of the greatest importance for those who already have a state of life which cannot be changed, or at least are not called by God to change their state. This reformation removes many abuses which, if not actually sinful, are at least the source of many evils.

[237] 2. **Fruits of this teaching.**—The aim of this instruction is to enable large numbers of persons who already have a wife and family to pursue perfection in their own way even while remaining in the world. Our own vocation requires us to invite and lead them to this perfection, as we are charged to do throughout our Constitutions. There is not doubt that if we tried to help and direct our neighbor by the program set out here, really outstanding results would ensue. Hence, this should be an important concern of all our men engaged in ministries.

[238] 3. **How to help those who already have a state of life.**—The method to use with this type of persons is the following. Besides the ordinary exercises on the mysteries of Christ's life, they should be given the Two Standards, the Three Classes, and also the Preamble for Making an Election. These latter exercises, even though less essential for them than for those deliberating about their entire state of life, are nevertheless unquestionably of great value for such persons, to encourage them toward at least the kind of perfection possible in their state and condition.

[239] 4. **The third time more helpful for them.**—However, for this task the second time of election is considerably less suitable than the third time with its two parts. What should be done is to take each item—for instance, the person's household or his expenditures—and examine it separately. After deliberating on one item the exercitant should go on to the next, spending on each an amount of time proportionate to its importance or difficulty. Thus, sometimes a single item might take a whole hour or even several hours, while at other times several items could be disposed of in a single hour.

CHAPTER 35: THE THIRD WEEK

[240] 1. **The choice of a more perfect life stabilized.**—In the Third Week the election of a more perfect life and the resolution to serve God is stabilized and confirmed by consideration of the great and wondrous example of the passion of our Lord and Savior. In the Passion, all his virtues shine forth in a far more visible and glorious way, challenging us more powerfully to his imitation. Thus a great treasure lies hidden here, and this is why we see that the saints devoted themselves especially to meditating on the Passion, as appears

from writings left by them. Hence, the exercitant should also be well instructed in how to meditate on the Passion, for it should be the soul's regular food.

[241] 2. **The same method of meditation as in the Second Week.**— The order and procedure for these meditations is the same as in the previous Week, viz., contemplation of the persons, their words, and their actions. In this Week, however, especially for less experienced persons, a way into contemplation should be opened up using the points that are commonly taught: Who suffers? What does he suffer? At whose hands? For whose sake?

[242] 3. **Composition of place.**—In the composition of place the exercitant should take up his position as though present in the mystery as it unfolds, just as if it took place for him alone, according to the words of St. Paul: "He loved me and gave himself up for me" [Gal. 2:20]. The soul should regard itself as being the cause of all the great sufferings and humiliations that the Son of God endured. Then it should consider that all its spiritual goods, all its grace, as well as its liberation from eternal evils and its hope of obtaining eternal goods, have come to it from Christ's merits. Indeed, it should consider that in suffering all these things Christ had before his eyes both ourselves and each one of our sins, praying for them, obtaining pardon for them and grace for us.

[243] 4. **Affections to be aimed at.**—Although the affection of compassion is quite excellent and should be earnestly petitioned, humbly longed for, and gratefully received, nevertheless there are other affections that should be cultivated at the same time and are of greater worth for our spiritual life.

[244] 5. **First, hatred for sin.**—The first is to feel how serious a matter it is to offend God, since in order to make satisfaction for it God's wisdom thought it meet to use the very blood and life of his Son. This consideration engenders a profound hatred for sin when the latter is seen as visited by God's justice with such severe punishment; for if this happens in the green wood, what will happen in the dry? [see Luke 23:31].

[245] 6. **Second, realization of God's goodness.**—Second, we should acknowledge and adore God's limitless goodness and wisdom in having devised so effective a means for melting human hearts and drawing them to himself by his love, as St. Paul says: "God commends his charity toward us in that when we were yet sinners," etc. [Rom. 5:8ff].

[246] 7. **Third, strengthening of hope.**—Third, here our hope also is strengthened; for, as St. Augustine says, he who gave what is greater—the blood of his only-begotten Son—will also give eternal glory, a smaller thing without doubt; hence, the blood of Christ should be regarded as an earnest and pledge both of God's love and of our future happiness.[11]

[247] 8. **Fourth, love for God.**—Fourth, and most importantly of all, our love for God is set ablaze by consideration of his vast goodness and of the

---

[11] See *City of God* xxii.24.

benefits he has bestowed on us—and bestowed in such a fashion.

[248] 9. **Fifth, enthusiasm for imitating Christ.**—Fifth, in this way everyone is also stimulated to perfect imitation of our Lord, as St. Peter says: "Christ also suffered for us, leaving you an example that you should follow his steps" [1 Pet. 2:21]. It would be disgraceful and intolerable that, while he deigned to suffer such humiliation in order to instruct us for our own salvation, we whose own salvation is at issue should decline to follow.

[249] 10. **Sixth, zeal for souls.**—Finally, we can and should conceive a great zeal for souls, seeing that God has valued them so highly, loved them so dearly, and purchased them at so high a price.

[250] 11. **Using Scripture passages.**—It is helpful during this Week to have a stock of Scripture texts bearing on the Lord's passion, from the Psalms, the prophets (especially Isaiah), or from the Gospels themselves and the letters of St. Paul—texts speaking of the immensity of Christ our Lord's sorrows and sufferings, or of his goodness, or of their wonderful effects in the restoration of the human race. These texts will be very helpful in the time outside meditation for stirring up the heart and also for dispelling a certain satiety which often sets in when one dwells for long periods on the same subjects. The director will be able to make his own collection of such Scripture texts or obtain one elsewhere —such texts are numerous throughout the Bible.

[251] 12. **Other matters can be found in the book of the Exercises; regulation of diet.**—The remaining matters pertaining to this Week are set out clearly and distinctly in the book of the Exercises in the meditations and Additions. Specifically, the Rules for Regulating One's Diet placed at the end of this Week should only be explained orally and not given in writing, since (among other reasons) they ought not to be given to all persons in the same way but adapted with discretion to each individual's character as well as to his physical and mental strength.

[252] 13. **When to present these rules.**—Note also that these rules should be taught not exclusively in the Third Week but even earlier at some suitable moment. But if this has not been done already it should be done now. It may be these rules were reserved till now so as not to overburden the exercitant during the earlier Weeks with excessive amounts of instruction over and above the meditations. This Week has considerably fewer such instructions and leaves the director more time for explaining these rules. For it is good that he have something new to bring each time he visits the exercitant.

CHAPTER 36: THE FOURTH WEEK

[253] 1. **The Fourth Week corresponds to the unitive way.**—The Fourth Week appears to correspond to the unitive way, for it is wholly concerned with love for God and longing for eternity, the exemplar of which

is set forth in the resurrection of Christ and the joys which have followed upon it even in this world. Other meditations may be added here on the glory of paradise and on the future happiness of the just, the pledge of which we have received in this mystery of Christ's resurrection, since, as St. Paul says, God has raised us up with him and seated us with him [Eph. 2:6]. Hence, we ought all the more to be stirred up to despise the things of earth and long for those of heaven, as St. Paul also says: "If you are risen with Christ, seek the things that are above, relish the things that are above," etc. [see Col. 3:1ff].

[254] 2. **Exercise on the Love of God.**—The exercise on the Love of God is most effective in exercising our love for God. It contains four extremely rich points which provide abundant material for meditation. It can be made in two ways. One is to make it on the same days as the mysteries of the Resurrection; thus, on the second day, after the mysteries of the risen life have begun, the meditation on loving God would also begin, with one or two hours being devoted to it each day apart from the meditation on the mysteries. Alternatively, the mysteries can all be gone through first, and then one or two full days be allotted to this meditation.

[255] 3. **Directions for making this meditation.**—When the exercitant embarks upon this meditation it is important to point out and explain to him what is said there about love depending more on deeds than on words, and consisting in a mutual sharing of resources and all other things. Thus the exercitant should realize that experiencing a mere tender affection is not enough and that he should not rest satisfied with this. What St. Gregory says is true: "The proof of love is the performance of deeds," and "Where love is present it works great deeds, and where it does no deeds it is not present."[12] Nothing more needs to be said about the Fourth Week.

CHAPTER 37: THE THREE METHODS OF PRAYER

[256] 1. **Valuable instruction.**—After the Exercises there are added a number of instructions of great value and assistance for spiritual progress. In the first place we find the three Methods of Prayer. These are given not so that everyone who finishes the Exercises should practice them (this is not necessary) but as a complement to the teaching on prayer and for the sake of less educated or capable persons who cannot keep up sufficiently continuous trains of thought in prayer to be able dwell for long periods on a single topic. For this reason the *Constitutions,* VII, 5.F, say that, while the full Exercises should be given only to a few persons, the First Week together with these Three Methods of Prayer can be given to larger numbers.

---

[12] Gregory the Great, *Hom. in Ev.* ii.30.

[257] 2. **First Method: going through the commandments, etc.**—The First Method is to go through the commandments of God or the Church, the seven capital sins, the three powers of the soul and the five senses—and this not so much speculatively as practically. Thus, in the case of the commandments, a person should reflect on how poorly he has kept them, resolving to keep them better in the future. Similarly with the other topics.

[258] 3. **The First Method for more capable persons.**—To raise these topics to a somewhat higher level with a more capable exercitant, the following method can be used. When praying on the commandments he should first consider a given commandment in itself—how good and just and holy it is. Secondly, how profitable is its observance. Thirdly, how well he has kept it up till now, thanking God if he has kept it well, or grieving and asking pardon if he has not. Fourthly, he should resolve to keep it perfectly and exactly in the future, and ask the grace for this in a colloquy. If his hour is not up by the time he has done this he should do the next commandment in the same way.

[259] 4. **On the capital sins.**—In the case of the capital sins, he can examine, first, how evil they are and how rightly forbidden. Secondly, how harmful they are if not avoided. Thirdly, how well he has avoided them up till now, or resolves to avoid them in the future.

[260] 5. **On the five senses.**—In the case of the powers of the soul and the senses, he can reflect, first, how noble and essential for us each of them is —the intellect, and all the others in order. Secondly, the purpose for which they were given. Thirdly, how Christ or the blessed Virgin employed them. Fourthly, how we ourselves have employed them: grieving if badly, etc. The same with our other powers and senses, one by one—including also our powers of speech, movement, and the like.

[261] 6. **Note on this method.**—Note that in considering how we have used these powers, or in meditating on the commandments and how poorly we may have kept them, and particularly in meditating on the capital sins, we should avoid equating this meditation with an examination of conscience as in preparation for confession, or making some special effort to elicit contrition. That is proper to the First Week. Our main intention here is to consider the subject matter and only incidentally to reflect upon ourselves. Hence this reflection should be done in a general way, not going too much into detail regarding particular sins.

[262] 7. **This method recommended by Father Francis Xavier.**—Father Francis Xavier is said to have recommended this type of prayer to all the souls he dealt with, even assigning as a penance to spend some time on it in the morning and in the evening.

[263] 8. **How long to dwell on these meditations.**—Although the book of the Exercises says to dwell on each point for the length of three Our Fathers, anyone who finds some devotion or spiritual help there should spend

longer, even if he is unable to finish off all the commandments. See the fourth Addition at the end of the First Week [76].

[264] 9. **Note on the Second Method.**—In the Second Method, note that if a single word yields no sense, several should be grouped together, v.g., "Who art in heaven" or "Hallowed be thy name." Other words furnish matter for meditation even when taken singly, v.g., "Our" and "Father."

[265] 10. **Other prayers.**—What is said of these prayers applies to other scriptural passages as well, especially the Psalms. Whole psalms or individual verses can be selected which offer rich nourishment to both mind and heart.

[266] 11. **How long to stay with the Methods of Prayer.**—Note also that if the exercitant does well with this kind of prayer and seems to have a grasp of it, he need not continue with it for long. It is enough if he learns the method for later use. The same is true of the First Method—unless, given the somewhat greater variety of matter in the First Method, it is worthwhile to do one exercise on the commandments, another on the powers of the soul, another on the senses, and so forth.

[267] 12. **Third Method of Prayer.**—In the Third Method we consider each word of a prayer for the length of time normally occupied by a single breath. Of course, if a person's devotion prompts him to dwell longer he may do so; but then he will be using the Second rather than the Third Method. The Third Method is helpful in learning to recite vocal prayers with proper attention and devotion, following the words of St. Paul: "I will pray with the spirit, I will pray also with the understanding" [1 Cor. 14:15]. Hence this exercise is most helpful for persons who are obliged to recite the canonical hours or other vocal prayers.

[268] 13. **Other methods not excluded.**—Even though these three methods are given here, we should not imagine that this excludes such other methods as are often taught by the Holy Spirit and employed by spiritually experienced persons, basing themselves on experience, reason, and sound doctrine; or such as individual persons have been found in practice to be useful for their own progress. This is to be understood of our own men also—of course always with the approval and consent of the superior or spiritual prefect, to whom each one should manifest his way of praying, especially if it is somewhat out of the ordinary. Moreover, not only will one or another of these three methods be suitable for different persons, but even the same person— depending on his state of mind or body—will find different ones more suitable at different times. For example, when a person is tired or unwell and not in a condition for lengthy meditation and cogitation, he will be helped more by the Second or Third Methods. This applies not only to the Fourth Week but to all other times.

CHAPTER 38: GIVING THE RULES

[269] 1. **Reason for the rules at the end of the Exercises.**—The additional rules at the end of the Exercises are placed there to be given not universally but in accord with individual persons' needs or even wishes arising from their particular devotion.

[270] 2. **Distribution of alms.**—Accordingly, the Rules for Distributing Alms should be given only to wealthy people who have the practice or possibility of giving alms. Similarly, there is no need for giving the Rules on Scruples to persons who are not troubled by them.

[271] 3. **Rules on Catholic doctrine.**—The rules on Catholic doctrine are of course helpful for strengthening and encouraging anyone's spiritual life. However, they should be given chiefly to those who live in places or with persons of suspect orthodoxy. Secondly, they should be given to all who are in ministry and handle the word of God, since these rules run directly counter to the opinions and statements of the heretics of our times.

CHAPTER 39: BRIEF EXPLANATION OF SOME REMARKS
IN THE DIRECTORY ABOUT THE THREE WAYS

[272] 1. **The purgative, illuminative, and unitive ways.**—In this directory, and in the course of giving the Spiritual Exercises, mention is made of the purgative, illuminative, and unitive ways and of how the sequence of the four Weeks corresponds to them. Some further clarification seems advisable here. For this correspondence should not be taken to mean that a person will have reached full and perfect purgation after going through the First Week, or perfect illumination after the Second and Third Weeks, or complete union with God after the Fourth Week. These all require much time, effort, and practice devoted to rooting out faults, subduing passions, and acquiring the virtues.

[273] 2. **The First Week corresponds to the purgative way.**—What is meant is this: there is a certain correspondence or analogy between the First Week and the purgative way. For the First Week consists altogether in thinking over and weighing one's past sins and in forming the greatest possible sorrow and contrition for them together with a fear of eternal punishment. The aim is to withdraw the spirit from love of all earthly things and to ground it in hatred and detestation for sin. Now all this corresponds to the soul's purgation.

[274] 3. **The Second and Third Weeks correspond partly to the purgative and partly to the illuminative ways.**—Similarly, in the Second and Third Weeks we consider the example of our Lord and Savior both in his life and in his passion, together with all the virtues which shone forth in ideal perfection in him. We we also learn therefrom what constitutes human

salvation and perfection, and what is the way to obtain eternal blessedness. Furthermore, when the soul has been cleansed, it becomes ready and fit to receive illuminations from God and the inpouring of his inward light. At the same time a certain vigor is engendered in the soul which drives out all concupiscence and makes the soul eager to endure poverty, contempt, and every kind of hardship; this vigor shakes off all negligence and disposes the soul to a watchful and strenuous pursuit of good works.

[275] 4. **The Fourth Week corresponds to the unitive way.**—Finally, in the Fourth Week, first through the Lord's Resurrection and Ascension, in which we can meditate at the same time our own future glory since, as Paul says, if Christ is risen we also shall rise [see 1 Cor 14:12–22]; and secondly through the Contemplation for Arousing Love in us, with its wealth of varied points and topics, unification with God is effected in the soul through the love which springs from meditation on God's goodness and benefits and on the greatness of what he has done and endured for our sake. It is effected also by longing for the glory of heaven and by consideration of God's presence in every thing and every place—rejoicing in his perfections and yearning to please him alone and for his own sake, now praising him, now extolling him, now marveling at his sublimity, and the like. All these elements correspond, as we have already said, to the unitive way.

[276] 5. **Two reasons for this correspondence.**—Thus, there are two reasons why the four Weeks are asserted to correspond to the three ways. Firstly, because of the topics treated in the individual Weeks which correspond to the three ways; and secondly because the four Weeks lay down the beginnings of each of the three ways. These will have to be followed up with time and effort if we wish to reach some degree of perfection. A final reason is that we receive instruction on the manner and method which we must subsequently follow in pressing forward on each of these ways.

[277] 6. **Should a person remain in one way or return to the earlier ones?**—From this it follows that even if a person has gotten a taste or sample of this unitive way in the Fourth Week, he should not for that reason stay there uninterruptedly, but should return to the earlier ways, applying himself for a long time and as an ordinary thing to the mortification of his passions, the practice of virtues, and other pursuits appropriate to the first two ways. Of course, it is not impossible but even a common occurrence for a person in one of the ways sometimes to experience affections characteristic of another way. These affections should not be rejected, provided they are not prematurely exercised as an ordinary thing, as was stated above.

[278] 7. **How to judge the fruit.**—In this matter it is not the length of time but the degree of progress which counts. For a person to aspire rashly to the unitive way would result in a great confusion which would completely block spiritual progress. It would also be a course exposed to dangers and

illusions. It would be like a person's wanting to move from the lowest to the highest class in school without passing through the intermediate grades, or move from the bottom to the top rung of a ladder without climbing the ones in between. Therefore, before professedly practicing this unitive way a person should have been thoroughly purified by exercises of the purgative way and have made good progress in the illuminative way as well. For lack of this, many persons, leaping rather than walking in the way of the Lord, are found after much time and various labors to be empty of virtue, impatient, wrathful, and otherwise imperfect.

[279] 8. **It depends upon the election of the Holy Spirit.**—Indeed, this advance to a higher way depends not so much upon our own choice, will, and effort as upon the guidance of the Holy Spirit, who is accustomed to "dispose these ascents" in the soul so that it can "go from virtue to virtue" [see Ps 84:6, 8]. In order to have surer guidance in this matter, however, and to avoid possible aberrations, the spiritual father who has charge of the soul should be consulted and everything done with his advice.

CHAPTER 40: REMINDERS FOR SOMEONE FINISHING THE EXERCISES

[280] 1. **Advice when the person leaves the Exercises.**—Upon moving from a warm to a cold room, a person can easily catch a sudden chill unless he takes care to preserve his heat. In the same way, a person finishing the Exercises and returning to his everyday life and dealings can all too easily lose in a quite short time the fervor and light he has received. This is especially true inasmuch as whatever good he may have received has not yet been solidified into a habit but is still a kind of impulse which can easily slacken or even die out altogether. When this happens, the entire fruit and the entire labor of the Exercises vanishes.

[281] 2. **The first thing to recommend to him.**—Hence, the first piece of advice for someone finishing the Exercises is that he should realize the great importance of this beginning and foundation of a good and spiritual life which by God's grace he has laid in the Exercises. He should receive it as an immense gift from God, and be convinced that all the lights and all the knowledge which he has acquired during the Exercises were bestowed on him by God with a very special love—and as such he ought to strive hard to preserve and protect them. He should also fear that, if he fails to live in the future as he has seen he ought to live, he will be the more severely punished by God because of his thanklessness and because "the one who knows the good and does not do it" [James 4:17] will have a heavier judgment.

[282] 3. **Second recommendation.**—Secondly, he should realize that what he as achieved up till now only amounts to the good seed being sown in his soul by God, with the result that, unless he tends and cultivates this seed

and brings it to maturity so that it will "give its fruit in due season" [Matt. 21:41], what has been done is of itself little or nothing. Hence, his first concern must be to prevent the seed from being snatched away by the birds, i.e., evil spirits; or being choked by thorns, i.e., worldly and corrupt thoughts and desires. He needs, therefore, to avoid not only sins but also the occasions of sins, especially of those to which he was prone before making the Exercises. It is against these he must particularly forearm himself since it will be so easy for him to backslide.

[283] 4. **Third recommendation.**—Thirdly, he should be urged to preserve and nourish his newly acquired devotion by means of religious and spiritual exercises. The following should be especially recommended. First, continuation of the practice of meditating for a half hour, or if possible even an hour, each day. Secondly, the daily examination of conscience for a quarter hour. Thirdly, weekly confession and Communion. Fourthly, the choosing of a regular confessor to take as his guide on the way of the spirit and with whom to discuss everything pertaining to his soul. Fifthly, frequent spiritual reading, along with the cultivation of good friendships and the strenuous avoidance of evil ones. Sixthly, a concern to grow daily in virtue, especially humility, patience, and charity. In sum, he himself should make an effort to reach the highest degree of perfection he can reach in his own state of life, in accord with the measure of God's grace.

[284] 5. **Additional particularized advice.**—These are the main general counsels which can be given to everyone. In addition, there are other pieces of advice which can be given to people according to their profession, state of life, or particular needs. Indeed, this advice can be expanded or intensified with persons of greater devotion and spiritual progress, as will easily be discerned by a good and competent director, assisted by the grace and light of our Lord Jesus Christ. To him be glory and honor forever. Amen.

Appendix 1: Letter of St. Ignatius to Manuel Miona[1]

May the grace and love of Christ our Lord be always for our favor and help.

I am very anxious to hear how you have been doing—and no wonder, seeing how indebted I am to you in spiritual matters as a son to his spiritual father. And since it is right for me to return the great love and goodwill which you have always had for me and shown in deeds, and since in this life I know of no way to repay even a particle of this debt except by putting you into spiritual exercises for a month with a person to be named for you, and since you yourself even promised me you would do so, I beg you by the service of God our Lord, if you have already tested and tasted these exercises, to write me about it; and if not, I beg you by his love and by the bitter death he underwent for us to enter into them. And if afterwards you regret that you did, then besides any penance you may wish to give me (and for which I am ready) take me for a hoaxer of spiritual persons to whom I owe everything.

Since I have written to one person for all, I have not written to you individually up till now. And so Favre will be able to give you any news about me you would like to have, and you can see it in my letter to him. For the second and the third time, and as many more times as I can, I beg you by the service of God our Lord to do what I have been saying to you—lest the Divine Majesty at the end demand of us why I did not beg this of you with all my strength, inasmuch as this is the very best thing that in this life I can think, perceive, or understand for helping a person benefit himself as well as bring fruit, benefit, and advantage to many others; for even if you felt no need for the former, you will see how immeasurably and incomparably you will be helped with regard to the latter.

For the rest, I conclude praying the immense clemency of God our Lord that he will bestow on us the grace to know his most holy will, and that he will bring us to fulfill it perfectly according to the talent entrusted to each, at least so he will not say to us, "You wicked servant, you knew . . . ," etc. [Luke 19:22–23].

Venice, November 16, 1536.

Entirely yours in the Lord,

Iñigo

---

[1] Monumenta Historica Societatis Iesu, *Sancti Ignatii de Loyola . . . Epistolae et Instructiones*, vol. 1, pp. 111–13; original in Spanish.

Appendix 2: Juan Alonso De Vitoria's Election of a State of Life[1]

Jesus, Son of the Virgin Mary,
to whose honor and glory be whatever I choose

I. IN THE WAY OF THE COMMANDMENTS

Advantages

1. Perfection and [eternal] glory if I keep them well.
2. The broader mode of proceeding in the way of the commandments.
3. More opportunity for helping oneself in bodily infirmities, although at times not.
4. More opportunity for almsgiving with one's temporal goods, without losing the ability to give spiritual goods as well.

Disadvantages

1. More opportunity for sinning through greater involvement with people and worldly affairs; less opportunity for rising again.
2. Great reversals, which even when accepted with patience are of little merit because they do not come because of God's affairs but because of my own, such as loss of property, insults, and similar things—which few like Job bear joyfully.
3. Having no time for God because of concern about supporting oneself and the similar things, which divide the heart which we ought to give totally to God, since he requires it of us.
4. Finally, it is almost impossible to detach oneself from worldly things and from the flesh when one is continually seeing and involved in worldly affairs and things attractive to the flesh.

II. IN THE WAY OF CHRIST'S COUNSELS

Advantages

1. Greater perfection if I follow them purely, and greater reward.
2. Greater spiritual gifts for falling more deeply in love with God and serving Him more, and living with more consolation in this exile.
3. Greater opportunity for arising again if I fall.

---

[1] Translated from Ignacio Iparraguirre, S.J., *Historia de los Ejercicios Espirituales de S. Ignacio de Loyola*, vol. 1: *Práctica de los Ejercicios de S. Ignacio de Loyola en vida de su autor* (Roma-Bilbao, 1946), pp. 259-63. Original in Spanish.

4. Fewer opportunities for sinning through the greater recollection and peaceful state I can maintain with a tranquil and pure conscience.

5. Contempt for the world and of all created things in it, which is a basis for better observance of the commandments, as the Lord teaches saying, "If you would be perfect, etc."

Disadvantages

1. My infirmities.
2. The differences from one another found in those who follow this way.
3. Its strictness—though bearable for one who follows it willingly.

WHEREFORE: it is my determinate will to follow this way of the counsels as providing more advantages for serving my God, to whom I offer myself totally and from whom I ask favor and help that I may put into effect whatever he is best pleased with, whenever he is best pleased. And I resolve before his Majesty and his heavenly and holy Mother and his entire imperial court that I will not alter this unless I see very clearly that it would be more acceptable to his majesty and service.

JUAN ALONSO DE VITORIA

III. IN RELIGIOUS LIFE

Advantages

1. The security and tranquillity of conscience in which one lives through the merit of obedience.
2. The merit of serving in God's household.
3. Sharing in all the prayers made throughout the whole order.
4. Living under rule even in matters regarding food and drink, which is an advantage for health.

Disadvantages

Fasts, disciplines and night watches—which, even if they were disadvantageous for me (which I do not find to be the case), touch only the body, and do not hurt the soul but rather make it purer.

IV. OUTSIDE RELIGIOUS LIFE

Advantages

Not being subject in such a degree—although because of its little merit this might better be termed a disadvantage than an advantage.

Disadvantages

1. Not being so far from the snares of the world.
2. The countless kinds of harms which can arise while going on pilgrimages.
3. The difficulty in recollecting one's spirit for prayer because of change of place

and other things.

SEEING the greater resources (in this case quite obvious) for serving my God better, it is my determinate intention that the preparation of my powers and soul should be for the service of my God in religious life. Offering myself wholly to him and submitting to his divine inspirations, I beg the grace to obtain this desire, and before him and his blessed and merciful mother and his heavenly court, I resolve, if it is pleasing to his service and divine providence, not to alter this decision for any reason unless I see very clearly that it is for his greater service.

JUAN ALONSO DE VITORIA

V. IN THE ORDER OF SAINT FRANCIS

Advantages

1. Its being so approved and ancient.
2. Its founder being such a great saint.
3. The great number of men and women saints who have belonged to his order.

Disadvantages

1. Its obliging its subjects to so many rules under pain of mortal sin.
2. Getting up at night for matins, which would be extremely harmful for my infirmities.
3. Lack of time for helping one's neighbor because of the long and laborious liturgical offices, etc.

VI. IN THE SOCIETY OF JESUS OUR LORD

Advantages

1. It imitates more closely Christ's way of life, authentically and without impositions.
2. Its great efforts on behalf of the salvation of the neighbor's soul.
3. Its holy procedure for ridding self of sin and helping oneself, through the meditations.
4. Taking no solemn vows until they see it is the better thing to do.
5. Not having any obligation to disciplines, fasts, night watching, beyond what Holy Mother Church requires or the Holy Spirit inspires each one to do for his own progress.
6. Not falling into apostasy [i.e., canonical desertion of religious life] or needing a papal brief when the superior sees that a person is not suited for religious life and dismisses him.

Disadvantages

Its lack of antiquity.

WHEREFORE, having noted the advantages and disadvantages on either side, I find that this Society is more suited to my character and constitution, since it is simpler and plainer and does not have so many obligations under pain of mortal sin. Hence, it is my determinate will to adopt it, if God approves. I beseech him as humbly as I can to deign to give me his favor and help so that I may put this into effect in his holy service, if it is for the greater glorification of his sacred Majesty. And thus, in the presence of his infinite goodness and of his most blessed and merciful Mother and the entire court of heaven, I resolve not to alter my decision for whatever cause, unless I see very clearly that it is against his divine providence and less for his service.

JUAN ALONSO DE VITORIA

[In the lengthy Section VII Vitoria employs the further methods of election given in nos. 184-187 of the Exercises. In Section VIII he takes up again the comparison of advantages and disadvantages to decide whether or not he ought to confirm his decision with vows. In Section IX he uses the same method in deciding that he will not delay carrying out his resolve. Then he continues:]

Jesus, Son of Mary, etc.

MOVED by just reasons and the desire of better serving my God to chose the above-mentioned state, for which I give measureless thanks to Jesus, God our Lord and Master, since, aware of my great unworthiness and lowliness, he has deigned to call me to a state perfect beyond all others and suited for being able to serve him better—moved, I say, by desire and longing to serve my God better, I wish to resign myself totally into the governance of holy obedience, and become a member of the family of the above-named holy Society—in order to live and die in it and observe perpetual obedience, chastity and poverty, and from this moment on to subject and resign myself entirely as a member of it, without retaining any power to dispose of myself or of whatever I may possess. To carry out and persevere in this decision, I beg the help of the Most Holy Trinity, with my Lady the Holy Virgin Mary, the 11,000 virgins, the spouse of Christ St. Catherine, and all the rest of the heavenly court as my intercessors, to all of whom with all my heart I commend and entrust myself so as to be directed in this decision to the glory and honor of almighty God.

JUAN ALONSO DE VITORIA

Jesus, Son of Mary

FATHER, our sovereign Lord and Redeemer, I, Juan de Vitoria, a great sinner and your most unworthy servant, recognizing, by the light of the grace which in your infinite goodness you granted for the enlightening of my mind (which I had blinded and darkened with the filth of my sins), that the lavish gifts which I have unworthily received until this day from your generous mercy would not be safe in such a worthless vessel as I am, have determined to present them to your goodness and sovereign mercy, my Lord, so that they might receive therefrom the life-giving dew of grace and bear fruit in an odor of sweetness before your divine Majesty.

And therefore, my Father and Lord, on this day sacred to my Lady the Virgin Mary, I offer you all my heart, will, and powers of soul, and all the natural, infused, and acquired gifts, for the service, glory and honor of your most holy name of Jesus, in whose Company and observant religious order I promise to him who is God and true man, to his most holy Mother my Lady the Virgin Mary, and the whole court of heaven which glorifies and serves you, my Lord, so that I might live and die and forever observe chastity, poverty and obedience, as understood by the said Company, from this present day of our Lady's solemn annunciation until the day I go to give an account to your Majesty of the talents entrusted to me. And so I offer myself as servant of said Company, in such wise that I be incapable of disposing of my person or of the life which I have or may have, now or at any other time, with no freedom of my own but at the will of and in submission to this Society, so long as the Superiors General, or those under whose obedience I may be, shall think good to keep me in this Society.

I likewise promise, my Lord and all my hope, before your holy Majesty and my Lady the Virgin Mary and your entire heavenly court, to observe forever perpetual chastity and poverty from this day forward, with your help and grace. And if the General and Superiors of this Society should at some time decide not to keep me for any reason, I promise to observe obedience nonetheless in whatever order or hermitage your Majesty thinks best. I promise that neither now nor at any time will I or anyone on my behalf ask permission or absolution in order to be released from these vows; and even though your vicars the Popes, my Lord and King, have power to grant this I renounce it and count it as non-existing, persuaded that thereby I will render and am rendering greater service to your Majesty. And with all the humility of which I am capable, I beg the grant of your grace and protection so that I may persevere and battle with strength and confidence, overcoming the stratagems of our chief foe, the ancient serpent.

Today, the glorious Annunciation of our Lady, 25 March 1549.

JUAN ALONSO DE VITORIA

Index of Names

Adam of Dryburgh, 84
Ambrose, St., 260, 329
Androzzi, Fulvio, S.J., 26
Apostolic Constitutions, 253
Aquaviva, Claudio, S.J., 2, 162, 289, 292
Aquinas, St. Thomas, 46, 48, 236, 245, 251, 253–54, 257, 259, 328, 330
Aristotle, 50, 136, 257, 274, 330
Augustine, St., 50, 57, 81, 243, 256, 259, 260, 275, 297, 316, 331, 341

Bencio, Girolamo, S.J., 199
Bernard of Clairvaux, St., 131, 245, 260, 313, 323
Blondo, Giuseppe, S.J., 220–27, 308
Bonaventure, St. (and Pseudo-Bonaventure), 80–82, 132, 157, 218, 236, 251, 256, 257, 275, 276, 314, 322, 332
Broët, Paschase, S.J., 115

Cajetan, Thomas de Vio, 52, 254
Câmara Luis Gonçalves da, S.J., 1, 29–31
Canisius, St. Peter, S.J., 41
Cassian, 245, 256, 258, 303, 313
Codazzo, Pietro, S.J., 30
Cordeses, Antonio, S.J., 265–85

David of Augsburg, 256, 332
Denis (Dionysius) the Carthusian, 89, 156, 217, 297
Dionysius the Areopagite, 103, 254, 262
Domènech, Jerónimo, S.J., 29, 71–75
Dominici, Jacopo, S.J., 289

Fabi, Fabio de, S.J., 65, 71, 114, 162, 191–203
Favre, Bl. Pierre, S.J., 29–30, 46, 78–80, 115, 351
Ferrer, St. Vincent, O.P., 68

Gelasius, Pope, 258

Gerson, Jean, 256, 332; supposed author of the *Imitation of Christ,* 29, 70, 113, 165, 202, 225, 296, 323
González Dávila, Gil, S.J., 2, 18, 20, 21, 67, 101, 115, 116, 133, 162, 234–64
Granada, Luis de, O.P., 113, 323
Gregory I, St., Pope, 144–45, 253, 343
Guibert, Joseph de, S.J., 3
Guy, Jean-Claude, S.J., 1

Helmi, Cesare, S.J., 26
Hilarion, St., 274
Hoffaeus, Paul, S.J., 87–100

Innocent III, Pope (Lotario de' Conti di Segni), 89, 156
Iparraguirre, Ignacio, S.J., 3–4, 35, 162, 352

Jerome, St., 272, 274

Kempis, Thomas à, 157; see also: Gerson, Jean
Kostka, St. Stanislaus, S.J., 65

Laínez, Diego, S.J., 42, 115
Leerno, Felipe, S.J., 24
Lipomani, Luigi, 157
Loarte, Gaspar, S.J., 25
Longridge, W.H., 2, 4
Loyola, St. Ignatius of, 1–2, 7–31, 76–77, 79, 84–85, 101–2, 109, 110, 115–17, 162, 178, 191–93, 220, 232, 235, 237, 239–40, 242–44, 252–54, 256, 260, 263, 290, 293–94, 299, 306–7, 313–14, 319, 326, 331, 351

Maggio, Lorenzo, S.J., 15
Martinengo, Girolamo, 30
Marulus (Marulić), Marcus, 156
Mary of Egypt, St., 274

357

Index of Subjects